Carla Falluomini
The Gothic Version of the Gospels and Pauline Epistles

Arbeiten zur Neutestamentlichen Textforschung

Herausgegeben im Auftrag des
Instituts für Neutestamentliche Textforschung
der Westfälischen Wilhelms-Universität
Münster/Westfalen

von David C. Parker und Holger Strutwolf

Band 46

Carla Falluomini

The Gothic Version of the Gospels and Pauline Epistles

Cultural Background, Transmission and Character

DE GRUYTER

ISBN 978-3-11-055273-7
e-ISBN (PDF) 978-3-11-033469-2
e-ISBN (EPUB) 978-3-11-039024-7
ISSN 0570-5509

Library of Congress Cataloging-in-Publication Data
A CIP catalog record for this book has been applied for at the Library of Congress.

Bibliographic information published by the Deutsche Nationalbibliothek
The Deutsche Nationalbibliothek lists this publication in the Deutsche Nationalbibliografie;
detailed bibliographic data are available on the Internet at http://dnb.dnb.de.

© 2017 Walter de Gruyter GmbH, Berlin/Boston
This volume is text- and page-identical with the hardback published in 2015.
Printing and binding: CPI books GmbH, Leck

♾ Printed on acid-free paper
Printed in Germany

www.degruyter.com

The Gothic Version of the Gospels and Pauline Epistles: Cultural Background, Transmission and Character

Carla Falluomini

To Bianca

Contents

a   General abbreviations —— XIII

b   Symbols —— XV

c   Manuscript sigla and abbreviations —— XVII

d   Notes —— XXI

Introduction —— 1

1   Wulfila and his context —— 4
1.1.   Wulfila's life and education —— 4
1.2   The cultural and religious background of Wulfila's activity —— 10
1.3   The Gothic alphabet —— 18
1.4   Christian vocabulary —— 22
1.5   Conclusions —— 24

2   The Gothic witnesses to the Gospels and Pauline Epistles —— 25
2.1   The manuscripts —— 27
2.1.1   *Codex Argenteus* —— 32
2.1.2.   *Codex Ambrosianus* C —— 34
2.1.3   *Codex Gissensis* —— 35
2.1.4   *Codex Carolinus* —— 36
2.1.5   *Codex Ambrosianus* A⁺ —— 38
2.1.6   *Codex Ambrosianus* B —— 39
2.2   Other witnesses —— 40
2.2.1   Tablet of Hács-Béndekpuszta (*Tabella Hungarica*) —— 41
2.2.2   *Codex Bononiensis* —— 42
2.2.3   *Gotica Vindobonensia* —— 43
2.2.4   *Gotica Parisina* —— 43
2.3   Scribal errors and interventions —— 44
2.4.   *Marginalia* —— 46
2.5   Relationships between the manuscripts —— 47
2.6   Editions of the Gothic texts —— 49
2.7   Recent tools for the study of the Gothic texts —— 51
2.8   Conclusions —— 51

3	'Helps for readers' and other codicological features —— 53
3.1	The Ammonian Sections and Eusebian Canons —— 53
3.2	The Euthalian Apparatus —— 54
3.3	Running titles —— 55
3.4	Superscriptions and subscriptions —— 55
3.5	Paragraphs —— 57
3.6	Punctuation —— 58
3.7	*Cola et commata* —— 59
3.8	Enlarged letters —— 61
3.9	Distinctive ink —— 62
3.10.	*Diple* —— 63
3.11	*Nomina sacra* —— 63
3.12	Numerals —— 64
3.13	*Diaeresis* —— 65
3.14	Liturgical indications —— 65
3.15	Conclusions —— 65
4	**Linguistic and stylistic features —— 66**
4.1	The Gothic rendering of the Greek text —— 69
4.1.1	Idiomatic features of the Gothic text —— 69
4.1.2.	Non-systematic renderings —— 72
4.1.3	Gothic renderings of two or more Greek forms —— 75
4.1.4	Parallel Gothic and Latin renderings —— 78
4.2	Lexis and style —— 80
4.3	Proper names —— 88
4.4	Conclusions —— 90
5	**The Greek *Vorlage* and the transmission of the Gothic text —— 92**
5.1	The history of research on the text-critical character of the Gothic version —— 93
5.2	The Gothic influence on the Latin text —— 101
5.3	The Latin influence on the Gothic text —— 105
5.4.	The Gothic text and Ambrosiaster —— 112
5.5	Parallel passages and parallel expressions —— 114
5.6.	Transmission in two witnesses —— 119
5.7	Marginal glosses —— 123
5.8	Glosses incorporated into the text —— 126
5.9	Conclusions —— 127

6	A different approach to the problem of the *Vorlage* —— 130
6.1	The Gothic Gospels —— 133
6.1.1	The Byzantine readings in Matthew and John —— 134
6.1.2	The non-Byzantine readings in Matthew and John —— 136
6.1.3	Significant textual features —— 138
6.2	The Pauline Epistles —— 141
6.2.1	The Byzantine readings in Romans and Galatians —— 141
6.2.2	The non-Byzantine readings in Romans and Galatians —— 141
6.2.3	Significant textual features —— 143
6.3	Conclusions —— 146

Appendix I
'Significant readings' —— 149

I.1	The Gospel of Matthew —— 149
I.2	The Gospel of John —— 153
I.3	The Epistle to the Romans —— 164
I.4	The Epistle to the Galatians —— 169

Appendix II —— 174

II.1	Table of the main codicological features of the Gothic manuscripts of the Gospels and Pauline Epistles —— 174
II.2	The Long Ending of Mark —— 175
II.3	The *Praefatio* to the *Codex Brixianus* —— 178

Bibliography —— 181

Index of biblical citations —— 206

Index of manuscripts —— 212

Index of names and subjects —— 215

Index of words —— 220

Plates —— 225

a General abbreviations

acc.	accusative
act.	active
adj.	adjective
ad loc. (= *ad locum*)	at the place
al. (= *alii*)	others
aor.	aorist
art.	article
c (superscript)	correction
ch.	chapter
co	the whole Coptic tradition (bo: Bohairic; sa: Sahidic; pt: part)
dat.	dative
dem.	demonstrative
f. (= *folium*)	leaf
fem.	feminine
gen.	genitive
Goth	the Gothic text
Goth.	Gothic
Gr.	Greek
impf.	imperfect
ind.	indicative
inf.	infinitive
it	the great part or all the manuscripts of the *Vetus Latina* (in superscript: the specific manuscript, see Jülicher *et al*. 1963–1976; VLD)
l.	line
lat	the great part of the *Vetus Latina* and Vulgate manuscripts
Lat.	Latin
latt	the whole Latin tradition (both *Vetus Latina* and Vulgate)
lit.	literally
m	the greatest part or the half of the Byzantine manuscripts, according to Hodges-Farstad 1985
𝔐	the text of the majority of the biblical manuscripts, among them there are always included the manuscripts of the Byzantine text type, see Nestle-Aland[28], 14*; Hodges-Farstad 1985
mg	marginal reading
mid/pass.	middle-passive
ms(s).	manuscript(s)
nom.	nominative
om. (= *omissum*)	omitted
opt.	optative
part.	particularly
partic.	participle
partit.	partitive
pass.	passive
pc (= *pauci*)	a few New Testament manuscripts

pers.	person
plur.	plural
pm (= *permulti*)	a great many of the New Testament manuscripts
pres.	present
pret.	preterite
pron.	pronoun
r	*recto*
refl.	reflexive
rell. (= *reliqui*)	the rest of the New Testament manuscripts
s (superscript)	reading in a supplementary (not original) part of a manuscript
sing.	singular
subst.	substantive
s.v. (= *sub voce*)	under the specified word(s)
sy	the whole Syriac tradition (superscript: 's' for Sinaitic; 'c' for Curetonian; 'h' for Harklean; 'p' for Peshitta)
v	*verso*
var	variants
var. lect. (= *variae lectiones*)	other readings of the New Testament tradition
vel	or
vg	the text of the Vulgate
vg^{cl}	1592 Clementine Vulgate edition
vg^{s}	1590 Sixtine Vulgate edition
vgst	see Weber *et al.* 1994
vg^{ww}	see Wordsworth-White 1889–1898
vid (= *videtur*)	apparent reading (but not certain)

b Symbols

$^{1\,2\,3}$ after a manuscript siglum	different correctors
$^{1\,2\,3}$ after a word	the first, second, third occurrence of the word in the same verse
* after a manuscript siglum	first hand
* before a word	the word or the sequence of words is not attested
+	addition
+ (superscript)	existence of *membra disiecta*
–	omission
|	separation between alternative readings in a group of variants
—	separation between variant groups in a single verse
( )	witnesses with slight differences
( ) in abbreviations	suspended letter(s)
( ) in translations	the words in brackets are not present in the text
‹ ›	editorial addition by conjecture or from a parallel source
‹ › after a letter or a word in Gothic alphabet	it shows the corresponding transcription in Latin alphabet
/	or
||	line division (in a manuscript)
]	separation between a reading and its variants
[*italics*] with reference to a part of a reading	words or letters of doubtful authenticity; glosses inserted into the text
[ ] in quotations of old texts	editorial deletion
[ ] in quotations of modern texts	addition
[ ] with reference to a grapheme	phonetical value
[...]	gap in quotations
<	derivation from
=	corresponding to
underline	used to draw attention to a form or to establish parallelisms

c Manuscript sigla and abbreviations

Gothic manuscripts
A	*Codex Ambrosianus* A⁺
Ambros.	*Ambrosianus*
B	*Codex Ambrosianus* B
C	*Codex Ambrosianus* C
CA	*Codex Argenteus*
CB	*Codex Bononiensis*
CC	the Gothic part of the *Codex Carolinus*
G	the Gothic part of the *Codex Gissensis*

Codex Ambrosianus A⁺	Milan, Biblioteca Ambrosiana, S 36 sup. + Turin, Biblioteca Nazionale Universitaria, F. IV. 1 Fasc. 10
Codex Ambrosianus B	Milan, Biblioteca Ambrosiana, S 45 sup.
Codex Ambrosianus C	Milan, Biblioteca Ambrosiana, I 61 sup., ff. 90–91
Codex Ambrosianus D	Milan, Biblioteca Ambrosiana, G 82 sup., ff. 209–210, 451–452, 461–462
Codex Ambrosianus E⁺	Milan, Biblioteca Ambrosiana, E 147 sup., ff. 77–78, 79–80, 111–112, 113–114, 309–310 + Vatican City, Biblioteca Apostolica Vaticana, Vat. Lat. 5750, ff. 57–58, 59–60, 61–62
Codex Argenteus	Uppsala, Universitetsbiblioteket, D G 1 + Speyer, Historisches Museum der Pfalz, s. n.
Codex Bononiensis	Bologna, Archivio della Fabbriceria della Basilica di San Petronio, Cart. 716/1, n°1, *olim* Cart. 353, cam. n°3
Codex Carolinus	Wolfenbüttel, Herzog August Bibliothek, Guelf. 64 Weiss., ff. 255–256, 277, 280
Codex Gissensis	Giessen, Universitätsbibliothek, 651/20
pap. 34	Naples, Biblioteca Nazionale 'Vittorio Emanuele', s. n.

Greek manuscripts

The Greek manuscripts are indicated with both the usual uppercase letters (Wettstein's cataloging system) and the Gregory-Aland numbers in the text, but only with the letters in the Appendices. This list excludes manuscripts cited in support of readings.

p^{29}	Oxford, Bodleian Library, Gr. bibl. g. 4 (P)
p^{38}	Ann Arbor/MI, University Library, Inv. Nr. 1571.
p^{46}	Dublin, P. Chester Beatty II + Ann Arbor/MI, University Library, Inv. Nr. 6238
p^{48}	Florence, Biblioteca Medicea Laurenziana, PSI X 1165
ℵ/01	*Codex Sinaiticus*; London, British Library, Add. 43725
A/02	*Codex Alexandrinus*; London, British Library, Royal 1 D VIII
B/03	*Codex Vaticanus*; Vatican City, Biblioteca Apostolica Vaticana, Vat. Gr. 1209
C/04	*Codex Ephraemi Rescriptus*; Paris, Bibliothèque Nationale de France, Gr. 9

D/05	*Codex Bezae*; Cambridge, Trinity College, Nn. II. 41
D/06	*Codex Claromontanus*; Paris, Bibliothèque Nationale de France, Gr. 107 + 107 AB
E/07	*Codex Basilensis*; Basel, Universitätsbibliothek, A.N. III. 12
E/08	*Codex Laudianus*; Oxford, Bodleian Library, Laudianus Gr. 35 [S. C. 1119]
F/09	*Codex Boreelianus Rheno-Trajectinus*; Utrecht, Universiteitsbibliotheek, 1
F/010	*Codex Augiensis*; Cambridge, Trinity College, B. XVII. 1
G/011	*Codex Seidelianus I*; London, British Library, Harley 5684 + Cambridge, Trinity College, B. XVII. 20
G/012	*Codex Boernerianus*; Dresden, Sächsische Landesbibliothek, A 145^b
H/013	*Codex Seidelianus II*; Hamburg, Staats- und Universitätsbibliothek, Cod. 91 in scrin. + *membra disiecta*
K/017	*Codex Cyprius*; Paris, Bibliothèque Nationale de France, Gr. 63
K/018	*Codex Mosquensis I*; Moscow, Gosudarstvennyj Istoričeskij Musej, V. 93
L/019	*Codex Regius*; Paris, Bibliothèque Nationale de France, Gr. 62
L/020	*Codex Angelicus*; Rome, Biblioteca Angelica, 39
M/0121+0243	*Codex Campianus*; Paris, Bibliothèque Nationale de France, Gr. 48
N/022	*Codex Petropolitanus Purpureus*; Saint Petersburg, Rossijskaja Nacional'naja Biblioteka, Gr. 537 + *membra disiecta*
P/024	*Codex Guelferbytanus* A; Wolfenbüttel, Herzog August Bibliothek, Guelf. 64 Weiss.
P/025	*Codex Porphyrianus*; Saint Petersburg, Rossijskaja Nacional'naja Biblioteka, Gr. 225
Q/026	*Codex Guelferbytanus* B; Wolfenbüttel, Herzog August Bibliothek, Guelf. 64 Weiss.
S/028	Vatican City, Biblioteca Apostolica Vaticana, Vat. Gr. 354
U/030	*Codex Nanianus*; Venice, Biblioteca San Marco 1397 [I.8]
V/031	*Codex Mosquensis II*; Moscow, Gosudarstvennyj Istoričeskij Musej, V. 9
W/032	*Codex Washingtonianus*; Washington/DC, Smithsonian Institution, Freer Gallery of Art, 06.274
Γ/036	*Codex Tischendorfianus IV*; Oxford, Bodleian Library, Auct. T. infr. 2.2 + Saint Petersburg, Rossijskaja Nacional'naja Biblioteka, Gr. 33
Θ/038	*Codex Coridethianus*; Tbilisi, Inst. rukop., Gr. 28
Λ/039	*Codex Tischendorfianus III*; Oxford, Bodleian Library, Auct. T. infr. 1.1
Π/041	*Codex Petropolitanus*; Saint Petersburg, Rossijskaja Nacional'naja Biblioteka, Gr. 34
Ψ/044	*Codex Athous Laurensis*; Athōs, Monē Megistēs Lavras, B' 52
33	Paris, Bibliothèque Nationale de France, Gr. 14

Old Latin manuscripts

The Old Latin manuscripts are cited both with the usual lowercase letters (Lachmann's custom) and the Beuron numbers in the text, but only with the abbreviation 'it' and the letters (superscript) in the Appendices.

a/3	*Codex Vercellensis*; Vercelli, Archivio Capitolare Eusebiano, s. n.
ar/61	*Codex Ardmachanus*; Dublin, Trinity College, 52
aur/15	*Codex Aureus*; Stockholm, Kungliga Bibliotheket, A.135

b/4	*Codex Veronensis*; Verona, Biblioteca Capitolare, VI
b/89	*Codex Budapestiensis*; Budapest, Országos Széchényi Könyvtár, Lat. 1
c/6	*Codex Colbertinus*; Paris, Bibliothèque Nationale de France, Lat. 254
d/5	the Latin part of the *Codex Bezae* D/05; Cambridge, Trinity College, Nn. II. 41
d/75	the Latin part of the *Codex Claromontanus* D/06; Paris, Bibliothèque Nationale de France, Gr. 107 + 107 AB
e/2	*Codex Palatinus*; Trent, Museo Nazionale, s. n.
e/76	the Latin part of the *Codex Sangermanensis*; Saint Petersburg, Rossijskaja Nacional'naja Biblioteka, Gr. 20
f/10	*Codex Brixianus*; Brescia, Biblioteca Queriniana, s. n.
f/78	the Latin part of the *Codex Augiensis* F/010; Cambridge, Trinity College, B. XVII. 1
ff^2/8	*Codex Corbeiensis*; Paris, Bibliothèque Nationale de France, Lat. 17225
g/77	the Latin part of the *Codex Boernerianus* G/012; Dresden, Sächsische Landesbibliothek, A 145^b
g^1/7	*Sangermanensis primus*; Paris, Bibliothèque Nationale de France, Lat. 11553
g^2/29	*Codex Sangermanensis secundus*; Paris, Bibliothèque Nationale de France, Lat. 13169
gat/30	*Codex Gatianus*; Paris, Bibliothèque Nationale de France, Nouv. acq. Lat. 1587
gig/51	*Codex Gigas*; Stockholm, Kungliga Biblioteket, A. 148
gue/79	the Latin part of the *Codex Carolinus*; Wolfenbüttel, Herzog August Bibliothek, Guelf. 64 Weiss., ff. 255–256, 277, 280
k/1	*Codex Bobiensis*; Turin, Biblioteca Nazionale Universitaria, G. VII. 15
l/11	*Codex Rehdigeranus*; Berlin, Staatsbibliothek, Preußischer Kulturbesitz, Depot Breslau, 5
m/*Speculum*	see Pseudo-Augustinus in Bibliography, I. Ancient sources.
q/13	*Codex Monacensis*; Munich, Bayerische Staatsbibliothek, Clm 6224
r^1/14	*Codex Usserianus primus*; Dublin, Trinity College 55
r^3/64	*Fragmenta Frisingensia*; Munich, Bayerische Staatsbibliothek, Clm 6436 + *membra disiecta*
t/56	*Liber Comicus Toletanus*; Paris, Bibliothèque Nationale de France, Nouv. acq. Lat. 2171
δ/27	*Codex Interlinearis Sangallensis*; Sankt Gallen, Stiftsbibliothek, 48

d Notes

The Gothic text is usually cited according to Streitberg-Scardigli 2000, corrected on the basis of Falluomini 1999 and Snædal 2013 A, I. In some cases, the text is given according to the manuscript(s), with diacritical marks and abbreviations.

Greek and Latin New Testament readings and witnesses are cited according to Aland *et al.* 1991, Aland *et al.* 1998–2005, Hodges-Farstad 1985, IGNTP 1984–1987, Jülicher *et al.* 1963–1976, Legg 1935, Legg 1940, Nestle-Aland[28], Robinson-Pierpont 2005, Swanson 1995–2005, UBS[4], VLD, Weber *et al.* 1994, Wordsworth-White 1889–1898, www.iohannes.com. The witnesses that are consistently cited are: the papyri, ℵ/01, A/02, B/03, C/04, D/05, D/06, F/010, G/012, K/018, L/019, L/020, N/022, P/025, W/032, Θ/038, Ψ/044, f¹, f¹³, 33, 1739, '𝔐' or '𝔪' (or *pm*) and – if different from 𝔐 or 𝔪 – 565, 579, 700, the *Vetus Latina* manuscripts a/3, ar/61, aur/15, b/4, b/89, c/6, d/5, d/75, e/2, e/76, f/10, f/78, ff²/8, g/77, g¹/7, gue/79, k/1, l/11, q/13, r¹/14, t/56, and the Vulgate (vg). Special attention will be given to the citations quoted by Chrysostom and Ambrosiaster. All the manuscripts that agree with the Gothic text are reported in the cases in which the Gothic readings are supported by few or none of the usually cited witnesses or diverge from 𝔐/𝔪.

The English translation of the New Testament verses follows the New Revised Standard Version with some adaptations in order to render the Gothic or the Greek text as literally as possible. The words not present in the Gothic text, but necessary for the meaning of the translation, are within brackets.

Introduction

The Gothic translation of the Bible was devised in the mid-fourth century by Wulfila (or Ulfila; ca. 311–383), bishop of those Goths (*Gothi minores*), who – according to the sources – settled first somewhere north of the Danube (modern southern Romania) and after 347/348 in Moesia Inferior (modern northern Bulgaria), and thus in the territory of the Roman Empire. The Gothic Bible was in use not only among Wulfila's Goths, but also among Visigoths and Ostrogoths, who carried it with them in the migrations to the west – respectively southern Gaul and Spain, and Italy – during the fifth century. It was probably also used by other Germanic peoples, such as the Vandals.

The translation of the Old Testament is lost, with the exception of a small fragment of Nehemiah. Of the New Testament there remain only long parts of the Gospels and of the Pauline Epistles. Moreover, several citations from the Old and New Testament are transmitted by a Gothic fragmentary text (part of a sermon or liturgical prayer). All these texts are preserved in manuscripts, most of which are palimpsests, produced very probably in Italy in the first half of the sixth century. Among the Gothic manuscripts, the *Codex Argenteus*, written in silver and golden ink on purple parchment, stands out for its magnificence. There are no doubts that it was prepared for a person of high rank, probably the Gothic King Theoderic. Two manuscripts are Gothic-Latin bilingual. It is worth noting that in both cases the Gothic text occupies the position of honour on the left.

The distinctive value of the Gothic version has been recognised by Germanic and New Testament philologists, linguists and historians since it was first published in the first half of the nineteenth century. It is indeed the oldest extant text – excluding the runic inscriptions – in a Germanic language and one of the oldest translations of the Holy Scriptures from the Greek.

The *Vorlage* of the Gothic version is lost. From a text-critical point of view, the Gothic text is close to the early Byzantine text form, mainly in the Gospels. Consequently, in several instances, it represents the oldest witness of the circulation of the Byzantine readings. The main problem for Gothic textual criticism concerns the origin of the non-Byzantine readings which are found in the Gothic version and particularly of those which agree with the 'Western' witnesses. The explanation of their presence remains controversial. However, the larger part of studies of Wulfila's *Vorlage* was undertaken in the first half of the twentieth century and represents, therefore, a perspective that reflects the textual theories regarding the formation of the Byzantine text promoted especially by Hermann von Soden. For this reason, a reevaluation of the Gothic readings in light of more recent hypotheses concerning the origin of this branch of the textual tradition seems necessary.

The use of the Gothic version as a New Testament textual witness has been conditioned by the Alands' judgment[1] on its textual value. Consequently, it has been omitted both in the critical apparatus of the latest editions of the *Novum Testamentum Graece*[2] and of *The Greek New Testament*.[3] It is, however, mentioned in the apparatus of *The Gospel according to St. Luke*[4] and it will be included in the apparatus of the *Novum Testamentum Graecum Editio Critica Maior*.[5]

In consideration of the relevance of the Gothic version from several perspectives, the scope of the present study is (1) to point out the historical and cultural context in which it was produced; (2) to provide up-to-date information about the Gothic witnesses to the New Testament; (3) to describe their codicological features; (4) to indicate the limitations of the Gothic version in representing its underlying Greek *Vorlage*; (5) to trace the history of text-critical research on the Gothic text; and finally (6) to offer a new evaluation of the Gothic readings in the light of current New Testament textual criticism.

I have many debts of gratitude to acknowledge. The first of these is due to †Piergiuseppe Scardigli, who introduced me to Gothic studies in 1988 and supported me over the years.

I greatly thank the Humboldt foundation, which allowed me to spend several months at the Institut für neutestamentliche Textforschung in Münster. I will be forever grateful to Holger Strutwolf, its Director, for having accepted me as a guest scholar and for his support, and to the researchers of this Institute. Among these, I would like to thank in particular Ulrich Schmid and Klaus Wachtel for their continued availability – even during lunch times – to discuss with

---

1 "Wenn die gotische Übersetzung [...] nicht wie die lateinische, syrische usw. Übersetzung als primärer Zeuge in den kritischen Apparaten des griechischen Neuen Testaments verzeichnet wird, sondern in der Regel beinahe beiläufig, dann eben deshalb, weil die Textvorlage in ihrem Grundcharakter genau bestimmt werden kann: Wulfila hat eine Handschrift des frühen byzantinischen Textes bei seiner Übersetzung zugrunde gelegt, so wie er uns in den griechischen Handschriften ebenfalls begegnet." (Aland-Aland 1989, 216).
2 With the exception of the mention of the existence of Mk 16:9 – 20, see Nestle-Aland[28], 76*, 174.
3 UBS[4].
4 IGNTP 1984 – 1987.
5 On this project, carried on by the researchers of the Institut für neutestamentliche Textforschung (INTF; Münster/Westf., Germany) and by the Institute for Textual Scholarship and Electronic Editing (ITSEE; Birmingham, UK), in collaboration with the International Greek New Testament Project (IGNTP) and several other scholars, see http://www.uni-muenster.de/INTF/ECM.html (7.11.2014).

me part of my text and for their useful suggestions. My deepest gratitude also goes to David C. Parker for his encouragement and help.

Furthermore, I wish to thank many other teachers, colleagues and friends for the critical reading of this volume and for their suggestions: Philip Burton, Vittoria Dolcetti Corazza, J. Albert Harrill, Michael W. Holmes, Antonio Piras, Roland Schuhmann and Magnús Snædal. Many thanks are due also to Francesco Lo Monaco and Gianluca Poldi, with whom I have examined the Gothic manuscripts in the Ambrosian Library of Milan. Of course, any errors in this book are entirely my own.

1 Wulfila and his context

Ancient authors considered the Gothic bishop Wulfila or Ulfila[6] to be the translator of the Bible into Gothic. The oldest sources are the reports of the fifth-century Church historians Philostorgios, Socrates and Sozomen.[7] According to Philostorgios, Wulfila "translated all the Scriptures into their [i.e of the Goths] language – with the exception, that is, of Kings. This was because these books contain the history of wars, while the Gothic people, being lovers of war, were in need of something to restrain their passion for fighting rather than to incite them to it – which those books have the power to do."[8] Auxentius of Durostorum, Wulfila's pupil, does not explicitly mention the translation of the Bible among the activities of his teacher. He reports more generally that Wulfila left "several tractates and many interpretations"[9] in Gothic, Greek and Latin.

The Gothic bishop also devised an alphabet in order to write down the translation. The memory of his achievement is not only attested by the authors of the fifth century, but continues until the Middle Ages.[10]

1.1. Wulfila's life and education

Two main periods of Wulfila's life may be discerned: one before and one after his crossing of the Danube in 347/348. In the first period, he and his people settled outside the Roman Empire. He lived somewhere in the southern part of the area associated with the so-called 'Sântana de Mureș' culture,[11] a territory which extended between the Dniester and Danube rivers and which covered the eastern part of the former Dacia, approximately corresponding with the fourth century

---

6 On the various renderings of the Gothic bishop's name, which means in Gothic 'little wolf', see Ebbinghaus 1991, 236–238.
7 Philost., *HE* II. 5; Socr., *HE* IV. 33; Sozom., *HE* VI. 37.
8 Philost., *HE* II. 5, translated by Heather-Matthews 1991, 144. It is impossible to determine whether the statement concerning the book of Kings is true because, with the exception of a fragment of the book of Nehemiah (see below, fn. 140) and some citations preserved in a Gothic sermon or liturgical prayer (see below 2.2.2), the Old Testament in Gothic is lost.
9 Max., *diss*. 33: *[Qui et ipsis tribus linguis] plures tractatus et multas interpretationes [uolentibus ad utilitatem et aedificationem sibi ad aeternam memoriam et mercedem post se dereliquid]*, translation in Heather-Matthews 1991, 150. However, none of these other works survive.
10 On Wulfila as inventor of the Gothic alphabet see Lendinara 1992; on Wulfila, the Goths and their conversion see Scardigli 1967.
11 Sîntana de Mureș in the pre-1989 Romanian spelling.

Gothia.¹² His village may have been in the regions of Moldavia or Wallachia, where archaeological evidence suggests there was a particular concentration of Gothic settlements.¹³

The date of Wulfila's birth has been extrapolated from Auxentius' statement that Wulfila *de lectore triginta annorum episkopus est ordinatus*.¹⁴ Since the *terminus post quem non* of his consecration is the death of Eusebius of Nicomedia in 341, who nominated him bishop, the year of Wulfila's birth is set between 306/307 and 311 (the latter is the traditional date).¹⁵ The place of his birth is unknown.

According to Socrates,¹⁶ he was a pupil of Theophilos, bishop of the *Gothia* (Θεόφιλος Γοτθίας), who attended the council of Nicaea in 325. If this is true, it is necessary to explain when Wulfila converted to the Homoean creed (which he followed until his death).¹⁷ Indeed, written sources provide two different pictures of his religious formation. The Nicene historians (Socrates,¹⁸ Sozomen¹⁹ and Theodoret²⁰) report his conversion from Nicene orthodoxy between 360 and 376; i.e. many years after his crossing of the Danube. The Arians Philostorgios²¹ and Auxentius²² do not mention this alleged conversion; a fact which seems to imply that Wulfila followed the Homoean docrine from the very beginning of

---

12 See Wolfram 1990, 33; Chrysos 1992, 187; Kokowski 2007, 222–223.
13 Heather 1991, 86. The Goths were not a unified political entity. They were divided into at least two tribal confederations in the fourth century: the Tervingi-Vesi and the Greuthungi-Ostrogothi. The Tervingi inhabited the eastern half of the old Roman province of Dacia; the Greuthungi lived beyond the Dniester eastward up to the Don. On this topic see Wolfram 1990, 34; Heather 1991, 331–333; Lenski 1995, 120.
14 Max., *diss.* 35: "he was at the age of thirty ordained bishop from the rank of lector", translated by Heather-Matthews 1991, 141. "The exact date is however affected by Auxentius' wish to assimiliate Ulfila's career to that of king David, who became king at 30 and reigned forty years", and "to Joseph" (Heather-Matthews 1991, 141, fn. 41); see also Ebbinghaus (1992, 98).
15 Regarding the date of Wulfila's consecration, on which the date of birth is based, see below, fn. 28.
16 Socr., *HE* II. 41.23; *Patrum Nicaen. Nom.* lxiv. Since Philostorgios (*HE* II. 5) called Wulfila "the first bishop of the Goths", it is not clear who Theophilos was (some modern historians make him bishop of the Crimean Goths); see Schäferdiek 1990 [1991], 37; Schwarcz 1999, 451.
17 On Wulfila's Homoean creed see Schäferdiek 1992, part. 42–43 (against Simonetti 1976); Brennecke 2007, 150–154. Wulfila's creed is reported by Max., *diss.* 40, see Heather-Matthews 1991, 135–143.
18 Socr., *HE* II. 41, 23.
19 Sozom., *HE* VI. 37, 8–9.
20 Theod., *HE* IV. 37, 1.
21 Philost., *HE* II. 5.
22 Max., *diss.* 40.

his career.²³ No conclusive answer concerning Wulfila's first doctrinal position may be given. In any case, political reasons could well explain the acceptance of this form of Christianity by the Goths, since it was supported by both emperors Constantius II and Valens, who permitted Wulfila and his followers to enter the Roman Empire.

Even if Wulfila's ancestors were among the Christian prisoners captured during the Gothic raids into Asia Minor shortly after the middle of the third century (they came from a village called Sadagolthina, in Cappadocia),²⁴ his social status was high, judging by his education and career.²⁵ Auxentius reports that Wulfila preached and wrote in Greek, Latin and Gothic²⁶, and that he attained the rank of reader (*lector*),²⁷ a reference which leads to the assumption that he was well educated.

According to Philostorgios,²⁸ Wulfila was sent to Constantinople before 341 as a member of a diplomatic mission, during which he was consecrated bishop of the Goths by Eusebius of Nicomedia, the emperor's leading bishop. After his consecration – Auxentius²⁹ reports – he "began to preach the Gospel" among the Goths. He "taught them to live by the rule of evangelic, apostolic and prophetic truth", a reference that seems to indicate lectures and/or interpretations of both the New ("evangelic, apostolic") and Old ("prophetic") Testament.

Seven years later, in 347 or 348, following persecutions by heathen Goths, he was forced to seek asylum within the imperial territory, together with his people,

---

23 See the discussion of the sources in Sivan 1996.
24 Philost., *HE* II. 5, see Heather-Matthews 1991, 143–145.
25 Difficulties emerge from the comparison between the different accounts of Wulfila's career given by the Church historians, see the bibliography quoted in the fn. 28.
26 Max., *diss.* 33: [...] *grecam et latinam et goticam linguam sine intermissione in una et sola eclesia Cristi predicauit* [...], see also above, fn. 9.
27 Max., *diss.* 35; see also above, fn. 14.
28 Philost., *HE* II. 5. Chronological problems arise from Philostorgios' statement, according to whom Wulfila was consecrated during Constantine's lifetime, whilst Eusebius (†341) was still bishop of Nicomedia. Auxentius, instead, puts Wulfila's consecration under Constantius II (Max., *diss.* 35); see also the discussion in Thompson 1966, xiv-xvii; McLynn 2007, 128. The traditional date of Wulfila's consecration is the year 341; see for instance Heather 1991, 142; Schwarcz 1999, 453. Schäferdiek (1990 [1991], 39–40 and 2001, 299) and Barnes (1990, 541–545) prefered to accept the year 336; Wolfram (1990, 87; 2013, 28) argues that Wulfila went to Constantinople between 332 and 337 with a Gothic delegation and in 341 to Antiochia, where he was nominated bishop of the Goths by Eusebius. Ebbinghaus (1992, 97, 100) suggested 336 or early 337 as the year of the consecration, which would have taken place in Nicomedia, not in Constantinople. Sivan (1996, 381–383) prefers generically to speak of a time between 337 and 341.
29 Max., *diss.* 35, translated by Heather-Matthews 1991, 141.

the so called *Gothi minores* 'lesser Goths'.[30] Received by Constantius II with honour and respect, they settled in Moesia Inferior, close to Nicopolis ad Istrum, at the foot of Mount Haemus (near modern Nikyup, northern Bulgaria), in the report of the Gothic historian Jordanes.[31] According to this latter source, descendents of this group still lived in the same area in the mid-sixth century, peacefully farming and tending cattle.

In Moesia, Wulfila continued to teach biblical texts and to govern his community.[32] His religious and political leadership emerges from the words of Auxentius,[33] who compares him to Moses, as well as from those of Philostorgios,[34] who reports that the emperor called him 'the Moses of our time'.[35] This juxtaposition, therefore, seems to highlight – beyond the literary *topos* – Wulfila's authority within his community, an authority which undoubtedly also had political echoes, as Theodoret[36] and Jordanes[37] later recognise.

In the following years, the Gothic bishop maintained contacts with the church and the court of Constantinople. At least two official visits are known: one in 360, when he attended the council of Constantinople, under the patronage of Constantius II (337–361), who – as it is known – favoured the Homoean position;[38] and the second in 383, when he died after having arrived "by imperial order to the city of Constantinople for the purpose of disputation".[39] One may speculate that there were other contacts in the early 360s – when the bishop of the Goths was involved in negotiations with the imperial court – but the sources are not consistent.[40] This relationship between Wulfila and the court and church of Constantinople, both before and after his entrance into the Roman Em-

---

30 Philost., *HE* II. 5; Max., *diss.* 37: *cum grandi populo*, see Heather-Matthews 1991, 151–152. According to Wolfram (1990, 90), the label *minores* is applied to the peoples settled within the imperial territories.
31 Jord., *Get.* LI. 267. On the Goths in Moesia, see Velkov 1989, 525–527; Wolfram 1990, 73, 89; Heather 1991, 96; Heather-Matthews 1991, 144, fn. 22.
32 Max., *diss.* 34.
33 Max., *diss.* 37.
34 *HE* II. 5.
35 This kind of juxtaposition is well attested in Greek authors of the fourth and fifth centuries, in which Moses was regarded as the prototype of the Christian leader and especially of the bishop, in other words as the embodiment of ecclesiastical leadership, see Rapp 2005, 127–131.
36 Theod., *HE* IV. 37, 3.
37 Jord., *Get.* LI. 267.
38 Sozom., *HE* IV. 24, 1; VI. 37, 9; Socr., *HE* II. 41; Theod., *HE* II. 28. On this occasion he subscribed to the formulas of Rimini, see Sumruld 1994, 39.
39 Max., *diss.* 39, translated by Heather-Matthews 1991, 142. Concerning the date of death, which has been disputed, see Thompson 1966, xv, xxi; Heather-Matthews 1991, 141; McLynn 2007, 126.
40 Sozom., *HE* VI. 37, 9, see Sivan 1996, 379.

pire, is not irrelevant for the text-critical history of the Gothic Bible. Indeed, it is certain that it was translated from a Greek *Vorlage*[41] and it is easy to speculate that this *Vorlage* came from this city.

When and where Wulfila started his translation of the Bible is a matter of conjecture. One might reasonably guess that the version was begun at least orally before the crossing of the Danube, during the time in which he was *lector* and missionary, and completed (transcribed?) in Moesia, in a politically more peaceful milieu.

Another open question concerns the authorship of the version. Even if Wulfila is the only translator of the Gothic Bible mentioned by ancient sources,[42] it is very likely that the Gothic bishop did not carry out the entire work alone. Divergences in the rendering of the Greek text would indeed suggest a team working under his supervision.[43] Among the possible helpers, there might have been Selenas (Σελῖνας), Wulfila's secretary (ὑπογραφεύς) and successor (διάδοχος) as bishop.[44]

Besides the *Gothi minores*, other Germanic peoples of Homoean faith used the Gothic Bible, which at a certain point may have also assumed a political and social identity role.[45] The missionary activity of the Visigoths (*Vesegothae*) in spreading their Christian belief is reported by Jordanes:[46] "Moreover, from the love they bore them, they preached the Gospel both to the Ostrogoths and to their kinsmen the Gepidae, teaching them to reverence this heresy, and they invited all people of their speech everywhere to attach themselves to this sect."

The use of the Gothic version outside Wulfila's community is attested by an amulet with some verses of John in Gothic script, found in the Hungarian cemetery of Hács-Béndekpuszta, dating from the last third of the fifth century.[47] It is the oldest witness to the diffusion of the Gothic Bible and – currently – the only one from eastern Europe. It is probably connected with the Ostrogoths.[48] Perhaps Ostrogoths were those peoples, settled near Tomi (Constanţa, on the Black Sea

---

41 See below 5. and 5.1.
42 See above, fn. 7.
43 Friedrichsen 1939, 259.
44 On Selenas, see Socr., *HE* V. 23 and Sozom., *HE* VII. 17; he "is said to have been involved in inter-Arian disputes in the difficult days in Constantinople following the Council of 381." (Wiles 1996, 48).
45 See Liebeschuetz 1990, 49–50; Heather 1991, 328; Gwynn 2010, 258–260.
46 Jord., *Get*. XXV. 133, translated by Mierow 1915, 88.
47 See below 2.2.1.
48 On Ostrogoths in Pannonia see Burns 1984, 150.

coast), who, according to Walafrid Strabo († 849),⁴⁹ still used in his time the Gothic translation in the liturgy.

The Gothic Bible was in use in southern Gaul during the reign of the Visigoths, as Salvian of Marseille (mid-fifth century) reports,⁵⁰ and perhaps later. Some Gothic words and biblical names are attested in two Latin manuscripts of French origin from the end of the eighth/beginning of the ninth century.⁵¹ Until the conversion to Catholicism of King Reccared I (589), who ordered that all Arian manuscripts (in Gothic?) should be collected and burned,⁵² the Gothic Bible was probably used also in Spain.

Wulfila's translation was almost certainly carried to Italy by Theoderic's Ostrogoths (489). It is not known when and where they came into contact with this version: one of the latest possible opportunities might have been during Theoderic's settlement at Novae (ca. 476–488),⁵³ not far from the settlement of the *Gothi minores* in Moesia. It is very likely that the Gothic text was also adopted by the Vandals, whose language was very similar to Gothic.⁵⁴ They might have become acquainted with the Gothic version when they settled in Pannonia, or after their migration to Spain, through the Visigoths, or finally later, after their migration to northern Africa, through the Ostrogoths, with whom the Vandals had many political contacts.⁵⁵ Whether other Germanic peoples – like the Burgunds, the Suebes and the Langobards – used this text before their conversion to Catholicism is impossible to ascertain (even if it is plausible).⁵⁶

---

49 Wal. Strabo, *exord.* VII.
50 Salv., *gub.* V. 2, 5.
51 See below 2.2.2 and 2.2.4.
52 Pseudo-Fredegar., *chron.* IV, 8.
53 On Theoderic at Novae (close to Svishtov, northern Bulgaria) see Burns 1984, 64, 123, 128, 190; Heather 1991, 275, 301; Prostko-Prostyński 1997.
54 On the Vandalic language see Francovich Onesti 2002, 200–202. It is also worth noting that many Goths served in the Vandalic army (see Proc., *BV* I. 8, 11–13).
55 See below 2.1.3.
56 Dennis H. Green (1998, 308) wrote concerning this topic: "This translation, probably accompanied by a vernacular liturgy, provided the linguistic basis for the spread of the new religion to other EG [East Germanic] tribes, for which Gothic served as a lingua franca." Regarding the Burgundian Church see Heil 2011.

1.2 The cultural and religious background of Wulfila's activity

As mentioned above, before moving into Roman soil, the Gothic bishop lived somewhere in the southern part of the area associated with the 'Sântana de Mureș' culture'.[57] A mixture of ethnic groups, religions and cultures emerges from the archaeological finds in these territories, which denote a close interaction – often difficult to evaluate – between their inhabitants, at least in the first half of the fourth century.[58] Evidence for this interaction also survives in the scanty written sources: Selenas, Wulfila's successor, was the son of a Phrygian mother and a Gothic father.[59] The Christian Sabas lived peacefully with Goths in a pagan community, where the people clearly sought to defend him from persecutors.[60] Furthermore, without intending to connect name forms with ethnic origin, it is interesting to note that the list of the martyrs burnt with the Goths Wereka and Batwins also comprehends Daco-Trakian, Illyrian, Latin and Greek names.[61]

A similar mixture is attested by the languages spoken in these territories during Wulfila's time: Latin, at least in the former Dacia; Greek, which was also the language used in the Greek colonies along the coast of the Black Sea; Gothic (and other East Germanic dialects) and the unattested languages spoken by Dacians, Sarmatians and other unidentifiable peoples living in the area (like Alans, Gepids, Thracians and perhaps Celts).[62] That Latin was still in use in Dacia, even after the withdrawal of the Roman administration (271), emerges from the Latin loan words attested in the Gothic version. These terms of Latin origin, which en-

---

57 See above 1.1.
58 Ionița 1997, 162. Interpretative difficulties are mainly the result of the formation of what can be called 'a Roman frontier culture'. As Linda Ellis (1996, 106) points out: "Identifying ethnicity during the fourth century using archaeological evidence in the Carpathian-Pontic region has proven especially difficult because finds, from both settlements and burials, have been attributed to four different cultures: Dacian, Roman, Sarmatian, and Germanic." On the relationship between Goths and Romans in the third and fourth century see Scardigli-Scardigli 1976, 261–295.
59 Socr., *HE* V. 23.
60 *Passio S. Sabae* 3.
61 Wereka and Batwins are named in a fragment from a Gothic calendar bound together with the Gothic Pauline Epistles in the ms. *Ambros.* A⁺, at f. 216r. The text – a translation of a now lost Greek model, probably not earlier than 419 – reports the notices of the martyrdom of many people burnt in a church during one of the Gothic persecutions. The names of these martyrs are preserved also in the form Οὐήρικας and Βαθούσης (with variants) in a Greek menologium, written around 400, see Achelis 1900; Ebbinghaus 1976; Ebbinghaus 1979 A; Schäferdiek 1988; Reichert 1989; Nigro 2012.
62 See Popescu 1973; Popescu 1976; Gerov 1980, 163; Lungu 2000, 113; Alexianu 2004.

tered into Gothic after the migration from northern Europe, testify to the close relationship between Goths, Romans and Daco-Romans. They belong particularly to the military sphere: some examples are the Gothic words *anno* 'wages' (< Lat. *annōna*), *kapillon* 'to cut hair' (< Gothic new formation based on Lat. *capillus* 'hair'), *sulja* 'sandal' (< Lat. *solea*), *militon* 'to serve as a soldier' (< Lat. *mīlito*) and perhaps *karkara* 'prison' (< Vulg. Lat. **carcara*). Other Latin loan words in Gothic suggest the Goths' fascination for the Roman lifestyle, e. g.: *anakumbjan* 'to recline at table' (< Lat. *accumbo*), *aurali* 'towel', 'napkin' (< Vulg. Lat. **ōrārium*), *mes* 'table', 'platter' (< Vulg. Lat. **mēsa*), *kubitus* 'company of people at a meal' (< Lat. *cubitus* 'reclining at a meal') and *lukarn* 'lamp', 'light' (< Lat. *lucerna* or better from Vulg. Lat. **lucarna*). The linguistic adaptation suggests that these words entered into Gothic through popular speech. They were probably adopted by Gothic soldiers who served in the Roman army during the third century and subsequently became part of the Gothic language.[63]

The conversion of the Goths, or at least part of them, took place within this multicultural and multilingual context. It was a complex and long process: different groups converted at different times and to different forms of Christian belief. The existence of Nicene and Homoean Goths is indeed attested contemporarily, without their relationship – whether peaceful or hostile – being clear.

The spread of Christianity among the Goths is, obviously, closely related on the one hand to its spread in the trans-Danubian territories, on the other to the political interests of the Gothic rulers. Concerning the diffusion of Christian faith north of the Danube (modern Romania) in the second half of the third and in the first half of the fourth century, the written sources are very scanty.[64] However, some archaeological evidence is preserved, especially objects with Christian symbols (crosses, fishes, doves).[65] Eastern territories close to the Black Sea (*Schy*-

---

[63] That these words entered into Gothic before Wulfila's translation emerges from their degree of integration into Gothic, see Corazza 1969; Scardigli 1973, 80–86; Green 1998, 202–209. On the Latin influence on some Gothic syntactical constructions before Wulfila's translation see Dolcetti Corazza 2004, 73, 85–87.

[64] Concerning the allusions of Tert., *adv. Jud.* 7, and Orig., *in Matth.* 24, 9, see Barnea 1987, 39–40; on the diffusion of Christianity north of the Danube, in territories close to Gothic settlements, see also Barnea 1977, 13; Rusu 1991; Zugravu 1997, 299–300; Madgearu 2004; Gudea-Chiu 2005; Popescu 2006; Ene 2009; Mitrea 2009, 135–136; in the Lower Danube region, see Cățoi 2009.

[65] Among them is the famous *tabella ansata* of Biertan (fourth century), with a Latin inscription and the monogram of Christ: it represents an important witness to the continuity of the use of the Latin in this area, see Popescu 1973, 77; Barnea 1987, 44. It is also notable that Christian objects are often found in the same places where Roman coins are present, a fact that reveals the connection between the Roman imports and the spread of Christianity, see Madgearu 2004, 42.

thia Minor) show clear traces of evangelisation – and connections with Asia Minor – already at the end of the third century, if not earlier.[66] Conversely, the southern and eastern territories of the 'Sântana de Mureș' culture' do not offer clear archaeological evidence of the spread of Christianity, even if the west-east orientation of some graves and their lack of grave goods might be ascribed to Christian influence.[67] The modest number of archaeological finds with Christian symbols in the northern Danubian area and the Christian terminology of Vulgar Latin origin suggest a slow penetration of the new faith, rather than a mass conversion led by the political authorities and realised by official missionaries. In other words, the picture that emerges from the archaeological evidence is that of a 'popular Christianity', spread by Christianised and Latinised inhabitants of the trans-Danubian territories, Roman prisoners, soldiers and traders. They could be regarded as the first vehicles of transmission of the Christian belief to the Goths.[68] Also some early Christian loan words in Gothic, which seem to stem from Latin,[69] might date back to these first contacts between Goths and Latinised Christians.

It is indeed very likely that a form of Christianity reached at least part of the Goths some decades before Wulfila's activity. Mention has already been made that Christian prisoners, among them Wulfila's ancestors, converted many Goths to the Christian faith during the last third of the third century.[70] Athanasius claimed – in the first third of the fourth century – that some Goths had already become Christian.[71] Furthermore, the existence of a bishop of the *Gothia* in 325 is attested by the list of the Nicene bishops.[72] In addition, the fact that Wulfila was a *lector* suggests the existence, in the trans-Danubian territories, of organised Christian communities (whose doctrinal status is not possible to determine), that used biblical texts.[73] It is difficult to ascertain whether they were in Latin or Greek, because on the one hand the official language of the Empire was

---

[66] Lungu 2000, 103–115.
[67] Ioniţa 1997, 165; Madgearu 2001, 62–69.
[68] See Barnea 1977, 23–24; Forlin Patrucco-Roda 1979; Zugravu 1997, part. 19–23; Popescu 2006, 632–633.
[69] See below 1.4.
[70] Philost., *HE* II. 5; see also Sozom., *HE* II. 6.
[71] Athan., *de incarn.* 51, 2.
[72] See above, fn. 16.
[73] Other missions in *Scythia* and *Gothia* were carried out by the heretical bishop Audius in the second quarter of the fourth century, see Heather 1986, 293, fn. 13; Schwarcz 1999, 452.

still Latin and the trans-Danubian region was deeply Latinised; on the other hand, Greek was the common language of the liturgy in the Eastern Empire.[74]

Constantine's intention to impose Christianity on those Goths with whom he made peace in 332 is attested by Socrates[75] (this reference does not contradict the affirmation that part of the Goths was already introduced to the Christian faith). After this treaty, the Roman regular interventions made it certainly easier for Christianity to take hold in the trans-Danubian territories.[76] Other references concerning the spread of the Nicene faith among the Goths are provided by Basil and the acts of the martyrs. According to Basil,[77] the Cappadocian Eutyches undertook a mission in the second half of the third century. Furthermore, the acts of the martyrs Sabas, Nicetas, Innas, Rimas and Pinnas indicate the existence of Nicene communities in *Gothia* in the second half of the fourth century.[78] Some decades later, John Chrysostom ordained priests, deacons and lectors and offered to the Gothic Nicene community of Constantinople a proper church, where he occasionally preached;[79] and in 404 he ordained the bishop Unila for a Gothic community in Crimea.[80]

Concerning the spreading of the Homoean doctrine in the trans-Danubian territories, and particularly among the different groups of Goths, the sources are scanty and their interpretation is controversial.[81] Regarding the time before Wulfila's activity as bishop nothing is known. After his consecration, according

---

74 On the diffusion of the Latin language in the lower Danubian territories in the fourth century, see Bardy 1948, 123–129, 146–148; Mihăescu 1978, part. 52–56; Liebeschuetz 1990, 136. It is worth noting that the first bishop of the Goths, Theophilos, bore a Greek name and that Wulfila himself, according to Auxentius, preached and wrote also in Latin and Greek (see above, fn. 9 and 26).
75 Socr., *HE* I. 18.
76 On the close relationship between the trans-Danubian territories and the Roman Empire, as result of Constantine's victory, see Popescu 2013, 595–614.
77 Bas., *epist.* 164, 2, translated by Heather-Matthews 1991, 118–125, see Schäferdiek 1990 [1991], 39; Wolfram 1990, 87.
78 Thompson 1966, 99; Schwarcz 1987, 112; Liebeschuetz 1990, 80; Schäferdiek 1990 [1991], 38–39; Heather-Matthews 1991, 109–117; Schäferdiek 1993; Girardi 2004, 157–171; Nigro 2012. Sabas' *passio* provides the best account of the life of a Gothic community in the lower Danube and it has been studied from several points of view; see for instance Thompson 1966, 64–77; Diaconu 1975; Rubin 1981, 36–41; Girardi 2009; Girardi 2012.
79 Joh. Chrys., *hom.* 8. On Chrysostom's attitude toward the Goths, see Liebeschuetz 1990, 169–170, 190–191; see also Albert 1984, 173–177; Schwarcz 1987, 112–113.
80 Joh. Chrys., *epist.* IX. 5, see Schäferdiek 1990 [1991], 37.
81 See Thompson 1966, 78–93; Zeev 1981; Burns 1984, 146–150; Heather 1986; Wolfram 1990, 93; Lenski 1995; McLynn 2007, 132–133.

to Socrates[82] and Sozomen,[83] Wulfila began to teach the Holy Scriptures to Athanaric's and Fritigern's peoples. The latter seems to have accepted Christianity – in the Homoean form endorsed by Valens – as a condition of entering the Roman Empire in 376.[84] The official conversion of the Gothic authorities, of course, may not represent the real beginning of the diffusion of Christianity among the Goths, which to some extent dates back to Wulfila's missionary activity and in part also to contacts with other Christianised peoples. The two waves of persecutions of the mid-fourth century[85] in the trans-Danubian territories led to the assumption that Christianity was much more widespread than the sources testify, particularly, but not only, amongst the lower social classes.[86]

From sporadic attestations in the sources it is possible to extrapolate that both the Homoean and Nicene communities of Goths were clearly structured in the mid-fourth century.[87] There are references to the existence of bishops, like Wulfila and Goddas[88] (if Nicene); priests, like the Homoean Wereka and the Nicene Guþþika;[89] and lectors, like Wulfila himself and the Catholic Sabas,[90] who worshipped in churches. Within the Homoean community – it is not known whether the Catholic community used the same forms – the Gothic designation for 'bishop' was *aipiskaupus* (< Gr. ἐπίσκοπος or Lat. *episcopus*), for 'deacon' was *diakaunus* (< Gr. διάκονος or Lat. *diaconus*), as it is possible

---

82 Socr., *HE* IV. 33, 6–7.
83 Sozom., *HE* VI. 37, 12–14.
84 Socr., *HE* IV. 33, 6–7, see Heather 1986, 315–316; Liebeschuetz 1990, 49.
85 They are dated 347/348 and 369/372 (Heather 1986, 316). According to Rubin (1981, 44), instead, three waves occurred: 347/348, 369 and 372.
86 Thompson 1966, 75–76; Wolfram 1990, 88, 91–92. The sources testify that the queen Gaatha was also an active Christian (perhaps Nicene), engaged in the *translatio* of relics, see Rubin 1981, 39–40; Wolfram 1990, 91–92.
87 On the basis of the peoples of Christian faith mentioned by different sources, Cățoi (2009, 200) observes: "On peut constater […] que l'Eglise était bien organisée en ces régions [i.e. in the northern Danubian territories], disposant d'une hiérarchie supérieure (évêques, prêtres et diacres), la hiérarchie inférieure aussi étant attestée (hypodiacres, lecteurs, diaconesses, exorcistes). […] [C]ette structure ecclésiastique, à solide organisation hiérarchique, ne saurait être une réalité récente à la fin du IIIe siècle. Pour parvenir à ce niveau, les communautés auraient besoin de deux générations au moins. Les premières formes d'organisation stable de l'Eglise au Danube remontent, selon toutes ces données, jusqu'à la première moitié du IIIe siècle."
88 On the bishop Goddas, who transported Sabas' relics to a certain place, see Thompson 1966, 161–165.
89 *Passio S. Sabae* 4.
90 *Passio S. Sabae* 2; see Heather-Matthews 1991, 112, fn. 21.

to infer from the terms used in Wulfila's translation, and for 'priest' was *papa* (< Gr. παπᾶς), attested in the Gothic calendar and in the deed of Naples.[91]

Nothing is known about the relationship between the Homoean and the Nicene communities of the Goths. An open question is whether there existed two different translations of the Scriptures or whether Wulfila's translation was used also by Nicene Goths. In any case, there is no reason to doubt that the extant Gothic manuscripts transmit part of Wulfila's version.[92] The old hypothesis[93] that the text preserves traces of the Homoean creed in Phil 2:6 does not find a general consensus today. In this passage, ἴσα (θεῷ) 'equal (with God)' has been translated with *galeiko* (*guda*) – from *galeiks*, generally used to render ὅμοιος 'similar' – instead of *ibna*. However, it is not certain whether *ibna* and ἴσος correspond perfectly; furthermore, the semantic value of the adverb *galeiko* is not easy to determine.[94] Moreover, it is worth noting the translation of Jn 10:30, 17:11, 21, 22, where a Gothic dual form is used to render a Greek plural, e. g.: *ik jah atta meins ain siju* 'my Father and I are one' for ἐγὼ καὶ ὁ πατὴρ μου[95] ἕν ἐσμεν (Jn 10:30). The fact that Wulfila has used the dual to indicate the close relationship between the Father and the Son could – paradoxically – be interpreted as a hint of their consubstantiality for the translator.[96] It seems risky therefore to draw doctrinal conclusions from these contradictory passages.

As mentioned above, in 347/348 Wulfila and his followers established themselves in Moesia Inferior, in the region of Nicopolis ad Istrum.[97] Again, a blend of

---

91 On the origin of these Gothic words see the bibliography in Lehmann 1986, *s.v.*
92 They are written in a specific alphabet attributed to Wulfila (see below 1.3.). Otherwise one should postulate two different translations and two inventors of two different alphabets.
93 Castiglioni 1835, *ad loc.*; Streitberg 1919 (= Streitberg-Scardigli 2000), *ad loc.*; Mirarchi 1976 B; with doubts Stutz 1966, 6–7.
94 Schäferdiek 1979, 130–131; Piras 2007, 44.
95 meins: μου] W* Δ 27 1243 700 it^e sy$^{s.p}$ co | *om.* p$^{66.75}$ ℵ A B D L Θ Ψ f^1 f^{13} 33 𝔐 lat Chrys.
96 Stutz 1966, 6–7; Piras 2007, 44.
97 Jord., *Get.* LI. 267, see above, 1.1. Archaeologists, however, point out that in the territory of Nicopolis the presence of the Goths does not emerge clearly from archaeological evidence. In other words, it is not possible to ascribe to the Goths particular ethnic elements of identification, a fact that denotes a high degree of assimilation between peoples of different origin, see Poulter 2007. At p. 175 the English scholar notes that the "'Foederati ware' [i.e. {0,0,0,100}/grey vessels] is, in decoration, as well as in form and fabric, closer to the pottery of the Sântana de Mureş/Cherneakov culture than to earlier Roman fine wares. [...] That 'Foederati ware' indicates the introduction of a new ceramic tradition, perhaps brought by potters from outside the Empire, remains an attractive explanation", but at p. 182 he concludes: "[t]hat the modest but large community outside Nicopolis in the fourth century contained Goths is an attractive idea [...], but the excavated evidence does not prove it. [...] On the lower Danube, there had always been a mixing of different populations, the exchange of technology and fashions."

languages and cultures characterises this territory. Both Latin and Greek were spoken, together with Thracian and other languages about which very little is known, and Gothic, after the arrival of the Goths from the trans-Danubian area.[98] Roman colonists settled here after the withdrawal from Old Dacia, so that Latin was not yet obscured by the Greek language.[99] Indeed, in the city of Nicopolis, inhabited by élites, the inscriptions (until the fourth century) are predominantly in Greek; in the countryside, conversely, they are mostly in Latin.[100] Furthermore, it is interesting to note that the bishops Valens of Oescus (343) and Domninus of Marcianopolis (367) have Latin names and Wulfila's pupil, Auxentius of Durostorum, spoke and wrote in Latin. Also written in Latin is the mid-fourth century inscription of Marcus Aurelius Maximus, found in the area near to Nicopolis, in which the Gothic word *bruta* 'daughter-in-law', instead of Lat. *nurus* is attested.[101] Some decades later, at the beginning of the fifth century, Laurentius (bishop of Novae) felt the need to translate into Latin two homilies by John Chrysostom.[102]

Considering this cultural picture, it is certainly possible – although no manuscript is preserved – that Latin versions of the Bible circulated in the lower Danubian territories. Their availability in this area is not without importance for the textual history of the Gothic version, because Wulfila may have also used a Latin exemplar to aid his translation. This is a *vexata quaestio*.[103] At any rate, these hints regarding the circulation of Latin versions mean that one should keep an open mind as to whether the Gothic bishop used them.

The first possible – although problematic – hint comes from Wulfila's creed,[104] which transmits two quotations from the New Testament (Lk 24:49

---

98 It is also likely that Gothic words without a clear etymology (and without a Germanic origin) could be loan words from some non-identified languages spoken in the Danubian area see e. g. *frasts* 'child', *kalkjo* 'whore', *siponeis* 'disciple' (Lehmann 1986, s.v.).
99 On multilingualism in this area see Mihăescu 1978, 52–56; Zgusta 1980, 134; Curcă 2009.
100 Bardy 1948, part. 148–149; Gerov 1980, 159–163; Vladkova 2007, 207–208.
101 See Velkov 1989, 526–527.
102 See Morin 1937, 308–309.
103 See below 5.1.
104 Wulfila's creed, reported by Auxentius of Durostorum soon after the death of his master and quoted by the Arian bishop Maximinus in the mid-fifth century, is in Latin (Gryson 1982 B, 149–171). Some problems arise from the indirect tradition: (1) both Auxentius and Maximinus may have changed Wulfila's words; (2) Wulfila may have translated the biblical passages into Latin directly from a Greek text (and not quoted from a Latin version). However, there is no evidence that the creed is a translation from Gothic or Greek and nothing suggests that the original language was not Latin, see Gryson 1980, 168; Schäferdiek 1992, 36 and fn. 61.

and Acts 1:8). Particularly interesting is the fact that the reading of Lk 24:49[105] agrees with the early Byzantine text and with the Old Latin mss. *Brixianus* (f/10) and *Monacensis* (q/13)[106] against the readings of the other *Vetus Latina* and Vulgate manuscripts. In other words, the text of the quotation belongs typologically to the same text type as Wulfila's translation; a fact that seems to suggest a common geographical origin.

Evidence of the circulation of Latin translations of the Bible – at least of the Psalms – emerges from epigraphic witnesses from the end of the fourth, or perhaps from the fifth century. Although they seem to be some decades younger than Wulfila's translation, two Latin inscriptions from Moesia Inferior suggest the existence of Latin-speaking Christian communities in this area at an earlier time.[107]

Moreover, some Gothic compounds or syntagmas reflect Latin formations, deviating from the Greek counterpart: *arma-hairts* 'merciful' (Eph 4:32), structurally similar to Lat. *miseri-cors* (vs. Gr. εὔσπλαγχνος); *godis wiljins* 'good will' (gen.; Lk 2:14), which corresponds to Lat. *bonae uoluntatis* (vs. Gr. εὐδοκίας); *gawairþi habandans* '(they) who have peace' (Rom 12:18) to Lat. *pacem habentes* (vs. Gr. εἰρηνεύοντες); *wairaleiko taujai* 'act like a man' (1 Cor 16:13) to Lat. *uiriliter agite* (vs. Gr. ἀνδρίζεσθε).[108] Other linguistic structures are similar[109] and even if it is not possible to discern whether they are the result of a Latin influence on the Gothic or of a common linguistic heritage – both Gothic and Latin are Indo-European languages – this similarity is to be noted. Furthermore, it is worth mentioning the use of *arka* 'ark' in Lk 17:27 (*galaiþ Nauel in arka* 'Noah entered the ark'), which may reflect the biblical usage of the Latin term *arca* (originally 'box', 'coffer', then Noah's 'ark'): *intrauit Noe in arcam* against the Gr. εἰσῆλθεν Νῶε εἰς τὴν κιβωτόν.[110]

As has been said, the possibility cannot be excluded that Wulfila may also have had available a Latin version of the Bible (or parts of it), which may have offered a suitable solution for the rendering of some difficult expressions or passages of the Greek text into Gothic.

---

105 Max., diss. 40: *Ecce ego mitto promissum patris mei in uobis uos autem sedete in ciuitatem Hierusalem quoadusque induamini uirtutem ab alto.*
106 The Byzantine text reads: Καὶ ἰδού, ἐγὼ ἀποστέλλω τὴν ἐπαγγελίαν τοῦ πατρός μου ἐφ' ὑμᾶς· ὑμεῖς δὲ καθίσατε ἐν τῇ πόλει Ἰερουσαλήμ, ἕως οὗ ἐνδύσησθε δύναμιν ἐξ ὕψους (Hodges-Farstad 1985). Both Latin manuscripts, which are textually very close to the Gothic version (see below 5.2), transmit *ecce* and *Hierusalem* (Jülicher et al. 1976).
107 Felle 2009, 240 and 242.
108 See Dolcetti Corazza 1997, 16, 23.
109 See below 4.1.4.
110 Dolcetti Corazza 2004, 79–80.

1.3 The Gothic alphabet

In the multicultural Danubian territories, where several writing systems and writing styles were in use, Wulfila devised a specific alphabet to write down his translation of the Bible.[111] It was an important cultural achievement because the Goths did not have a written tradition, even if they probably knew and used the Germanic runes.

No Gothic manuscripts from Wulfila's time survive. The Gothic alphabet is known from manuscripts produced in the Latin west about 150 years later.[112] It comprises 27 signs, 25 of which have both a phonetic and numeric value. Two signs are used only as numerals: 𐍁 (90) and 𐍊 (900).

𐌰[113]	𐌱	𐌲	𐌳	𐌴	𐌵	𐌶	𐌷	𐌸	𐌹
1	2	3	4	5	6	7	8	9	10
‹a›	‹b›	‹g›	‹d›	‹e›	‹q›	‹z›	‹h›	‹þ›	‹i›
[a/a:]	[b]/[β]	[g]/[ɣ]	[d]/[ð]	[e:]	[kʷ]	[z]	[h]/[x]	[θ]	[i]

𐌺	𐌻	𐌼	𐌽	𐌾	𐌿	𐍀	𐍁	𐍂
20	30	40	50	60	70	80	90	100
‹k›	‹l›	‹m›	‹n›	‹j›	‹u›	‹p›		‹r›
[k]	[l]	[m]	[n]	[j]	[u/u:]	[p]		[r]

111 Socr., *HE* IV. 33; Sozom., *HE* VI. 37. A collection of the ancient sources regarding Wulfila as inventor of the Gothic alphabet can be found in Lendinara 1992, 217–225. The bibliography on the Gothic alphabet is vast and opinions on the origin of the Gothic letters are divergent: see e.g. von Friesen-Grape 1927; Boüüaert 1950; Marchand 1959; Viehmeyer 1971; Gendre 1976; Ebbinghaus 1979 B; Cercignani 1988; Ebbinghaus 1997 [1995]; Scardigli 1998; Mees 2002–2003; Raschellà 2008; Granberg 2010; Raschellà 2011.

112 See 2.1.

113 The original, Wulfilian shape of this letter was probably in three strokes, as the Greek *alpha:* 𐌰, as it is occasionally attested in the Gothic witnesses (among them the tablet of Hács-Béndekpuszta and the marginal glosses).

ε/s	T	Y	F	X	Θ	ᛉ	↑
200	300	400	500	600	700	800	900[114]
⟨s⟩	⟨t⟩	⟨w⟩	⟨f⟩	⟨x⟩	⟨ƕ⟩	⟨o⟩	
[s]	[t]	[w/y]	[f]	[x]	[hʷ]/[xʷ]	[o:]	

There is no doubt, on the basis of the shape of the letters and of their numerical value, that the primary source of the Gothic script was the Greek alphabet, in its majuscule or – less likely – cursive variant. As in the Greek script, the digraphs ΓΓ ⟨gg⟩ and ει are used respectively for [ŋg] and [i:].[115] Additional letters, which may stem from the Latin alphabet and/or from the runes (their origin is still disputed), are: (1) u [kʷ]; h [h/x]; G [j]; n [u]; ᛉ [o:] and (2) ᚱ [r]; ꜰ [f]. The introduction of the first group of letters is due to the fact that the Greek sound system and, consequently, the Greek alphabet, were defective in respect to the Gothic sound system. The letter h [h/x] stems undoubtedly from the Latin alphabet. It is interesting to observe that its form is uncial or cursive, i.e. non-epigraphic (H); a fact which points to the possibility that Wulfila found the model of this letter in a Latin manuscript. In any case, its presence in the *tabella Hungarica* indicates that it was already among the Wulfilian signs and was not introduced under western influence. The introduction of ᚱ [r] may instead be explained with the fact that the shape of Greek P [r] was unsuitable, because it was too similar to Latin P [p]. Wulfila avoided also the Greek letters H [e:] and C [s], which could be confused with the Latin letters of the same shape but different phonetic value (H [h], C [c]), preferring to use the shapes є and ε. This is a clear sign of the acquaintance of Wulfila and at least some other Goths (those who copied and read the Gothic manuscripts) with Latin writings. The reason for the replacement of ꜰ [f] is obscure (perhaps the Greek Φ [f] was too similar to ψ [θ]?). Finally, there is no explanation as to why two letters – ψ [θ] and ο [hʷ/xʷ] – have a Greek shape but a totally different phonetic value within the Gothic sound system. The value of ᚾ ⟨ai⟩ and ᚾn ⟨au⟩ is also controversial. Some scholars claim that they were diphthongs; other scholars prefer the view that they represent monophthongs, respectively [ε/ɛ:] and [ɔ/ɔ:].[116]

---

114 The phonetic value has been reconstructed especially on the basis of the Gothic rendering of Greek biblical names, see Marchand 1973, 23–34; Braune-Heidermanns 2004, 27–84. Some doubts, however, remain.

115 [ŋ] is usually rendered with Γ ⟨g⟩ plus the velar consonant. However, in a few instances, [ŋ] appears as ᚾ ⟨n⟩, undoubtedly as result of Latin influence. Regarding this and other graphic and phonetic features, as the assimilation of ⟨h⟩ at the end of a word and its omission, see the survey of Francovich Onesti 2007.

116 See the bibliography in Braune-Heidermanns 2004, 38–46; Piras 2007, 77.

Two types of ⟨s⟩ are attested in the Gothic witnesses: ϵ and s.[117] The origin of the shape ϵ may be the Greek Σ (used in inscriptions) or the rune for [s]; the letter s is undoubtedly of Latin origin. It seems to have been introduced – for an obscure reason – in a later period, probably in Italy. It is interesting to note that this introduction cannot have been polygenetic. In other words, the manuscripts that exhibit this letter are in some way related.

The Gothic manuscripts transmit two types of writings, which differ in the inclination of the axis of the letters: one is upright and one is sloping.[118] They share some common features: the letters are written between a bilinear system,[119] with only six or seven projecting above and below; each letter is drawn individually and not joined to another.[120] In the first studies of Gothic writing, scholars claimed that the sloping script was older than the upright one.[121] According to this opinion, the upright script was developed in Italy under the influence of the Latin uncial, because of the presence in the manuscripts with this script of the Latin-modelled s ⟨s⟩ and of the suspension of final -*m*[122] (as well of final -*n*). These two codicological elements point – doubtless – to a Latin influence on the Gothic manuscripts. Their introduction, however, should be dissociated from the introduction of the upright script. Indeed, both the Gothic scripts seem to derive from Greek models and would therefore

---

117 ϵ is attested in the ms. *Ambros.* B (see plate 4), in the Old Testament ms. *Ambros.* D, in the *Codex Bononiensis*, in the deeds of Naples (pap. 34) and Arezzo (now lost), in the marginal glosses of the mss. *Ambros.* A⁺ and Verona, Biblioteca Capitolare, LI (49)⁺; s is attested in the mss. *Argenteus* (see plate 1), *Gissensis* (see plate 2), *Carolinus* (see plate 3), *Ambros.* A⁺, *Ambros.* C (and in the marginal glosses of the *Argenteus*), see below 2.1.
118 The sloping type is attested in the ms. *Ambros.* B (see plate 4), in the *Codex Bononiensis*, in the deeds of Naples and Arezzo, in the marginal glosses of the mss. *Ambros.* A⁺ and Verona, Biblioteca Capitolare, LI (49)⁺; the upright type in the mss. *Argenteus* (see plate 1), *Gissensis* (see plate 2), *Carolinus* (see plate 3), *Ambros.* A⁺, *Ambros.* C (and in the marginal glosses of the *Codex Argenteus*); see below 2.1. The letters do not slope (or only slightly) in *Ambros.* D.
119 In the luxurious *Codex Argenteus* (2.1.1) the bilinear system is effectively drawn.
120 Cursive elements are attested in the deed of Naples, where two or more strokes of single letters are drawn at one time (facsimile in Tjäder 1954, 116–121). Cursive connections of letters do not however occur in any known Gothic manuscripts or documents.
121 Old references call the sloping script 'Type I' and the upright script 'Type II', see for instance Fairbanks-Magoun 1940, 315–316. The label 'S-type' for the upright script and 'Σ-type' for the sloping script (Ebbinghaus 1997 [1995], 83) should be rejected because the letter ϵ was very probably also used in the upright script (Falluomini 2010 B, 31).
122 This is a scribal practice typical of the Latin manuscripts, where there is an abundance of endings in -*m*, see Fairbanks-Magoun 1940, 316. Both -*m* (͞) and -*n* (͞) are written above or instead the preceding letter at the end of the line.

be old (Wulfilian):[123] the model of the upright type would be the Greek biblical majuscule;[124] those of the sloping type, the sloping majuscule.[125] The new form of s may have been introduced at a certain moment in the use of the upright script and from this point have become connected with this type.[126]

The correspondence between the Gothic upright script and the biblical majuscule is striking: the execution of the letters, the contrast between thin and thick strokes, and the serifs at the beginning and the end of the horizontal strokes are very similar. Both Gothic scripts are attested at the same time in Ostrogothic Italy, with different functions. The careful and harmonic upright script was employed for the production of precious and refined manuscripts; conversely, the sloping script was in use for writing less valuable manuscripts and glosses.[127]

Wulfila took not only the writing system from Greek models, but also the marks of punctuation, citation, paragraph, suspension, *nomina sacra* and, perhaps, the Ammonian and/or Euthalian Sections.[128] In addition to the translation of the Bible and the formation of an alphabet for the Goths, Wulfila also created a scriptorium, where parchment and ink were prepared, and where Gothic scribes were instructed to write his new alphabet.[129] This achievement may lead to the assumption that some experts, possibly from Constantinople,[130] helped in copying and book production.

---

123 Cavallo 1994 (orally, conference at the University of Florence); Ebbinghaus 1997 [1995], 92–93.
124 See the script of the fourth-century manuscripts *Sinaiticus* (ℵ/01) and *Vaticanus* (B/03), Cavallo 1967, 58 and 55.
125 See the script of the *Codex Washingtonianus* (W/032), fifth century (but see the doubts expressed in Schmid 2006).
126 Falluomini 2006, 35.
127 See Scardigli 1998, 456. But the 16 *marginalia* of the *Codex Argenteus* are in the upright variant.
128 See below 3.
129 Most of the words concerning the semantic field of book production are of Gothic origin (e.g. *boka* 'letter', *bokos* 'book(s)', *meljan* 'to write', *swartizl* 'ink'), see Lehmann 1986, s.v.; a loan word is Goth. *maimbrana* 'parchment', which may stem either from Lat. *membrāna* or Gr. μεμβράνα, see Corazza 1969, 59–60.
130 On Wulfila's close relationship with this city, see above 1.1.

1.4 Christian vocabulary

One of Wulfila's main achievement consisted in the creation of a new language to express peculiar biblical concepts which were foreign to Gothic culture.[131] The starting point for Wulfila's linguistic reflection may have been his time spent as *lector*, when he – at least orally – translated the Bible for his community. Wulfila's solutions to the rendering of Christian terms are diverse. He introduces into his version loan words, loan meanings, loan translations and mixed forms.

The Christian loan words in Gothic are few and concern biblical and technical terms, which could not be easily or satisfactorily rendered by purely native words. Some are of Semitic origin and passed into Gothic through the Greek, e.g.: *abba* 'father' (< ἀββα), *kaurban* 'gift to God' (< κορβᾶν), *manna* 'manna' (< μάννα), *pasxa/paska* 'Easter' (πάσχα), *rabbei* 'rabbi' (< ῥαββεί). Other words go back directly to the Greek, such as *aiwlaugia* 'blessing' (< εὐλογία), *aiwxaristia* 'thanksgiving' (< εὐχαριστία), *anaþaima* 'curse' (< ἀνάθεμα), *hairaiseis* 'heresies' (nom. plur. < αἱρέσεις), *paintekuste* 'Pentecost' (< πεντηκοστή), *parakletus* 'comforter' (< παράκλητος), *paraskaiwe* 'preparation' (< παρασκευή), *psalmo* 'psalm' (< ψαλμός).[132] Most of these terms – probably introduced into Gothic for the first time by Wulfila – follow a mixed Greek-Gothic declension.

It is worth noting that a group of Christian terms may have both Greek and Latin origin:[133] *aggilus* 'angel' (< Gr. ἄγγελος or Lat. *angelus*), *aipiskaupus* 'bishop' (< Gr. ἐπίσκοπος or Lat. *episcopus*), *aiwaggeljo* 'Gospel' (< Gr. εὐαγγέλιον or Vulg. Lat. **ēuangelio*), *apaustaulus* 'apostle' (< Gr. ἀπόστολος or Lat. *apostolus*), *diabaulus/diabulus* 'devil' (< Gr. διάβολος or Lat. *diabolus*). Furthermore, the word *aiwaggelista* 'evangelist' seems to be an old – pre-Wulfilian – borrowing from Lat. *ēuangelista* (vs. Gr. εὐαγγελιστής), as well as *praufetja* 'prophecy' from Lat. *prophētia* (vs. Gr. προφητεία).[134] All these words express basic concepts

---

131 Scardigli (1967) speaks of Wulfila's 'Germanisation of the Gospel' and 'Germanisation of Christianity' to underline a gradual process of assimilation and elaboration of Christian concepts in order to mediate them to the Goths; see also Dolcetti Corazza (2011, 73), who points out the influence of both Latin culture, on the lowest social niveau, and Greek, on the intellectual élite.
132 Beside the religious vocabulary, there are also other borrowings in the Gothic text, which render referents (originally) foreign to the Gothic culture, e.g.: *bwssaun* for βύσσος 'fine linen' and *gazaufwlakio* (dat.) for γαζοφυλάκιον 'treasury'; see Gaebeler 1911; on their adaptation, see Scardigli 1973, 122.
133 According to Corazza (1969, *s.v.*) they are old borrowings from Latin, see also Jellinek 1923 and the bibliography quoted in Lehmann 1986, *s.v.*, where a Greek derivation is not entirely excluded.
134 Details in Corazza 1969, *s.v.*; Lehmann 1986, *s.v.*

of the Christian faith and at least some of them may have been present in the Gothic language before Wulfila's translation, as a result of the contacts with Latin-speaking Christians already in the trans-Danubian territories.[135] They are integrated into the Gothic morphological system, even though, in some cases, there are discrepancies in their flexion.[136]

Wulfila's general tendency is, however, to avoid the use of (new) loan words, preferring loan meanings. They are the result of a process whereby previous existing Gothic forms acquired new meaning through the influence of a certain model, e.g.: *daupjan*, originally 'to immerse', came to mean 'to baptise', for βαπτίζω. Other examples are the words *ahma* 'spirit', *frauja* 'Lord', *gagups* 'devout', 'pious', *gup* 'God', which prior to the introduction of the Christian faith were probably employed in a pagan context; subsequently, they acquired a new Christian meaning and were used respectively for πνεῦμα, κύριος, εὐσχήμων and θεός.

The linguistic ability of Wulfila emerges particularly in the use of loan translations. In many cases Wulfila coined new compounds, such as *alabrunsts* 'burnt offering', formed by *ala-* 'all' and *-brunsts* (connected etymologically with *brinnan* 'to burn'), which renders ὁλοκαύτωμα; *allwaldands* 'almighty', a compound of *all-* 'all' and *waldands* (derived from *waldan* 'to rule', 'to control'), which translates παντοκράτωρ; *wailamerjan* 'to preach good news' (formed by *waila* 'well' and *merjan* 'to proclaim', 'to announce'), rendering of εὐαγγελίζω; *hleiprastakeins* 'feast of tabernacles' (formed by *hleipra* 'booth', 'tent' and *-stakeins*, connected etymologically with *staks* 'mark', 'puncture'), which translates σκηνοπηγία (Lat. *scēnopēgia*).[137] It is interesting that Wulfila offers a loan translation of σκηνοπηγία to his audience, who could understand this new formation by means of the preceding introductory sentence: *dulps Iudaie* '(the) festival of (the) Jews' (ἡ ἑορτὴ τῶν Ἰουδαίων).

Loan translations are, for the most part, learned formations, which are mostly restricted to the religious vocabulary and clearly modelled upon the Greek. Wulfila paid close attention to the Greek derivational structure and attempted to preserve it as closely as possible. Mixed forms are also occasionally attested,

---

135 Dolcetti Corazza 2004, 82–84; Dolcetti Corazza 2011, 70–71. However, since all the Gothic manuscripts have been produced in the Latin west, the Latinised forms might be later introductions.
136 See Snædal 2013 A, II *s.v.* Moreover, it is interesting to note that there are two Gothic variants for 'Gospel' (*aiwaggeli* and *aiwaggeljo*), as well as for 'epistle' (*aipistaule*, derived from Gr. ἐπιστολή, and *aipistula*, which shows influence of Lat. *epistula*) and for 'prophet' (*praufetes*, from Gr. προφήτης, and *praufetus*, analogical reformation on the basis of other words in *-us*).
137 See Lehmann 1986, *s.v.*

such as ψευδαπόστολος 'false apostle', which is rendered as *galiuga-apaustaulus*, composed of *galiug* 'falsity' and the loan word *apaustaulus* 'apostle'. Such words presumably needed, at least initially, a conceptual explanation through the help of instructed churchmen.[138]

1.5 Conclusions

The territories in which Wulfila lived, north and south of the Lower Danube, were characterised by the coexistence of several cultures and languages. Their echo is present in Wulfila's trilingual education, in his alphabet, devised on the basis of Greek and Latin letters and runes, and in the religious vocabulary of his version, which includes Greek and Latin terms.

The principal aim of the Gothic translation was undoubtedly to provide the recently Christianised Goths with the Holy Scriptures in their mother tongue, to be used for both worship and evangelisation. Five steps of Wulfila's work may be postulated: (1) an oral translation of at least some parts of the Bible, as he was *lector* in the area north of the Danube; (2) the creation of a proper alphabet (although it is impossible to say for certain where and when this occurred); (3) the production of a written prototype of the translation, perhaps with the help of other persons (again, it is not possible to state where and when this occurred); (4) the organisation of a scriptorium, to produce one or more copies of the final form of the translation (probably in Moesia, in a politically stable context); and finally, (5) the training of the clergy to read and explain the Scriptures.

In addition to the missionary purpose behind his translation, one can postulate that Wulfila saw his work as a way to elevate Gothic to the rank of other written languages; a process which might be connected with claims to reinforce the identity of his people within the Christian world. Possessing biblical books in their own language and script might have served to offer a picture of the Goths as a Christian community to the rest of the Empire. Indeed, the juxtaposition of 'Goths' and 'Christians' might have contributed to their better integration into Roman culture, removing – at least partially – the image of the Goths as a cruel enemies. On the other hand, the Gothic Bible may have become a key to preserving the ethnic (in a broad sense) and religious identity of the Goths within a multicultural environment, not only in the mid-fourth century Danubian region but also later, in the Ostrogothic kingdom of Italy.[139]

---

[138] On the Gothic compounds see Dolcetti Corazza 1997; Casaretto 2004 and 2010.
[139] See below 2.1.

2 The Gothic witnesses to the Gospels and Pauline Epistles

Six fragmentary manuscripts, produced in, or connected with, the Ostrogothic kingdom of Italy, transmit parts of the Gothic version of the New Testament:[140] the *Codex Argenteus*, the *Ambrosianus* C and the *Gissensis* transmit portions of the Gospels and the *Codex Carolinus*, the *Ambrosianus* A⁺ and the *Ambrosianus* B preserve parts of every Pauline Epistle, except for Hebrews.[141] Furthermore, some literal citations from the Gospels (Matthew and Luke) and from the Pauline Epistles (Romans, 1 and 2 Timothy), which undoubtedly go back to the Gothic version, are reported by the anonymous text preserved by the *Codex Bononiensis*.

The circulation of the Gothic version is also testified to by the Hungarian tablet of Hács-Béndekpuszta (last third of the fifth century), the only witness of the Gothic version which is of non-western origin.[142] Other witnesses to the diffusion of the Gothic text, perhaps related to the Visigothic kingdom of southern Gaul, are a few words preserved by two manuscripts of the Carolingian period.[143]

Some verses of Matthew, John and Romans survive as citations in the so-called *Skeireins*, a Gothic commentary on the Gospel of John. This text is possibly

---

140 Only small fragments of the Gothic translation of the Old Testament are preserved, i.e. Nehemiah 5:13–18; 6:14–7:3; 7:13–45, transmitted by the *Codex Ambrosianus* D (Milan, Biblioteca Ambrosiana, G 82 sup., f. 209–210, 451–452, 461–462; palimpsest). Some literal citations from Genesis, Psalms and Daniel are reported by the text of the *Codex Bononiensis* (see Falluomini 2014). It is worth noting that this text also transmits citations from the Acts of the Apostles (with its title in dative: *tojam apaustaule*, f. 1v, l. 2, a perfect translation of Πράξεις Ἀποστόλων) and the First Epistle of Peter (see Falluomini 2014). The twenty-seven marginal glosses – most of them illegible today – to the Latin Arian homilies preserved in the margins of the ms. Verona, Biblioteca Capitolare, LI (49) + Venice, Biblioteca Giustiniani Recanati, s. n. (end of the fifth/beginning of the sixth century, see Gryson 1982 A, 77–92; known as *Gotica Veronensia*), do not actually testify to the diffusion of the Gothic New Testament, since they may be free annotations. According to Marchand (1973 A, 468), followed by Snædal (2002, 5–6), "[...] the notes are not lectionary headings, as some have thought, but are simply *ad hoc* indications of the contents of the manuscript." Other Gothic texts are the short subscriptions in the deeds of Naples and Arezzo (see Tjäder 1954, papyri 8† and 34) and the Gothic calendar (see Schäferdiek 1988). On the typology of the Gothic manuscripts and their cultural context, see Scardigli 1994. The Gothic *corpus*, with the exception of the text of the *Codex Bononiensis*, is edited by Streitberg-Scardigli 2000.
141 The Epistle to the Hebrews was probably never translated into Gothic, see below 6.2.3.
142 See below 2.2.1.
143 See below 2.2.3. and 2.2.4.

a translation of a work by Theodore of Heraclea,[144] and therefore the citations may translate the citations of the Greek original and not date back to Wulfila's version.

Around three-fifths of the Gospels and around two-thirds of the Pauline Epistles survive, most of them transmitted by a *codex unicus*:

Mt	1:21 (CB); 1:23 (CB); 5:15–6:32, 7:12–10:1 (CA; 7:15 also CB); 10:23–11:25 (CA); 13:28 (CB); 25:38–26:3, 26:65–69 (C); 26:70–27:1 (CA+C); 27:2–19, 27:42–66 (CA)
Jn	5:45–7:52, 8:12–11:47, 12:1–49, 13:11–19:13 (CA)
Lk	1:1–10:30 (CA; Lk 10:18 also CB), 14:9–16:24, 17:3–20:46 (CA); 23:11–14 (isolated words) (G); 24:13–17 (isolated words) (G)
Mk	1:1–6:30, 6:53–12:38, 13:16–29, 14:4–16, 14:41–16:20 (CA)
Rom	1:8 (CB); 6:23–8:10 (A; 7:24 also CB); 8:34–11:1, 11:11–33 (A); 11:33–12:5 (CC); 12:8–16 (A); 12:17–13:5 (A+CC); 13:6–14:5 (A); 14:9–20 (CC); 15:3–13 (CC); 16:21–24 (A)
1 Cor	1:12–25, 4:2–12, 5:3–6:1, 7:5–28, 8:9–9:9, 9:19–10:4, 10:15–11:6, 11:21–31, 12:10–22, 13:1–12, 14:20–27, 15:1–35, 15:46–47 (A); 15:48–16:11 (A+B); 16:12–22 (B); 16:23–24 (A+B)
2 Cor	1:1–7 (B); 1:8–4:10 (A+B); 4:11–18 (B); 5:1–9:7 (A+B); 9:8–11:13 (B); 12:1–13:13 (A+B)
Eph	1:1–2:20 (A+B); 2:21–3:8 (B); 3:9–4:6 (A+B); 4:7–16 (A); 4:17–5:3 (A+B); 5:4–11 (B); 5:17–29 (A); 6:8 (B); 6:9–19 (A+B); 6:20–24 (B)
Gal	1:1–7, 1:20–21 (B); 1:22–2:9 (A+B); 2:10–16 (B); 2:17 (A+B); 2:18–4:18 (A); 4:19–23 (A+B); 4:24–5:16 (B); 5:17–6:18 (A+B)
Phil	1:14–2:8, 2:22–25 (B); 2:26–4:6 (A+B); 4:7–17 (B)
Col	1:6–9 (B); 1:10–29 (A+B); 2:11–19 (B); 2:20–3:8 (A+B); 3:9–4:3 (B); 4:4–13 (A+B); 4:14–19 (B)
1 Thess	2:10–5:21 (B); 5:22–28 (A+B)
2 Thess	1:1–6 (A+B); 1:7–2:4 (A); 2:15–3:6 (B); 3:7–18 (A+B)
1 Tim	1:1–9 (A+B); 1:10–17 (B); 1:18–3:4 (A+B); 3:5–16 (A); 4:1–8 (A+B); 4:9–5:3 (B; 4:10 also CB); 5:4–10 (A+B); 5:11–14, 5:16–20 (A); 5:21–6:14 (A+B); 6:15–16 (B)
2 Tim	1:1–4 (A); 1:5–18 (A+B); 2:1–20 (B); 2:21–4:11 (A+B; 3:5 also CB); 4:12–16 (A)
Tit	1:1–8 (B); 1:9–10 (A+B); 1:11–2:1 (A)
Phlm	1:11–23 (A)

---

144 See Schäferdiek 1981, 187. This commentary is transmitted by a manuscript that is now divided: Milan, Biblioteca Ambrosiana, E 147 sup., ff. 77–80, 111–114, 309–310 + Vatican City, Biblioteca Apostolica Vaticana, *Vat. Lat.* 5750, ff. 57–62 (*Ambros.* E⁺).

2.1 The manuscripts

Regarding the dating of the manuscripts, chemical, palaeographical, codicological and cultural analyses point to the first half of the sixth century. Carbon-14 analysis of the *Codex Argenteus* parchment, carried out in 1998 by Göran Possnert in Uppsala, offers evidence that it is "from the 6th century, not later than 550".[145]

Two codices (*Carolinus* and *Gissensis*) are bilingual (Gothic-Latin). The Latin script allows these manuscripts to be dated to the first two decades of the sixth century (*Carolinus*) or a little later (*Gissensis*). Other codicological features of the *Carolinus* point to the sixth century: first, the form of the Latin *nomina sacra*;[146] second, the usage of the enlarged and protruded letter at the beginning of a new paragraph combined with the double vertical bounding lines that delimit the text area.[147] The only internal feature which permits – even roughly – dating the monolingual manuscripts is the usage of an enlarged letter at the beginning of a new section of the text within a line; a feature that seems to be typical of sixth-century Latin manuscripts.[148]

The dating offered by the Latin scripts of the bilingual texts and by the codicological features of the Gothic manuscripts is supported by cultural considerations. There is no doubt that the *Codex Argenteus* was copied in northern Italy, because of its codicological and textual relation with the Latin *Codex Brixianus* (f/10).[149] From the magnificence of the *Argenteus*, scholars have inferred that it was devised for a person of high rank – probably Theoderic the Great († 526) and/or the palatine church – and that it was therefore produced in Ravenna, the Ostrogothic capital.[150] The other manuscripts share with the *Argenteus* many paleographical and codicological features, so that it is possible to assume that they were also produced in a similar cultural *milieu*, i.e. in northern Italy, where the majority of these were later rewritten and Gothic centers of power were well attested.

---

145 Possnert-Munkhammar 1999–2000, 59.
146 See Traube 1907, 214–215 and 237; see also below 2.1.4.
147 This emerges from the examination of the manuscripts edited in CLA, see details in Falluomini 2006, 9.
148 See below 3.8.
149 Brescia, Biblioteca Queriniana, s. n. (CLA III, 281, first half of the sixth century); see below 5.2.
150 The bibliography on the *Codex Argenteus* and its connection with Ravenna is vast: see, for example, Tjäder 1972; Scardigli 1973, part. 330–337; Munkhammar 2011 A; Munkhammar 2011 B, part. 49–60.

The Gothic manuscripts can therefore be considered to have been copied in the Ostrogothic kingdom (493–553), and principally during the reign of Theoderic (493–526). He, indeed, seems to have paid great attention to the promotion of both culture and literature, at least during the first decades of his reign. During this period, characterised by peace and wealth, the transmission of Late Antique texts continued without interruption, as the magnificent Latin manuscript production testifies.[151] At the same time both Roman intellectuals – like Boethius, Symmachus and Cassiodorus[152] – and the 'Ostrogothic Geographers' guaranteed a vivacious cultural life at Theoderic's court.[153] In any case, the end of the Greek-Gothic war (553) represents the *terminus post quem non* for the production of manuscripts in Gothic language. After the war, indeed, there were no longer the conditions – the Gothic audience and the support of the Gothic ruling class – for their copying.

The production of the Gothic manuscripts can be seen as the result of a cultural, religious and political programme: on the one hand, to lend prestige and authority to the Gothic version and the Arian Church; on the other hand, to preserve the cultural and religious heritage of the Goths, as part of their identity.[154] Seven new buildings were erected in Ravenna for Arian worship during the first decades of the Ostrogothic kingdom (three of them still survive: the palatine

---

[151] On Theoderic and the promotion of Gothic culture see Scardigli 1973, part. 181; Luiselli 1982, 62–75; Moorhead 1986, 112–122; on book production in the Ostrogothic period see Cavallo 1983; Cavallo 1984; Cavallo 1992; Pecere 1993; Bertelli 1998, 54–59.
[152] At the command of King Theoderic, he wrote a history of the Goths, now lost (it survives only in Jordanes' abridgment), focussed upon the Gothic past and the centrality of the Amal family. See Cassiod., *var.* 9.25.4–6: *Iste Hamalos cum generis sui claritate restituit, euidenter ostendens in septimam decimam progeniem stirpem nos habere regalem. Originem Gothicam historiam fecit esse Romanam colligens quasi in unam coronam germen floridum quod per librorum campos passim fuerat ante dispersum. Perpendite, quantum uos in nostra laude dilexerit, qui uestri principis nationem docuit ab antiquitate mirabilem, ut, sicut fuistis a maioribus uestris semper nobiles aestimati, ita uobis antiqua regum progenies inperaret.* On this topic see Merrills 2005, 101–115.
[153] According to Cassiodorus (*var.* 9.24.8), Theoderic was interested in the courses of the stars, the tides of the sea and the study of natural science. The bibliography concerning the cultural life at the time of the Ostrogoths is vast: see for instance Deichmann 1980; Luiselli 1992, part. 690–696; Pecere 1993; Bertelli 1998, 54–59, Hen 2007, 39–53; concerning the 'Ostrogothic Geographers', who produced a geographic survey of the known world, see Staab 1976.
[154] As John Moorhead (1986, 115) has pointed out, "Gothic Arianism seems to have been seen as something which distinguished them from the Catholic Romans"; see also Burns 1984, 161; Moorhead 1992, 95; Heather 1996, 317; a different opinion can be found in Amory 1997, 236–276; an intermediate position in Brown 2007, 424: "[T]he Arian Church was a rallying point for several decades but [...] it was never the dominant ethnic marker. It lost its importance with time". The term 'Arian' is here used in general for 'Homean'.

church Sant'Apollinare Nuovo, Spirito Santo and the Arian baptistery; a further four are mentioned by the sources),[155] a fact which suggests the interest of the Ostrogothic rulers, in particular Theoderic, in strengthening his 'national' Church.[156] Behind the erection of prestigious buildings and the production of manuscripts of great quality like the *Codex Argenteus*, written on purple parchment, one can therefore see a cultural emulation of the apparatus of the Catholic Church and the desire to create an Arian ecclesiastical power parallel to the Catholic one.[157] From this perspective, the careful preservation of Wulfila's version – used primarily for liturgical purposes[158] – may offer a further legitimisation to the existence of the Gothic Church.

The bilingual codices may have principally served practical purposes. It is worth noting the 'place of honour' of the Gothic text in these bilinguals, on the left of the Latin version.[159] The Latin text, then, occupies the position usually destined for the target language, a feature which suggests a primarily Latin-speaking audience for these manuscripts, possibly Latin-speaking Goths (or people that could understand both Gothic and Latin, like the Vandals in the case of the *Gissensis*),[160] Latin-speaking Arians or – less probably – Romans interested

---

155 On the destiny of the Gothic churches after the Greek-Gothic war and their rededication to the Orthodox worship by the archbishop Agnellus see Sörries 1983, 271–289; Mauskopf Deliyannis 2010, part. 144.
156 See Scardigli 1973, 330–337; Brown 2007, 419. Several studies have been concerned with the Arian buildings in Ravenna and Theoderic's building programme in general; see for instance Cecchelli 1960, 767–768; Lusuardi Siena 1984; Johnson 1988; Moorhead 1992, 89–97; La Rocca 1993; Saitta 1993, 103–138; Wood 2007; Mauskopf Deliyannis 2010.
157 The magnificence of the *Argenteus* demonstrates visually, on the one hand, the power of its commissioner(s) and owner(s), expressed through this kind of refined book production; on the other hand, it reflects the progressive sacralisation of the biblical book as a medium for ideological values. Petrucci (1973, 965–967) argued that a cult of the sacred book characterised early Christian and medieval manuscript production and reception. The ideological values of the text were expressed not only by the text itself but also by the external features (ornamentation and script) of the book which transmitted it.
158 Concerning the 'helps for readers' attested in the Gothic manuscripts see below 3. On the few traces of Gothic liturgical customs (the only direct reference is in Salv., *gub*. V. 2, 5), see Gamber 1988, 28–31.
159 From an investigation of the bilingual manuscripts produced between the fourth and the sixth centuries (listed in the CLA), it emerges that the text in the original language is usually placed to the left of the translation (on the same page or on opposite pages). For instance, in the bilingual Virgil manuscripts, the Latin text is always placed on the left side of the Greek translation. Among the bilingual manuscripts of the Bible, only in the *Codex Laudianus* E/08 (sixth-seventh century, perhaps written in Sardinia) is the Greek text placed on the right side of the Latin. The same picture emerges from the manuscripts listed in Parker 1992, 50–69.
160 See below 2.1.3.

in understanding the Gothic Bible.[161] Indeed, the youngest generation of Goths, growing up in a Latin environment, probably spoke Latin better than Gothic. Some evidence suggests that intermarriage between Romans and Goths was allowed, particularly at the highest levels of political life, and that the male partner tended to be a Goth.[162] This fact implies that subsequent children, who learned more easily the language of the mother, (also) spoke Latin. Moreover, besides Gothic Arians, the presence of Latin Arians must also be accounted for.[163] That they must have existed emerges from the production of some Latin manuscripts with Arian texts, such as the mss. Milan, Biblioteca Ambrosiana, C 73 inf.,[164] and Verona, Biblioteca Capitolare, LI (49)⁺.[165] In such political and religious conditions, the production of bilingual manuscripts appears as a natural consequence.

The Gothic-Latin manuscripts seem, therefore, to be the result of a process of integration and acculturation between Goths and Romans. How such bilingual manuscripts were read is an open question. It has been noted that translations

---

161 Such as the *patricius Ciprianus*, who was *instructus trifariis linguis* (Cassiod., *var.* 5.40.5), and his children. Regarding to them, Cassiodorus (*var.* 8.21.7) wrote that *pueri stirpis Romanae nostra lingua loquuntur*. However, this seems to have been unusual; in fact, this is the only known example.

162 Moorhead 1992, 84–85. Cassiodorus addressed many letters to Goths, and there is no indication that he expected his readers to have trouble with Latin. Furthermore, Amalasuintha, Theoderic's daughter, knew Gothic, Latin and Greek (Cassiod., *var.* 10.4.6 and 11.1.6) as well as his nephew Theodahad (Cassiod., *var.* 10.3.4). Among the ten Gothic members of the church of St. Anastasia in Ravenna, who signed a document in 551 (see Tjäder 1954, pap. 34), only four wrote in Gothic and six in Latin. Gothic probably remained the language of the army, from which the Romans were, of course, excluded (Proc., *BG* 1.10.10).

163 Very little is known about the existence of Latin Arian communities during the time of the Ostrogothic kingdom. Knut Schäferdiek (2009, 226) wrote on this topic: "Zur arianischen Kirche zählten [...] sicher auch lateinischsprachige Christen aus der Tradition des lateinischen Arianismus und vielleicht auch solche, die während der Zeit der gotischen Herrschaft übergetreten sind." The possibility that some Catholics wanted to change their belief emerges from the words of Ravenna's bishop Petrus († 520), who, speaking to his audience, said: *Ab omni herese seruate uos, cauete ab Arriana dogmata, sanctam et incontaminatam catholicam fidem tenete!* (Agn., *lib. pont.* 52). However, it is to be noted that, according to Procopius (*BG* 6.6.18), envoys of the Goths told Belisarius that no Romans had changed religion, whereas some Goths did (see also Cassiod., *var.* 10.26.3). On Arian literature and Arian-Catholic relationships in Italy see Zeiller 1905; Meslin 1967; Gryson 1982 B; Moorhead 1992, 89–97; Hen 2007, 54–56.

164 Northern Italy, sixth century; *Expositio Euangelii secundum Lucam*, see Gryson B 1982, xxii-xxiii.

165 Verona?, Ravenna?, end of the fifth or beginning of the sixth century. It transmits homilies, sermons and some tractates on different topics, see Gryson B 1982, xviii-xx. The manuscript contains marginal annotations in Gothic, see above, fn. 140.

often followed the readings in Hebrew or Greek in bilingual communities.¹⁶⁶ A similar liturgical practice may have been used in front of a Gothic-Latin audience. To this purpose the texts were segmented into short phrases or clauses, clearly marked by their disposition on the writing space.¹⁶⁷

These bilinguals also testify to the existence of Gothic and Latin scribes who worked side by side, as happened during the production of the Latin manuscript of Orosius (prepared in the workshop of the Goth Uiliaric, probably in Ravenna).¹⁶⁸ In such a context, Gothic scribes may have learned Latin scripts and customs of book production and applied them to the production of Gothic manuscripts, such as the letter s ‹s› in Latin form;¹⁶⁹ the suspension of -*m* at the end of the line; the numeration of the quires in the lower right-hand corner of the last page;¹⁷⁰ the Latin formulation of superscriptions and subscriptions,¹⁷¹ and perhaps the running titles¹⁷² and the habit of placing numerals between points.¹⁷³

Finally, it is interesting to note that four of the six extant Gothic New Testament manuscripts were palimpsested between the seventh and the first half of the eighth century, most likely in northern Italian writing centres. The important scriptorium of the monastery of Bobbio (near Piacenza, northern Italy), Columban's foundation under Langobardic patronage, was very probably the place where the *Codices Ambros. A⁺*, *Ambros.* B and *Ambros.* C were rewritten.¹⁷⁴ The re-use of the *Codex Carolinus* should, however, not be claimed for Bobbio, since the manuscript is never attested in its catalogue; the most plausible guess is that it was reused in an important Late Antique northern Italian center

---

166 See Gamble 1995, 230.
167 See below 3.7.
168 The Orosius manuscript – Florence, Biblioteca Medicea Laurenziana, Pluteo LXV. 1 (first half of the sixth century, CLA III, 298) – bears an inscription at f. 114v: *confectus codex in statione magistri Uiliaric antiquarii*. On this manuscript and its possible relationship with the *Codex Argenteus* see Tjäder 1972.
169 See above 1.3.
170 This usage is typical of the Latin manuscripts. Conversely, in the Greek manuscripts of the fourth-sixth centuries, the quires are numbered in the upper – rarely in the lower – right-hand corner of the first page of each, see Lowe 1961, 281; Agati 2003, 266–268.
171 See below 3.4.
172 See below 3.3.
173 On the codicological features of the Gothic manuscripts that may derive from Latin usages, see Falluomini 2006, 7.
174 Beeson's claim that all the Gothic manuscripts were rewritten in Bobbio (1946, 166) is now mitigated, see van den Hout 1950, and more recently Zironi 2004, 52, 63–68; Lo Monaco 2006, 56, fn. 9.

firmly connected to the Ostrogothic kingdom, such as Verona, Pavia, Brescia or Milan.[175]

2.1.1 Codex Argenteus

Uppsala, Universitetsbiblioteket, D G 1, 187 leaves
<http://www.ub.uu.se/samlingar/verk-och-samlingar-i-urval/silverbibeln> (plate 1) + Speyer, Historisches Museum der Pfalz, 1 leaf

This manuscript preserves portions of the four Gospels in the order Matthew-John-Luke-Mark.[176] The last folio was found in 1970 in St. Afra's chapel of Speyer cathedral (Germany).[177] This discovery is particularly important from a text-critical point of view, because it transmits the most part of the Long Ending of Mark (16:9–20).[178] The original manuscript comprised 336 leaves.[179]

It is the surviving part of a luxurious codex, written in silver ink on purple parchment,[180] with some parts in golden ink.[181] The writing area (13 x 21 cm; 20 lines per page)[182] corresponds to the Golden Section, that is, the height relates to the breadth in the same way as the sum of the height and breadth relates to the height. At the bottom of each page, arcade-like frames, designed in silver ink with great regularity and care, contain the parallel Ammonian Sections. The margins of the Uppsala leaves have at some point been cut by the bookbinder; those of the original manuscript were wider, as can be inferred by the leaf found in Speyer.[183]

---

175 Falluomini 1999, 28; Zironi 2004, 54 (about Verona).
176 See below 6.1.3.
177 See Scardigli 1971; Stutz 1971; Scardigli 1973, 302–380; Stutz 1973; Tjäder 1974. It was probably removed from the rest of the manuscript at an early stage, but not all scholars agree on this point; see the different opinions discussed in Munkhammar 2011 B, 74–77, 81–86. On linguistic aspects of the text, see also Pollak 1973; Snædal 2013 B.
178 The Speyer fragment begins with *twaim ize* (12–20); the foregoing part (9–12, down to *afaruh þan þata*) is preserved in the last page of the Uppsala manuscript, see Appendix II.2.
179 von Friesen-Grape 1928, 35.
180 On manuscripts written on purple parchment, see Petitmengin 1985, 99; McGurk 1994, 23. That purple was considered a symbol of the royal power by Theoderic emerges from the fact that he used to clad himself in this colour (see Cassiod., *var.* 9.24.9).
181 See below 3.9.
182 von Friesen-Grape 1928, 11.
183 The measurements of the Speyer leaf is around 21,70 cm x 26,60 cm; the other extant leaves measure 19,75–20 cm x 24,25–24,50 cm; the writing area is 13 x 21 cm, see Scardigli 1973 (= 1971), 344 (who reported the measurement taken by the discoverer Franz Haffner).

The script is of the upright type, executed with an extremely regular and accurate design, with the help of two ruled lines. Two hands have been identified: the first hand copied the Gospels of Matthew and John; the second hand the Gospels of Luke and Mark.[184] ‹s› has the Latin form (s); suspensions for -*n* (⁻) and -*m* (⁻) are attested at the end of the line. Sixteen *marginalia* are preserved, written in silver ink and in the upright script.[185]

The high quality of the manuscript suggests – as already said – that it was made for King Theoderic and/or the Gothic palatine church. It may therefore be assumed that it was produced in Ravenna in the first quarter of the sixth century, a dating confirmed by the carbon-14 analysis.[186] Close to the *Codex Argenteus* – from a codicological and textual point of view – is the *Codex Brixianus* (f/10), a purple manuscript written in silver ink, probably produced in a sixth-century scriptorium in northern Italy. It contains at the bottom of each page the canon tables, similar to those of the *Argenteus*. Furthermore, this codex transmits a mixed text – i.e. an Old Latin text heavily overlaid with Vulgate readings[187] – and shows several peculiarities shared with the text of the *Argenteus*, by which it seems to have been influenced.[188] The similarities between the two manuscripts suggest that the *Codex Brixianus* is a copy of part of a bilingual Gothic-Latin Gospel book, of which the *Codex Argenteus* represents the Gothic part.

The earliest history of the manuscript is unknown. According to Otto von Friesen and Anders Grape,[189] St. Liutger, a pupil of Alcuin, brought the manuscript at the end of the eighth century (possibly 795) from Italy to his newly founded Werden monastery (near Cologne). There it was found in 1554 (or perhaps earlier) by Georg Cassander and Cornelius Wouters. The first mention of this manuscript is by Johannes Goropius Becanus, who published his *Origines Antwerpianae* in 1569. He quoted the Lord's Prayer and parts of the Gospel according to Mark. At the beginning of the seventeenth century the codex was in Prague in the collection of Rudolf II. It was taken by the Swedish army in 1648 during the Thirty Years' War and incorporated into the library of Queen

---

184 von Friesen-Grape 1928, 112.
185 See below 2.4. and 5.7.
186 See above 2.1.
187 Burton 2000, 27.
188 Burkitt 1899, with whom all subsequent scholars agree. See also below 5.2.
189 von Friesen-Grape 1928, 122–126; Tjäder 1974, 90–91; on the possibility that the manuscript was taken by Charlemagne to Aachen before it came to Werden see Andersson-Schmitt 1975–76, 16–21. On the relationship between Charlemagne, the Carolingians and the Gothic culture see Zironi 1998.

Christina. Following the abdication of the queen, it passed to her librarian, Isaac Vossius, who took it to Holland. After passing through several hands, in 1662 the manuscript was purchased by the Swedish High Chancellor Magnus Gabriel De la Gardie who, in 1669, donated it to the library of Uppsala University, where it is now preserved.[190] The *editio princeps* was published by Franciscus Junius in 1665.

The first complete palaeographical and codicological study of the manuscript was undertaken by Otto von Friesen and Anders Grape; their results were published together with a {0,0,0,100} and white facsimile of the codex in 1927. A new colour facsimile was published online in the website of the Uppsala Library in 2011.[191] The manuscript is now kept unbound, with each bifolio stretched in its own folder.

2.1.2. *Codex Ambrosianus* C

Milan, Biblioteca Ambrosiana, I 61 sup., ff. 90–91 – palimpsest

This manuscript preserves the verses Mt 25:38–46, 26:1–3, 26:65–75, 27:1, part of which (Mt 26:70–27:1) are transmitted also by the *Argenteus*. There are – apparently – no common errors or interpolations, but only divergences in regard to some readings.[192]

The manuscript has 17 lines per page. The script is of the upright type but it diverges slightly in the proportion of the strokes from the other examples of Gothic writing. ‹s› has the Latin form (s); suspensions for -*n* and -*m* are present, at the end of the line, but they are apparently marked by a unique sign (⁓). Unlike the *Argenteus*, the text is not divided according to the Ammonian Sections.

The place of its production is unknown. Northern Italy is the safest guess, since the manuscript shares some paleographical and codicological features with the other Gothic codices.[193] It was probably rewritten in the second half of the seventh century at the monastery of Bobbio, where it is recorded in the catalogue of 1461.[194] Curiously, the *textus superior* is a Latin Matthew Gospel.

Since 1606, these leaves belong to the Biblioteca Ambrosiana. The *scriptio inferior* was discovered and deciphered in the years 1814–1817 by Angelo Mai,

---

190 For the history of this manuscript see Munkhammar 2011 B, part. 69–74.
191 See http://app.ub.uu.se/arv/codex/faksimiledition/contents.html (19.11.2014).
192 Streitberg 1919, *ad loc.*; see also below 5.5.
193 See the overview in Falluomini 2006, 35 and 36–37.
194 Catalog number: 6; see CLA III, 351; Zironi 2004, 131; Lo Monaco 2006, 62.

Prefect of the Library. They were printed in 1819 by Mai and Carlo Ottavio Castiglioni.¹⁹⁵ A facsimile edition was published in 1936 by Jan de Vries. The leaves are now kept unbound.

2.1.3 *Codex Gissensis*

Giessen, Universitätsbibliothek, 651/20 (now lost), part of a bifolio <http://bibd.uni-giessen.de/papyri/images/pbug-inv018 – 1.jpg and http://bibd.uni-giessen.de/papyri/images/pbug-inv018 – 2.jpg> (plate 2)

This is the central upper part of the last bifolio of a quire of a Gothic-Latin manuscript. Only some final words of the Gothic columns (Lk 23:11 – 14; 24:13 – 17) and some initial words of the Latin one (Lk 23:3 – 6; 24:5 – 9) are preserved. The corresponding passages are lost in the *Codex Argenteus*.

The fragment was found in Egypt, in the territory of Shêkh 'Abâde (close to the ancient city of Antinoopolis) and purchased by the Deutsches Papyruskartell in 1907 or 1908. It entered the collection of the University Library in 1908, where it received both the signature 651/20 and PbuG2 Inv. Nr. 18. During the Second World War the fragment was placed in the vaults of the Dresdner Bank in Giessen: here it was – apparently – destroyed in 1945 following floodings of the Lahn River.¹⁹⁶ Only photos survive.

The Gothic text is written in the upright script. The letter ‹s› has the Latin form (s); no nasal suspensions are present in the few words attested at the end of the Gothic column. The Latin script is an accurate and elegant uncial of the sixth century. The place of production is unknown, but the palaeographical connection with the remaining manuscripts – i.e. the presence of s ‹s› – suggests an Italian origin either of its ancestor or of the manuscript itself. It is possibly connected with the Vandal kingdom of Africa, where it may have been used by the Arian Church.¹⁹⁷ In this case, considering that the Vandal kingdom ended in 534, the dating may be confined to the first third of the sixth century.

---

195 On Carlo Ottavio Castiglioni and the discovery of the Ambrosian palimpsests see Bolognesi 1999.
196 See CLA VIII, 1200.
197 The arrival of this manuscript or of its ancestor from Italy may be connected with the wedding of Theoderic's sister Amalafrida with the Vandal King Thrasamund in 500. According to Procopius (*BV* I. 8, 11–13), the princess was accompanied by 6000 of her people. It is a reasonable guess that her dowry also included a Gothic Bible. Other suggestions about the direct arrival

The two texts are arranged on facing pages: the Gothic text on the left, the Latin on the right. The Latin text is written *per cola et commata*, a fact which leads to the assumption that the Gothic text too was written in a similar way. The writing area was probably enclosed by two bounding lines, judging from the layout of the Latin column. On the Latin left margin (the Gothic left margin is lost) small numbers indicate the Ammonian Sections. From a text-critical point of view, it is worth noting that the Latin part – a *Vetus Latina* text with Vulgate readings (Beuron siglum: 36) – preserves some readings in common with the *Codex Brixianus:* this is not to exclude that, like the *Brixianus*, the Latin *Gissensis* may also have been made to conform to the Gothic text.[198]

It was edited in 1910 by Paul Glaue and Karl Helm. Subsequent editions have been published by Scardigli and Manfredi in 1991 and Snædal in 2003.

2.1.4 *Codex Carolinus*

Wolfenbüttel, Herzog August Bibliothek, Guelf. 64 Weiss., ff. 255–256, 277, 280 <http://diglib.hab.de/mss/64-weiss/start.htm> – palimpsest (plate 3)

This Gothic-Latin manuscript preserves about 40 verses from Romans 11–15. The Gothic and Latin texts are arranged in two columns of 27 lines, placed side by side on the same page: the Gothic on the left, the Latin on the right, both written *per cola et commata* in short sense lines.[199]

The Gothic is written in an accurate upright script. ‹s› has the Latin form (s); suspensions for *-n* (⁻) and *-m* (⁻) are present, at the end of the line. There are numbers on the left margin of the Gothic column, within a frame of strokes, which correspond approximately with the Euthalian sections.[200]

The Latin script is a careful uncial of the old type with some elements which anticipate the new uncial.[201] According to Friedrich Kauffmann,[202] the *Carolinus* dates back to the fifth century and is therefore the oldest Gothic manuscript. His opinion is based on the fact that it is bilingual and arranged *per cola et commata*, and that the Latin script is an uncial of the old type. However, other elements

---

of the manuscript from Italy to Antinoopolis – for instance in connection with Goths in exile – seem to be less likely.
198 See below 5.2.
199 See below 3.7.
200 See below 3.2.
201 Details in Falluomini 1999, 49.
202 Kauffmann 1911 A, 403.

point to the sixth century rather than to the fifth: the combination of double bounding lines plus enlarged and protruded letter at the beginning of a new paragraph (.|..|) and the Latin contractions $\overline{dns}$ (*dominus*) – instead of $\overline{dms}$ –, $\overline{ni}$ (*nostri*), $\overline{sco}$ (*sancto*) and $\overline{scam}$ (*sanctam*). Furthermore, the bilingualism of the manuscript and the position of the Latin text (the target language) suggest that it was destined for an established bilingual audience and therefore that it was produced at least a generation after the arrival of the Goths in Italy. Since the passage from the old to the new uncial occurred between the fifth and the sixth century, one must take into account the possibility that the Latin scribe learned an outdated style from an elderly teacher or that the scribe himself was elderly. On the basis of such paleographical, codicological and cultural features, the manuscript can therefore be dated to the beginning/first two decades of the sixth century.

Part of the text (Rom 12:17–13:5) is also preserved by the *Codex Ambros. A⁺*: both have been copied directly or indirectly from the same ancestor,[203] which was probably not written *per cola et commata* in the manner as the *Carolinus*.[204] Moreover, it was very likely monolingual, as some problems in the arrangement of the text show.[205] The Latin text is a witness to the *Vetus Latina* (sigla: w or gue/ 79); some readings that diverge from the Latin tradition and agree with the Gothic version suggest the influence of the latter.[206]

Although it is possible that this manuscript was prepared for personal reading or study, the careful division of the text in *cola et commata*, paragraphs and sections suggests that it was intended primarily for liturgical reading. Private usage must posit one or more Latin speaking persons with sufficient interest and economic resources to afford the copying of such an accurate manuscript, such as the *patricius Ciprianus* and his children.[207] Even if this suggestion is very attractive, there is not sufficient evidence to support it.

The manuscript was rewritten with the text of Isidore of Sevilla's *Etymologiae* in the first half of the eighth century in a northern Italian scriptorium, where old Greek and Latin codices were also present.[208] This place was probably not Bob-

---

[203] See below 2.5.
[204] The evidence for this is an error in the arrangement of the text, see below 3. 7.
[205] In some cases, in order to keep the text within the writing space, both scribes wrote the letters smaller and – the Latin scribe – under the line. If the ancestor had been bilingual, such a clumsy arrangement would probably have been removed in the subsequent copy.
[206] See below 5.2.
[207] See above, fn. 161.
[208] The Gothic-Latin leaves were rebound together with leaves that came from a Greek manuscript containing Galen (beginning of the sixth century), two Greek Gospel books (of the fifth

bio, where this codex is never attested (it is not listed in Bobbio's catalog of 1461). Furthermore, from a palaeographical and textual viewpoint, it diverges from the *Etymologiae* manuscripts produced or preserved in Bobbio.[209] Its earlier history is unknown. At some point the manuscript arrived at the Benedictine abbey of Wissembourg (Alsace); in 1690 it was purchased, with other manuscripts of this abbey, by Anton Ulrich, Duke of Braunschweig-Lüneburg.[210] The theologian Franz Anton Knittel discovered the *scriptio inferior* in 1755 and published the Gothic-Latin text – which received the denomination *Codex Carolinus* in honour of the Duke of Braunschweig-Lüneburg, Karl I – in 1758. Subsequent editions have been published by Henning in 1913 and Falluomini in 1999.

2.1.5 *Codex Ambrosianus* A⁺

Milan, Biblioteca Ambrosiana, S 36 sup., 102 leaves + Turin, Biblioteca Nazionale Universitaria, F. IV. 1 Fasc. 10, 4 leaves – palimpsest

This manuscript preserves long parts of the Pauline Epistles (except Hebrews, which was absent from the beginning, since there is not sufficient room for it in the manuscript). Portions of the text are in common with the *Carolinus* (Rom 12:17–13:5) and the *Ambros.* B (long parts of the Epistles).[211]

The number of the lines per page varies from twenty-one to nineteen. The text is written *per cola et commata* down to 1 Cor 5:4 (f. 49r); in this part two marginal bounding lines delimit left and right the writing space. Subsequently, the text is marked by punctuation and the marginal bounding line is therefore single. Marginal numbers, corresponding approximately with the Euthalian sections,[212] are attested. The text is written in the upright script, apparently by three scribes: the most part of the text has been copied by the third scribe. The space between the letters, in the part of the text written in the colometrical arrangement, is slightly broader than in the other extant manuscripts. ‹s› has the Latin shape (s). Suspensions for -*n* (͞) and -*m* (͞) are present at the end of the

---

and sixth centuries; they are the Greek New Testament manuscripts Q/026 and P/024, see Aland-Aland 1989, 122), a list of Matthew's chapters (of the sixth/seventh century), two Latin Bibles (of the fifth and sixth centuries) and Ambrosiaster's *Commentarius in epistulam Paulinam ad Romanos* (sixth century), see Falluomini 1999, 19.

209 See details in Falluomini 1999, 28.
210 For the history of this find see Butzmann 1964, 3–8; Milde 1972, xxvii-xxxii.
211 See below 2.5.
212 See below 3.2.

line. There are fifty-three marginal glosses, some of which are illegible today, written in the sloping type, perhaps by different hands.[213] This evidence suggests that the manuscript was used for private reading – probably in addition to a liturgical use – possibly inside a religious community. The lack of particular care in its production (different layout of the writing, different number of the lines per page, few punctuation[214]) indicates that it was prepared for persons interested more in the text than in the aesthetic quality of the manuscript.

The origin of the manuscript is uncertain. Northern Italy (and perhaps Ravenna) is the most likely guess, judging from the similarities with the other Gothic manuscripts.[215] It was rewritten in the second half of the seventh century with the text of Gregory the Great's *Homiliae in Ezechielem*, possibly in Bobbio (it is listed in the catalog of 1461).[216] Since 1606, the leaves have been preserved in the Biblioteca Ambrosiana. The *scriptio inferior* was discovered and deciphered in the years 1814–1817 by Angelo Mai.[217] The text of the Epistles was published between 1829 and 1839 by Carlo Ottavio Castiglioni. The four leaves from Turin were found by Ingo Reifferscheid in 1866. They contain part of Galatians and Colossians.[218] The facsimile edition was published in 1936 by Jan de Vries. Both the Milan and Turin leaves are preserved unbound. The Gothic script is illegible in several parts, particularly in the Turin leaves, badly damaged by the fire of the library in 1904.

2.1.6 *Codex Ambrosianus* B

Milan, Biblioteca Ambrosiana, S 45 sup., 78 leaves – palimpsest (plate 4)

This manuscript preserves the Pauline Epistles, with the exception of Romans and Philemon (and Hebrews). It shares some errors and interpolations with *Ambros.* A⁺, from which it also differs in some significant readings. They probably belong to different branches of the tradition.[219]

The number of the lines per page varies from twenty-one to eigthteen. The text has been written in the sloping script by an expert scribe. The shape of ‹s›

---

213 See below 2.4. and 5.7.
214 See below 3.6.
215 Overview in Falluomini 2006, 35 and 36–37.
216 Catalog number: 73 or 74; see CLA III, 364; Zironi 2004, 67, 132; Lo Monaco 2006, 62.
217 On Mai's work see Lo Monaco 1996, 682, 689.
218 For the history of the Turin leaves see Bellocchio-Dolcetti Corazza 2009.
219 See below 2.5.

is old (ε).²²⁰ The contractions for *Iesus* and *Xristus* diverge from those used in the other codices.²²¹ The marginal indication in Gothic script – *laiktsjo* or *laiktjo*²²² 'reading', 'lesson' (from Lat. *lectio*) –, which is present forty-four times, is a clear reference to the liturgical use of the manuscript (the hand seems to diverge from the text hand). On the margins there are also several marks, composed of horizontal strokes. They probably serve to divide the text and/or highlight some passages inside the page. Marginal numbers are also attested, which correspond partially to the Euthalian Apparatus.²²³

The place of its writing is uncertain. Some codicological elements in common with the other codices would point to northern Italy.²²⁴ Elias Avery Lowe suggested Verona, on the basis of the similarity between the script of this codex and that of the *Gotica Veronensia*.²²⁵

The *textus superior* transmits St. Jerome's *Explanatio in Isaiam*.²²⁶ It was very probably written in Bobbio in the second half of the seventh century (it is listed in Bobbio's catalog of 1461²²⁷). The leaves arrived at the Biblioteca Ambrosiana in 1606. Angelo Mai discovered and deciphered the *scriptio inferior* between 1814 and 1817. The text of the different Epistles was published between 1829 and 1839 by Carlo Ottavio Castiglioni. Jan de Vries published the facsimile edition in 1936. The manuscript is now kept unbound. Several parts of the *scriptio inferior* are illegible today.

2.2 Other witnesses

Other witnesses which testify to the circulation and usage of the Gothic version of the New Testament are the tablet of Hács-Béndekpuszta (now lost), the recently discovered *Codex Bononiensis*, the *Gotica Vindobonensia* in Gothic script and the *Gotica Parisina* in Latin script.

---

220 See above 1.3.
221 See below 3.11.
222 The first form occurs in 1 and 2 Corinthians (first part); the second one in the other occurrences (included 2 Corinthians), see Snædal 2013 A, II, *s.v.* The hand seems to be the same.
223 Braun 1898, 439–440, see below 3.2.
224 Falluomini 2006, 35 and 36–37.
225 CLA IV, 504; see also Ferrari 1976, 273; Zironi 2004, 63; see also above, fn. 140.
226 See Zironi 2004, 63–64, 66.
227 Catalogue number: 87; see CLA III, 364; Zironi 2004, 132; Lo Monaco 2007, 62.

2.2.1 Tablet of Hács-Béndekpuszta (*Tabella Hungarica*)

Lost

Brought to the attention of scholars in 1989 by Ernst A. Ebbinghaus,[228] this lead tablet (about 5,5 x 5,5 cm) was found between 1954 and 1958 in the Hungarian cemetery of Hács-Béndekpuszta.[229] It was folded and positioned in the hands of a young man (it was found in the pelvis of the skeleton). The grave had been opened by "treasure-hunters", who "attempted to unfold the tablet and in the process it broke into an indeterminate number of small pieces. Some of the pieces were recovered in the salvage excavation while an unknown number is now lost."[230] The fragments were preserved for a while at the Institute of Archaeology of the Hungarian Academy of Sciences. They are now lost; only photos survive.[231]

The fragment transmits part of John 17:11–12.[232] The nature of the text and the position of the tablet suggest that it was used as an amulet, destined to invoke protection in the afterlife. The tablet is dated to the last third of the fifth century.[233] It testifies to the circulation of the Gothic Bible outside the western Ostrogothic and Visigothic kingdoms. From a graphic viewpoint, the axis of the letters is both upright and sloping, a fact that may depend on the type of writing material. Some graphemes show older shapes: ‹a› is in three traits and ‹s› has the Greek or runic shape (ε).

The first notice of this fragment was published by Salamon in 1978, who interpreted the letters as runes.[234] The identification of the text is due to Harmatta in 1996; the most recent analysis of the fragments has been conducted by Scardigli.[235]

---

228 Ebbinghaus 1989.
229 Salamon 1977 [1978], 37.
230 Ebbinghaus 1989, 80.
231 Székely 1977 [1978], plates 17–20.
232 János Harmatta (1996) recognised some words as belonging to these verses, transmitted also by the *Codex Argenteus*. It is to be noted that "the text of Jn 1:1–14 began to be used in amulets in the late antique world. No other amulets specifically transmit Jn 17:11–12, as far as it is known." (Don C. Skemer, mail comunication, 4th Feb. 2013).
233 Salamon 1977 [1978], 37–40.
234 Salamon 1977 [1978], 38; see also Kiss 1995, 286.
235 Streitberg-Scardigli 2000, 507–514.

2.2.2 Codex Bononiensis

Bologna, Archivio della Fabbriceria della Basilica di San Petronio, Cart. 716/1, n° 1 (*olim* Cart. 353, cam. n°3), central bifolio – palimpsest

Some citations from the Gospels (Matthew and Luke) and the Epistles (Romans, 1 and 2 Timothy) – in addition to other passages from the Old and New Testament[236] – are transmitted by a fragmentary and anonymous Gothic text, very probably part of a sermon or liturgical prayer, discovered in 2010.[237] The fragment consists of an internal bifolio (the second or third of the quire),[238] which has subsequently been used as the cover of a book of accounts. It belonged to the Bolognese family of Foscarari (1635 is the date on the cover).

The manuscript was written in the first half of the sixth century, very probably in northern Italy (Verona?).[239] The script is the sloping variant.[240] The Gothic text was overwritten in the seventh century with the text of Augustinus' *De civitate Dei*.[241] Regarding the composition of the text, nothing is known, but it may have been written in Ostrogothic Italy. The author knew very well the Holy Scriptures and almost certainly used as his source an exemplar of the Gothic Bible that circulated in Italy.[242] There are no doubts that the text served for liturgical purposes.

The first transcription and edition was published in 2013 by Finazzi-Tornaghi (who called the text *Gothica Bononiensia*); a new transcription and edition has been made by Falluomini (2014).

---

236 See Falluomini 2014.
237 The fragment was found in Bologna by Armando Antonelli (see Antonelli 2009), but the *scriptio inferior* was uncovered by Maddalena Modesti and Annafelicia Zuffrano (see Aimi-Modesti-Zuffrano 2013, 324).
238 The topic of the text(s) does not help to establish whether the two leaves transmit parts of the same text or parts of two different texts.
239 Some codicological features diverge from those of the manuscripts that are certainly produced in Ravenna: the ‹s› has not the Latin shape and only the nasal suspension for -*n* is present, within the line (not at the end of the line as in the other Gothic manuscripts), see the palaeographical and codicological analysis in Falluomini 2014.
240 See above 1.3.
241 Aimi-Modesti-Zuffrano 2013, 331.
242 See Falluomini 2014.

2.2.3 *Gotica Vindobonensia*

Vienna, Österreichische Nationalbibliothek, 795, f. 20r and 20v

Some Gothic words belonging to Lk 9:28 and perhaps to Lk 15:32, and the title of Luke's Gospel – in addition to some numerals of Genesis and part of Gothic alphabets – are preserved in this manuscript, which dates from the very last years of the eighth century or the first years of the ninth.[243] The Gothic text was inserted slightly later.

The features of the Gothic script[244] and the form of the title[245] are different from those of the Gothic manuscripts of Ostrogothic origin. This fact suggests a different writing place of the *Vorlage* of the Gothic notes, perhaps identifiable with the Visigothic kingdom of southern Gaul. It is an interesting witness – even if only an indirect one – to the circulation of the Gothic Bible outside Ostrogothic Italy.

This material was discovered and edited first by W. Grimm in 1828; the facsimile edition was published by Unterkircher in 1969. A recent edition has been offered by Zironi in 2007.

2.2.4 *Gotica Parisina*

Paris, Bibliothèque Nationale de France, Lat. 528, f. 71v.

Seven Gothic biblical names (six of them extrapolated from Jesus' genealogy; Gospel of Luke, ch. 3), written in Latin letters, are transmitted by this manuscript, from the end of the eighth or the very beginning of the ninth century. The Gothic notes are not much younger. They were published in 1984 by Bischoff,[246] their discoverer, and subsequently by Zironi in 2009.

---

[243] See Unterkircher 1969, 37; Bischoff 1980, 118–119; Diesenberger-Wolfram 2004, 102–103; Zironi 2007; Zironi 2009, 253–265.

[244] In particular, the old Gothic ε ‹s› appears in the upright form, see Falluomini 2010 B, 34–35.

[245] See below 3.4.

[246] Bischoff 1984. See also Zironi 2009, 265–268.

2.3 Scribal errors and interventions

The Gothic manuscripts, like every manuscript tradition, are not free from scribal errors or interventions. The text transmitted by two witnesses occasionally shows some divergences, which evidently denote that the readings of one or both manuscripts have been altered.[247] This leads one to suppose that also in other passages transmitted by a *codex unicus*, the text might have been modified in respect to the Wulfilian original.

Some errors found in the Gothic manuscripts are typical of scribal transmission and are unintentional: haplography, dittography, homoeoteleuton, permutation or confusion between letters or signs of similar shape, omission or addition of letters and confusion between sounds.[248] In rare cases they have been corrected, mostly with erasures and rewriting or additions (generally above the line).

Very few cases of homoeoteleuton are attested. An example is found in the *Codex Argenteus*, at Jn 10:18, where the Gothic reading corresponding to (ἀπ' ἐμοῦ) ἀλλ' ἐγὼ τίθημι αὐτὴν ἀπ' ἐμαυτοῦ '(from me) but I lay it down of my own accord'[249] is missing. This kind of error could theoretically go back to the Greek *Vorlage*, even if it seems unlikely, because the sense of the sentence is defective without these words, a fact which would probably have generated suspicion in the mind of the translator. It is more difficult to judge the cases in which the homoeoteleuton is also attested by some Greek manuscripts and the meaning of the sentence is not defective. An example occurs in Jn 15:16: here the Gothic text omits the words which correspond to (ὑμᾶς) καὶ ἔθηκα ὑμᾶς '(you) and I appointed you',[250] as do the Greek mss. Δ/037, 565, 1424, f¹³. It is not possible to establish with confidence whether this error goes back to the *Vorlage* or not.[251]

The manuscripts also contain permutations or confusion between letters or signs, sometimes corrected by the scribes, such between ƕ ⟨a⟩ and ι ⟨i⟩; ι ⟨i⟩ and ᚢ ⟨u⟩; ᚢ ⟨u⟩ and ƕ ⟨a⟩; τ ⟨t⟩ and ᚷ ⟨g⟩; м ⟨m⟩ and и ⟨n⟩. However, with few exceptions,[252] most of the errors in the Gothic manuscripts do not generate

---

247 See below 5.6.
248 Some errors and confusion between ⟨e⟩/⟨ei⟩/⟨i⟩ or between ⟨au⟩/⟨u⟩ and ⟨u⟩/⟨o⟩ may reflect changes in the pronunciation of the scribes (in respect to Wulfila's Gothic?), see Marchand 1973 B, 50–53; D'Alquen 1974; Braune-Heidermanns 2004, 29–46; Francovich Onesti 2007, 8–9.
249 Streitberg-Scardigli (2000, *ad loc.*) reconstructed (*af*) *mis, akei ik lagja þo af* (*mis silbin*).
250 Streitberg-Scardigli (2000, *ad loc.*) reconstructed (*izwis*) *jah gasatida izwis*.
251 The homoeoteleuton in Jn 19:3, instead, goes probably back to the Greek *Vorlage*.
252 See for instance Jn 19:5, where the Gothic transmits <u>sa ist</u> *sa manna* 'this is the man' instead of *<u>sai ist</u> sa manna* 'here is the man' (in both cases with the insertion of the copula *ist*, see

new meaningful variants and are not important for the history of the biblical text. They simply create incorrect or – in the worst cases – unintelligible words, difficult to emend and restore to the original form, especially if they are *hapax legomena*.²⁵³

An alteration of the meaning of the text is caused by confusion between the *nomen sacrum* īs ⟨is⟩ (the contracted form of *Iesus*) and the personal pronoun ῒs ⟨ïs⟩ 'he', for example, in Mk 9:39, Mk 10:18 and 42 (ῒs 'he' instead of īs 'Iesus') and Jn 18:1, Mk 1:42 (īs 'Iesus' instead of ῒs 'he'). More difficult is the judgment concerning other instances, e.g.: *gibau* (1ˢᵗ pers. sing. pres. opt. act. of *giban* 'to give'; Jn 13:29), which corresponds to δῶ (vs. the correct form δῷ: Goth. *gibai*, 3ʳᵈ pers. sing. pres. opt. act. of *giban*). In this case there are two possible explanations, both of them having the same degree of plausibility: (1) the translator used an uncial *Vorlage* without iota adscript or subscript; or (2) a Gothic scribe – at which point in the tradition it is impossible to state – misread and/or miswrote n ⟨u⟩ of *gibau* for ι ⟨i⟩ of *gibai*.²⁵⁴

Some errors in the writing of [ŋg] as ⟨ng⟩, [ŋk] as ⟨nk⟩ and [ŋkʷ] as ⟨nq⟩ instead of – respectively – ⟨gg⟩, ⟨gk⟩ and ⟨gq⟩ (in the *Codex Argenteus*, particularly in Luke) are very probably the result of Latin influence.²⁵⁵ The omission or erroneous addition (*hypercorrectismus*) of ⟨h⟩ might also indicate the weakness of this sound in the Ostrogothic language of the sixth century, as well as in the Latin of the time.²⁵⁶

Other unintentional or intentional interventions – such as the substitution of synonyms, variations in word sequence, insertion or omission of words and harmonisation of parallel passages – are not easily recognisable in the Gothic version, since its Greek *Vorlage* is unknown.²⁵⁷ In some cases, the insertion or omission of words could be the result of scribal activity within the Gothic transmission. It is worth noting that, at the beginning of sentences, the Gothic version occasionally presents a copulative, conclusive or continuative conjunction, with-

---

below 4.1.4.(2); Gr. ἰδοὺ ὁ ἄνθρωπος; Lat. *ecce homo*). The error *sa ist* for *sai ist* is very probably due to haplography.
253 See for instance *aibr* 'offering', only in Mt 5:23 (possibly a corrupt form for *tibr*) or *plapja* 'street', only in Mt 6:5 (perhaps an error for *platja*).
254 The miswriting *u* ⟨u⟩ for *i* ⟨i⟩ and vice versa are attested in *laustim* (2 Cor 12:18, Ambros. B) for *laistim*, *Teimaiþaiu* (2 Cor 1:19, Ambros. A⁺) for *Teimauþaiu*; *gatraiau* (2 Cor 10:2, Ambros. B) for *gatrauau*.
255 See above 1.3.
256 On this topic see Marchand 1973 B, 53–54; on the Latin influence on the Gothic orthography see in particular Francovich Onesti 2007.
257 On this topic see below 5. and 6.

out a Greek (or Latin) model.²⁵⁸ In the absence of correspondences in other traditions, it is possible to suppose that this feature could date back to an autonomous insertion by a Gothic scribe (or by Wulfila himself?), who added a coordinate element to the narration. However, it is perfectly possible also that this element – for the same narrative reason – was already in the lost Greek *Vorlage* and therefore present in Wulfila's translation. Other changes are due to the occasional insertion of glosses into the text and the conflation of variants.²⁵⁹ Furthermore, as in other biblical traditions, the context or the parallel passages may have led to changes in the original text. The result of the harmonisation to parallel passages is particularly difficult to detect. It could already date back to the Greek *Vorlage* or be due to the activity of the Gothic scribes who were familiar with different accounts of the same story.²⁶⁰

2.4. Marginalia

The *Argenteus* and the *Ambros.* A⁺ exhibit *marginalia*, sixteen and forty-four respectively. Regarding the *Codex Argenteus*, there are fifteen proper glosses, which are mostly synonyms or variants to the readings of the text.²⁶¹ A further marginal annotation contains some words overlooked by the scribe, who perhaps added it later.²⁶² In the text, over the glossed word, there is a mark – a waved dash with a dot below – which refers to the existence of a marginal annotation. A similar sign is over the gloss. All the *marginalia* are written in the upright script and in silver ink. In some cases, they have apparently been written by hands that are different from those that wrote the text and similar to the one that wrote the Ammonian Sections. This fact, as well as the use of silver ink, would point to a glossatory activity inside the scriptorium in which the manuscript was produced. Furthermore, there is evidence that some glosses were incorporated into the text of the *Argenteus*.²⁶³ Therefore, it is possible that its model was a manu-

---

258 See below 4.1.2.(6).
259 See below 5.8.
260 See below 5.5.
261 See below 5.7.
262 The addition of the words overlooked by the scribe is in Mk 2:13 (f. 61v). The proper glosses are in Mt 6:24 (f. 6r); Lk 3:14 (f. 129v); Lk 5:28 (f. 139v); Lk 6:27 (f. 143v); Lk 6:40 (f. 144v); Lk 6:49 (f. 146r); Lk 7:32 (f. 149r); Lk 8:27 (f. 153v); Lk 9:13 (f. 158r); Lk 9:34 (f. 160r); Lk 16:13 (179v); Mk 1:6 (f. 57v); Mk 1:11 (f. 57v); Mk 5:4 (f. 31v); Mk 12:24 (f. 45v).
263 See below 5.8.

script with marginal glosses: some of these crept into the text and others were written in the margins.

Among the forty-four *marginalia* of the *Ambros.* A⁺ forty-three are proper glosses, written in the sloping script,²⁶⁴ and one is a word that belongs to the text.²⁶⁵ It has been overlooked and subsequently added in the margin probably by the scribe himself. Its script is upright, as in the text. The proper glosses are written perhaps not all by the same hand, judging from f. 189v, where the two marginal annotations diverge from a palaeographical viewpoint. Some of these are closed by a short doodle.²⁶⁶ The glosses are mostly synonyms or variants to the readings of the text.²⁶⁷

2.5 Relationships between the manuscripts

Regarding the relationship between the Gothic witnesses only a few considerations are possible. The text in common between the *Argenteus* and the *Ambros.*

---

264 See above 1.3.
265 The overlooked word is in 1 Cor 9:7 (56v/183). The glosses are often illegible. According to Streitberg (1919, *ad loc.*), they are in the external margins of Rom 9:13 (f. 23r/68; refused by Snædal 2013 A, I, XVII); 1 Cor 9:9 (f. 56v/183); 1 Cor 9:19 (f. 58r/136); 1 Cor 9:21 (f. 58r/136); 1 Cor 9:22 (f. 58r/136); 1 Cor 10:30 (f. 61r/162); 1 Cor 13:3 (f. 67r/84); 1 Cor 13:5 (f. 67r/84); 1 Cor 14:21 (f. 70r/86); 1 Cor 15:33 (f. 74v/145); 2 Cor 1:8 (f. 82r/168); 2 Cor 2:11 (f. 84v/181); 2 Cor 2:15 (f. 85r/178); 2 Cor 3:14 (f. 86v/133); 2 Cor 5:12 (f. 90r/138); 2 Cor 6:16 (f. 92v/105); 2 Cor 12:7 (f. 104v/115); 2 Cor 12:15 (f. 105v/83); Eph 1:9 (f. 110v/149); Eph 1:14 (f. 111r/134); Eph 1:19 (f. 111v/135); Eph 2:3 (f. 112r/88); Eph 2:3 (f. 112v/89); Eph 2:10 (f. 113r/90); Eph 3:10 (f. 115r/166); Eph 4:8 (f. 116r/120); Eph 4:13 (f. 116v/121); Eph 6:11 (f. 122r/184); Gal 2:5 (f. 127v/175); Gal 2:6 (f. 127v/175); Gal 2:6 (f. 127v/175); Gal 2:8 (f. 127v/175); Gal 4:3 (f. 129v/171); Gal 4:13 (f. 133r/186); Gal 4:19 (f. 133v/187); Gal 4:21 (f. 133v/187); Gal 6:3 (f. 137r/48); Col 3:5 (f. 155v/6); 1 Tim 1:5 (f. 177v/39); 1 Tim 1:9 (f. 177v/39); 1 Tim 1:18 (f. 179r/17); 1 Tim 3:11 (f. 181v/30); 1 Tim 5:18 (f. 185v/43); 1 Tim 5:23 (f. 186r/23); 1 Tim 6:6 (f. 187r/13); 2 Tim 3:2 (f. 195v/191); 2 Tim 3:9 (f. 196r/188); 2 Tim 3:10 (f. 196v/189); 2 Tim 3:13 (f. 196v/189); 2 Tim 4:6 (f. 198r/200); Tit 1:16 (202v/193); Philm 12 (209r/194); Philm 14 (209r/194).
266 The reading of the glosses is very difficult, because they have suffered from scraping. A campaign of multispectral imaging with the goal to recover the cancelled or scarcely visible glosses was carried out on some sheets of this palimpsest in March and November 2012, by a team from the University of Bergamo (Gianluca Poldi and Francesco Lo Monaco, with the collaboration of Agostino Osio) and myself. The manuscript was studied inside the Biblioteca Ambrosiana using Canon and Nikon high resolution cameras with proper lenses and band-pass filters. A UV lamp (max emission peak 365 nm) with MPX technology was employed together with a halogen lamp to obtain images in UV reflected, UV induced fluorescence and diffused light. In some cases the photos allow one to read parts of the *scriptio inferior* that are otherwise illegible.
267 See below 5.7.

C is very short and the leaves of the *Argenteus* which correspond to the few words of the *Gissensis* are lost. Tracing a stemma of the textual relationship between the Gospel manuscripts is therefore not possible.

The difficulty in tracing a stemma of the Pauline manuscripts lies in the fact that the *Carolinus* and the *Ambros.* B do not share any common parts of the text. The collation of the text shared by *Carolinus* and *Ambros.* A⁺ (Rom 12:17–13:5) and by *Ambros.* A⁺ and *Ambros.* B (long portions of the Epistles, excluding those to the Romans and Philemon) shows some common errors and textual divergences.[268] The obvious conclusion is that these manuscripts derive from the same ancestor, either directly or through intermediate copies. No sure clue of their dependence from intermediate manuscripts is however attested.[269]

Three marginal glosses of *Ambros.* A⁺ correspond to readings of the text in *Ambros.* B.[270] According to Friedrichsen, the composition of the glosses seems to point

> to two originals of close kinship, yet differing in occasional readings and renderings, and to the probability that Codex [*Ambros.*] A was subsequently annotated, the notes being mainly of variant renderings, usually synonyms found in other portions of the text, and occasionally [...] from a sister manuscript like Codex [*Ambros.*] B.[271]

Another possibility is to postulate a common ancestor with marginal glosses. The scribe of *Ambros.* B would have chosen generally the reading of the text and in three cases those of the margin, while the scribe of *Ambros.* A⁺ would have copied faithfully the text of the ancestor and then its glosses. This possibility, however, seems less likely because the glosses belong – apparently – to different hands, diverse from those of the text. Furthermore, they are not disposed regularly on the page.

The codicological analysis of the manuscripts may help to add some details to the picture: the ancestor of the *Carolinus* was not written *per cola et commata* in the same manner as this manuscript and very likely was not bilingual, as indicated by an error of the *Carolinus* which could be made only from a copy with a

---

268 Details in Friedrichsen 1939, 62–86.
269 According to Streitberg (1919 = 2000, *ad loc.*), the *Ambros.* A⁺ transmits in 1 Tim 3:3 *ak sutis, [qairrus], ni sakuls* vs. the *Ambros.* B: *ak sutis, [airkn[i]s], ni sakuls* 'but patient [gentle (A)/pure (B)], not a brawler' (ἀλλὰ ἐπιεικῆ, ἄμαχον). However, the reading *airkn[i]s* does not exist (refused by Snædal 2013 A, I, *ad loc.*, who suggests to read *qairrus* in both manuscripts; Snædal's suggestion has been confirmed by my autoptic examination of the *Ambros.* B); furthermore one of the readings might already have been present in their common ancestor.
270 See below 5.7.
271 Friedrichsen 1939, 73.

different text arrangement.[272] The text division of the ancestor was perhaps similar to that of *Ambros.* A⁺ (I part, down to 1 Cor 5:4). Moreover, it is worth noting that the *Ambros.* A⁺ (II part, from 1 Cor 5:4) and the *Ambros.* B do not show the articulated system of division of the text attested in the *Carolinus*. One may not exclude that *Ambros.* A⁺ was copied from two different manuscripts: the first was used down to 1 Cor 5:4, i.e. for the part written in colometrical arrangement; the second for the rest.

To be cautious, it is only possible to trace a stemma of the relationship between the *Carolinus* and the *Ambros.* A⁺ (1) and another one of the relationship between the *Ambros.* A⁺ and the *Ambros.* B (2), manuscripts which have common parts of text:

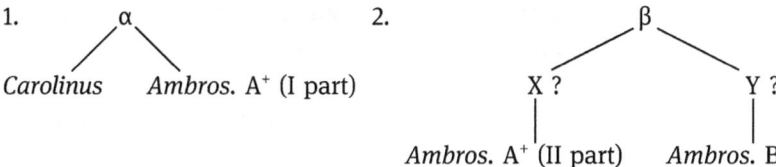

A possible stemma which takes into account the three manuscripts is:

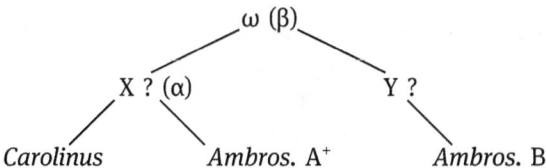

where ω is the common ancestor, monolingual and in *scriptio continua*; X is a monolingual manuscript, written not *per cola et commata* as the *Carolinus* but rather as *Ambros.* A⁺ (I part). Many doubts, however, still remain.

2.6 Editions of the Gothic texts

Many editions of the Gothic texts have been published since the *editiones principes*, which generally closely followed the discovery of each single Gothic witness. The first one dates back to Hans Georg von der Gabelentz and Julius Löbe in 1836, subsequently reprinted in 1843–1846 in Leipzig and in 1848 in

---

272 See above 3.7.

Migne's *Patrologia Latina* (volume 18). It was accompanied by a faithful Latin translation, various comments and grammatical notes which are still useful today.

The Gothic texts were reedited by Andreas Uppström between 1854 and 1868 (posthumously), with introduction and notes. In 1857 Hans Ferdinand Maßmann proposed a new edition, with grammar and dictionary. The Gothic text was accompanied by an extensive introduction and parallel Greek and Latin texts. Friedrich Ludwig Stamm's edition appeared in 1858, with a brief introduction on the manuscripts and on Wulfila. Numerous editions of this text were made: from the third (in 1865) onwards it was edited by Moritz Heyne, and from the tenth (in 1903) onwards by Ferdinand Wrede. These editions remain useful because of the subsequent deterioration of the Gothic manuscripts.

In 1875 Ernst Bernhardt provided the first attempt to offer the Greek *Vorlage* of the Gothic text. This edition, with a long introduction and numerous notes, is still interesting.[273] It was used by Gerhard H. Balg in his edition of the Gothic Bible in 1891. This latter is accompanied by a dictionary and numerous linguistic reflections.

In 1908 Wilhelm Streitberg published a new critical edition of the Gothic Bible, accompanied by a reconstruction of its Greek *Vorlage*.[274] This became the standard edition of the Gothic text, reprinted in 1919^2 (with corrections of the Gothic text and notes on the basis of Wilhelm Braun's new examination of the Pauline manuscripts in 1911 and 1912, and the addition of the text of the *Codex Gissensis*), 1950^3 (with corrections of printing errors), 1960^4, 1965^5 (revised by Ernst A. Ebbinghaus), 1971^6 and finally 2000^7. This latter, edited by Piergiuseppe Scardigli, is integrated with the Gothic texts discovered after 1965, i.e. the Speyer fragment, the Hács-Béndekpuszta tablet and the *Gotica Parisina*. Both Streitberg's Gothic and Greek texts have remained unaltered. Furthermore, although it is not presented as a critical edition, Magnús Snædal, as the source of his concordance (1998; rev. in 2005^2 and 2013^3), offers a revision of Streitberg's text – on the basis of a rereading of the facsimiles – and proposes several corrections to the previous editions.

---

273 See below 5.1.
274 The reconstruction of the Greek *Vorlage* was based on different premisses in respect to Bernhardt's reconstruction; see below 5.1.

2.7 Recent tools for the study of the Gothic texts

A valuable resource for the study of the Gothic Gospels and Pauline Epistles is the online text of the Gothic Bible, based on Streitberg's edition of 1919, available at http://www.wulfila.be/ (hosted by the University of Antwerp; last modified in 2006). It offers the Gothic text, the Greek text according to Nestle-Aland$^{26/27}$ (*sic*) and the Latin Clementine Vulgate (of course both of them diverge in many instances from the Gothic), together with modern translations in English, Dutch and French. It provides also lexical and morphosyntactic analyses – with links to digital facsimile editions of Streitberg's *Gotisches Elementarbuch* (1920^5) and of Streitberg's *Gotisch-griechisch-deutsches Wörterbuch* (1910) – and highlights variations between divergent manuscript readings. It permits also the search for all the words which contain a certain phonetic/graphic sequence.

The most recent grammars of the Gothic language are those by Roland Schuhmann (forthcoming) in German, André Rousseau (2013) in French, Antonio Piras (2007) in Italian, Thomas O. Lambdin (2006) in English, and the revision of Wilhelm Braune's grammar by Frank Heidermanns (2004) in German. Another useful tool for investigating the Gothic text is *A Concordance to Biblical Gothic* by Magnús Snædal (2nd revised edition: 2005; 3rd revised edition: 2013), which also offers grammatical notes for each entry.

Among the dictionaries, special mention deserves that of Gerhard Köbler (1989^2), which gives a translation of the items into German and English and a list of the occurrences of each word. It is available at http://homepage.uibk.ac.at/~c30310/gotwbhin.html. The most recent etymological dictionary of the Gothic language was edited by Winfrid P. Lehmann in 1986, on the basis of Sigmund Feist's etymological dictionary (3rd revised edition: 1939). There is also available the *Bibliographia Gotica Amplificata*, by Christian T. Petersen, which provides a list of studies (up to 2005) on the Gothic Bible in different fields. Online reproductions of the Gothic manuscripts are available only for the *Argenteus* (with the exclusion of the Speyer leaf), *Gissensis* and *Carolinus*.[275]

2.8 Conclusions

Among the Gothic manuscripts the *Codex Argenteus* may be considered as an example of a high class of book production. The elegant bilingual *Carolinus* and *Gissensis* are also the product of well organised scriptoria, where Gothic and

---

[275] See the respective descriptions of these manuscripts above.

Latin scribes worked together. Beside these, there are manuscripts less accurate in their writing, perhaps destined for the 'daily' liturgical usage.

Some of the manuscripts are closer related than others. The *Argenteus*, *Carolinus* and *Ambros.* A⁺ exhibit the ‹s› in Latin shape and the abbreviation for *-m*. These features may be considered innovations in regard to the Wulfilian scribal practice of Greek origin. Ravenna seems to be the most probable place for their production.

The existence of glossed manuscripts (*Argenteus* and *Ambros.* A⁺) indicates undoubtedly that the biblical text was also read and used outside the strict liturgical contexts. This fact is clearly testified by the text (a sermon? a prayer?) transmitted by the *Codex Bononiensis*, in which several biblical passages are cited verbatim. Significant also are the indirect witnesses, which denote the interest of cultivated Carolingian readers for Gothic antiquities.

3 'Helps for readers' and other codicological features

Like Greek and Latin manuscripts, the Gothic ones also provided some 'aids for readers'. Some of these help to find a book or a passage of the text; others were used for public – as well as for private – readings of the manuscript, usually written in *scriptio continua*. Not all of these features seem to date back to Wulfila's time. In some cases their introduction may be connected with the influence of the Latin scribal usages. This suspicion derives from the discrepancy between the features attested in the Gothic codices and those of the fourth-century Greek biblical manuscripts – under the assumption that Wulfila found the model for these 'helps' in one or more Greek manuscripts – and conversely the agreement with features typical of the Latin manuscripts.

How the Goths read the Holy Scriptures is unknown. It has been noted[276] that ἀναγινώσκω 'to read (aloud)' was translated into Gothic with *siggwan* 'to sing' (Eph 3:4; + *bokos* 'books' in Lk 4:16 and 2 Cor 3:15, where the reference is to the Old Testament) and *ussiggwan* 'to sing' (Lk 6:3, 10:26; Mk 2:25, 12:10, where the reference is to the Old Testament; Col 4:16; 1 Thess 5:27). Therefore, the reading of the Gothic texts seems to have been a type of cantillation or psalmody. However, it cannot be excluded that there were divergences in the reading of different parts of the Scriptures.[277]

3.1 The Ammonian Sections and Eusebian Canons

The texts of both the *Codex Argenteus* and the Latin part of the *Codex Gissensis* (the beginning of the Gothic text is entirely lost but it was certainly disposed as its Latin counterpart) are divided according to the Ammonian Sections.[278] The number of each section is written in the left margin of the page, within a frame of strokes. The first letter of a new section is enlarged and protruded into the margin (in *ekthesis*), if it coincides with the beginning of a new

---

[276] Scardigli 1973, 120.
[277] On the development of Christian psalmody see Gamble 1995, 228. He points out that "[t]he chant [...] was the way the public reading of scripture was done in the early church, and it served primarily the hermeneutical purpose of making the semantic structure and substance of the text accessible to the hearer."
[278] On this topic see Metzger 1981, 42; Metzger-Ehrman 2005, 38; Parker 2008, 315–316.

line.[279] The first line of a new section is written in different ink,[280] in order to highlight its beginning. The short extant part of the *Ambros. C* does not indicate the Ammonian Sections, which are attested only in the parallel part of the *Argenteus*. In the lower margin of each page, the *Argenteus* offers also the relevant Eusebian Canons, written within silver arcades (the contracted Evangelists' names are in golden ink).[281]

Whether the Ammonian Sections and Eusebian Canons were inherited from Wulfila's time or were introduced later into the Gothic manuscripts is impossible to determine. This system, which permitted the easy comparison of parallel passages, was elaborated – according to the tradition – by Eusebius of Caesarea († ca. 340). It is therefore fully plausible that Wulfila knew and used it.

3.2 The Euthalian Apparatus

The manuscripts of the Pauline Epistles (*Carolinus, Ambros.* A⁺ and *Ambros.* B) exhibit a system of textual division that corresponds – despite several discrepancies – to those attributed to a certain Euthalius (or Evagrius) and generally dated to a period between the fourth and the sixth century (though the fourth century is the usually accepted date).[282] The numbers of the sections are written in smaller script on the left margin of the page, within a frame of strokes. In twenty cases out of twenty-eight the numbers attested in the *Ambros.* A⁺ correspond to the numbers or to the liturgical indication *laikt(s)jo* of the *Ambros.* B.[283] The num-

---

279 But there are some exceptions in the *Codex Argenteus:* at f. 8r, l. 17 (Mt 7:28) begins a new Ammonian Section with a new line, but the first letter is neither enlarged nor protruded.
280 See below 3.9.
281 A similar design is attested also in the *Codex Brixianus* (see above 2.1.1.) and in the *Codex Rehdigeranus* (Berlin, Staatsbibliothek, Preußischer Kulturbesitz, Dep. Breslau 5; see Nordenfalk 1938, 264; CLA VIII, 1073). This latter is dated palaeographically to the seventh or eighth century; it transmits an Old Latin text of the Gospels (ms. l/11) overlaid with Vulgate readings (Burton 2000, 27). The design of the arcades is simpler and less accurate in respect to the *Argenteus* and *Brixianus*. The parchment is not coloured and the ink is brown. The earliest history of this manuscript is unknown; in the middle of the fifteenth century it was in Aquileia (northern Italy), see Vogels 1913, v-vi.
282 The origin of this kind of apparatus is controversial; on the topic see Metzger 1981, 42–43; Metzger-Ehrman 2005, 40, fn. 60; Willard 2009, 111–134; Parker 2008, 268–270; Scherbenske 2013.
283 Braun 1898; Marchand 1956 (see the criticism by Willard 2009, 106).

bers attested in the *Carolinus* show some divergences from the Euthalian Apparatus, divergences which may go back to scribal errors.²⁸⁴

It is not possible to say with safety whether the system dates back to Wulfila's time or was introduced later into the Gothic manuscripts, since its origin is unknown. However, the slight divergences attested in the Gothic witnesses suggest that it is an old tradition, which suffered some corruption during its transmission.²⁸⁵

3.3 Running titles

Running titles in the top margin of the leaf are attested in some of the Gothic manuscripts.²⁸⁶ The formula is short and simple: *þairh* 'according to' (equivalent to κατά) and the abbreviation for the name of the evangelist in the Gospels; *du* 'to' (equivalent to πρός) and the abbreviation for the name of the addressee in the Pauline Epistles.²⁸⁷ This peculiarity is rarely attested in Greek manuscripts, even though it is present in the oldest ones of Wulfila's time.²⁸⁸ It is instead common in Latin codices. It is therefore possible both that the running titles in the Gothic manuscripts reflect an old Greek usage and that they were introduced under the influence of Latin models, as an aid for readers.

3.4 Superscriptions and subscriptions

The Gothic manuscripts which preserve the beginning and/or the end of a book²⁸⁹ transmit superscriptions and subscriptions. They are longer and more

---

284 Falluomini 1999, 137–138.
285 On the first letter of a new section see below 3.8.
286 *Codex Argenteus*, *Ambros.* A⁺ and *Ambros.* C. It is not possible to verify if they were present in the *Carolinus*, because the top margin has been cut; doubts remain on the *Gissensis* (see Ebbinghaus 1989, 276–278). In the *Ambros.* A⁺ the drawing of the titles is careless and variable in the form, see also Friedrichsen 1939, 87–88.
287 The preposition *þairh* is on the verso page and the abbreviation for the name of the evangelist in the following recto page every two pages (flesh side); *du* and part of the name of the addressee is on the verso page and the rest on the following recto page.
288 Among sixty-seven Greek biblical manuscripts of which the top margin remains, only three have running titles, i.e. the *codices Sinaiticus* (ℵ/01), *Vaticanus* (B/03) and *Bezae* (D/05), see Parker 1992, 16–20.
289 *Codex Argenteus*, *Ambros.* A⁺ and *Ambros.* B; on this topic see also Friedrichsen 1939, 86–87.

complex than those of the Greek manuscripts[290] and reflect the Latin formulas (with different syntax), e. g.: *aiwaggeljo þairh lukan anastodeiþ* '(the) Gospel according to Luke begins' (CA, f. 118r), which corresponds to Lat. *incipit euangelium secundum lucam*. The influence of the Latin usage is therefore very likely. It is worth noting that the *Codex Vindobonensis 795* (f. 20v)[291] seems to transmit the original Gothic superscription: *aiwaggeljo þairh lokan* '(the) Gospel according to Luke'. The only subscription of the Gospels is preserved by the Speyer fragment: *aiwaggeljo þairh marku ustauh. wulþus þus weiha guþ. amen.* '(the) Gospel according to Mark ends. Glory to you, holy God. Amen'.

The superscriptions and subscriptions of the Epistles show some divergence between the *Ambros.* A⁺ and the *Ambros.* B, e. g.: *aipistaule pawlaus du aifaisium anastod<e>iþ* '(the) epistle of Paul to (the) Ephesians begins' (*Ambros.* A⁺) against the simple *du aifaisium anastodeiþ* '(the epistle) to (the) Ephesians begins' (*Ambros.* B); *aipistaule pawlaus du þaissalauneikaium ·b· anastodeiþ* (*Ambros.* A⁺) '(the) second epistle of Paul to (the) Thessalonians begins' against the simple, original *du þaissalauneikaium anþara* the (*Ambros.* B) '(the) second (epistle) to (the) Thessalonians'. This formula is attested also in the *Ambros.* A⁺: *du teimauþaiau anþara* lit. '(the) second (epistle) to Timothy' (*Ambros.* B is lost).

Generally, the subscriptions of the *Ambros.* A⁺ show the conflation of different types of subscriptions attested in the Greek and Latin manuscripts, e. g.: *du kaurinþium ·a· ustauh* || *du kaurinþium frume melida ist* || *us filippai swe qeþun sumai* || *iþ mais þugkeiþ bi silbins* || *apaustaulaus insahtai* || *melida wisan us asiai* lit. '(the) first (epistle) to (the) Corinthians ends. (The) first (epistle) to (the) Corinthians is written from Philippi, as some people said; but it is better to think, according to (the) declaration of (the) apostle himself, (that) was written from Asia' (*Ambros.* B is lost); *du kaurinþium · b · ustauh* || *du kaurinþium · b · meliþ ist* || *us filippai makidonais* lit. '(the) second (epistle) to (the) Corinthians ends. (The) second (epistle) to (the) Corinthians is written from Philippi of Macedonia' (*Ambros.* A⁺);[292] a simpler formula is transmitted by the *Ambros.* B: *du kaurinþaium anþara ustauh* '(the) second (epistle) to (the) Corinthians ends'.

---

290 In the oldest manuscripts of the Greek Bible the titles of the books were usually short and simple; only the content of the book was given, e. g.: (εὐαγγέλιον) κατὰ [...] or πρὸς Ῥωμαίους (see Metzger 1981, 40). In Latin, instead, they were introduced by *incipit* [...] or *explicit* [...]. *Explicit* (of a certain book) and *incipit* (of the subsequent book) were often united in the oldest Latin manuscripts, as well in the Greek-Latin bilingual *Bezae* (D/05) and *Claromontanus* (D/06).
291 See above 2.2.3.
292 Among the Greek manuscripts listed by Swanson (2005, 186), only K/018 exhibits a similar subscription.

As in the Greek manuscripts, the words that signal the end of a book and the beginning of the following book are separated and written on different pages: [...] *ustauh* '*explicit*' is written at the end of a certain book and [...] *anastodeiþ* (*/dustodeiþ*) '*incipit*' at the beginning of the following page. They are framed by short strokes or *diple*, both in the Gospels and in the Epistles.

3.5 Paragraphs

The division of the text into paragraphs is well attested in all the Gothic manuscripts. Paragraph marks – which, according to the Greek usage, consist of a horizontal stroke with a *diple* or dot in the middle (–·–) – signal the end of a paragraph.[293] They are placed in the left margin, between the last line of one text section and the first line of the new section which begins a new line. The system probably dates back to Wulfila's time, even if some subsequent variations in the length of the paragraphs were introduced. Indeed, textual breaks represent a scribal or editorial evaluation of sense units and may be easily changed in the course of the text transmission.[294]

A comparison between the manuscripts which exhibit the same portion of text (*Codex Argenteus* and *Ambros.* C; *Carolinus* and *Ambros.* A⁺; *Ambros.* A⁺ and *Ambros.* B) shows several divergences in the textual division. It is more detailed in the *Argenteus*, *Carolinus* and *Ambros.* B[295] than in the other manuscripts. Moreover, in the *Argenteus*, the beginning of a new paragraph usually coincides with the beginning of an Ammonian Section.[296] A paragraph, however, may include more Ammonian Sections.

The first letter of a new paragraph which begins a new line is generally protruded and enlarged.[297]

---

[293] On paragraph division see recently Porter 2009, 183.
[294] See Goswell 2009, 135–136.
[295] According to Braun (1898, 439–440), there are different paragraph marks in the *Ambros.* B: one more complex, composed by a horizontal sign with a stroke in the middle and shorter strokes above and below, would denote a textual division of first rank; a simpler horizontal sign with a stroke in the middle would mark a division of second rank. However, such a distinction is doubtful.
[296] But there are some exceptions: with Jn 8:14 (97r, l. 10) begins a new paragraph but not an Ammonian Section.
[297] The only exception among the Gothic NT manuscripts is the first part of *Ambros.* A⁺, see below 3.8.

3.6 Punctuation

The Gothic manuscripts offer two marks of punctuation: a double point (:) to indicate the end of a long sense unit, considered as a part of a phrase complete in its grammatical constituents, and a single middle point (·) to signal the end of a shorter sense unit.[298] The double point, therefore, corresponds to a major transition of thought and may identify the end of a paragraph or an Ammonian/Euthalian Section. In several cases, however, the single point is used where the double point is expected (the opposite is much rarer). In the *Ambros. A*⁺ the double point is not attested. From 1 Cor 5:4, a space of ca. two/three letters marks the end of the *commata* and a single point indicates that of the *cola*.

The general criterion of division seems to be rhetorical and emphatic. This is evident, for instance, in some passages in which the division of the text reveals the emphasis of the reading, for example in Mt 5:37 (CA, f. 3r, l. 5–6):

sijaiþ þan waurd ïzwar · ja · ja · ne · ne

'but let your word be · yes · yes · no · no'

In enumerative passages in particular, the usage of the high point was determined by the rhythm of the declamation, as in Lk 6:14–16 (CA, f. 142r, l. 17–20 and f. 142v, l. 1–5):

seimon þanei jah namnida paitru jah andrai an broþar ïs · ïakobu · jah ïohannen · filippu jah barþulomaiu · maþþaiu jah þoma(n) · ïakobu þana alfaius · jah seimon þana haitanan zeloten · ïudan ïakobaus · jah ïudan ïskarioten · saei jah warþ galewjands ïna[299]

'Simon whom he also named Peter and Andrew his brother · James · and John · Philip and Bartholomew · Matthew and Thomas · James (son) of Alphaeus · and Simon who (was) called (the) Zealot · and Judas (brother) of James · and Judas Iscariot · who also became a traitor'

However, the segmentation of the text is, in some cases, difficult to explain. Indeed, parallel passages of the *Codex Argenteus* show some inexplicable discrepancies between their punctuation.[300]

---

298 Occasionally in Matthew (*Codex Argenteus*), if the *colon* ends in the middle of the line, there is a short horizontal line after the double point; see for instance Mt 7:29 (f. 8v, l. 1); Mt 8:12 (f. 9v, l. 4); Mt 9:8 (f. 12r, l. 9); Mt 11:17 (f. 38r, l. 8).
299 On the addition of *ina* see below 5.5.
300 Werth 1967, 525–523. Discrepancies in the punctuation can also be observed in the Greek and Latin manuscripts. Malcolm B. Parkes (1992, 70) pointed out that "two copies of the same

The uniform presence of punctuation marks and their attestation in the Greek scribal tradition lead to the assumption that they were introduced into the Gothic manuscripts in the first phase of their production.[301]

3.7 *Cola et commata*

The practice of dividing the text into sense lines through their different disposition in the writing area is attested in the bilingual *Carolinus* and *Gissensis* and in the first part of the monolingual *Ambros*. A⁺ (down to 1 Cor 5:4, f. 49r). The beginning of the *comma* is indented (| |..) in comparison to the beginning of the *colon* (|..|), by help of two vertical bounding lines, which delimited the writing area left and right.[302]

Rhetorical emphasis and writing space determined the different length of the *cola* and *commata*. The text common to the *Carolinus* and the *Ambros*. A⁺ (Rom 12:17–13:5), which derives from the same (now lost) ancestor, is disposed in a slightly different way, the writing area of the latter being larger. The beginnings of the *cola* correspond, whereas those of the *commata* often diverge:[303]

Rom 12:20

Carolinus
(f. 256v, l. 15–18)

Ambros. A⁺
(f. 31v, l. 20–21 and f. 32r, l. 1)

Jabai gredo fijand þeina(n)a
    mat gif ïmma
iþ jabai þaursjai
    dragkei ïna

jabai gredo fijand þeinana
    mat gif ïmma
iþ jabai þaursjai dragkei ïna

'If your enemy hungers || give him food; || if he thirsts, ||[304] give him drink'

---

text could exhibit differences of punctuation in situations where we would expect the grammatical and rhetorical structure to be identical."

301 Moreover, it is interesting to note that Jesus' genealogy (Lk 3:23–38; f. 130v-132v) is disposed in two columns, as in the oldest Greek manuscripts *Sinaiticus* (ℵ/01), *Alexandrinus* (A/02) and *Bezae* (D/05). The writing area of the *Argenteus* is divided into two columns: in the first there is the word *sunaus* (gen. of *sunus* 'son'); in the second there is the name of the ancestor.
302 The double vertical bounding lines are typical of manuscripts which transmit a text divided in sense lines, in order to guide the disposition of the text, see Raffaelli 1984, 8.
303 See Kauffmann 1911 A, 413.
304 This division is absent in the *Ambros*. A⁺.

In the *Carolinus*, the redactor has paid particular attention to the segmentation of the text, creating parallelisms and respecting the syntactical rule of the conjunctions, such as *iþ* 'but', 'however', *aþþan* 'but', 'then', 'however', *duþþe* 'therefore', 'because' and *unte* 'since', 'until', 'indeed', 'because', *ak* 'but', and other elements of the sentences, such as negations and relative pronouns. They are always placed at the beginning of a new line.[305] It is likely, however, that the common ancestor of the *Carolinus* and the *Ambros*. A⁺ was not divided into *cola et commata*, at least not in the same manner as the *Carolinus*. There is evidence that the colometrical arrangement of *Carolinus*' model diverged: at the beginning of a new line (f. 277v, Rom 12:2, l. 2) the Gothic scribe wrote a letter (*þ*), later erased, belonging to the preceding word. This error could arise only if the two words were near each other. In other words, if the model was written in the same manner as the *Carolinus*, this error would not have been possible.[306]

The origin of this text division is controversial. According to the tradition, it was introduced into the Greek manuscripts of the Pauline Epistles by Euthalius (or Evagrius).[307] A similar textual arrangement was used by Jerome as he translated the Prophets.[308] The uncertainty about its origin does not allow one to speculate about the period in which this system was introduced into the Gothic manuscripts.[309]

The division of the text into sense lines was considered – at the beginning of the studies on the Gothic manuscripts – as a sign of the greater antiquity of the bilingual *Carolinus* and *Gissensis*[310] in respect to the other manuscripts. This

---

305 Details in Falluomini 1999, 142–145.
306 Details in Falluomini 1999, 127.
307 See also above 3.2.
308 See Vezin 1987, 56–57: "Le sens de l'expression *per cola et commata* est difficile à cerner. [...] Quand saint Jérôme parle de copier un texte *per cola et commata*, il doit avoir à l'esprit de le disposer de telle manière que chaque partie du discours soint transcrite sur une seule ligne, ou bien, si cela est impossible, sur deux ou plusieurs lignes, mais en faisant ressortir l'indépendance de chaque membre ou de chaque incise par un artifice graphique. [...] Le nombre de manuscrits de la *Vetus latina* remontant au Vᵉ ou au VIᵉ siècle [several manuscripts with poetic books of the Old Testament, the first part of the Evangeliar of Sarezzano (CLA III, 436a) and the Latin parts of the *Carolinus* and *Gissensis*] qui présentent une telle disposition laisse penser que d'autres contemporains de saint Jérôme ont employé cette technique et que l'ermite de Bethléem n'a fait que s'approprier une idée qui était dans l'air."; on this topic see also Müller 1964; Metzger 1981, 39; Petitmengin 1985, 103–105; Parkes 1992, 65; McGurk 1994, 13–14.
309 Marchand (1956, 166) claimed that this system went back to Wulfila himself. It is of course possible, but it cannot be verified.
310 Glaue-Helm 1910; Kauffmann 1911 A, 403. Furthermore, it should be noted that the palaeographical analysis of the *Gissensis* points clearly to the sixth century, see Falluomini 2010 A, 316–317 (with further bibliographical references).

practice, however, is undoubtedly due to the need to facilitate the comparison between the Gothic and Latin texts and it is not a criterion for dating these manuscripts. Indeed, it is attested principally in the Greek-Latin bilinguals[311] and in the manuscripts destined for schools,[312] where the parallel texts are placed in two columns, on the same page or on opposite pages.[313] The beginning of each *colon* or *comma* corresponded in the parallel versions, helping the reader to correlate the two texts. That this division is found also in the two Gothic-Latin manuscripts is therefore not surprising.

The layout of the page, with the beginnings of the paragraphs and the *cola* and *commata* distinguished graphically, allowed recognition of the hierarchy of the sense units, facilitating the identification of the relationships between the grammatical elements of the sentence. Great consideration was therefore given to the readability of the text. This arrangement may have been intended particularly for public reading.[314] Indeed, this refined textual articulation, individuating graphically the clause and grammatical units, helped the reader to comprehend – and, in the case of the bilingual manuscripts, to compare – the two texts. Moreover, the use of such a system, which involves a waste of parchment and a careful layout, is evidence of the wealth of the commissioners of these manuscripts.

3.8 Enlarged letters

Enlarged letters, hanging in the left margin at the beginning of a new line in order to highlight the beginning of a new section or paragraph,[315] are found in the Gothic manuscripts, with the exception of *Ambros.* A⁺ (I part).[316] Since this

---

311 According to Dahl (1979, 95), the colometrical arrangement of the Gothic and Latin texts of the *Carolinus* may go back to that of the ancestor of the Greek-Latin bilinguals. The investigation of the *Carolinus*, however, does not support this idea.
312 See Daris 2000, 173–174.
313 See Parker 1992, 50–69.
314 On the colometrical arrangement as an aid for public reading see Gamble 1995, 229–230.
315 More rarely, in the *Codex Argenteus*, the enlarged and protruded letters, in silver ink, are not combined with Ammonian Sections or paragraphs marks, but they correspond to the beginning of new sentences. See for instance f. 6v, l. 16 (Mt 6:31); f. 123v, l. 12 (Lk 2:1); f. 51v, l. 16 (Mk 8:31).
316 The first letter of a new paragraph or section protrudes into the margin but is not enlarged. See for instance f. 22r, l. 3 (Rom 8:35); f. 32r, l. 6 (Rom 13:1), against the parallel *Carolinus* (f. 256v, l. 26), which has enlarged initials; f. 40r, l. 3 (Rom 16:22). But at l. 9 (Rom 16:24) the letter ᚨ ⟨a⟩ seems to be slightly larger than usual.

usage is attested also in the Greek manuscripts,³¹⁷ it might date back to Wulfila's time. Their purpose was clearly connected with the readability of the manuscript, permitting the easy identification of a new portion of text.

The use of enlarged letters in the middle of the line is, however, typical of Latin manuscripts from the second half of the fifth century onwards, becoming usual in the sixth century.³¹⁸ It is not testified uniformly in the Gothic NT manuscripts: it is attested only in the *Argenteus* (I hand, occasionally), *Ambros.* A⁺ (II part, occasionally) and *Ambros.* B (slightly). It is clearly not present in the manuscripts written in sense lines (*Carolinus* and *Gissensis*), where initial letters of each new paragraph or section are placed totally (*Carolinus*) or partially (Latin part of the *Gissensis*) outside of the first vertical line (.| |) and are totally (*Carolinus*) or partially (Latin part of the *Gissensis*) enlarged.

3.9 Distinctive ink

Distinctive golden ink – as opposed to the silver ink of the majority of the text – is used in the *Codex Argenteus* to highlight the first three lines of each Gospel,³¹⁹ the first line of the Ammonian Sections (in instances in which an Ammonian Section begins a new line the paragraph mark is also in golden ink), the first line of the *Pater noster*³²⁰ and the contractions of Evangelists' names in the Eusebian Canon Tables. The use of a different colour helped the readers to segment the text and consequently to change the reading intonation.

Also the *Codex Gissensis* – at least the Latin part – seems to have been written with two inks, because the first line of the Ammonian Sections are discolored – judging from the pictures – in comparison to the rest of the text.³²¹ This may be an indication that such a line was written in a different colour, perhaps red. In this case, it is likely that the Gothic part also had the same feature.

The use of distinctive ink as an indicator of unit divisions is attested in the Hebrew, Greek and Latin traditions, particularly in deluxe copies.³²²

---

317 Metzger 1981, 32; Comfort 2005, 53.
318 However, amongst the Greek manuscripts, the *Codex Washingtonianus* (W/032, usually dated in the fifth century) exhibits slightly enlarged letters in the middle of the line.
319 The first three lines of the Gospels of Luke and Mark are in gold. It is then reasonable to think that the lost beginnings of Matthew and John were also written in the same manner.
320 Mt 6:9 (f. 4v, l. 20).
321 Snædal 2003, 18.
322 As, for instance, the *Codex Bezae* (D/05, from the fifth century, where the first three lines of each book are in red ink, see Metzger-Ehrman 2005, 70) or the *Codex Purpureus Rossanensis* (Σ/

3.10. *Diple*

The citations from the Old Testament are indicated in the Gothic manuscripts by the *diple* (>) or an enlarged point (a corruption of the *diple*, often attested in the *Argenteus*), set on the left margin along the cited text. This mark, which permitted quick recognition of the quotations, is attested also in Greek manuscripts. Therefore its use may go back to Wulfila's time. The citations from the Old and New Testament reported in the text of the *Codex Bononiensis* are indicated by a horizontal stroke (sometimes with an oblique sign in the middle).

3.11 *Nomina sacra*

Nomina sacra are always used for the names 'God', 'Lord', 'Jesus' and 'Christ' in all their declined forms when they refer to Christian appellatives.[323] It is interesting to note that the name of the 'Holy Spirit' is never contracted, a fact which Ludwig Traube[324] explained as a reflex of the Arian belief, which regarded the Holy Spirit as being subservient to God and to Christ. Another possible explanation is that Wulfila's *Vorlage* did not have such a contraction, which appears later in the Greek manuscripts.[325] It is curious that in the bilingual *Carolinus* – where the texts are arranged in parallel columns – the Gothic part (Rom 14:17, f. 255r l. 15) offers *in ahmin weihamma* 'in (the) Holy Spirit' and the Latin one the contracted forms *in sp(irit)u s(an)c(t)o*.

As in Greek and Latin manuscripts, the contracted forms are marked by a horizontal superscribed stroke:

042, written in the sixth century in silver and gold ink on purple vellum, see Metzger-Ehrman 2005, 84); see also Petitmengin 1985, 101; Tov 1998, 128–129.
323 The words are not contracted when they do not have 'sacred' referents, as in Lk 19:33 (*fraujans* 'human masters', plur.; *Codex Argenteus*, f. 104r, l. 6). Some miswritings occur, as in 2 Cor 4:4, where *guþ* 'god' is contracted even if it is related to Satan (in both *Ambros*. A⁺ and *Ambros*. B); or in 2 Tim 2:21, where *fraujin* 'Lord' (*Ambros*. B) is not contracted. In these instances, the scribes probably did not pay close attention to what they were copying. Similar miswritings frequently appear in Greek manuscripts, see Hurtado 2006, 126–127. Concerning the *nomina sacra*, see Traube 1907; Turner 1924; Metzger 1981, 36–37; Gamble 1995, 74–78; Hurtado 2006, 95–134.
324 Traube 1907, 272.
325 Turner 1924, 65, 67.

	Nom./Voc.	Gen.	Dat.	Acc.
'God'	ḡb̄ g(u)þ	ḡb̄s g(u)þ(i)s	ḡb̄a g(u)þa	ḡb̄ g(u)þ
'Lord'	f̄a f(rauj)a	f̄ins f(rauj)ins	f̄in f(rauj)in	f̄n/f̄an f(rauj)n f(rauj)an
'Jesus'	īs i(esu)s	īnis i(es)uis	īua i(es)ua	īn i(es)u
'Christ'	x̄s x(ristu)s	x̄ins x(rist)aus	x̄in x(rist)au	x̄n x(rist)u

It is noteworthy that the contractions of the indirect forms of *guþ* 'God' (gen. *gudis*, dat. *guda*) attest -*þ*- instead of -*d*-, a reflexion of their fixity in Gothic. The form īs ‹is› has been occasionally confused with i̅s ‹is› 'he', causing changes in the meaning of the text.[326] In the *Ambros.* B the contractions for *Iesus* and *Xristus* are īu̅ ‹ius› and x̄u̅ ‹xus› instead of i̅ε ‹is› and x̄ε ‹xs›.[327] It is furthermore remarkable that these contractions are also found in non-biblical manuscripts such as the *Codex Bononiensis* and the *Ambros.* E⁺; a fact that denotes how the Gothic scribes were acquainted with this practise. Their visual emergence in the written page could represent a practical guide to facilitate the reading of the text.

3.12 Numerals

As in the Greek manuscripts, numbers can be expressed by letters, which represent a numeric value, or as words. They are always expressed by letters when they refer to the Ammonian and Euthalian Sections, are reported in the Eusebian Canons, and mark the signatures of the quires. The numbers present in the text – when they are expressed by letters – are placed between points and are highlighted by a horizontal stroke. This usage seems to be a combination of the Greek usage (a horizontal stroke) and the Latin one (the points).[328]

---

326 See above 2.3.
327 Ebbinghaus 1997 [1995], 92.
328 See Thompson 1912, 91; Metzger 1981, 9.

3.13 *Diaeresis*

Two dots are regularly placed over an initial *i*, such as *ïn* 'in', *ïmma* 'him', *ïs* 'he', *ïudan ïskarioten* 'Judas Iscariot'. This practice allowed recognition of the beginning of the word within the *scriptio continua* and therefore represented a useful aid for the reader. The *diaeresis* above -*i*- is also used to indicate that this vowel is not part of a diphthong. Both the usages are well attested in the Greek manuscripts and therefore there is no doubt that their introduction goes back to Wulfila' time.

3.14 Liturgical indications

The only clear liturgical indications are offered by the *Codex Ambros. B*. In forty-four cases, on the external margin of the page, it exhibits the indication *laiktsjo* or *laiktjo*[329] 'reading, lesson' (doubtless a borrowing from Lat. *lectio*), together with a horizontal stroke.[330]

3.15 Conclusions

The Gothic manuscripts were used in the liturgy, as emerges from several features: beside the proper punctuation or the arrangement in lines according to sense units, there are further pragmatic aids to draw the attention of the reader in order to permit an easier division of the text and consequently to facilitate its legibility: (1) the paragraph signs; (2) the enlarged letters; (3) protruded letters (in *ekthesis*) and (4) the distinctive ink. The articulate visual construction of the text indicates undoubtedly – at least in some of the Gothic manuscripts – the care of their redactors/scribes and the importance of the commissioners and of the audience for which they were produced.

Moreover, from a codicological point of view, features which date back to the Greek tradition – and are therefore inherited from Wulfila's time – are attested together with features of Latin origin. These latter are the result of the influence of Latin models, with which the Goths came into contact in the west; a fact which denotes a close relationship between Gothic and Latin scribes and the existence of scriptoria, where Goths and Romans worked side by side.

---

[329] See above, fn. 222.
[330] According to Braun 1898, 435–436 (in the facsimile by de Vries the paragraph mark is often not visible).

4 Linguistic and stylistic features

Like many ancient translations of the Bible, such as the Old Latin ones and the Vulgate, the Gothic version is very literal: the Greek *Vorlage*[331] is rendered word for word and in the same order.[332] It has been noted that "every word of the Greek text, excepting the definite article, is normally represented in the Gothic, even particles like μεν, δε, αν".[333] This might suggest that the first stage of Wulfila's translation consisted in the interlinear rendering of the model. In any case the translator has adjusted the Gothic text, in order to use it as proper text. Indeed, attention is paid to the idiomatic collocation of discourse particles, which differ from the corresponding Greek particles and reflect undoubtedly the Gothic word order.[334]

The closeness of the Gothic version to the Greek text has been differently judged by scholars. The positions oscillate between the claim that the translation was almost unintelligible to the Goths and the opinion that it was idiomatic and in accordance with Gothic linguistic rules.[335] It is true that the Gothic translator renders the Greek text faithfully, without additions or interpretations, free renderings or free circumlocutions. He tried scrupulously to reproduce the Greek text as closely as possible, perhaps forcing in some cases – where it was possible or necessary – his own language, but saving the general intelligibility of the text.[336] In doing so, the Gothic bishop showed respect for the sacred text, a respect which characterised the oldest biblical versions. Furthermore, lacking a written Gothic tradition before Wulfila's work, the prestige of the Greek text was certainly taken as the linguistic model. However, that the translation is not slavish is evident in the rendering of the Greek terms. Wulfila searched for the exact equivalent of the Greek words, varying the translation according to the context in which they occur and using idiomatic expressions where they

---

331 For the type of text used by Wulfila see below 5. and 6.
332 But not necessarily against the idiomaticity, see below 4.1.1.
333 Friedrichsen 1926, 15.
334 See above 4.1.1.(1). As Friedrichsen (1926, 19) pointed out, "[t]he Gothic translation is thus certainly not an interlinear version, although one is tempted to wonder whether the text that has come down to us did not owe its humble beginnings to a strictly interlinear gloss of which we have [...] a conspicuous example."
335 A survey of the different opinions can be found in Stolzenburg 1905; Curme 1911; Scardigli 1973, 116–132; Piras 2007, 61–67.
336 Stutz 1966, 47; Piras 2007, 61–62.

were necessary.[337] In other words, Wulfila tried to mediate between his adherence to the source text and the constraints of his own language.

Particularly thorny is the question concerning the idiomatic quality of the Gothic syntax, since the comparison of Wulfila's version with independent (i.e. non-translated) Gothic texts does not offer sufficient elements of judgement.[338] Generally, Wulfila followed the Greek syntax closely, a fact which led to the assumption that the Gothic translation does not reflect natural usage.[339] As far as the word order is concerned, it was relatively free in Gothic, being an inflected language; a circumstance which allowed the translator to follow the word order of the *Vorlage*. However, some word positions in the sentence – in particular of the pronouns – seem to be more usual (unmarked?), as emerges from the translation of passages without Greek or Latin textual variants.

It seems reasonable that the Gothic version, although perhaps not completely idiomatic, could perform its function of mediating the Greek text to the Goths. In similar ways, both the *Vetus Latina* and the Vulgate display a high degree of literalism and are heavily skewed by Greek.[340] Familiarity with the biblical text led to the subsequent absorption of scriptural expressions, which in some cases were considered more correct than those used by the classical writers.[341] The same phenomenon may have happened with respect to the Gothic version: that some words, expressions and syntactical constructions have become part of the Gothic language after a period of use in religious – above all liturgical and missionary – contexts.[342]

---

337 See below 4.2.
338 On the originality of the *Skeireins* see above 2; the deeds of Naples and Arezzo are too short to offer indication about the Gothic syntax, and the text of the *Codex Bononiensis* is mainly formed by scriptural citations (see above 2.2.2).
339 See for instance Stutz 1966, 48: "Die gotische Bibel bietet also nur teilweise ein idiomatisches, weithin jedoch ein gräzisierendes Gotisch. Wer ihre Syntax untersucht, erfaßt zur Hälfte ein von Goten tatsächlich gesprochenes Idiom, zur andern Hälfte beschreibt er das Bibelgriechische in gotischer Verkleidung." The bibliography on different aspects of the Gothic syntax is vast: see for instance Stolzenburg 1905; Kapteijn 1911–1912; Ferraresi 2005; Buzzoni 2009; Pagliarulo 2011 and the Gothic bibliography collected by Petersen 2005.
340 See Burton 2000, 172–191.
341 See Piras 2009, 163. Concerning aspects of translation theory in biblical texts, see Burton 2000, 80–84 and related bibliography.
342 With regard to this point, it is worth noting that the language of the text of the *Codex Bononiensis* is very close to the language of the biblical manuscripts (which is supposed to reflect Wulfila's language).

Both Indo-European languages, Gothic and Greek share many grammatical similarities.[343] However, Gothic displays fewer verbal forms in comparison with Greek.[344] Synthetically, the Gothic noun has five cases (nominative, genitive, dative, accusative and vocative) and two numbers (singular and plural). The verb is characterised by three numbers (singular, plural and dual, attested also in the pronominal declension), two tenses (present, preterite), three moods (indicative, optative and imperative[345]). The synthetic passive is attested only in the indicative and optative present. There are deviations between the Gothic and the Greek texts in the rendering of some syntactical constructions (such as the interrogative, the accusative plus infinitive, the genitive absolute, the hypothetical subordinate) and in the use of the infinitive. In such cases, the translator chose, from time to time, between several possible Gothic constructions, selecting the one most appropriate to the context.

Not surprisingly, the language and the style of the Gothic translation of the Pauline Epistles are different from those of the Gospels, reflecting the discrepancies between the language and style of the corresponding Greek texts. It is likely that Wulfila had more difficulty translating Paul's expressions, since they are less simple than those of the Gospels. Therefore, it cannot be excluded that – particularly in the Epistles – he might have also consulted a Latin version, in order to render some difficult passages more clearly.

---

[343] There are several grammars of the Gothic languages, amongst which (here in the latest revised edition): Wright-Sayce 1954; Mossé 1956; Krahe-Seebold 1967; Krause 1968; Mastrelli 1980; Streitberg-Stopp 1981; Rauch 2003; Braune-Heidermanns 2004; Lambdin 2006; Piras 2007; Schuhmann forthcoming.

[344] Since the word order of the Gothic version is strictly adherent to the Greek, the syncretism in the Gothic nominal inflection may have produced in some (few) cases a different interpretation (for the Gothic audience) than that intended in the *Vorlage*, see Snædal 2007. An example is in Gal 5:6: *ak galaubeins þairh friaþwa waurstweiga* 'but faith through effective love' (ἀλλὰ πίστις δι' ἀγάπης ἐνεργουμένη 'but faith operating through love'), where "*waurstweiga* 'effective' [...] is most normally taken to be an acc. sg. fem. (instead of nom.) and so an attribute to *friaþwa* 'love' rather than to *galaubeins* 'faith'." (Snædal 2007, 95). However, as the Icelandic scholar points out, this passage is problematic. Some manuscripts, with which the Gothic text often agrees (p^{46}, H/015, Ψ/044, 642), transmit ἐνεργουμένης, referred to ἀγάπης. Therefore, it is not entirely to exclude that Wulfila intended *waurstweiga* as attribute to *friaþwa*. The Gothic translation would probably have been the same.

[345] The imperative is only used in the present active.

4.1 The Gothic rendering of the Greek text

Limitations in identifying the underlying Greek text of the Gothic readings are due – as would be expected – to some linguistic features of the Gothic in respect to the Greek.[346] In several instances, a Gothic reading may correspond to two or more Greek readings. Moreover, in the case of some non-systematic renderings – without apparent Greek or Latin parallels – it is not possible to evaluate whether they reflect idiomatic features of the Gothic language or a Greek or Latin lost tradition.[347]

4.1.1 Idiomatic features of the Gothic text

Certain divergences between the Gothic and Greek texts occur regularly. They are, therefore, expected to be idiomatic.

1. The Gothic particles *aþþan* 'but', 'but then', 'however', *iþ* 'but', 'however', *þaruh* 'therefore', 'then' and *unte* 'since', 'for', 'until', 'indeed', 'because' are always at the beginning of the sentence. Their position differs regularly from those of the Greek particles which they usually render (γάρ, δέ, οὖν), e.g.:

> Mt 7:15 *iþ innaþro sind wulfos* translates ἔσωθεν δέ εἰσιν λύκοι 'but inwardly (they) are wolves'
>
> Jn 6:19 *þaruh farjandans* renders ἐληλακότες οὖν 'then having rowed'
>
> Rom 13:3 *aþþan wileis* corresponds to θέλεις δέ 'but (do you) will'
>
> 1 Cor 11:23 *unte ik andnam* renders ἐγὼ γὰρ παρέλαβον 'for I received'

Their position in the sentence is undoubtedly idiomatic.

2. Gothic indefinite and interrogative pronouns in the singular form are often constructed with the genitive partitive plural, as well as some adjectives of quantity and numerals, e.g.:

> Lk 4:2 *dage fidwor tiguns* 'forty of (the) days' renders ἡμέρας τεσσεράκοντα 'forty days'
>
> Mk 5:25 *qinono suma* 'a certain of (the) women' translates γυνή τις 'a certain woman'

---

346 Friedrichsen 1977.
347 The following survey does not pretend to be complete, but only reports the more frequent discrepancies between Gothic and Greek.

Rom 13:1 *all saiwalo* 'every of (the) souls' renders πᾶσα ψυχή 'every soul'

3. Gothic lacks a morphological distinction between perfective and non-perfective forms. However, the perfective forms are often rendered – although many examples to the contrary are attested – with verbs prefixed by *ga-*,[348] e.g.:

Lk 4:9 *gasatida* for ἔστησεν '(he) set'

Lk 9:16: *gaþiuþida ins jah gabrak jah gaf siponjam* '(he) blessed them and broke and gave to (the) disciples', rendering of εὐλόγησεν (aor.) αὐτοὺς καὶ κατέκλασεν (aor.) καὶ ἐδίδου (impf.) τοῖς μαθηταῖς. The first two verbs are compounded with *ga-* (*gaþiuþjan* and *gabrikan*); the third verb is the preterite of *giban*.

Eph 1:20 *gawaurhta* for ἐνήργησεν '(he) worked'

4. Gothic lacks a future tense. The category of the future is developed late in the Germanic languages compared to other Indo-European cognates such as Greek and Latin. The Greek future is translated into Gothic mostly by the present, occasionally by the optative and the modal verbs *skulan* 'should', *duginnan* 'to begin', *haban* 'to have', *munan* 'to intend' plus infinitive, e.g.:

Jn 16:22 *iþ aftra saihva* (pres.) *izwis* renders πάλιν δὲ ὄψομαι ὑμᾶς 'but (I) will see you again'

Lk 6:25 *gretan duginnid* translates πεινάσετε '(you) will be hungry'

Mk 4:13 *hvaiwa allos þos gajukons kunneiþ* (opt.) renders πῶς πάσας τὰς παραβολὰς γνώσεσθε 'how will (you) understand all the parables'

5. Gothic lacks a mediopassive voice. The reflexive meaning is rendered in some cases through the corresponding active form and the reflexive pronoun, e.g.:

Jn 6:20 *ni ogeiþ izwis* renders μὴ φοβεῖσθε 'do not be afraid'

6. Synthetic passive forms, inherited from Indo-European, are attested only in the present tense (indicative and optative). In the preterite, passive forms are usually translated by the preterite participle and the auxiliaries *wisan* 'to be' (in a stative sense) or *wairþan* 'to become' (in a dynamic sense),[349] e.g:

---

[348] For a discussion of the various opinions on the aspectual value of the Gothic prefix *ga-*, see Scherer 1964, Trovato 2009 and the bibliography cited here.

[349] Among the several studies on this topic, see Streitberg 1891; Schröder 1957; Abraham 1992; Ferraresi 2005, 121–124; Pagliarulo 2008. According to Dolcetti Corazza (2004, 85–86), they might have been modelled upon the passive periphrastic constructions of the Vulgar Latin.

2 Cor 11:25 *usbluggwans was* (from *wisan*) renders ἐλιθάσθην '(I) was beaten'

Gal 2:13 *miþgatauhans warþ* (from *wairþan*) renders συναπήχθη '(Barnabas) was carried away with'

7. Some Gothic substantives are employed in the singular to render Greek substantives in the plural and vice versa, most probably according to idiomatic usage, e.g.:

Jn 12:3 *skufta* (sing.) 'hair' translates θριξίν (plur.)

Lk 4:17 *bokos* (plur.) 'book' (lit. 'letters') renders βιβλίον (sing.). The singular form *boka* is used to translate 'letter' (= γράμμα)

2 Cor 11:10 *in landa* (sing.) *Akaje* 'in (the) region of (the) Achaians' vs. ἐν τοῖς κλίμασιν (plur.) τῆς Ἀχαΐας 'in the regions of Achaia'

8. Different tenses of the Greek text, attested in a unique narrative sequence, are rendered with the same tense in Gothic,[350] e.g.:

Mt 26:71 *gasahv* (pret.) *ina anþara jah qaþ* (pret.) renders εἶδεν (aor.) αὐτὸν ἄλλη καὶ λέγει (pres.) 'another (maid) saw him and said'

Lk 1:46–47 *mikileid* (pres.) [...] *jah swegneid* (pres.) translates μεγαλύνει (pres.) [...] καὶ ἠγαλλίασεν (aor.) '(my soul) magnifies [...] and (my spirit) rejoices'

9. The Gothic dual of pronouns or verbal forms is habitually used to render the Greek plural related to two people (the dual is lost in New Testament Greek), e.g.:[351]

Mt 9:27 *armai uggkis* renders ἐλέησον ἡμᾶς 'have mercy on us'

Mk 1:17 *hirjats afar mis jah gatauja iggis* corresponds to δεῦτε ὀπίσω μου καὶ ποιήσω ὑμᾶς 'follow me and (I) will make you'

1 Cor 9:6 *ik jah Barnabas ni habos waldufni* renders ἐγὼ καὶ Βαρναβᾶς οὐκ ἔχομεν ἐξουσίαν 'Barnabas and I have no power'

10. The Gothic demonstrative pronoun neuter singular renders the Greek neuter plural, e.g.:

---

350 According to Piras (2009, 165–167), the Greek text would reflect a Hebraic construction (*waw*-conversive).
351 However, there are some occurrences of the use of Gothic plural where the dual would be expected, such as Lk 2:48 and 49. On the dual in Gothic, see Seppänen 1985.

Jn 15:17 *þata* anabiuda izwis 'this (I) command you' vs. ταῦτα ἐντέλλομαι ὑμῖν 'these (I) command you'

Lk 4:28 hausjandans *þata* 'hearing this' vs. ἀκούοντες ταῦτα 'hearing these'

11. The name of a country is usually rendered into Gothic by the name of its inhabitants, e.g.:

Mt 11:22 *Twrim jah Seidonim* 'for Tyrians and Sidonians' vs. Τύρῳ καὶ Σιδῶνι 'for Tyre and Sidon'

1 Cor 16:1 aikklesjom *Galat(i)e*[352] 'to (the) churches of (the) Galatians' vs. ταῖς ἐκκλησίαις τῆς Γαλατίας 'to the churches of Galatia'

4.1.2. Non-systematic renderings

In some instances, the divergences between Gothic and Greek renderings are difficult to explain and evaluate because they are non-systematic. They might reflect either idiomatic features of the Gothic language or a lost Greek tradition.

1. The word order with possessive, demonstrative and personal pronouns diverges in several cases – apparently – from Greek models, e.g.:

Mt 7:24 *waurda meina* 'my words' translates μου τοὺς λόγους
(but in several cases the word order possessive pronoun plus substantive is attested)[353]

Mt 10:23 in *þizai baurg* 'in this city' renders ἐν τῇ πόλει ταύτῃ
(vs. *managein þizai* 'to this people' for τῷ λαῷ τούτῳ in 1 Cor 14:21)

Jn 18:22 *qiþandin imma* lit. 'saying he' (absolute dative) translates αὐτοῦ εἰπόντος (vs. *imma qiþandin* lit. 'he saying' for αὐτοῦ λέγοντος in Lk 9:34[354])

In most of the cases, personal and possessive pronouns[355] follow verbs and nouns. This position seems therefore to be the unmarked one.[356]

---

352 *Galate* in the *Ambros.* A⁺; *Galatiais* in the *Ambros.* B.
353 See the occurrences in Snædal 2013 A, II, *passim*.
354 It is, however, to be noted that the order λέγοντος αὐτοῦ is also attested (ms. 892).
355 Unless they are in the nominative case; see for instance Jn 18:25 *iþ is afaiaik* 'but he denied' vs. ἠρνήσατο οὖν ἐκεῖνος.
356 The different word order between the *Ambros.* A⁺ and the *Ambros.* B in Gal 6:11 is remarkable: it agrees with the Greek text in the *Ambros.* B (*hvileikaim bokom izwis gamelida* 'what large letters (I) wrote to you', in agreement with πηλίκοις γράμμασιν ὑμῖν ἔγραψα D/06, F/010, G/012,

In very rare cases, the word order of other parts of the discourse diverges, e.g.:

> Mk 2:4 *lag sa usliþa* (nom.) 'the paralytic laid' vs. ὁ παραλυτικὸς κατέκειτο (Lat. parallel: *iacebat paralyticus* ff²/8; vs. *paralyticus iacebat*, with variants)
>
> Mk 6:5 *handuns* (acc.) *galagjands* 'having laid (the) hands' vs. ἐπιθεὶς τὰς χεῖρας (no Latin parallels to the Gothic reading)

2. A participle plus the conjunction *jah* or *-uh* 'and' (= καί)³⁵⁷ plus the finite verb is attested in correspondence with a Greek participle plus the finite verb, e.g.:

> Mt 8:14 *qimands Iesus* [...] *jah gasahv* lit. 'having entered Jesus [...] and (he) saw' renders ἐλθὼν ὁ Ἰησοῦς [...] εἶδεν lit. 'having entered Jesus [...] (he) saw' (no Latin parallels to the Gothic reading)
>
> Mk 8:1 *athaitands siponjans qaþuh du im* lit. 'having called (the) disciples and (he) said to them' translates προσκαλεσάμενος τοὺς μαθητὰς λέγει αὐτοῖς 'having called (the) disciples, (he) said to them' (no Latin parallels to the Gothic reading)

This Gothic construction, however, could reflect a Hebraic one, rendered in Greek as 'participle plus conjunction καί and finite verb', a construction which tended to be replaced, predominantly by removing the conjunction.³⁵⁸ Therefore, it cannot be excluded that the Gothic version reflects a lost Greek variant with this peculiar construction.

The Greek participle plus the finite verb may also be rendered by two finite verbs connected with the conjunction *jah* or *-uh* 'and', e.g.:

> Jn 12:14 *bigat þan Iesus asilu jah gasat ana ina* lit. 'then Jesus found (a) donkey and sat upon it' for εὑρὼν δὲ ὁ Ἰησοῦς ὀνάριον ἐκάθισεν ἐπ' αὐτό 'then Jesus, having found (a) donkey, sat upon it' (many Old Latin manuscripts transmit a parallel construction: *inuenit* [...] *et sedit*)
>
> Jn 19:2 *uswundun wippja us þaurnum jah galagidedun imma ana haubid* lit. '(the soldiers) wove (a) crown of thorns and put (to) him on (the) head' renders πλέξαντες στέφανον ἐξ ἀκανθῶν ἐπέθηκαν αὐτοῦ τῇ κεφαλῇ '(the soldiers,) having woven (a) crown of thorns,

---

d/75, g/77, f/78, r³/64 or πηλίκοις ὑμῖν γράμμασιν ἔγραψα *rell.*), while the *Ambros.* A⁺ (*hvileikaim bokom gamelida izwis*) probably reflects a more natural construction.

357 Of course, the insertion of the conjunction *jah/-uh* between participle and finite verb has nothing to do with the insertion of the conjunction *jah/-uh* at the beginning of a sentence, see below 4.1.2.(6).

358 Piras 2009, 167–168. On this Gothic construction see also Henss 1957.

put (it) on his head' (Latin parallels: <u>ornauerunt</u> [...] <u>et</u> capiti eius <u>superposuerunt</u> e/2; <u>texuerunt</u> [...] <u>et inposuerunt</u> capiti eius f/10, in capud eius q/13).³⁵⁹

3. The Greek present participle, used as imperative, is rendered in some cases by a Gothic participle, as in Rom 12:9 <u>fijandans</u> ubila lit. '<u>hating</u> (the) evil (things)' (= ἀποστυγοῦντες τὸ πονηρόν/<u>odientes</u> malum), in others by an optative present, as in Mt 9:13 appan <u>gaggaiþ</u>³⁶⁰ (2ⁿᵈ pers. plur.) ganimiþ lit. 'but <u>go</u>, learn' (vs. πορευθέντες δὲ μάθετε; <u>euntes</u> autem discite).

4. In rare cases the proper name is placed before the verb, e.g.:

> Jn 5:46 jabai allis <u>Mose</u> galaubidedeiþ 'but if (you) believed <u>Moses</u>' vs. εἰ γὰρ ἐπιστεύετε Μωϋσεῖ (no Latin parallels to the Gothic reading)
>
> Jn 18:25 iþ <u>Seimon Paitrus</u> was standands 'then <u>Simon Peter</u> was standing' vs. ἦν δὲ Σίμων Πέτρος ἑστώς (no Latin parallels to the Gothic reading)

5. In rare cases the pronominal subject is made explicit and often placed before the verb, e.g.:

> Lk 7:50 iþ <u>is</u> (3ʳᵈ pers. sing.) qaþ 'but <u>he</u> said' vs. εἶπεν δέ (parallel to the Gothic reading is ipse autem dixit f/10; see also dixit autem Iesus c/6, e/2; var. lect.)
>
> Mk 1:7 <u>ik</u> (1ˢᵗ pers. sing.) ni im wairþs '<u>I</u> am not worthy' vs. οὐκ εἰμὶ ἱκανός (no Latin parallels to the Gothic reading)

The personal pronoun is often added before a noun in the vocative, occasionally in correspondence with the Greek definite article, e.g.:

> Lk 4:23 <u>þu</u> (2ⁿᵈ pers. sing.) leiki hailei lit. '<u>you</u>, physician, heal' vs. ἰατρέ θεράπευσον (no Latin parallels to the Gothic reading)
>
> Eph 5:25 <u>jus</u> (2ⁿᵈ pers. plur.) wairos frijoþ lit. '<u>you</u>, husbands, love', vs. οἱ ἄνδρες ἀγαπᾶτε (no Latin parallels to the Gothic reading)

It is also interesting to note that in very rare cases the Gothic text adds 'Jesus' as subject without Greek or Latin parallels, e.g.:

> Lk 20:23 <u>Iesus</u> qaþ du im '<u>Iesus</u> said to them' vs. εἶπεν πρὸς αὐτούς '(he) said to them' (no Latin parallels to the Gothic reading)

---

359 The Gothic text has a different construction: *imma* (dat. sing.) is connected with the verb (*galagidedun*), against αὐτοῦ/*eius* (gen. sing.), which are connected with the substantive (κεφαλῇ/*capiti*/*capud*).

360 See also the reading *ite* in the Old Latin ms. k/1 (= Syriac versions).

Mk 4:1 *aftra Iesus dugann* 'again Jesus began' vs. πάλιν ἤρξατο 'again (he) began' (= *et iterum coepit Iesus* f/10; – *Iesus cet.*)

There is a suspicion that the original addition was the personal pronoun ⟨is⟩ 'he', misread/miswritten as 'Jesus', in the contracted form I̅S̅ ⟨is⟩.[361]

6. In some cases, at the beginning of clauses, the Gothic text transmits a copulative (particularly frequent is the coordinating enclitic *-uh* 'and'), conclusive or continuative conjunction, without (apparently) Greek or Latin parallels,[362] e.g.:

Jn 14:9 *baruh qaþ imma Iesus* 'and then Jesus said to him' vs. λέγει αὐτῷ ὁ Ἰησοῦς

Mk 2:6 *wesunuh þan sumai* 'and moreover some were' vs. ἦσαν δέ τινες

Rom 7:2 *jah auk ufwaira qens* 'and thus (a) married woman' vs. ἡ γὰρ ὕπανδρος γυνή

2 Cor 6:8 *jah þairh wulþu jah unswerein* 'and in honour and dishonour' (*Ambros.* A⁺) vs. *þairh wulþu jah unswerein* 'in honour and dishonour' (*Ambros.* B), which corresponds to διὰ δόξης καὶ ἀτιμίας

These particles have a clear connecting function. However, it is worth noting that the tendency to remove original *asyndeta* and to add connecting particles (γάρ, δέ, καί, οὖν) is well attested also in the Greek New Testament tradition.[363] Therefore, it is difficult to evaluate whether the insertion of these elements originates from a lost Greek reading or is an independent addition within the Gothic tradition.

4.1.3 Gothic renderings of two or more Greek forms

When the Greek tradition is divided and transmits two or more variants which could have the same translation in Gothic, it is not possible to determinate the Greek reading underlying Wulfila's translation, e.g.:

1. Gothic has only one past tense (preterite), which may render the Greek imperfect, the aorist, the non-resultative perfect, the pluperfect and occasionally the historical present, e.g.:

---

[361] See above 3.11.
[362] See also above 3.11.
[363] Zuntz 1946, 188–215.

Mt 27:49 *qeþun* '(they) said' may render both ἔλεγον (impf.) and εἶπαν (aor.)

Mk 4:40 *qaþ* '(he) said' may translate ἔλεγεν (impf.), εἶπεν (aor.) or λέγει (pres.)

Mk 5:9 *frah* '(he) asked' may render both ἐπηρώτα (impf.) and ἐπηρώτησεν (aor.)

2. The Gothic present may render both the Greek present and future, e.g.:

Mt 5:39 *stautai* may render both ῥαπίσει (fut.) '(whoever) shall strike' and ῥαπίζει (pres.) '(whoever) strikes'

Mk 2:20 *fastand* may translate both νηστεύσουσιν (fut.) '(they) will fast' and νηστεύουσιν (pres.) '(they) fast'

3. The Gothic present participle may translate both the Greek present and aorist participle, e.g.:

Lk 5:13 *attaitok imma qiþands* may render both ἥψατο αὐτοῦ λέγων (pres.) lit. '(he) touched him, saying' and ἥψατο αὐτοῦ εἰπών (aor.) lit. '(he) touched him, having said'

Mk 3:8 *gahausjandans* may render both ἀκούοντες (pres.) 'hearing' and ἀκούσαντες (aor.) 'having heard'

4. Gothic lacks a definite article. The demonstrative pronoun is used with anaphoric and emphatic value to both render the Greek definite article and the demonstrative pronouns αὐτός, οὗτος and ἐκεῖνος, e.g.:

Mt 26:71 *qaþ du þaim jainar* may correspond both to λέγει τοῖς ἐκεῖ and to λέγει αὐτοῖς ἐκεῖ '(she) said to them who (were) there'

Jn 16:11 *þis fairƕaus* may render both τοῦ κόσμου τούτου '(of) this world' and τοῦ κόσμου '(of) the world'

When the Greek tradition is divided with respect to the attestation of the article, it is impossible to say which variant corresponds to the Gothic version, e.g.:

Jn 11:24 *Marþa* 'Martha' may render both ἡ Μάρθα and Μάρθα

Mk 3:20 *managei* 'crowd' may render both ὁ ὄχλος and ὄχλος

The demonstrative pronoun in Gothic, however, very probably renders the article or the demonstrative pronoun in Greek, e.g.:

Mt 27:1 *allai þai gudjans* (*Ambros. C*) reflects πάντες οἱ ἀρχιερεῖς 'all the chief priests' vs. *allai gudjans* (*Codex Argenteus*)

2 Cor 7:8 *unte jabai gaurida izwis in þaim bokom* (Ambros. B) 'for even if I made you sorry with the letter' reflects ὅτι εἰ καὶ ἐλύπησα ὑμᾶς ἐν τῇ ἐπιστολῇ vs. *unte jabai gaurida izwis in bokom* (Ambros. A⁺)

It is not possible to determine whether the Wulfilian reading had the article or not.

5. The rendering of the Greek prepositions or particles is not uniform but depends on proper uses in Gothic, often difficult to evaluate. It is not possible to assess which Greek preposition or particle was attested in Wulfila's *Vorlage* in cases where the Greek tradition offers two semi-equivalents, e.g.:

Lk 4:35 *usgagg us þamma* 'come out of this' may render both ἔξελθε ἀπ' αὐτοῦ and ἔξελθε ἐξ αὐτοῦ

Lk 6:9 *qaþ þan Iesus* 'then Jesus said' may render both εἶπεν δὲ ὁ Ἰησοῦς and εἶπεν οὖν ὁ Ἰησοῦς

Mk 1:45 *ana auþjaim stadim* 'in desert places' may correspond both to ἐπ' ἐρήμοις τόποις and to ἐν ἐρήμοις τόποις

6. The Greek *praesens historicum* is very rarely translated with the present; it is usually rendered by the preterite. Therefore, when the Greek tradition is divided between present and past forms, the Gothic may render either, e.g:

Mk 2:8 *qaþ* (pret.) *du im* '(he) said to them' may render both λέγει (pres.) αὐτοῖς and εἶπεν (aor.) αὐτοῖς

Mk 5:15 *atiddjedun* (pret.) '(they) came' may render both ἔρχονται (pres.) and ἤρχοντο (aor.)

7. It is not possible to determine whether the Gothic translation corresponds to a substantive participle or a relative clause when the Greek tradition is divided, because both are rendered into Gothic with a relative clause, e.g.:

Mk 4:9 *saei habai* lit. 'he who has' may translate both ὁ ἔχων and ὃς ἔχει

8. It has been noted above that the word order with possessive, demonstrative and personal pronouns is partially independent in Gothic.[364] Therefore, the Gothic text cannot be used reliably to reconstruct the underlying Greek text, particularly when the tradition is divided, e.g.:

---

364 See above 4.1.2.(1).

Mt 5:39 *þeina kinnu* '<u>your</u> cheek' may translate both <u>σου</u> σιαγόνα and σιαγόνα <u>σου</u>

Jn 6:27 *gibiþ izwis* '(the Son of Man) will give <u>you</u>' may translate both <u>ὑμῖν</u> δώσει and δώσει (or δίδωσιν) <u>ὑμῖν</u>

Jn 6:60 *þata waurd* '<u>this</u> word' may render both ὁ λόγος <u>οὗτος</u> and <u>οὗτος</u> ὁ λόγος

9. The rendering of the genitive of the Greek possessive pronoun is not regular. It can be translated by the reflexive possessive adjective *sein-*, declined in the proper case, or by the genitive of the personal pronoun *is*. The difference in their use is not clear, e.g:

Mt 9:11 μαθηταῖς <u>αὐτοῦ</u> '<u>his</u> disciples' is rendered by *siponjam <u>is</u>*, but in Mt 9:37 μαθηταῖς <u>αὐτοῦ</u> by *siponjam <u>seinaim</u>*

Jn 18:1 μαθηταῖς <u>αὐτοῦ</u> '<u>his</u> disciples' is translated as *siponjam <u>seinaim</u>*, but in the same verse μαθηταὶ <u>αὐτοῦ</u> is translated as *siponjos <u>is</u>*

4.1.4 Parallel Gothic and Latin renderings

Some Gothic renderings have parallels in the Latin versions. They may be the result of an independent approach to the Greek text, which has led to identical translations. However, there is another possibility: the Gothic-Latin parallels may be the consequence of Wulfila's use of a Latin version to find a suitable – or a more suitable – rendering of some Greek forms and expressions. A Latin influence in a post-Wulfilian period seems instead less likely for cultural reasons.[365]

1. The Gothic relative clause often renders the Greek substantive participle,[366] as in the Latin versions, e. g.:

Mt 7:26 *hvazuh <u>saei hauseiþ</u>* 'and everyone <u>who hears</u>' renders πᾶς <u>ὁ ἀκούων</u> (Lat. *omnis <u>qui audit</u>*)

Jn 5:45 *<u>saei wrohida</u> izwis Moses* lit. '<u>who accuses you</u> (is) Moses' translates ὁ <u>κατηγορῶν</u> ὑμῶν Μωϋσῆς (*<u>qui accuset</u> uos Moyses* in c/6, f/10, l/11; *<u>qui accusat</u> uos Moyses* in ff²/8, vg; *<u>qui</u> uos <u>accuset</u> Moyses* in a/3, aur/15, b/4, d/5, e/2, q/13)

---

365 See above 2.1.
366 See above 4.1.3.(7).

2. The auxiliary verb *wisan* 'to be' is added in some cases of Greek elliptical constructions, often with Latin parallels, e.g.:

> Mt 10:32 *in andwairþja attins meinis saei in himinam ist* lit. 'before my Father who is in heavens' (as Lat. *coram patre meo qui est in caelis* in b/4, ff¹/9, h/12, l/11, q/13; *coram patre meo qui in caelis est* in aur/15, c/6, d/5, f/10, vg) renders ἔμπροσθεν τοῦ πατρός μου τοῦ ἐν οὐρανοῖς lit. 'before my Father who in heavens'.

> Rom 11:33 *hvaiwa unusspilloda sind stauos is* 'how unspeakable are his judgments' (as Lat. *quam inscrutabilia/incomprehensibilia sunt iudicia eius*, respectively in ar/61, f/78, m/*Speculum* and t/56) for ὡς ἀνεξεραύνητα τὰ κρίματα αὐτοῦ[367] lit. 'how unsearchable his judgments'

3. The Greek *praesens historicum* is usually rendered into Gothic by the preterite, as often happens also in Latin.[368]

> Jn 7:6 *qaþ* (pret.) '(he) said' / *dixit* (a/3, c/6, r¹/14) vs. λέγει (pres.)

> Mk 1:30 *qeþun* (pret.) '(they) said' / *rettulerunt* (c/6, f/10, ff²/8, r¹/14) vs. λέγουσιν (pres.)

4. The resultative Greek perfect is occasionally rendered through a present, as in Latin, e.g.:

> Rom 14:14 *jag gatraua* 'and (I) believe' renders καὶ πέπεισμαι 'and (I) am persuaded' (Lat. *et confido*)

5. The *schema Atticum*, ie. a neuter plural with a singular verb, is not attested in Gothic. The Greek New Testament tradition tends to regularise this construction, producing a variant with the verb in the plural. The Gothic verb is always plural, so that it may render either of the Greek variants, e.g.:

> Mt 6:28 *blomans* (plur.) [...] *wahsjand* (plur.) *nih arbaidjand* (plur.) *nih spinnand* (plur.) '(the) lilies [...] (they) grow; (they) neither toil nor spin' may translate both τὰ κρίνα [...] αὐξάνουσιν· οὐ κοπιῶσιν οὐδὲ νήθουσιν (plur.) and τὰ κρίνα [...] αὐξάνει· οὐ κοπιᾷ οὐδὲ νήθει (sing.) (Lat. *lilia* [...] *crescunt non laborant neque neunt*, with variants)

> Mk 3:11 *ahmans* (plur.) [...] *gasehvun* (plur.), *drusun* (plur.) 'spirits [...] (they) saw [...], (they) fell down' may render both τὰ πνεύματα [...] ἐθεώρουν, προσέπιπτον (plur.) and τὰ πνεύματα [...] ἐθεώρει, προσέπιπτεν (sing.) (Lat. *spiritus* [...] *uidebant, procidebant*)

---

[367] The fact that *unusspilloda* 'unspeakable' has not the same meaning of ἀνεξεραύνητα or *inscrutabilia/incomprehensibilia* is not relevant here, see 6.2.2.(3).

[368] See above 4.1.3.(6). Pakis (2010) gave evidence for the agreement between the Gothic and Latin renderings of the Greek *praesens historicum*, but he – prudently – did not draw any conclusions regarding their relationship.

Also the Latin verb is often plural.

6. The Greek construction τοῦ plus the genitive of the proper noun is rendered with *sunaus* (genitive of *sunus* 'son') plus the genitive of the proper noun, as in part of the Old Latin tradition, e.g.:

> Lk 3:26 *sunaus Mahaþis sunaus Mattaþiaus sunaus Saimaieinis* 'son of Maath, son of Mattathias, son of Semein' renders τοῦ Μάαθ τοῦ Ματταθίου τοῦ Σεμεΐν (as Lat. *filius/filii* plus the genitive of the proper noun in, respectively, ff²/8, r¹/14 and e/2, f/10).³⁶⁹

In other cases the translation is literal, as in several Latin witnesses, e.g.:

> Lk 6:15 *Iakobu þana Alfaius*³⁷⁰ 'James (son) of Alphaeus' renders Ἰάκωβον τὸν τοῦ Ἀλφαίου (as *Iacobum Alphei* – with some orthographical variants – in the Latin tradition)
>
> Mk 2:14 *Laiwwi þana Alfaiaus* 'Levi (son) of Alphaeus' renders Λευὶν τὸν τοῦ Ἀλφαίου (as *Leui Alphei* – with some orthographical variants – in aur/15, f/10, l/11, q/13, vg)

The possibility that Wulfila has used a Latin Bible as linguistic model for these constructions has to be seriously taken in account.

4.2 Lexis and style

As noted above,³⁷¹ the majority of the Christian terms are likely to date back to Wulfila's translation activity. They are the result of the introduction of a new specific vocabulary for which there were no existing equivalents in Gothic. The linguistic interventions of the Gothic bishop, however, went beyond the introduction of these terms. He usually took care – when possible – to render the various derivatives of a single Greek stem by derivatives of a single Gothic stem, e.g.: βάρ-ος, βαρ-ύς, ἀ-βαρ-ής, βαρ-έω, ἐπι-βαρ-έω are translated respectively with *kaur-ei/kaur-iþa* 'burden', *kaur-us* 'burdensome', *un-kaur-eins* 'not burdersome', *kaur-jan* 'to burden', *ana-kaur-jan* 'to put a burden upon'. Furthermore, Wulfila's creations may reflect the morphological and semantic structure of Greek words, e.g: *liugna-waurds* 'lie-telling', composed of **liugna* (or **liugn*) 'lie' and a derivate of *waurd* 'word', is a loan translation of ψευδο-λόγος; *silba-siuneis* 'eyewitness', formed by *silba* 'self' and **siuneis* lit. 'one who

---

369 Friedrichsen (1926, 175) claimed that "perhaps *filii* (e f) is after Gothic". It is possible but not necessary.
370 On divergences in the orthographical rendering of the proper names see below 4.3.
371 See 1.4.

sees', is a loan translation of αὐτό-πτης.[372] The Gothic translator was also careful to render Greek compound verbs with prepositional elements by analogous formations, e.g: *us-hrainjan* 'clean out' corresponds to ἐκ-καθαίρω, *us-bruknan* 'break off' to ἐκ-κλάω, *us-letan* 'shut out' to ἐκ-κλείω. The Gothic-Greek correspondence cannot be due to chance, but it is the result of a deliberate technique of rendering which denotes a deep respect to the model.

In several cases, it is impossible to determine whether a term has changed its value by its use in the biblical text or whether the translator used it in an unusual sense. Indeed, both semantic extensions and specialisations are well-documented linguistic phenomena of the translation. The usage of *þiudos*, plural of *þiuda* 'people', to render Ἕλληνες[373] might be an example of semantic specialisation of the Gothic term in its biblical usage. It is, however, not possible to establish this with certainty, since only religious texts are preserved.

Generally speaking, the translation reveals a great uniformity of vocabulary, especially of technical Christian terms, in respect to the Greek.[374] Polysemous Greek terms are translated by different Gothic words, according to the context, e.g.: ἄγγελος, with the meaning of 'messenger', is translated as *airus*;[375] with the meaning of 'messenger of God', it is rendered by the loan word *aggilus*. The Gothic equivalents of λόγος are: *waurd* in the meaning of 'word', *sagiþa* (*hapax*) in the sense of 'reason', 'way', 'manner' and finally *raþjo* as 'account'.[376] According to the different meanings, γυνή is translated as *qens* 'wife' and *qino* 'woman'.[377] Βασιλεία is translated as *þiudinassus* 'kingdom', 'reign' (connected with *þiudans* 'king') and *þiudangardi*, which indicates properly the 'kingdom' (composed by *þiudans* 'king' and *gard-* 'house', 'court').[378] The Greek verb γαμέω, used indifferently in relation to a man or a woman, is rendered by the active form *liugan* 'to marry (a woman)' or passive 'to marry (a man)'.

From such examples, it is clear how Wulfila searched for the exact Gothic equivalent on the basis of the contextual meaning of the Greek term. This fact is particularly evident from the rendering of the Greek discourse markers into

---

372 See Dolcetti Corazza 1997, 100.
373 With the exception of 1 Cor 1:22, where Ἕλληνες is translated as *Krekos*; in singular it is attested the form *Kreks* 'Greek'.
374 See Friedrichsen 1926, part. 23–34.
375 Similarly, the Latin versions transmit *nuntius* (Lk 7:24 and 9:52).
376 The beginning of John's Gospel is lost and it is not possible to establish how Wulfila translated λόγος in that context.
377 The same approach was adopted by Old Latin translators, who distinguished between *mulier* 'woman' and *uxor* 'wife', see Burton 2000, 88.
378 Both are attested in the *Pater noster*, as translation of βασιλεία: in Mt 6:10 there is *þiudinassus* and in 6:13 (Byzantine text) *þiudangardi*.

Gothic. For instance, δέ may be translated as *iþ, þan, aþþan, þanuh, þaruh, jah, -uh*, according to its value as marker of strong or slight antithesis or continuity.³⁷⁹ In so doing, Wulfila shows a linguistic sensibility and a (relative) independence in respect to the *Vorlage*, a fact which indicates his attention to the intelligibility of the translation.

In some cases, it is difficult to judge the reason behind a particular lexical choice, due to the paucity of extant Gothic texts and, consequently, the limited knowledge of the different nuances of the Gothic terms. Some scholars have expressed the opinion that the translation was carried out by a team under Wulfila's supervision, a fact that could well explain some different renderings of the same Greek word used in the same context.³⁸⁰ It is highly likely, but not verifiable.

Occasionally, divergences in the translation of – apparently – non-polysemous Greek words may be well explained by stylistic devices. In some cases the same Greek term occurring in near verses is translated with different Gothic words which are supposed to be synonyms, as in:

Mt 5:23 – 24:
δῶρον [...] δῶρον [...] δῶρον: *aibr*³⁸¹ [...] *giba* [...] *giba* 'offering', 'gift'
(Lat.: *munus* [...] *munus* [...] *munus*)

1 Cor 15:49:
εἰκόνα [...] εἰκόνα: *manleikan*³⁸² [...] *frisahts* 'representation', 'effigy'
(Lat.: *imaginem* [...] *imaginem*)

In other cases, the reason for the use of a different term is unclear, e.g.: *gud-hūs* (lit. 'house of God', 'temple'; *hapax*) renders ἱερόν 'temple' in Jn 18:20 (Lat. *templum*), a term which is usually translated as *alhs* (twenty times). This peculiar rendering has been explained by Friedrichsen as "the result of the substitution [...] of a word more familiar to the reviser or scribe than the reading of the traditional or Wulfilian text."³⁸³ He suggested the influence of the Latin expression *domus dei* – unattested, however, in the corresponding passage of the Latin versions – as the model for the Gothic word. One might ask why the usual *alhs* has been substituted only in this case and not elsewhere.

---

379 See Friedrichsen 1961, 90 – 111, who, however, based his investigation on Streitberg's reconstructed Greek text.
380 See Friedrichsen 1961, 103 – 104; Gryson 1990, 13; Scardigli 1994, 139; Piras 2007, 47.
381 This is a *hapax* of obscure etymology, perhaps a corruption of *tibr*, see Lehmann 1986, s.v.
382 *Ambros.* B; *mannleikan* in the *Ambros.* A⁺.
383 See Friedrichsen 1926, 119.

The different renderings of ἀρχιερεύς 'high priest' is worthy of note: it is translated as *gudja*, which represents the old, non-Christian word for 'priest', *ufar-gudja*, *reikista gudja*, *maista gudja*, *auhumista gudja* and *auhumists weiha*, where the first part renders the value of 'high'.[384] Different renderings of ἀρχιερεύς, which are often attested in the same manuscript, are also transmitted by Old Latin versions: *pontifex*, *pontifex sacerdotum*, *princeps*, *princeps sacerdotum*, *sacerdos*, *summus sacerdos*. The expressions *auhumista gudja* and *auhumists weiha* could be modelled upon *summus sacerdos*.[385] In this case, the Latin influence might go back to Wulfila's time and to his efforts in finding the most suitable rendering of the Greek technical terms. To postulate a subsequent influence of the Old Latin versions – during the Visigothic and Ostrogothic reigns – is not necessary.

The Gospel of John exhibits the greatest number of different translations within a few verses, which may be explained as a *variatio*:[386]

7:32 *auhumista gudja*: *pontifex/princeps* (*sacerdotum*)
7:45 *auhumista gudja*: *pontifex/princeps sacerdotum*
11:47 *auhumista gudja*: *sacerdos* (a/3, e/2, r¹/14); *pontifex/princeps sacerdotum* (*rell.*)
12:10 *auhumista gudja*: *princeps* (*sacerdotum*)
18:3 *gudja*: *pontifex/princeps sacerdotum*
18:10 *auhumista gudja*: *pontifex/princeps* (*sacerdotum*)
18:13 *auhumists weiha*: *summus sacerdos* (r¹/14); *pontifex/princeps sacerdotum* (*rell.*)
18:15 *gudja*: *pontifex/princeps sacerdotum*
18:15 *gudja*: *pontifex/princeps sacerdotum*
18:16 *gudja*: *pontifex/princeps sacerdotum*
18:19 *auhumista gudja*: *summus sacerdos* (r¹/14); *pontifex/princeps sacerdotum* (*rell.*)
18:22 *reikista gudja*: *pontifex/princeps sacerdotum*
18:24 *maista gudja*: *pontifex/princeps sacerdotum*
18:26 *maista gudja*: *pontifex/princeps sacerdotum*
18:35 *gudja*: *pontifex/princeps sacerdotum*
19:6 *maista gudja*: *sacerdos* (a/3); *pontifex/princeps sacerdotum* (*rell.*)

---

384 Regarding the first part of these expressions: *ufar* 'over', *reikista* < *reikists* 'noblest', 'highest', *maista* < *maists* 'greatest', 'best'; *auhumista* < *auhumists* 'highest' (and *weiha* < *weih-* 'holy'), see details in Lehmann 1986, *s.v.* The forms in *-a* (weak declension of the adjective) are generally preceded by the article/demonstrative pronoun.
385 Friedrichsen 1926, 169–171; Velten 1930, 339.
386 See also Scardigli 1973, 108–109: "Lesen wir den ganzen Abschnitt Jo. 18,19–19,6, so stellen wir mühelos fest, daß Wulfila sehr darauf achtete, seine Adjektive mit rhetorischem Effekt zu setzen." The expressions *maista gudja* (3 times), *reikista gudja* (*hapax*), *auhumists weiha* (*hapax*) are attested only in John. There are apparently no divergences in the Greek tradition, which reports ἀρχιερεύς (with the exception of 7:32 and 18:22, where the mss. 1519 and 0290* transmit ἱερεύς), see www.iohannes.com (27.12.2013), from which the following Latin readings are cited. The forms are given here in nominative.

It is also worth noting that only in Gal 4:6 πατήρ 'father' is translated with *fadar*, instead of the usual word *atta*, a hypocoristic/nursery word. The term is attested in the clause *abba fadar* 'Abba Father', as rendering of αββα ὁ πατήρ. The reason behind this lexical choice could be euphonic: Wulfila probably wanted to avoid the sequence **abba atta*. As a solution, he uses the old word *fadar*, a *hapax* of Indo-European origin. According to some scholars,[387] *fadar* would have belonged, at Wulfila's time, to the Gothic religious (non-Christian) vocabulary – possibly used in the meaning of 'spiritual father' (a kind of shaman?) – and therefore would have not been suitable in the translation of the Bible. Another nursery word used by the translator is *mammo* 'flesh' (*hapax*), translation of σάρξ 'flesh', usually rendered by *leik*, a term that translates also σῶμα 'body' and πτῶμα 'corpse'. The use of *mammo* in Col 1:22 – *in leika mammons* 'in (the) body of flesh' (= ἐν τῷ σώματι τῆς σαρκὸς) – is easily explained by the context, since the normal translation of σάρξ, i. e. *leik*, was already employed to translate σῶμα.

Another interesting case is the rendering of (ὁ) δαιμονιζόμενος 'possessed by a demon' (mid/pass. partic. from δαιμονίζομαι). The Greek form is attested eight times in the passages that are preserved in Gothic:

Mt 8:16 *daimonarjans*: *daemonia habentes/d(a)emoniacos/var. lect.*
Mt 8:28 *daimonarjos*: *daemonia habentes/habentes daemonia/daemoniaci*
Mt 8:33 *daimonarjans*: *qui daemonia (daemonium) habebant/daemoniacis/qui daemonizati erant*
Mt 9:32 *daimonari*: *daemonium (daemonem) habentem/daemoniacum*

Mk 1:32 *unhulþons habandans*: *qui d(a)emonia habebant/daemonia habentes*
Mk 5:15 *þana wodan*: *qui a daemonio uexabatur/qui uexabatur a daemonio/daemoniacum*
Mk 5:16 *þana wodan*: *daemonium habuerat/uexabatur a daemoniis/daemonio uexauatur/daemoniaco*

Jn 10:21 *unhulþon habandins*: *d(a)emonium habentis/daemonium habentes/demoniaci*

In Matthew there is always the same Gothic rendering: *daimonareis* (in declined forms), an integrated loan word from Lat. *daemonarius* or less likely from Gr. δαιμονιάρι(ο)ς 'one possessed'.[388] Its use in these contexts, however, seems to be independent from the Latin version(s), where other forms occur. *Daimonareis* is attested also in Lk 8:36 as translation of ὁ δαιμονισθείς (aor. partic. pass. from δαιμονίζομαι). In Mark other renderings are present, a discrepancy difficult to explain. Worthy of note is the expression *unhulþons habandans* (Mk 1:32, acc. plur.) '(those) who have demons', which corresponds literally to δαιμόνια ἔχοντας and

---

387 See Scardigli 1973, 69–70; Ebbinghaus 1974, 97–101.
388 Corazza 1969, 93; Lehmann 1986, *s.v.*

is also attested in Jn 10:21 (gen. sing.). There are many possible explanations for this divergent rendering: (1) the translator wanted to offer a parallel to the previous expression (in the same verse of Mark): *allans þans ubil habandans*, 'all who have diseases' (πάντας τοὺς κακῶς ἔχοντας); (2) he found the (unattested) readings δαιμόνια ἔχοντας in his Greek *Vorlage*; (3) he was influenced by the corresponding Latin passage, where *daemonia habentes* (Old Latin mss. aur/15, d/5, f/10, l/11; vg) is attested. This last possibility is worth considering. The Latin expression may have been used by the translator or a subsequent revisor as model to render the Greek word. One may ask why this expression was not introduced already in Matthew (different times in the translation process? different translators?). Furthermore, in Mk 5:15 (τὸν δαιμονιζόμενον) and 5:16 (τῷ δαιμονιζομένῳ), the Gothic text offers another translation: *þana wodan* (acc. sing.) 'him (who was) possessed', a substantive adjective from **woþs* 'possessed', attested also in Mk 5:18 (*saei was wods* 'he who was possessed') as translation of ὁ δαιμονισθείς. The reason behind the use of different Gothic words to render the same Greek term is unclear.

There are other cases where two forms – generally one indigenous and one loan word – are used to render a foreign word: συναγωγή 'synagogue' is translated in Gothic as *swnagoge* (fifteen times), a loan word from the Greek, and by *gaqumþs* (five times), a compound formed with the prefix *ga-* 'together' and a derivative of the verb *qiman* 'to come' (which also renders other Greek terms: συνέδριον 'council' and ἐπισυναγωγή 'assembly', 'gathering'). The reason for their use by the translator is not clear. In some rare cases, such as Mt 6:2 (*in gaqumþim jah in garunsim*, translation of ἐν ταῖς συναγωγαῖς καὶ ἐν ταῖς ῥύμαις 'in the synagogues and in the streets'), the choice of *gaqumþs* instead of *swnagoge* might have been conditioned by the assonance with the following *garuns*. Stylistic variation could be the reason for the use of both forms in Lk 4:15–16: *in gaqumþim ... in swnagogein* for ἐν ταῖς συναγωγαῖς ... εἰς τὴν συναγωγήν 'in the synagogues... to the synagogue'.

Another example of double rendering is that of μαμ(μ)ωνᾶς 'mammon', 'accumulation of riches', translated with *mammona* and *faihuþraihns*. It is curious that in Mt 6:24 (CA, f. 6r), *mammonin*, dat. of *mammona*, is glossed on the margin with *faihuþra⟨ihna⟩* (the parchment has been cut); in the parallel passage Lk 16:13 (CA, f. 179v), *faihuþraihna*, dat. of *faihuþraihns*, is glossed with *mammonim*, probably a miswriting for *mammonin*.[389] It is not clear whether the hand of the

---

389 *Mammona* follows the weak declension, as do many loan words. Desinences in *-im* are not attested in this declension.

glosses is the same or not. Again, the reason behind the different renderings of the same Greek form is unclear.

It is notable that parallel passages often offer different translations. For instance, καθήμενον ἐπὶ τὸ τελώνιον 'sitting at the custom place' is rendered as *sitandan at motai* lit. 'sitting at (the) custom' in Mt 9:9 and Mk 2:14 and as *sitandan ana motastada* 'sitting at (the) custom place' in Lk 5:27. In the first case, the term *mota* 'custom' is used extensively also for 'receipt of custom'; in the latter, *motastaþs* is a compound of *mota* 'custom' and *staþs* 'place'. Another example is the rendering of πέδαις 'fetters' (dat. plur.), which is translated with *fotubandjom* lit. 'fetters for the feet' in Lk 8:29 and *eisarnam bi fotuns gabuganaim* lit. 'irons (which are) bowed around (the) feet' in Mk 5:4. In the same verse, Mk 5:4, τὰς πέδας (acc. plur.) is rendered as *þo ana fotum eisarna* lit. 'the irons around (the) feet'. In this case, the easiest conjecture is that the Gothic language did not have a proper term to explain the reference expressed by πέδη 'fetter'.

It is difficult to see the reason behind the divergences in the translation of the same Greek syntagm also in:

Mt 9:12
οἱ κακῶς ἔχοντες.
þai (dem./art.) *unhaili* (subst.) *habandans* (pres. partic.)
lit. 'those who have unhealthiness'
(Lat.: *male habentes/habentibus*)

Lk 5:31
οἱ κακῶς ἔχοντες·
þai (dem./art.) *unhailans* (adj.)
lit. 'those unhealthy'
(Lat.: *qui male habent/male habentibus/male habentes*)

Mk 2:17
οἱ κακῶς ἔχοντες
þai (dem./art.) *ubilaba* (adv.) *habandans* (pres. partic.)
lit. 'those who have badly'
(Lat.: *qui male habent/male habentibus/male habentes*)

The Gospel of Mark seems to offer the more literal translation among these passages. Why the renderings diverge is impossible to determine. Again, the hypothesis of different translators and/or of different times of the translation might be possible explanations. Less likely is the idea of a later revisor who changed Wulfila's translation: the tendency among scribes – as it is well known – is indeed harmonisation, and not the introduction of differences between parallel passages.

Several expressions of the Gothic version are surely idiomatic, e.g.: βεβλημένην καὶ πυρέσσουσαν lit. 'lying and having a fever' (Mt 8:14) is translated as *ligandein in heitom* lit. 'lying in fevers' (Lat. *iacentem et (-et k/1) febricitantem*);[390] εἰς ἄγραν 'for (a) catch' (Lk 5:4) as *du fiskon* 'in order to fish' (Lat. *in capturam/ad capiendum/ad piscandum*);[391] ἐν μακέλλῳ 'in (the) meat market' (1 Cor 10:25) as *at skiljam* 'at (the) butchers' (Lat. *in macello*). The count of the years is often rendered by the count of the winters, according to the usage of the Germanic cultures, as in Mt 9:20 · *ib · wintruns* (acc. plur.) '12 winters' (= δώδεκα ἔτη), Lk 8:42 *wintriwe twalibe* (gen. plur.) 'twelve winters' (= ἐτῶν δώδεκα).[392] The independent use of such expressions argues against a slavish rendering of the Greek text.

From the lexical point of view, the translator is often close to the style of the Greek text. Negative compounds are often rendered by negative compounds in Gothic. It is well evident in the list of the sins: the Greek text offers several negative compounds, formed by *alpha privativum*:[393] 2 Tim 3:2 [...] ἀπειθεῖς, ἀχάριστοι, ἀνόσιοι, 3:3 ἄστοργοι, ἄσπονδοι, [...], ἀκρατεῖς, ἀνήμεροι, ἀφιλάγαθοι. Similarly, the Gothic text offers negative forms, composed with the negative prefix *un-*: 2 Tim 3:2 [...] *ungahvairbai, launawargos, unairknans*,[394] 3:3 *unhunslagai, unmildjai*, [...], *ungahabandans sik, unmanariggwai, unseljai* 'disobedient, ungrateful, unholy, 3.3. inhuman, implacable, [...], profligates, brutes, haters of good'. Only in one case (*launawargos*) does the Greek term formed by ἀ- not correspond with a Gothic term formed by *un-*. This parallelism seems not to be a coincidence, but rather a stylistic device adopted by Wulfila in order to maintain a similar rhythm to that of the *Vorlage*.

The 'poetic' style of Wulfila's translation has often been emphasised by scholars, who have pointed out, beside the use of *variatio*, also that of the alliteration.[395] Many examples of alliterative clauses are attested in the Gothic text, e.g.:

---

390 But in Mk 1:30 κατέκειτο πυρέσσουσα is translated with *lag in brinnon* 'laid in fever'.
391 The reading *ad piscandum* (e/2) is parallel to the Gothic one. It is not necessary to suppose a Latin influence on the Gothic version or the opposite as Friedrichsen (1926, 169–186) did. Indeed, he postulated a close connection between the *Codex Argenteus* and e/2, but his claim does not seem persuasive (see Burkitt 1927, 90–97; Burton 2002, 404).
392 But in Mk 5:42 ἐτῶν δώδεκα 'twelve years' is rendered with *jere twalibe* 'twelve years' (gen. plur.).
393 See Dolcetti Corazza 2011.
394 *Ambros.* A⁺; *unairknai* in the *Ambros.* B.
395 Stolzenburg 1905, 155; Kapteijn 1911–1912, 342; Stutz 1966, 53–54.

<u>w</u>ulfos <u>w</u>ilwandans (Mt 7:15)
jah <u>w</u>arþ skura <u>w</u>indis mikila jah <u>w</u>egos <u>w</u>altidedun in skip (Mk 4:37)
<u>m</u>alma <u>m</u>areins (Rom 9:27)
fair<u>w</u>eitjan du <u>w</u>lita Mosezis in <u>w</u>ulþaus <u>w</u>litis (2 Cor 3:7)
in <u>d</u>raggka aiþþau in <u>d</u>ailai <u>d</u>agis <u>d</u>ulþais (Col 2:16)

However, it is difficult to determine whether the alliteration is the result of Wulfila's conscious choice or is accidental. A similar claim also concerns the occasional use of the *figura etymologica*, as in Mt 5:16 <u>liuhtjai liuhaþ</u> izwar 'let your light shine' (Gr. λαμψάτω τὸ φῶς ὑμῶν; Lat. *luceat lux uestra*) or in Mt 6:19 ni <u>huzdjaiþ</u> izwis <u>huzda</u> 'do not <u>store up</u> for yourselves <u>treasures</u>' (Gr. μὴ <u>θησαυρίζετε</u> ὑμῖν <u>θησαυρούς</u>; Lat. *nolite <u>thesaurizare thesauros</u>*). Indeed, the strict adherence to the *Vorlage* did not allow a great freedom in the lexical choice.

4.3 Proper names

Biblical proper names are transliterated according to the phonetic correspondences between Gothic and Greek.[396] It is worth noting that the Gothic forms often oscillate in the same manuscript, e.g.: Βαρθολομαῖον is attested once as *Barþulomaiu* (acc.; Lk 6:14, CA) and once as *Barþaulaumaiu* (acc.; Mk 3:18, CA); Βηθσαϊδά(ν) is transmitted as *Baidsaiidan* (acc.; Lk 9:10, CA), *Baiþsaidan* (voc.; Lk 10:13, CA), *Beþsaeida* (dat.; Jn 12:21, CA); the epithet of Jesus's betrayer, Iscarioth, is attested in several orthographic forms: *Iskariotes* (nom.; Jn 12:4, CA), *Iskarjotes* (nom.; Jn 14:22, CA), *Iskarioteis* (nom.; Mk 14:10, CA), *Iskariotu* (acc.; Jn 6:71, CA), *Iskarioten* (acc.; Lk 6:16 and Mk 3:19, CA), *Skariotau* (dat.; Jn 13:26, CA).

The reasons that may explain the different orthography of the proper names are: (1) the Greek manuscripts offered different variants of the same name;[397] (2) the Gothic scribes were not confident with the foreign names and therefore the possibility of errors during the process of copying increased in the course of the transmission; (3) the Gothic scribes were influenced by the corresponding Latin forms. Each of these reasons and their combination may explain the proliferation of orthographic variants.

In regard to the name 'Iscarioth' in Jn 13:26, the Greek manuscripts offer the forms Ἰσκαριώτου (with ℵ/01, B/03, C/04, L/019, Θ/038, Ψ/044, 33) and Ἰσκα-

---

396 See Marchand 1973; Solari 1974.
397 On this topic see Krašovec 2010.

ριώτῃ (p⁶⁶, A/02, K/017, W/032, f¹, f¹³, 565, 700, 𝔐).³⁹⁸ The Latin manuscripts transmit *Scarioth* (a/3, aur/15, e/2, ff²/8, r¹/14), *Scariotae* (b/4), *Scariothae* (c/6, f/10, l/11, q/13), *Scariotis* (vg^mss), *Iscariotae* (vg^mss), *Scariothis* (g¹/7, g²/29, gat/30), *Scariothi* (δ/27). The Gothic form *Skariotau* may be explained in different ways: as an influence of the Latin orthography, where the forms *Scariot-* are well attested; or as a simple error of the Gothic scribe, who miswrote/misread the sequence *seimonisiskariotau* (Σίμωνος Ἰσκαριώτη) of the model in *Seimonis Skariotau*; or, finally, as a rendering of Σκαριώθ-, unattested in this passage but usual in D/05 (see Lk 6:16). The individuation of the Greek model of the biblical names is therefore often difficult.³⁹⁹

In rare instances, the form of the biblical name is unusual. *Nauel* 'Noah' (and *Nauelis*, gen.; Lk 3:36, Lk 17:26–27, CA) does not correspond to any Greek (Νῶε) or Latin (*Noe*) models and reflect an unattested *Νῶελ/*Noel, with an -*l* suffix, perhaps in analogy with other biblical names in -*l*.⁴⁰⁰ Among the peculiar Gothic forms, there is the name *Aizoris* (Lk 3:33, CA), which would render *Ἐσώρ, an altered form of Ἐσρώμ (or Ἐζρώμ, Ἐσρών, Ἐσζρώμ, with other variants). It is also worth noting that the spelling of Mary as Jesus' mother, *Mariam* or *Maria* (= Μαριάμ/Μαρία), is different from that of other figures named Mary, i.e. *Marja*⁴⁰¹ (= Μαρία). This latter form shows an adaptation to the Gothic sound system, particularly evident in the oblique cases (gen. *Marjins* vs. *Mariïns*; dat. *Marjin* vs. *Mariïn*; acc. *Marjan* vs. *Marian*). The reason for such distinction is unknown.

Another peculiar feature is that the name of the city of Capernaum has always (twelve times) the form *Kafarnaum*, which corresponds to Καφαρναούμ – attested also in the oldest biblical witnesses (usually in א/01, B/03, often in D/05, W/032) against the Byzantine Καπερναούμ (usually with A/02, C/04) – and to the Latin form *Capharnaum*. The reason is unknown. Either the Gothic form reflects an old Greek form or it has been influenced by the Latin spelling. Con-

---

398 Miswriting in D/05: απο καρυωτου; see www.iohannes.com for the Greek and Latin variants.
399 Difficulties also arise in identifying the model of Hebrew-Greek expressions. For instance, *lima* (Mt 27:46, Mk 15:34, CA) corresponds to λιμά. However, in some cases, Goth. *i* renders Gr. ε or ει. Thus, it is not excluded that *lima* is a Gothic rendering of λεμά or λειμά, i.e. Greek variants attested in these passages. It is instead possible to exclude that the Gothic renders λαμα, attested in some manuscripts.
400 See Solari 1974, 337. It is worth noting that this form also occurs in the text of the *Codex Bononiensis* and therefore represents a clear indication that the citations of this text derive from the Gothic biblical manuscripts.
401 With the exception of Mk 6:3, where *Marjins* is referred to Jesus's mother.

cerning the second hypothesis, however, one might ask why just the spelling of this city would have been changed according to the Latin.[402]

The form *Mambres* (*Ambros.* B) / *Mamres* (miswriting, *Ambros.* A⁺) 'Mambres' in 2 Tim 3:8 is also worth noting. It renders Μαμβρῆς (with F/010, G/012, d/75, g/77, vg, Cyprian, Lucifer, Augustine, Ambrosiaster), against Ἰαμβρῆς of the remaining tradition. Whether this is the Wulfilian form or not is impossible to state.

Proper names are often integrated into the Gothic declension system, such as Καϊάφας 'Caiaphas' that is rendered as *Kajafa* (nom.) / *Kajafin* (dat.), according to the Gothic weak declension. More often they have a mixed Greek-Gothic declension.

4.4 Conclusions

With some exceptions, it is very often possible to determine the underlying Greek text of the Gothic version with a high degree of plausibility.

Those cases where it is not possible include the attestation of connecting particles. Connecting particles – particularly the coordinating enclitic *-uh* 'and' – are common at the beginning of a sentence, often without Greek or Latin parallels. In these instances it is not possible to determine whether the Gothic readings go back to a lost Greek variant or are insertions that occurred in the course of the Gothic manuscript transmission. Indeed, the addition of connecting particles reflects a typical scribal feature, i.e. the tendency to remove original *asyndeta*, attested also in the Greek manuscripts. The reason for such additions may be a voluntary attempt to connect two semantically related sentences or the involuntary result of the insertion of a cohesive-continuative element by someone who read or dictated the text.

The adherence of the Gothic word order to the Greek, where there are apparently no variations in the Greek tradition, is strict. However, on some occasions, the Gothic text diverges from the Greek tradition without any apparent model. The discrepancies mostly concern the position of personal, possessive and demonstrative pronouns. Some possibilities may be taken into account in order to suggest the reason for the changes: (1) the Gothic text reflects the idiomatic use better than the order modeled upon the Greek (in this case the attested word order goes back to Wulfila himself); (2) the Gothic text renders the word order of a lost (or not identified) Greek manuscript; (3) subsequent copyists

---

402 See for instance Mt 8:28: the Gothic *Gairgaisaine* renders Γεργεσηνῶν of part of the Greek tradition; the Latin form is *Gerasenorum*.

have changed the word order of the Wulfilian version, influenced by similar passages, by idiomatic uses of the Gothic or by the Latin version(s). Such divergences imply that the word order of the Gothic translation – in presence of pronouns – is not a reliable witness to the word order of the underlying Greek text.[403]

Also particularly thorny are the linguistic variations which involve the same Greek expressions in parallel passages. It is more probable that they reflect Wulfila's original, rather than being later changes. Indeed, scribal tendency is to adopt parallel expressions. The different translations of non-polysemous Greek words is occasionally difficult to assess. In some cases the synonymic *variatio* may be the reason for the discrepancies. Different translators and different times in the translation are other possible explanations. Finally, in some cases, subsequent modifications of Wulfila's version cannot be excluded.

There is a general consensus regarding the competence and faithfulness of the Gothic translation. The translator's deliberate decision to be literal does not contrast with the main scope of his work: to be intelligible to his audience, while at the same time remaining close to the *Vorlage*. Wulfila distinguished the various senses of the one Greek term, in order to give the more accurate Gothic rendering. Some of his loan words or creations, as well as some constructions, may have been at the very beginning of their use difficult to understand or even incomprehensible for the Goths without further explanation. However, even if such terms may have sounded alien to the ears of their audience, they may have found a kind of justification in the aura of mystery surrounding the new cult.[404]

Furthermore, the possibility cannot be excluded that Wulfila's translation formed, among the Christian Goths, a *Sondersprache*, different lexically and syntactically from the Gothic language commonly used.[405] Wulfilian coinages and biblical expressions may have become constituents of a special Christian language, which the Gothic missionaries helped popularise and render comprehensible. How deeply such language was understandable for the Goths of the sixth century who copied Wulfila's version is impossible to determine with certainty. The presence of glosses in the Gothic manuscripts[406] seems to indicate that some words were obsolete or obsolescent. However, the fact that the text of the sixth century *Codex Bononiensis* – probably part of a sermon or liturgical prayer – reports citations of the Gothic Bible suggests that Wulfilian Gothic was still understood and in use at least in liturgical contexts.

---

403 On Wulfila's *Vorlage* see below 5.
404 Piras 2007, 62.
405 Regarding the Latin Christian *Sondersprache* see Mohrmann 1968 and Burton's considerations (2000, 153–154).
406 See above 2.4.

5 The Greek *Vorlage* and the transmission of the Gothic text

The Gothic translation of the Gospels and Pauline Epistles does not reflect the text of any existing model in its entirety. However, no one has ever doubted – on the basis of linguistic and textual affinities between the Gothic and Greek texts – that Wulfila used a Greek *Vorlage*.

Some very rare variants, errors or misreadings of the Greek model are attested in the Gothic text, for instance: Goth. *jabai* 'if' (Mt 6:24, CA), which renders εἰ, attested in ℵ/01, L/019, Σ/042, 543 and 1675 for the correct ἤ 'or' of the other Greek manuscripts; Goth. *beidandans* 'were waiting' (Lk 1:10, CA), which translates προσδεχόμενον, with Y/034 and 131 (προδεχόμενον 1241; προσδεχόμενος 1[184]), for the correct προσευχόμενον 'were praying'; Goth. *fodeins* 'food' (Lk 7:25, CA), which corresponds to τροφῇ, for the correct τρυφῇ 'luxurious living', 'luxuriousness'. Some other Gothic readings seem to go back to a misunderstanding of the Greek model, written – very likely – in uncial and without critical signs, in accord with the fourth-century customs of writing. An example is Goth. *jau* (interrogative particle; Rom 7:25, *Ambros. A⁺*), which renders the Greek interrogative particle ἆρα against the correct form ἄρα 'therefore' (both written APA in the Greek manuscripts). The reason for the confusion between these Greek readings, either already present in Wulfila's *Vorlage* or misread from a correct exemplar by the Gothic translator, is clearly their palaeographical or phonetical similarity. From this evidence it is possible to draw the conclusion that either Wulfila used only one Greek manuscript as *Vorlage* or that – in case he used more – he did not collate them. It is unlikely that such rare or erroneous Greek forms were present in all the hypothetical exemplars which lay in front of Wulfila. The presence of these erroneous forms indicates also that Wulfila's text or, rather, the text passed on by the Gothic extant manuscripts, was not revised or collated – at least completely – with other Greek or Latin manuscript(s) in the course of their transmission. Otherwise these passages would have very likely been emended.[407]

From a text-critical point of view, the Gothic text agrees primarily with the Byzantine text type (also called Antiochian, Syrian, Koine). However, many

---

[407] That these wrong readings stem from a secondary revision of the Gothic text with a Greek manuscript seems unlikely. On this hypothesis, see Friedrichsen 1926, part. at p. 223 ("We shall be much nearer the truth if we ascribe these errors to post-Wulfilian revisions with Greek MSS."), 224–226. Why should a hypothetical revisor change the correct text inserting meaningless readings?

Gothic readings agree with readings of the 'Western' and/or Alexandrian text types.⁴⁰⁸ The origin of such readings and particularly of the 'Western' ones is very controversial and is still a matter of discussion.⁴⁰⁹ Indeed, the individuation of the Greek text underlying Wulfila's version is complicated by the fact that the original translation might have undergone alteration during the period of almost one hundred and fifty years between Wulfila's translation, undertaken in Moesia (or already before his crossing of the Danube), and the extant Gothic manuscripts, copied in Italy.

Scholarship is divided between two opinions: that the 'Western' readings were already attested in the Greek *Vorlage* or that they entered into Wulfila's version during the transmission of the Gothic text, through a revision on the basis of the Latin version(s). This second hypothesis has dominated the history of research and the perception of the textual value of the Gothic text.

5.1 The history of research on the text-critical character of the Gothic version

Scientific examination of the text-critical character of the Gothic version began with Hans Georg von der Gabelentz and Julius Löbe,⁴¹⁰ and Hans Ferdinand Maßmann.⁴¹¹ According to these scholars, Wulfila's version was based on the contemporary text which circulated in Constantinople, subsequently interpolated with Latin readings.

In 1875 Ernst Bernhardt published the Gothic text together with its alleged Greek *Vorlage*. His bilingual edition was anticipated in 1864 and in 1868 by two text-critical studies on the Gothic translation. In the first study, he gave a list of readings which, in his opinion, had entered into the Gothic text through

---

408 This opinion is definitely accepted in the New Testament criticism since Westcott-Hort 1882, 158, see below 5.1. See Metzger-Ehrman 2005, 276–280 for a survey of the main textual streams. The term 'text type' is considered largely inappropriate today (even if it is still in use in New Testament scholarship), because it reflects old text-critical views, see Strutwolf 2006 in Parker 2008, 174.
409 It is to be pointed out that there is often confusion, in studies on the Gothic version, between 'Western' readings and Old Latin readings, which are frequently used as synonyms. Indeed, 'Western' readings are testified not only by the Old Latin versions (known as *Vetus Latina*), but also by the Greek-Latin bilinguals (D/05, D/06, F/010, G/012), as well as by the Sinaitic and Curetonian Old Syriac text (sy^s, sy^c), see Metzger-Ehrman 2005, 276–277.
410 Von der Gabelentz-Löbe 1836, 470–489; see also the notes to the text. This work was used by Tischendorf 1869–1872.
411 Maßmann 1857, lxxxiii-lxxxviii.

Latin influence, and specifically through the *Codex Brixianus* (f/10),⁴¹² a thesis which was sustained also in his later work.⁴¹³ Furthermore, he pointed out the strict correspondence between the Gothic text of the Gospels and the corresponding text of the *Codex Alexandrinus* (A/02), concluding that Wulfila had followed an exemplar of this type for his translation of the Gospels.⁴¹⁴ Concerning the Gothic Epistles, instead, Bernhardt noted the similarities between the Gothic text and that of the 'Western' mss. D/06, F/010 and G/012.⁴¹⁵ In his edition, therefore, the Greek *Vorlage* of the Gospels was based principally on the *Codex Alexandrinus* and that of the Epistles on the 'Western' manuscripts. Moreover, he advanced the opinion that Wulfila also used a Latin version as an aid for his translation, although he did not exclude the possibility of a successive influence of Latin version(s) on the Gothic text in Italy.⁴¹⁶

Subsequently, the text-critical character of the Gothic text was discussed by Brooke F. Westcott and Fenton J. A. Hort. According to these scholars, the Gothic text is

> largely Syrian and largely Western with a small admixture of ancient Non-Western readings. Whether the copies which furnished the Western element were obtained by Ulfilas in Europe or brought by his parents (*sic*) from Cappadocia, cannot be determined: in either case they were Greek not Latin.⁴¹⁷

Some years later, Caspar R. Gregory also concluded that "[u]sus est textu Graeco, maxima ex parte Antiocheno, cum multis lectionibus Occidentalibus, nonnullis antiquis non-Occidentalibus."⁴¹⁸

Subsequent text-critical studies of the Gothic version were conducted by Friedrich Kauffmann, who between 1898 and 1911 published a series of articles on this topic. Particularly noteworthy is the article of 1898, in which he highlighted the agreement between the Gothic text of Matthew and the corresponding quotations of John Chrysostom. In the same article, he severely criticised Bernhardt's work, particularly his claim that the Gothic text was close to the *Codex*

---

412 Bernhardt 1864, 12: "Als Quelle der Interpolation [...] erscheint vorzüglich die Handschrift von Brescia, f".
413 Bernhardt 1868. This claim was later demolished by Burkitt 1899, see below 5.2.
414 Bernhardt 1864, 23–28; Bernhardt 1875, xxxix.
415 Bernhardt 1875, xxxix.
416 Bernhardt 1875, xxxviii-xxxix; xlix.
417 Westcott-Hort 1882, 158.
418 Gregory 1894, 1108; Gregory 1902, 730: "Der griechische Text, den er [Wulfila] für das Neue Testament benutzte, scheint in der Hauptsache antiochenisch gewesen zu sein, aber mit vielen westlichen Lesarten und mit einigen alten nicht-westlichen."

Alexandrinus (A/02). Kauffmann's theories were based on the fact that the Gothic text of the Old Testament (Nehemiah) does not agree with the text of the *Alexandrinus*, that this manuscript has a different layout and, finally, that it was written and preserved in Egypt.[419] Furthermore, he added some observations which are indicative more of his willingness to refute Bernhardt's theories than to approach the text from a scientific point of view: "Man beachte ferner Joh. XIX, 40 θεου A [/02] für Ιησου der übrigen codd.; es fehlt zwar die gotische übersetzung, aber man darf mit sicherheit behaupten, das hier der Gote es nicht mit A[/02] gehalten hat."[420] In a subsequent work, Kauffmann continued the comparison of the Gothic text with the quotations of Chrysostom, putting in evidence their agreement.[421] He also advanced the hypothesis that the Gothic text suffered a process of Latinisation in the course of its transmission.[422]

Successive studies of the text type of Wulfila's *Vorlage* – mostly concentrated in the first half of the twentieth century – were based on the textual theories regarding the formation of the Byzantine text proposed by Westcott and Hort[423], accepted and developed by Hermann von Soden[424] and Burnett H. Streeter.[425] As is known, these scholars claimed that the Byzantine text was the result of a revision made by one or more editors (Lucian of Antioch, † 312, according to von Soden[426] and Streeter[427]); a revision that, with several subsequent alterations, became the prevailing text of the Byzantine Church.

Von Soden also argued that Wulfila's *Vorlage* was a text similar to that used by Chrysostom, "einen K-Text, in den hin und her I-Lesarten eingedrungen waren."[428] Following von Soden's arguments, Wilhelm Streitberg, in his 1908 edition, reconstructed Wulfila's Greek *Vorlage* of the Gospels on the basis of the text transmitted by the Greek manuscripts S/028, and V/031, E/07, G/011 and F/09, H/013 (manuscripts which, according to von Soden, better testify the recension of Lucian) together with the manuscripts K/017, U/030, Γ/036, Λ/039 and Π/041, which represent texts close to the Koine, as well as the citations of John

---

419 Kauffmann 1898, 146–147.
420 Kauffmann 1898, 147.
421 Kauffmann 1903, 433.
422 Kauffmann 1903, 453, 457–458.
423 Westcott-Hort 1882, 135–143
424 von Soden 1907, 712–893.
425 Streeter 1924, 112–121.
426 von Soden 1907, 1471.
427 Streeter 1924, 112–113.
428 von Soden 1907, 1469. According to him, 'K' represents the Koine, which is attested in several forms; 'I' is the Palestinian-Jerusalem recension, edited by Eusebius of Caesarea and Pamphilus.

Chrysostom.⁴²⁹ The reconstruction of the Greek model of the Pauline Epistles was based upon the manuscripts K/018, L/020, P/025, dating from the ninth century, and M/0121+0243, from the tenth century, and Chrysostom's citations.⁴³⁰ In his work, Streitberg did not therefore take into any account Bernhardt's opinion regarding the agreement of the Gothic version with the *Codex Alexandrinus*.

To explain the deviations of the Gothic from the Byzantine text, particularly evident in the Pauline Epistles, Streitberg claimed either the influence of the Old Latin version(s) or the presence of foreign elements, i.e. non-Byzantine readings, already in the Greek *Vorlage*. However, according to him, "die Wahrscheinlichkeit spricht meist für die erste Annahme [i.e. for the influence of the Old Latin version(s)], besonders in dem Fall, wenn dem Text von it [= *Itala*, i.e. *Vetus Latina*] nur reine *H-Hss. [H is used for Hesychius, i.e. Alexandrian recension] zur Seite stehn."⁴³¹ In other parts of his introduction to the critical edition, he stressed the influence of the Old Latin version(s) on the Gothic text.⁴³²

Adolf Jülicher disputed Streitberg's position in 1910.⁴³³ He invited caution in attributing all the non-Byzantine readings to post-Wulfilian changes, claiming that they may have been already present in Wulfila's *Vorlage*.⁴³⁴ If the non-Byzantine readings – he pointed out – are also attested in other eastern traditions (Armenian, Syriac, Coptic), they cannot be considered as the result of post-Wulfilian modifications under Latin influence. Furthermore, a mixed text was also offered by the citations of John Chrysostom.⁴³⁵ According to him, Streitberg's reconstructed Greek *Vorlage* was to be considered more a step backwards rather

---

429 Streitberg 1908, xxxix.
430 Streitberg 1908, xl.
431 Streitberg 1908, lxv.
432 Streitberg 1908, lxv: "In den Paulinen ist der Einfluß der altlateinischen Bibel auf den got. Text besonders stark" (reference to Kauffmann 1903, 453–462); at p. xl: "die gotische Fassung der paulinischen Briefe hat gleich den Evangelien, jedoch in noch höherm Maße, eine umgestaltende Einwirkung von seiten der altlat. Übersetzungen erfahren."
433 Jülicher 1910, 370–371, 379 ("Für mich unterliegt es keinem zweifel, dass die griechische vorlage des Ulfila dem jetzt gotisch überlieferten texte viel ähnlicher gesehen hat, als sie es bei Streitberg tut."); see also Jülicher 1912, 372–381.
434 Jülicher 1910. He stated at p. 371: "[I]ch will damit [...] nicht spätere eindringlinge lateinischer herkunft in den Ulfilas-text ableugnen, ich warne nur vor dem vorurteil von dem Streitberg sich beherscht zeigt, wonach eine lesart des Goten, die nicht durch einen zweifellosen K-zeugen, dagegen durch einen oder mehrere Lateiner bezeugt ist, sofort dem verdacht nachulfilanischen ursprungs verfällt."
435 Jülicher 1910, 370.

than forwards in comparison to Bernhard's text.⁴³⁶ Jülicher's study was heavily criticised by Kauffmann in 1911 (B), who again argued that the Gothic text had been revised after Wulfila's death. Jülicher replied that the 'Western' readings of the Gothic text do not necessary support the hypothesis of a Latin influence; they may stem from Wulfila's *Vorlage*.⁴³⁷

The second edition of Streitberg's work appeared in 1919.⁴³⁸ He maintained his position regarding the origin of the non-Byzantine readings of the Gothic text, claiming the influence of the *Vetus Latina* and of the parallel passages to explain their origin.⁴³⁹

In an article of the same year, Hans Lietzmann pointed out that the manuscripts chosen by Streitberg date back to the ninth century and may therefore transmit a different text from Wulfila's *Vorlage*. He rejected Kauffmann's and Streitberg's hypothesis of a Latinisation of Wulfila's text and offered another explanation, by postulating a mixed text, i.e. a Byzantine text with 'Western' readings, or a bilingual edition.⁴⁴⁰ In particular, he spoke of an "abundance of variants" which characterised the Byzantine tradition and evidenced the possibility that the Gothic version reflects one of the lost witnesses of this mixed tradition.⁴⁴¹

Lietzmann sent a copy of his article to Streitberg, who answered in a letter dated 1ˢᵗ June 1919, reaffirming the opinion that almost all divergences between the Gothic text and the Byzantine manuscripts used in his own edition have to be considered post-Wulfilian changes.⁴⁴²

Two lengthy studies by George W. Friedrichsen, focused on the Gothic text, should be considered milestones in the history of Gothic criticism. The first, dat-

---

436 Jülicher 1910, 365: "[S]eine [i.e. Streitberg's] reconstruction des griechischen grundtextes selber muss ich gegenüber der Bernhardtschen eher für einen rückschritt als für einen fortschritt ansehen."
437 Jülicher 1912, 376.
438 The Greek text remained unaltered in the second edition, even though Streitberg declared himself to be unsatisfied (1919, xi-xii) "Hätte ich freie Hand gehabt, so würde ich ihn an mancher Stelle umgestaltet haben."
439 Streitberg 1919, viii-ix: "Bis auf wenige, für die Textgeschichte meinst belanglose Ausnahmen führen sie alle Abweichungen auf zwei Ursachen zurück: auf den Einfluß fremder Bibeltexte, in der Regel der altlateinischen Übersetzung und auf die Einwirkung der Parallelstellen."
440 Lietzmann 1919, 275–276.
441 Lietzmann 1919, 264: "Fülle von Varianten" [...] "Die Koine hat gar wild gewuchert, und neben tausend verschollenen ist der gotische Text einer der wenigen erhaltenen dieser so wandlungsfähigen Zeugen."
442 Streitberg asserted (in Scardigli 2003, 709): "Denn das steht mir heute fester als je, daß der Text Wulfilas im Laufe der Zeit starke Veränderungen erfahren hat, vorab natürlich in Italien und durch den Einfluß der altlateinischen Bibel."

ing from 1926, offers a stylistic analysis of the Gothic Gospels. Friedrichsen's main task was to scrutinise "all the passages where the Gothic rendering seems to depart from the basic norm, and [...] every rendering that varies from the usual rendering of the same Greek word or sense."[443] His point of departure is the observation of the great uniformity in the rendering of the Greek text into Gothic. He considered the Gospel of Matthew to be "[closer] to the original than [...] the other three Gospels, showing in this respect a more primitive technique or, alternatively, less traces of revisional disturbance."[444] He also argued that the Gospel of Luke exhibited the greatest amount of linguistic and stylistic variations compared to the other Gospels.[445]

On the basis of his linguistic analysis, Friedrichsen concluded that the Gospels of Luke and Mark had suffered the influence of the *Vetus Latina* to a far greater degree than the other Gospels. He claimed that these two texts go back to a Visigothic Latinised revision, whilst the Gospels of Matthew and John are more adherent to the Wulfilian original.[446] It is true that the texts of Luke and Mark show some divergences compared to the other Gospels in the rendering of Greek readings, as Friedrichsen pointed out. No evidence, however, supports the opinion that the freedom of rendering and the lexical choice which characterise Luke and Mark depend on their revision. Friedrichsen did not take into sufficient account the easiest explanation: the different style might be the result of different moments in the making of the Gothic translation, as well as the work of different translators. Furthermore, the text of Matthew is the most lacunose of the extant Gothic Gospels and it is not statistically relevant. Despite his claim that "[i]n most cases [...] where the C. A. [i.e. *Codex Argenteus*] presents a Western [...] type of reading, it is impossible to say whether this derives from the Wulfilian Greek, or from a later revision with a Greek ms of Western character, or from the Old Latin version", he concluded that "[t]here is no doubt that the Old Latin is in many cases responsible".[447] Friedrichsen did not deny the possibility that the occasional agreements between Gothic and Latin renderings depended on Wulfila's use of a Latin version, or that both the Gothic and the Latin texts render independently the same Greek form.[448] However, he preferred to conclude that "[t]he latinization of the Gothic was largely an accomplished fact."[449]

---

[443] Friedrichsen 1926, 7.
[444] Friedrichsen 1926, 158.
[445] Friedrichsen 1926, 119.
[446] Friedrichsen 1926, 161, 243.
[447] Friedrichsen 1926, 10 (both quotations).
[448] Friedrichsen 1926, 194; Friedrichsen 1939, 260.

5.1 The history of research on the text-critical character of the Gothic version — 99

Friedrichsen's subsequent study (1939) is devoted to the Pauline Epistles. Starting from the claim that K/018, L/020, (M/0121 + 0243), P/025 and the text of Chrysostom[450] are the closest witnesses to the Gothic text, he stressed even more the Latin influence on this. According to him,[451] "[t]he original version is based on a fourth-century Byzantine text, and where the Ambrosian text departs from the T.R. [i.e. *Textus Receptus*] it is largely due to the influence of the Old Latin represented especially by the Claromontanus [D/06]." He concluded:

> If there is one fact in connexion with the origins of the Gothic Epistles that may be affirmed without hesitation, it is that they were done into Gothic from the Byzantine text represented by KLP and Chrysostom. The readings which agree with the text of D*EFG defg alone are secondary, and belong to the later history of the Gothic text west of Constantinople. The hypothesis of an original of mixed type, recovered by retranslating the existing Gothic into Greek, of the kind postulated by A. Jülicher and, more recently, by H. Lietzmann, is unsupported by any existing evidence [...].[452]

A brief note by James W. Marchand in 1957 (re)introduced the idea that the Gothic version may reflect lost readings. According to this scholar, "[t]he appearance of the same readings in the Gothic, Syriac, Armenian and Old Church Slavonic versions makes [the] assumption of Latin influence unnecessary and unlikely."[453]

In a study published in 1961, Friedrichsen reviewed and partially criticised the apparatus of Streitberg's edition of the Gothic Bible.[454] He seemed to be more cautious in respect to his previous opinions concerning the post-Wulfilian Latinisation of the Gothic text, at least in regard to the text of the Gospels. He claimed that

> [t]he Old Latin version undoubtedly exercised great influence on the post-Wulfilian text, but its influence was casual, and it is not possible to know, in the absence of indicative evidence, whether a Gothic non-Syrian reading was so from its origin, or whether an original Gothic Syrian reading was subsequently altered to agree with an Old Latin non-Syrian text.[455]

---

449 Friedrichsen 1926, 167.
450 Friedrichsen 1939, 20. On p. 9 he wrote: "The text of Chrysostom, therefore, whilst admissible to membership of the group KLMP Chr., with which the Gothic shows the closest affinity, cannot be accorded any special privilege over the other members of the group."
451 Friedrichsen 1939, 31.
452 Friedrichsen 1939, 257.
453 Marchand 1957, 234.
454 See Friedrichsen 1961, 36 ("[H]e [i.e. Streitberg] produces a mutilated and distorted picture of the documentary attestation"), 63.
455 Friedrichsen 1961, 64.

Concerning the text of the Epistles, Friedrichsen reasserted his position.[456] However, it is worth noting that he pointed out the mixed character of Wulfila's *Vorlage*, "which retained many older readings."[457]

The possibility that at least part of the non-Byzantine readings of the Gothic Gospels may reflect the readings of Wulfila's *Vorlage* was for many years almost ignored by Gothic scholars. Instead, the assumptions expressed by Friedrichsen in his earliest studies became the *communis opinio* in Gothic literature.[458]

A renewed perspective of the problem was presented by Roger Gryson in 1990. In agreement with Jülicher and Lietzmann, the Belgian scholar pointed out that almost all the 'Western' readings of the Gothic version are found also in Greek witnesses of other textual traditions and in the eastern versions.[459] Therefore, he claimed – on the basis of the analysis of the first chapter of the Gospel of Mark – that the non-Byzantine readings of the Gothic version may be old readings, going back to the Greek tradition.[460]

---

456 Friedrichsen 1961, 87–88.
457 Friedrichsen 1961, 5, 73.
458 See for instance Metzger 1964, 82: "For the basis of his version Ulfilas used that form of Greek text which was current in Byzantium about A.D. 350, belonging to the early Koine type of text. Western readings, particularly in the Pauline Epistles, were subsequently introduced from Old Latin manuscripts."; Hunter 1969, 347: "Thus during the period which elapsed between the original translation by Ulfilas and the production of the *Codex Argenteus* in the first half of the sixth century, a number of western readings from the Latin Bible infiltrated into the predominantly Byzantine text of the Gothic Gospels," and further at p. 355 "[t]he comparison between the Greek text of Streitberg's edition [which is, however, an editorial reconstruction !] and the Gothic text will provide an indication of the extent to which the original translation has been disturbed, usually by conformation to the Old Latin."; Klein 1992, 339: "It is widely held that the Gothic Gospels are [...] translations of their Greek Vorlage with the intrusion, in a considerable number of cases, of 'Western' readings, i.e. readings based on pre-Vulgate Latin versions of the text with which the Goths would have become familiar in Italy and France in the 6th century A.D." More cautious was Vööbus' claim (1954, 309): "[T]hat the Gothic version has experienced in its history a Latinization of its text, appears to be as good as certain. But it cannot be stated with any certainty at what point in the history of this version the Latin version began to exercise its influence."
459 Gryson 1990, 28.
460 "Pourquoi veut-on que la version gotique soit allée chercher dans un modèle latin ce que les autres ont lu de toute évidence dans un modèle grec?" (Gryson 1990, 28).

5.2 The Gothic influence on the Latin text

The textual, other than codicological,[461] affinities between the *Argenteus* and *Brixianus* f/10 are undeniable. Francis C. Burkitt's review/article of 1899 offered a new evaluation of the relationship between these two manuscripts. He gave a series of examples in which the *Brixianus* differs from the other Latin manuscripts and agrees instead with the Gothic text, arguing that this latter has influenced the Latin text and not the contrary, as Bernhardt[462] supposed.

Among the parallels which are exclusive for the *Argenteus* and *Brixianus*, there is the reading of Mt 6:24: *ufhauseiþ* '(he) will obey' = *obediet* vs. *sustinebit* (k/1, vg), *patietur* (rell.). The Greek tradition offers ἀνθέξεται, from ἀντέχομαι 'to hold against', 'to withstand'; the Gothic text and the *Brixianus*, instead, render ἀνέξεται, a forms that evidently goes back to an error or misreading of the Greek *Vorlage*.

Another example is in Mt 9:8. The *Argenteus* transmits *ohtedun sildaleikjandans* lit. '(they) feared marvelling' (= *timuerunt admirantes*) and the *Brixianus* has *admirantes timuerunt*. In this case there is a conflation, with syntactical change, of two readings of the Greek tradition: ἐφοβήθησαν '(they) feared', attested by א/01, B/03, D/05, several minuscules and the Latin witnesses, and ἐθαύμασαν '(they) marvelled', transmitted by C/04, K/017, L/019, N/022, Θ/038 and the Byzantine manuscripts, as well as Chrysostom's citations. No other Latin manuscript but f/10 offers the reading *admirantes*.

In Jn 6:66, the *Brixianus* follows the Gothic *uzuh þamma mela* lit. 'and from that time' in the rendering of ἐκ τούτου 'from that (time)': *ex hoc ergo tempore*, against the remaining Latin tradition (*exinde* e/2; *ex hoc* in the other manuscripts).

A further example is in Jn 7:12: the Gothic text transmits *sunjeins* 'true, truthful', the *Brixianus* has *uerax*, against the extant Greek and Latin traditions which report ἀγαθός/*bonus*. A possible explanation of this reading: the Gothic translator misread or found in his *Vorlage* ΑΛΗΘΗΣ (= Goth. *sunjeins*), instead of ΑΓΑΘΟΣ.[463]

In Mk 4:24, at the end of the verse, there is the insertion of *þaim galaubjandam* '(to you) who believe' in Gothic and *credentibus* in the *Brixianus*, against τοῖς ἀκούουσιν '(to you) who listened' of the Byzantine text (part of the Greek

---

461 See above 2.1.1.
462 Bernhardt 1868.
463 Francini (2009 B, 100) prefers to explain the Gothic rendering as a "result of theological interpretation, either on the part of the translator or [...] on the part of a later scribe in the course of textual transmission."

tradition does not have any kind of addition). The explanation proposed by Friedrichsen to justify this reading is persuasive.[464] It would go back to a plain scribal error of the Gothic tradition: the correct translation of τοῖς ἀκούουσιν would have been *þaim gahausjandam*, which was wrongly transcribed as *þaim galaubjandam*. This error would have arisen from the context rather than from a misreading, since the Gothic letters h ⟨h⟩ and ᚨ ⟨l⟩, s or ε ⟨s⟩ and ʙ ⟨b⟩ are not particularly similar. The reading of the Latin text, *credentibus*, was subsequently modelled upon the Gothic one.

Burkitt, examining the peculiar readings of the *Brixianus* which differ both from the Old Latin and the Vulgate and agree instead with the *Argenteus*, claimed that this Latin manuscript is a copy of a bilingual ancestor "with the Gothic left out".[465] The relationship between the *Argenteus* and the *Brixianus* in the Gospels of Matthew and John was further investigated by Kauffmann, who, in agreement with Burkitt, recognised the influence of the Gothic text on the Latin.[466] Subsequent investigations by Odefey,[467] Friedrichsen[468] and Francini[469] have confirmed Burkitt's idea.[470]

The adjustments of *Brixianus*' model in accordance with the *Argenteus* is particularly interesting both from a text-critical and cultural point of view, and has many implications. The Gothic version was indeed the leading text, as in the bilingual *Carolinus* and *Gissensis*, where the Gothic texts are in the position of honour, to the left of the Latin.[471] Moreover, it is worthy to note that the Latin part of the bilingual *Carolinus* also exhibits some readings which agree with the Gothic text against the majority of the Latin witnesses, e.g.: Rom 12:3 *þairh anst gudis* = *per gratiam dei* (with t/56, vg^{ms}, Augustine), against *per gratiam* of the remaining tradition; Rom 13:1 *ufarwisandam* = *sublimibus*, against *sublimioribus* of the other witnesses; Rom 14:14 *þairh sik silbo* = *per se ipsum* (with Rufinus, Augustine^{mss}, Pelagius^B), against *per ipsum/per illum* of the majority of the Latin witnesses; Rom 14:18 *in þaim* = *in his* (with b/89, vg^{mss}), against *in hoc* of the Latin tradition; Rom 15:8 *Xristu Iesu* = *Christum Iesum* (with ar/61, t/56, vg), against *Iesum Christum/Christum* of the Latin tradition; Rom 15:9 *in þiudom frauja* = *in*

---

464 Friedrichsen 1926, 136.
465 Burkitt 1899, 131.
466 Kauffmann 1900, 324.
467 Odefey 1908, 96–106 (for Luke).
468 Friedrichsen 1926, part. 194–196.
469 Francini 2009 A, 259–264 (for John).
470 See also Burton (2002, 400), who affirms that the *Brixianus* is "definitely Gothic-influenced".
471 See above 2.1.3. and 2.1.4.

gentibus domine (with ar/61, t/56, vg^(mss)), against *in gentibus* of the other witnesses. These agreements might be explained through the influence of the Gothic on the Latin text.⁴⁷²

Also of particular significance is the agreement between the readings transmitted by the Latin *Gissensis* (with the *Brixianus* and few other witnesses) and the Byzantine text, against D/05 and the majority of the Latin witnesses: Lk 24:6 *non es⟨t⟩* (with aur/15, q/13, vg; οὐκ ἔστιν); Lk 24:9 *a monu⟨mento⟩* (with aur/15, q/13, vg; ἀπὸ τοῦ μνημείου). The agreement between the Latin *Gissensis* and the Byzantine text may be explained by the influence of the Gothic version on the Latin part, rather than by the direct influence of the Byzantine text or the Vulgate. Indeed, it should be noted that there are cases in which the Latin *Gissensis* diverges from the Vulgate and agrees with the Byzantine text: Lk 23:4 *pilatus au⟨tem⟩* (ὁ δὲ Πιλᾶτος); 23:5 *quia comm⟨ouet⟩* (ὅτι ἀνασείει); 23:5 (- *et*) *incipiens a* (ἀρξάμενος ἀπό); 24:7 *et tertia die* (καὶ τῇ τρίτῃ ἡμέρᾳ). This fact leads to postulate a Gothic influence on the Latin part.⁴⁷³

The textual adjustments between Gothic and Latin texts imply bilingual redactor(s), who were able to understand both languages and worked together in the same scriptorium.⁴⁷⁴ Another aspect to consider is that a Gothicised Latin version – with many Byzantine readings – may have altered the transmission of the Latin (primarily 'Western') text. In addition to the *Brixianus* (or its model), the Latin *Carolinus* and the Latin *Gissensis*, the text of other manuscripts might have been influenced by the Gothic version.

Philip Burton, in an article in 1996, pointed out the similarities between the text of the ms. Vienna, Österreichische Nationalbibliothek, 563 (Beuron siglum: 43), from the fifth century, and the Gothic text, arguing that these agreements may be due to influence from the Gothic. This scholar excludes, however, the possibility that the ms. 43 might derive from the model of the *Brixianus*. Both manuscripts "seem to have Gothicised independently".⁴⁷⁵ On the basis of Burton's observations a problem arises: if the ms. 43 belongs to the period before

---

472 The close affinity between the Gothic text and the *Liber Comicus Toletanus* (t/56) is worth noting. The latter is the Hispano-Mozarabic lectionary of the church of Toledo, the ancient capital of the Visigothic kingdom of Spain. The text, transmitted by a manuscript of the eleventh century, contains Old Latin readings (Metzger 1977, 304). Did the Gothic text influence these readings?
473 See Falluomini 2010 A, 328.
474 See also above 2.1.
475 Burton 1996 A, 155.

the beginning of the Ostrogothic kingdom of Italy (493), it is not clear in which cultural context the Gothic influence may have occurred.[476]

Moreover, according to Friedrichsen, the *Codex Palatinus* (e/2) is a copy of the Latin half of a lost bilingual manuscript (called Palatinian Bilingual). The Gothic text would have influenced the Latin counterpart.[477] Among the examples that the scholar offered, there is Lk 1:9: *sors illi exiit* (e/2), where *illi* is considered an intrusion after Goth. *imma* (*hlauts imma urrann* lit. '(the) lot went out for him').[478] Friedrichsen's claim was criticised by Burkitt and recently by Burton.[479]

Finally, it is worth noting that also the *Codex Monacensis* (q/13),[480] written around 600, transmits many variants in common with the Gothic version and with the Latin Arian texts. Some examples:[481] in Jn 9:15 the ms. q/13 transmits *dixit et illis*, in agreement with the Gothic text *qaþ jah þaim* lit. '(he) said also to them' (= εἶπεν καὶ αὐτοῖς, attested in A/02, 0211, f^{13}, 124, 788, 1346), against the remaining Latin tradition, which omits *et*. In Jn 18:20 the ms. q/13 exhibits *semper Iudaei*, in agreement with Goth. *sinteino Iudaieis* 'always (the) Jews' (= πάντοτε οἱ Ἰουδαῖοι, attested in C^3/04^3, D^s/05^s, Δ/037, Ψ/044, m, sy^h), against the Latin tradition, which transmits *omnes Iudaei* or *uniuersi Iudaei* (= πάντες οἱ Ἰουδαῖοι, attested in the remaining Greek witnesses). In Jn 19:3 the Gothic text, following the early Byzantine tradition, exhibits a homoeoteleuton: the words that correspond to καὶ ἤρχοντο πρὸς αὐτόν are lacking in Gothic (with A/02, D^s/05^s, Δ/037, Ψ/044, f^1, m, f/10, q/13, sy^p). Their omission in q/13, as well in f/10, seems not to be a coincidence. A connection between the text of q/13 and the Gothic text (or its Greek *Vorlage*) is not to be excluded.

---

[476] A reevaluation of the dating of this fragment through a new palaeographical and codicological analysis might be interesting in the light of Burton's observations.
[477] Friedrichsen 1926, 169–186, 195. The Gothic part, in its turn influenced by the Latin, is represented by the Gospel of Luke in the *Codex Argenteus*, see below 5.3.
[478] Friedrichsen 1926, 174. The Greek text has ἔλαχε.
[479] Burkitt 1927; Burton 2002, 416–417.
[480] Munich, Bayerische Staatsbibliothek, Clm 6224. The origin of this manuscript is disputed. Both northern Italy and Pannonia are considered plausible centres of its production, see Fischer 1972, 36; Burton 2000, 24.
[481] The following examples are taken from the Gospel of John, because for this text exists a recent collation of Greek and Latin variants (see www.iohannes.com). The ms. δ/27 is left out from the following comparison being the Latin part of a Greek-Latin bilingual. Its coincidence with the ms. q/13 may therefore depend on the agreement of q/13 with its Greek counterpart (Δ/037).

5.3 The Latin influence on the Gothic text

There is a widespread agreement among scholars that the Latin tradition has influenced the Gothic text. That Gothic manuscripts exhibit Latin palaeographical and codicological elements is a matter of fact; this influence goes back, in all probability, to the period of the Ostrogothic kingdom of Italy.[482] More problematic is the possible textual influence of the Latin tradition. Connected with this issue are two difficult items: (1) the interpretation of the *Praefatio* to the *Codex Brixianus*;[483] and (2) the presence of Gothic readings which agree exclusively with Latin witnesses.

The *Praefatio* to the *Codex Brixianus* is a Latin text written on a bifolio, bound with the Gospel book (f/10) into the *Codex Brixianus* and dated palaeographically to the sixth century (first half?). The period of its composition is uncertain: it was written after 405, because it quotes Rufinus' translation of Pseudo-Clement's *Recognitiones*.[484] Also the place of its composition is completely obscure, although Ostrogothic Italy is the most likely guess. To claim that this text was composed elsewhere would indicate that it had been brought to Italy and that the critical study of the Gothic Bible, suggested by its content, had already begun before the Ostrogothic migrations. The *Praefatio* makes reference to some glosses or important passages – the term used is the Goth. *uulthres*, explained with Lat. *adnotationes* – and to the comparison between the Gothic (biblical?) text and the Greek and Latin ones. These references are not clear, since no extant manuscript displays a system of glosses such as the one described here:

> Nam et ea conuenit indicare pro quod in uulthres factu‹m› est latina uero lingua adnotatio significatur. Quare id positum est agnosci possit ubi littera .gr. super uulthre inuenitur. Sciat qui legit quod in ipso uulthre secundum quod Graecus continet scribtum est. Ubi uero littera .la. super uulthre inuenitur secundum latina‹m› lingua‹m› in uulthre ostensum est. Et ideo ista instructio demonstrata[ta] est ne legentes ipsos uulthres non perciperent pro qua ratione positi sint.[485]

---

482 See above 2.1.
483 See Appendix II.3.
484 On the *Praefatio*, see Henss 1972. It should be noted that this text is not a preface to the Gospel book. The person who bound the two texts together evidently knew that these were in some ways related.
485 Metlen's translation (1938, 357) is: "In this connection (nam) it will also be useful (conuenit) to explain these [idiomatic expressions, etymologias linguarum] in a measure (i.e., where it is particularly necessary for the understanding) by adding wulthres – which means in Latin adnotatio –, so that it may be understood why a particular [Gothic] rendering (etymologia = it) was used. [Hence] where the symbol .gr. is found on top of a wulthre, the reader may know that the corresponding wulthre is a [literal] rendering of the Greek text. Where, on the other hand, the

The text of the *Praefatio* is difficult to understand in some passages. Bernhardt proposed the interpretation of *uulthres* as a *terminus technicus*[486] referring to "die richtigen lesarten";[487] Burkitt considered them as "readings",[488] Kauffmann[489] as "gute lesart", Friedrichsen[490] as "renderings", Scardigli[491] as "die auffälligsten Varianten", Henss[492] as something similar to the *scholia*; Minis[493] as something "wertvoll, wichtig". More generally, this passage seems to highlight the need to dedicate philological attention to the origin of some Gothic readings.[494]

Kauffmann attributed the *Praefatio* to two clerics, Sunnja (Sunnia) and Friþila (Fretela), to whom Jerome addresses an epistle to answer their questions concerning his translation of the Psalms (their epistle is lost).[495] According to Kauffmann, they made a bilingual – or even a trilingual – critical edition of Wulfila's text.[496] This hypothesis, however, is advanced without any evidence, as Jülicher[497] and Friedrichsen[498] pointed out.

The content of the *Praefatio* most likely refers to a biblical text in Gothic with text-critical notes (what else may be compared with a corresponding Greek and Latin text?). Whether this text has to be identified with a bilingual edition or with

---

symbol .la. is found above a wulthre, the latter exhibits the Latin form. The foregoing explanation has been given lest those who read these wulthres fail to understand the reason for the same." The round and square brackets are Metlen's. See Appendix II.3.

486 The word is attested in Gal 2:6, in the expression *wulþrais* (Ambros. A⁺) or *wulþris* (Ambros. B) *ist*, translation of διαφέρει 'it makes a difference', 'it matters', 'it is of importance'. Here *wulþrais/wulþris* (*hapax*) is genitive singular of the substantive *wulþrs* 'significance', 'importance', 'value'. In Mt 6:26 *wulþrizans sijuþ* translates διαφέρετε '(you) are more valuable', where *wulþrizans* is a comparative, nominative plural, of the adjective *wulþrs* (*hapax*) 'valuable', 'important'.
487 Bernhardt 1875, xl.
488 Burkitt 1899, 131.
489 Kauffmann 1900, 315.
490 Friedrichsen 1926, 199, 204–211.
491 Scardigli 1973, 189.
492 Henss 1972, 69.
493 Minis 1977, 25.
494 Friedrichsen 1926, 200; see also Henss 1972, 82: "Mittels systematischer Glossierung werden Belege dafür erbracht […], daß die gotische Bibel eine adäquate und konkurrenzfähige Übersetzung darstellt: Was sie vom Original und der lateinischen Bibel unterscheidet, ist nur von untergeordnetem, linguistischem Belang und erklärt sich ganz natürlich aus der Vielfalt der Sprachen." According to Scardigli (1973, 184), the *Praefatio* was "eine Art Manifest und Programm einer Schule".
495 Hier., *epist.* 106.
496 Kauffmann 1900, 316; Kauffmann 1911 B, 120, 132.
497 Jülicher 1910, 380–387 and Jülicher 1912, 380–381.
498 Friedrichsen 1926, 198–199.

a Gothic glossed manuscript is impossible to ascertain.[499] In any case, this document is an important witness to the philological study and linguistic reflections on the Gothic text.

Undoubtedly some readings of the Gothic version diverge from the Greek tradition and are supported only by Latin witnesses, e.g.:[500]

Lk 1:3

(Nestle-Aland[28]) ἔδοξε κἀμοί
'it seemed good to me also'

(Goth) *galeikaida jah mis jah ahmin weihamma*
lit. '(it) seemed good to me also and to (the) Holy Spirit'

(f/10) *placuit et mihi*
'it seemed good to me also'

The Gothic version adds *jah ahmin weihamma*, with the Old Latin mss. b/4, g¹/7, q/13 and the Vulgate mss. B, G, O (+ *et spiritui sancto*), reminiscent of Acts 15:28 (ἔδοξεν γὰρ τῷ πνεύματι τῷ ἁγίῳ), against the Greek and Latin traditions. It is impossible to establish whether this reading goes back to Latin influence or to independent harmonisation of the Gothic text. Finally, both traditions might reflect a lost (or unidentified) Greek reading.

Lk 1:29

(Nestle-Aland[28]) διεταράχθη ἐπὶ τῷ λόγῳ αὐτοῦ καὶ διελογίζετο ποταπὸς εἴη ὁ ἀσπασμὸς οὗτος.
'But she was greatly troubled at his saying and pondered what sort of greeting this might be.'

(Goth) *gaþlahsnoda bi innatgahtai is jah þahta sis ƕeleika wesi so goleins þatei swa þiuþida izai*

(f/10) *turbata est in introitu eius et erat cogitans qualis esset ista salutatio quod sic benedixisset eam*
'But she was greatly troubled at his entrance and pondered what sort of greeting this might be, why (he) thus blessed her'

---

[499] For a bilingual edition, see Burkitt 1899, 131; Kauffmann 1900, 316; Friedrichsen 1926, 197; different positions are held by Henss 1972, 89; Minis 1977, 28; Gryson 1990, 25.
[500] As Friedrichsen (1926, 119) noted, they are mainly attested in the Gospel of Luke. According to this scholar, the model of Luke and Mark had a Visigothic origin. There is, however, no reason to support this claim, see above 5.1.

According to Friedrichsen,[501] the original Gothic reading *bi waurda is* 'at his word', which translated ἐπὶ τῷ λόγῳ αὐτοῦ, was replaced by *bi innatgahtai is* 'at his entrance' after the Old Latin *in introitu* (a/3, aur/15, b/4, ff²/8, g¹/7, q/13, r¹/14; *introitum* l*/11*; *ad introitum* e/2; vs. *in uerbo* f/10, *in sermone* c/6, vg, *super uerbo* d/05) *eius* (- *eius* d/5, l/11). The following *ƕeleika wesi so goleins þatei swa þiuþida izai* is the result of a conflation of two readings: the original one would be *ƕeleika wesi so goleins*, rendering of ποταπὸς εἴη ὁ ἀσπασμὸς οὗτος of the Greek manuscripts, which is attested also in part of the Old Latin tradition: *qualis esset ista salutatio* (c/6, vg); *qualis sit salutatio heac* (d/5). The second part, *þatei swa þiuþida izai*, would have been originally a gloss modelled on the Old Latin reading *quod sic benedixisset eam* (a^{vid}/3^{vid}, b/4, ff²/8, l/11, q/13) / *quid sic benedixisset eam* (aur/15) / *quod ita eam benedixis‹set›* (r¹/14) / *quia sic benedixit eam* (e/2). The same conflation of the Gothic text is found also in the Old Latin mss. f/10 and g¹/7: *qualis esset haec salutatio* (+ *et* g¹/7) *quod sic benedixisset eam*. Friedrichsen is likely right in this explanation. However, there is another possible explanation: both *bi innatgahtai is* and *þatei swa þiuþida izai* might go back to lost Greek variants that influenced also the Latin tradition.

Lk 1:63

(Nestle-Aland²⁸) καὶ αἰτήσας πινακίδιον ἔγραψεν
'and having asked for a writing tablet (he) wrote'

(Goth) *iþ is sokjands spilda nam gahmelida*
lit. 'but he, having sought (a) writing tablet, took (it) and[502] wrote'

(f/10) *et postulans pugillarem scribsit*
'and having asked for a writing tablet (he) wrote'

The Gothic *sokjands* 'having sought' is, according to Friedrichsen, "an inaccurate reproduction of the Palatinian [= e/2] *petiit*".[503] Burton suggests instead that this reading may go back to an unattested Greek variant ζητήσας 'having sought', instead of αἰτήσας 'having asked', "palaeographically unproblematic, and efficient as an explanation for the various readings in the Latin and Gothic."[504] The addition of *nam* '(he) took' is also very interesting. It seems to reflect a conflation of variants: *[nam] ga-h-melida* or *[nam] jah melida*[505] might be influenced by *ac-*

---

501 Friedrichsen 1926, 221.
502 The presence of the conjunction 'and' is not certain; see the following discussion.
503 Friedrichsen 1926, 174.
504 Burton 2002, 400.
505 The form *gahmelida*, emended as *gamelida* '(he) wrote' (Streitberg 1919, *ad loc.*) or interpreted as *ga-h-melida* 'and (he) wrote' (Streitberg 1920, 161), might also be a misreading/miswriting

*cepit pugillarem/pugillares et scripsit*⁵⁰⁶ of the Latin tradition (it is attested in b/4, ff²/8, l/11, q/13, r¹/14). However, a common Greek model of *nam/accepit* is not entirely to be excluded.

A long addition, common to the Gothic and part of the Old Latin tradition, is attested in Lk 9:43:

> (Goth) *Qaþ Paitrus: Frauja, duƕe weis ni mahtedum usdreiban þamma? Iþ Iesus qaþ: þata kuni ni usgaggiþ nibai in bidom jah in fastubnja*
> lit. 'Peter said: "Lord, why could we not cast it out?" Then Jesus said: "This kind cannot be driven out by anything but prayers and fasting"'

> (f/10) *Dixit Petrus: Domine quare nos non potuimus eicere eum? Ad ille dixit: hoc genus non exiet nisi in orationibus et ieiuniis*

The text of the *Brixianus* (f/10) depends undoubtedly on the Gothic text, as the reading *ille* for *Iesus* reveals: it reflects the frequent confusion between the abbreviation of *Iesus* and the pronoun *is* 'he' attested in the Gothic manuscripts.⁵⁰⁷ The discrepancy between *fastubnja* (sing.) and *ieiuniis* (plur.) may be explained as a misreading/miswriting by the Gothic scribe of an original *fastubnjam* (plur.), perhaps with the abbreviation of *-m* over the line.

A similar addition – suggested by the parallel passages Mt 17:19–21⁵⁰⁸ and/ or Mk 9:28–29⁵⁰⁹ – is attested in other Old Latin manuscripts (c/6, e/2, ff²/8, r¹/14), with some variants:

qaþ / dixit] e/2 | + *ei* c/6, ff²/8, r¹/14

duƕe weis ni mahtedum usdreiban þamma / quare nos non potuimus eicere eum] c/6 (*propter quid ... illud*), e/2 (*illum*), ff²/8 (*illum*), r¹/14

iþ Iesus qaþ / ad ille dixit] *quibus dixit* c/6, e/2, ff²/8, r¹/14

---

of *jah melida* 'and (he) wrote' – with a change of ᚷ ‹j› (*jah*) in r ‹g› (*gah*) – by a scribe who also knew the Latin uncial (where a letter similar to ᚷ has the value of ‹g›).
506 Friedrichsen 1926, 174–175.
507 Friedrichsen 1939, 213. It is worth noting that the *Codex Argenteus* transmits the correct form *Iesus*, in the contracted form i̅s̅ ‹is› (f. 161r, l. 10). Therefore, the text of the *Brixianus* either does not depend directly on that of *Argenteus*, but on a Gothic manuscript with i̇s ‹is› 'he', or it is based on a misreading of i̅s̅ ‹is›; see also above 3.11.
508 Mt 17:19: διὰ τί ἡμεῖς οὐκ ἠδυνήθημεν ἐκβαλεῖν αὐτό; 20. Ὁ δὲ Ἰησοῦς εἶπεν αὐτοῖς ... 21. τοῦτο δὲ τὸ γένος οὐκ ἐκπορεύεται εἰ μὴ ἐν προσευχῇ καὶ νηστείᾳ, attested in part of the Greek tradition, among which the Byzantine one, see Nestle-Aland²⁸, *ad loc*.
509 Mk 9:28: ὅτι ἡμεῖς οὐκ ἠδυνήθημεν ἐκβαλεῖν αὐτό; 29. καὶ εἶπεν αὐτοῖς, τοῦτο τὸ γένος ἐν οὐδενὶ δύναται ἐξελθεῖν, εἰ μὴ ἐν προσευχῇ καὶ νηστείᾳ, attested in part of the Greek tradition, among which the Byzantine one, see Nestle-Aland²⁸, *ad loc*.

> *þata kuni ni usgaggiþ nibai in bidom jah in fastubnja* / *hoc genus non exiet nisi in orationibus et ieiuniis*] *quoniam huiusmodi* (*eiusmodi* ff²/8) *orationibus* (*-ne* ff²/8) *et ieiuniis eicitur* (*eicietur* c/6, *eiciuntur et ieiunio* ff²/8) c/6, e/2, ff²/8, r¹/14

The main question is whether this addition in the Gothic text stems from a lost Greek reading or is dependent on the Latin influence. Both claims are possible.

Regarding the convergence of the Gothic and Latin texts, the studies of Burton offer some important considerations. In two articles from 1996 and 2002 the British scholar, analysing the Gothic and Latin readings and renderings, suggests the possibility that the agreements between the Gothic and Latin translations could arise from an independent translation of the same Greek readings, now lost or unidentified.[510] The 'Western' readings in the Gothic version are not necessarily a sign of Latin influence because they might have entered directly through the Greek. However, he does not deny the possibility of reciprocal influences between the versions.[511] In the latter study, Burton offered a detailed analysis of the possible relationship between the Gothic and Latin texts in order to verify Friedrichsen's idea concerning the existence of the Palatinian Bilingual.

Burton invites caution because some readings shared by the Gothic and Latin versions may go back to lost Greek readings. For instance, he proposes a different explanation to Friedrichsen's thesis of interaction between Gothic and Latin in Lk 2:8.

(Goth) *jah hairdjos wesun ... bairwakjandans*
(Lat) *erant autem pastores ... uigilantes* (*pernoctantes* e/2)
'and shepherds were ... staying awake (through the night)'

against the Greek tradition:

(Nestle-Aland²⁸) καὶ ποιμένες ἦσαν ... ἀγραυλοῦντες
'and shepherds were ... living in the fields'

According to Friedrichsen,[512] ἀγραυλοῦντες 'living in the fields' was replaced by the Gothic translator with a word more in keeping with the following context, after Lat. *uigilantes*. Burton, instead, suggests that both the Gothic and the Latin readings might also derive from a variant ἀγρυπνοῦντες 'staying awake', which fits the sense perfectly and is palaeographically very easy to explain. He concludes by stating that "[i]t is impossible to tell here whether the similarity

---

510 Burton 1996 B, 88, 96; Burton 2002, 398.
511 Burton 2002, 417.
512 Friedrichsen 1926, 175.

is the result of interaction between the two versions, or whether the same reading had coincidentally insinuated itself into both traditions separately."[513]

As previously seen, Friedrichsen[514] claimed that the Epistles have been heavily influenced by the Latin version(s) because they differ from the Byzantine text in several passages.[515] However, the Gothic readings which agree only with witnesses of the Latin tradition against the Greek manuscripts are very few. Among these, there is a reading in Rom 11:33, transmitted by the bilingual *Carolinus*. The Gothic diverges from its Latin counterpart and apparently does not find correspondence in the Greek tradition: *unusspilloda* (CC) 'unspeakable' vs. ἀνεξεραύνητα 'unsearchable' (= gue/79: ‹in›*scrutabilia*). The Gothic reading corresponds to ἀνεκδιήγητα. This variant is attested only in a quotation of Zeno, *tract.* 1, 34, 1, 2 (*inenarrabilia*) and in some Patristic allusions (Hier., *in Is.* 2, 49: *iudicia magna sunt et inenarrabilia* and Oros., *hist.* 7, 41: *ineffabilia* sunt iudicia dei). In this case the influence of the Latin tradition is not to be excluded.[516]

Some other readings, shared only by the Gothic and the 'Western' manuscripts, are difficult to assess.[517] An example is in 2 Cor 4:17: *unte þata andwairþo hveilahvairb jah leiht aglons* 'for this present momentary and light affliction', which renders τὸ γὰρ παραυτίκα πρόσκαιρον καὶ ἐλαφρὸν τῆς θλίψεως (D*/ 06*, F/010, G/012 with the Latin tradition), against τὸ γὰρ παραυτίκα ἐλαφρὸν τῆς θλίψεως of the remaining witnesses. The presence of these 'Western' readings may have two possible explanations: either they were already present in Wulfila's Greek *Vorlage* or in the Latin version which he probably used, or they entered into the Gothic text subsequently, through unsystematic glosses.[518] One explanation does not exclude the other. Conversely, there are not sufficient elements to assume a complete revision of Wulfila's text.

According to Friedrichsen,[519] some other Gothic renderings have been influenced by Old Latin versions. However, the examples that he offered are not really convincing and may have different explanations. For instance, regarding *in gardan lambe* 'in (the) sheepfold' (Jn 10:1; εἰς τὴν αὐλὴν τῶν προβάτων; *in cohortem ouium* b/4, c/6, e/2, ff²/8, q/13; *in aula ouium* r¹/14; *in ouile ouium rell.*), he suggest-

---

513 Burton 2002, 398; see also Burton 1996 B, 88–89.
514 Friedrichsen 1939, *passim*; see above 5.1.
515 For another perspective see below 6.
516 The agreement with Zeno Veronensis is particular interesting, since Verona was an important centre of Gothic culture, see Zironi 1997. On the Latin ms. Verona, Biblioteca Capitolare, LI (49)⁺ with Gothic glosses, see above 2, fn. 140.
517 Friedrichsen 1939, 257, see above 5.1.
518 Against the assumption of a complete or systematic consultation of the Latin version see also Friedrichsen 1939, part. 178–179.
519 Friedrichsen 1926, 172–183; Friedrichsen 1939, 172–243.

ed that the weak form *garda*, a *hapax*, "possibly translates *cohortem*, replacing an original *awistr*".[520] This latter word is also a *hapax*, rendering of αὐλή in Jn 10:16. In this case, there is no reason to postulate the Latin influence, because both Gothic terms may have covered the semantic value of αὐλή. Furthermore, concerning the shared rendering,[521] there is nothing against the possibility that the similarities between Gothic and Latin loan translations and constructions arose previously, in the course of Wulfila's work, by using a Latin model in addition to the Greek *Vorlage*.[522] Finally, some coincidences in the translations might be due to chance.

5.4. The Gothic text and Ambrosiaster

Friedrichsen,[523] developing Bernhardt's suggestion,[524] claimed an influence of the exegetical – mostly Latin – literature to explain particular renderings of the Gothic text of the Pauline Epistles. He quoted fifty-eight examples in which the Gothic text, deviating from the literal rendering of the alleged Greek *Vorlage* (i.e. Streitberg's text), seemed to be conditioned by Latin commentaries and, principally, by Ambrosiaster's writings.[525]

An example is in 1 Cor 13:12: δι' ἐσόπτρου ἐν αἰνίγματι 'through a mirror in an obscure manner' (Lat. *per speculum in aenigmate*) is rendered in Gothic with *þairh skuggwan in frisahtai*. The problem lies in the rendering of αἴνιγμα 'obscure saying', 'enigma', 'obscure thing' through Goth. *frisahts*. This term is the usual translation of εἰκών 'image', 'figure', 'likeness', τύπος 'figure', 'image', 'example', ὑπόδειγμα 'sign suggestive of anything', 'delineation of a thing', 'representation', 'figure', 'copy', example' and ὑποτύπωσις 'an outline', 'sketch', 'example', 'pattern'. According to Friedrichsen,[526] the reading *in frisahtai* has been suggested by commentaries: *'Uidemus nunc per speculum in aenigmate; tunc*

---

520 Friedrichsen 1926, 174.
521 As *unhulþon habandins/unhulþons habandans* 'having demons' for δαιμονιζομένου (Jn 10:21, *d(a)emonium habentis* lat) and τοὺς δαιμονιζομένους (Mk 1:32, *daemonia habentes* aur/15, d/5, f/10, l/11, vg) or *gawairþeigai sijaiþ* 'be at peace' for εἰρηνεύετε (Mk 9:50, *pacati estote* k/1).
522 See above 1.2.
523 Friedrichsen 1939, 214–231; see also Alcamesi 2009.
524 Bernhardt 1975, 1.
525 He stated, however, that "some of the [...] passages admit of alternative explanations; they may, for instance, be reminiscent, or contextually interpretative [...]; they may be from the Latin text not from Commentaries; or they may exhibit inaccuracy or error." (Friedrichsen 1939, 216).
526 Friedrichsen 1939, 221.

uero facie ad faciem.' Apertum est nunc imagines uideri per fidem, tunc res ipsas (Ambrosiaster);[527] *Quasi paruuli, qui non possumus serena cordis acie perfectae lumen perspicere claritatis, per speculum legis quasi rerum imaginem contemplamur* (Pelagius).[528] As a matter of fact, the entire Gothic expression *þairh skuggwan in frisahtai* is obscure. The value of *skuggwa* itself is problematic; it is attested only once in the extant Gothic text and therefore its meaning is not certain. On the basis of the other Germanic languages, it seems to have the sense of 'shadow'.[529] A translation of the passage might therefore be 'through (a) shadow in (an? the?) image'. It cannot be excluded that Wulfila interpreted the context in order to render this peculiar expression.

Another example is in Eph 2:3. The gloss in the margin of *Ambros.* A⁺ (f. 112v/ 89), *ussateinai urrugkai* 'depraved (?) seed', would be, according to Friedrichsen,[530] related to the reading of the text – *wesum wistai barna hatize* lit. '(we) were by nature children of wraths' (= ἤμεθα τέκνα φύσει ὀργῆς in the Greek text) – and influenced by Ambrosiaster's commentary: '*Et eramus natura filii irae, sicut et caeteri.' Naturae enim cum mala uoluntas supponitur, fit natura irae, id est, quae ultioni subiicienda sit, immutata non substantia, sed mala uoluntate. Hoc enim deputatur naturae, quod sequitur; unde ait in Esaia: 'Semen pessimum'*.[531] Two difficulties arise: the term *urrugkai*, a *hapax* of uncertain origin,[532] has an obscure meaning; the expression *semen pessimum*, an allusion to Isaiah (1:4 and 14:20), seems to have been popular in the commentaries[533] and therefore may have circulated independently from Ambrosiaster's quotation.

In 1 Tim 1:19, in correspondence to περὶ τὴν πίστιν ἐναυάγησαν and *circa fidem naufragauerunt*, the Gothic text offers *bi galaubein naqadai waurþun* lit. 'concerning faith (they) became naked'. The difficult point is that *naqadai* 'naked', 'unclad' (nom. plur.) renders usually γυμνοί. Friedrichsen[534] explained this reading through the influence of Ambrosiaster's commentary: *qui deserentes fidem naufragi facti sunt, id est, nudi ueritate*.[535] However, he added that the same comparison was made also by Chrysostom. It should be noted that in the other attestation of ναυαγέω 'to suffer shipwreck' (2 Cor 11:25), the Gothic version ex-

---

527 Ambrst., *in epist. Paul., ad loc.*
528 Pel., *exp. epist, ad loc.*
529 See Lehmann 1986, s.v.
530 Friedrichsen 1939, 225.
531 Ambrst., *in epist. Paul., ad loc.*
532 Lehmann 1986, s.v.
533 It is attested, for instance, also in Aug., *contra adv. leg. et proph.* 22:46; Hier., *in Is.* 16:57.
534 Friedrichsen 1939, 230.
535 Ambrst., *in epist. Paul., ad loc.*

hibits a curious circumlocution *usfarþon gatawida us skipa* lit. '(I) made (a) departure from (the) ship'. It seems likely that this Greek verb did not have a synthetic translation in Gothic. An interpretation of this passage by Wulfila himself, in order to render the meaning of the Greek text, cannot be excluded.

It is difficult to decide whether these renderings – as well as the other readings reported by Friedrichsen – are significant or not. Claiming the influence of Latin commentaries on the Wulfilian version, one must also assume a really sophisticated back translation of the exegetical passages into Gothic and a careful system of substitution of the original readings.[536]

5.5 Parallel passages and parallel expressions

It is well known that one of the most common interferences in manuscript transmission concerns the influence of parallel passages or parallel expressions. In every biblical tradition (Greek, Latin, etc.) the scribes tended to conform similar passages to one another, in order to harmonise the text. This happened also in the Gothic tradition.

The main difficulty concerning the Gothic text lies in determining at which point of the tradition the harmonisation occurred. Indeed, it may have been introduced in the course of the Gothic transmission or have been already attested in the Greek *Vorlage* (the hypothesis that Wulfila altered the Greek text in order to harmonise it before the translation is less plausible). For instance, in Lk 7:48 and Mk 2:9 the Gothic text transmits *afletanda þus frawaurhteis þeinos* 'your sins are forgiven you'. The Gothic text adds *þeinos* (= σου), a reading attested respectively also in the mss. 28, 903, 1071 (Lk 7:48) and f[13] (Mk 2:9). The expressions *afletanda þus frawaurhteis þeinos* and ἀφίενταί σου αἱ ἁμαρτίαι σου occur also in other Gospel passages, namely Mt 9:2, Lk 5:20 and Mk 2:5. In Mt 9:2 and Mk 2:5 the Greek tradition divides: however, the addition of σου is found in the Byzantine manuscripts, with which the Gothic text usually agrees. This insertion is attested also in some Old Latin manuscripts and other traditions: f/10, ff²/8, gat/30, l/11, sy, arm, slav (Lk 7:48); a/3, b/4, c/6, f/10, ff²/8, q/13, vg^{mss}, sy^p, co (Mk 2:9). The issue is whether *þeinos* is an internal Gothic addition on the basis of the Gothic parallel passages or whether Wulfila found σου in his Greek *Vorlage*. Both possibilities are plausible. To claim Latin influence, even if possible, is not necessary.

---

536 It should furthermore be noted that the Gothic text diverges from the Latin text used by Ambrosiaster in several passages, see Appendix I, *passim*.

Other examples put clearly in evidence the difficulty of making judgments concerning the readings due to parallel passages and expressions. For instance, in Mk 2:26 the Gothic text adds *ainaim* 'alone' (*þanzei ni skuld ist matjan niba ainaim gudjam* 'which it is not lawful to eat but for the priests <u>alone</u>'), while the greatest part of the Greek manuscripts transmit οὓς οὐκ ἔξεστιν φαγεῖν εἰ μὴ τοὺς ἱερεῖς. This addition may have been suggested to a Gothic scribe by the parallel passage Lk 6:4 *þanzei ni skuld ist matjan nibai ainaim gudjam*, which corresponds to οὓς οὐκ ἔξεστιν φαγεῖν εἰ μὴ <u>μόνους</u> τοὺς ἱερεῖς (with p⁴, ℵ/01, A/02, B/03, L/019, W/032, Θ/038, Ψ/044, 0233, f¹, f¹³, 33, 𝔐, (lat), syᵖ, syʰ, co) or εἰ μὴ <u>μόνοις</u> τοῖς ἱερεῦσιν (with D/05, 157, 1215, 1443, 1505, 2487, *l*²⁵³, *l*⁷⁵¹, *l*⁹⁵⁰, it; the parallel passage Mt 12:4 is lost in Gothic). However, the possibility that Wulfila's *Vorlage* transmitted a harmonised reading in Mk 2:26 is not to be excluded: the variant <u>μόνοις</u> τοῖς ἱερεῦσιν is indeed attested in 543, f¹³, while τοῖς ἱερεῦσιν <u>μόνοις</u> in Δ/037, 33, 106, 569, 579, saᵐˢˢ, bo. The Gothic version may render both the Greek readings, even if the Gothic word order reflects better <u>μόνοις</u> τοῖς ἱερεῦσιν. Finally, it may have been introduced under the influence of the Latin reading *quos non licebat manducare nisi <u>solis</u> sacerdotibus*, attested in Mk 2:26 (it, vgᵐˢˢ).

Another example is in Mk 1:8. The Gothic text transmits *aþþan ik <u>daupja</u> izwis in watin* 'but I <u>baptise</u> you in water' against ἐγὼ μὲν <u>ἐβάπτισα</u> ὑμᾶς ὕδατι of the Greek tradition (*daupja* is a present indicative, which may reflect both βαπτίζω and βαπτίσω,⁵³⁷ vs. the aorist indicative ἐβάπτισα). It is worth noting that there are some variants to the Greek readings: βαπτίζω ὑμᾶς, transmitted in 5; ὑμᾶς βαπτίζω in D/05, 837;⁵³⁸ ὑμᾶς βαπτίσω in 565. There are different possible reasons for the Gothic present tense: (1) it may reflect a Greek variant (βαπτίζω or βαπτίσω); (2) it may be the result of the influence of parallel passages: Mt 3:11, Jn 1:26 and Lk 3:16.⁵³⁹ The verse Lk 3:16 reports *ik allis izwis watin <u>daupja</u>*, which corresponds to ἐγὼ μὲν ὑμᾶς ὕδατι <u>βαπτίζω</u> (this word order is attested in Θ/038, 1220, a/3, b/4, c/6, ff²/8, q/13). The Gothic text of the parallel passages Mt 3:11 and Jn 1:26 is lost. The corresponding Greek text is: (Mt 3:11) ἐγὼ μὲν ὑμᾶς <u>βαπτίζω</u> ἐν ὕδατι, quoted also in the *Skeireins* 3:10 (*aþþan ik in watin izwis daupja*), and (Jn 1:26) ἐγὼ <u>βαπτίζω</u> ἐν ὕδατι. The harmonisation of the parallel passages may have been already present in Wulfila's lost *Vorlage* or it may be the result of changes within the Gothic transmission. Finally, (3) the Gothic text of Mk 1:8 may have been influenced by the Latin tradition, which exhibits a present form:

---

537 See above 4.1.1.(4).
538 The different Gothic word order is not problematic: in presence of pronouns, it may differ from the Greek model, see above 4.1.2.(1).
539 Dawson 2002, 10–13.

ego baptizo uos in aqua (b/4, c/6, t/56), *ego quidem uos baptizo in aqua* (d/5) and, in agreement with the Gothic construction, *ego quidem baptizo uos in aqua* (f/10, l/11). Again, more than one explanation of the Gothic reading is possible.

Other readings are difficult to assess. In Rom 14:11 the Gothic text of the bilingual *Carolinus* transmits *all kniwe biugiþ* 'every knee shall bow', which differs in word order both from the majority of the Greek manuscripts (κάμψει πᾶν γόνυ) and from the Latin tradition, including the parallel part (*flectet omne genu*). The Gothic variant reflects πᾶν γόνυ κάμψει, transmitted by the minuscules 330 and 2400. It is also a quotation of Is 45:24, attested in Phil 2:10 (πᾶν γόνυ κάμψῃ; lost in Gothic). The Gothic reading may therefore reflect a rare, harmonised Greek variant or be the result of the harmonisation of the parallel passages within the Gothic tradition. The possibility that it better represents the Gothic word order is less plausible, because the order verb-subject is common in Gothic.[540]

The reading *afstassais bokos* 'writ of divorce' in Mt 5:31 diverges from that of the Greek manuscripts (ἀποστάσιον). Nevertheless, it finds a parallel in a citation of Chrysostom (ἀποστασίου βιβλίον). The mss. 1170 and 1604 report βιβλίον ἀποστασίου as well the Latin tradition (*libellum repudii*), going back to Dt 24:1 (βιβλίον ἀποστασίου). The Greek expression is attested also in Mt 19:7 and Mk 10:4 (both βιβλίον ἀποστασίου): the first passage is lost in Gothic; the second reports *bokos afsateinais*. The origin of the Gothic reading in Mt 5:31 is impossible to state with certainty. The agreement in the word order with the quotation of Chrysostom suggests the possibility that Wulfila found this reading in his *Vorlage*.[541]

In other cases, changes within the Gothic tradition appear the most likely explanation. In Mt 27:42 the insertion *ei gasaihvaima* (pres. opt.) 'that (we) may see' before *jah galaubjam* (pres. ind.) *imma* 'and (we) will believe in him' seems to go back to the parallel passage Mk 15:32, *ei gasaihvaima jah galaubjaima*, which corresponds to ἵνα ἴδωμεν καὶ πιστεύσωμεν. It is interesting to note that in Mt 27:42 the *Codex Brixianus* (f/10) transmits *ut uideamus et credamus*, where both the verbs are conjunctive.[542] The interpolation ἵνα ἴδωμεν is attested, beside the Gothic text and f/10, also in the Greek ms. 1574 and in a manuscript of the

---

540 See for instance Lk 3:6: *gasaihviþ all leike* 'all flesh shall see' in correspondence to ὄψεται πᾶσα σάρξ.
541 See also Kauffmann 1898, 179.
542 According to Burkitt (1899, 132–133) the Latin text was influenced by the Gothic, see above 5.2. The picture is further complicated by the reading of the Old Latin manuscript 43 (fifth century), which reads *et uideamus et credamus*, where the first *et* might be a miswriting of *ut*. According to Burton (1996), the text of this manuscript could have been influenced by the Gothic version.

Peshitta.⁵⁴³ The different moods of the verbal forms in Matthew suggest that *ei gasaihvaima* is a secondary addition to the Gothic text, perhaps deriving from a gloss. The possibility that the Gothic text reflects a Greek reading seems less plausible.

In Lk 6:16 (*saei jah warþ galewjands ina* lit. 'who also became traitor him') the addition of the personal pronoun *ina* (acc. sing.) is probably the result of the influence of the parallel passages Mt 27:3 (*sa galewjands ina* 'who betrayed him' = ὁ παραδιδοὺς αὐτόν; see also Jn 18:2 *sa galewjands ina*) and Mk 3:19 (*saei jah galewida ina* 'who also betrayed him' = ὃς καὶ παρέδωκεν αὐτόν). The Gothic text of Lk 6:16 does not seem to be grammatically correct: here *galewjands* is used as substantive not as present participle. The first part (*saei jah warþ galewjands*) agrees with ὃς καὶ ἐγένετο προδότης (A/02, D/05, Q/026, Θ/038, Ψ/ 044, f¹, f¹³, 33, 𝔐, itᵈ against ὃς ἐγένετο προδότης p⁷⁵ᵛⁱᵈ, א/01, B/03, L/019, W/ 032, 579, lat, syˢ·ᵖ). The Old Latin d/5 and e/2 transmit respectivelly *qui etiam et qui tradidit eum* / *qui tradidit illum*; f/10 reports *qui fuit traditor eius*. It is also possible that *ina* represents a miswriting for *is* 'his' (gen. sing.); in this case, the Gothic would agree with f/10.⁵⁴⁴

Another example of internal Gothic addition is attested in Mk 2:12: *hauhidedun mikiljandans* '(they) glorified praising/having praised' for δοξάζειν. The verb *mikiljan* 'to praise' is a synonym of *hauhjan* and renders δοξάζειν in the parallel passages Mt 9:8 and Lk 5:26. The addition of *mikiljandans* seems therefore be due to the influence of the parallel form.

The harmonisation of parallel passages inside the Gothic tradition is the reason for the discrepancy between the text of the *Codex Argenteus* and that of the *Ambros. C*:⁵⁴⁵

Mt 26:70
Both the *Argenteus* and the *Ambros. C.* read the verb *laugnida* in correspondence to ἠρνήσατο.

Mt 26:72 and 26:75
The manuscripts transmit two different forms, both attested in the parallel passages:

Mt 26:72	Mk 14:70
jah aftra afaiaik (CA)	
jah aftra laugnida (C)	*iþ is aftra laugnida* (CA)
καὶ πάλιν ἠρνήσατο	ὁ δὲ πάλιν ἠρνεῖτο
'and again (he) denied'	'but again he denied'

---

543 Legg (1940, *ad loc.*) listed also the *Diatessaron*.
544 On the textual affinities between the Gothic text and f/10 (*Codex Brixianus*) see above 5.2.
545 On the text of the *Ambros. C* see also Cipolla 1990.

Mt 26:75	Jn 13:38	Mk 14:72
afaikis mik (CA)	þu mik afaikis (CA)	
inwidis mik (C)	σύ με ἀπαρνήσῃ⁵⁴⁶	inwidis mik (CA)
ἀπαρνήσῃ με	'you will deny me'	ἀπαρνήσῃ με (𝔐)⁵⁴⁷
'(you) will deny me'		'(you) will deny me'

The verb ἀρνέομαι 'to deny' is translated with different Gothic verbs in the extant parts of the Gothic Bible: *afaikan*, *inwidan* and *laugnjan*; ἀπαρνέομαι with *afaikan* and *inwidan* (the difference of meaning is not clear). Therefore, in Mt 26:72 and 75, it is not possible to restore the original Wulfilian reading with confidence. Either variant of the Gothic manuscripts could be correct. The parallel passages (Jn 13:38; Mk 14:70, 72) may have offered the alternative forms.

It is also difficult to assess the isolated reading in Mt 5:44 *þiuþjaiþ þans wrikandans izwis* 'bless those who persecute you', that corresponds to an unattested εὐλογεῖτε τοὺς διώκοντας ὑμᾶς, against εὐλογεῖτε τοὺς καταρωμένους ὑμᾶς of the Greek tradition. The Gothic reading is probably the result of the influence of the Gothic parallel passage Rom 12:14 (*þiuþjaiþ þans wrikandans izwis*), unless it goes back to a harmonised (now lost or unidentified) Greek variant.

The case of Lk 9:50 is different: *ni ainshun auk ist manne saei ni gawaurkjai maht in namin meinamma* lit. 'there is indeed no one of the men (people?) who does not (a deed of) power in my name', which renders an unattested οὐδεὶς γάρ ἐστιν ἀνθρώπων ὃς οὐ ποιήσει δύναμιν ἐπὶ τῷ ὀνόματί μου. The Gothic passage recalls Mk 9:39 *ni mannahun auk ist saei taujiþ maht in namin meinamma* 'there is indeed no one who does (a deed of) power in my name', rendering of οὐδεὶς γάρ ἐστιν ὃς ποιήσει δύναμιν ἐπὶ τῷ ὀνόματί μου. It is worth noting that the reading of Luke finds a parallel in the Old Latin mss. a/3, b/4, c/6, e/2, l/11, and r¹/14: *nemo est enim* (*enim est* e/2; *est autem* r¹/14) *qui non* (- r¹/14) *faciat uirtutem in nomine meo* (+ *et poterit male loqui de me* a/3, r¹/14). The Gothic addition may depend on the Latin influence or on a common (lost or unidentified) Greek reading. In this case a parallel harmonisation within the Gothic tradition seems unlikely.

To conclude, the origin of the influence of parallel passages in the Gothic text may have several explanations: it may be due to an internal Gothic harmonisation, to a harmonised Greek *Vorlage*, or to the influence of a harmonised

---

546 Reading attested in the Greek ms. W/032 and in the Old Latin b/4, ff²/8, r¹/14, see www.iohannes.com (30.12.2013). However, it is possible that the Gothic reading renders ἀπαρνήσῃ με, attested in other manuscripts, because the Gothic word order with pronouns is not a reliable witness to the word order of the Greek *Vorlage*; see above 4.1.2.(1).

547 Other variants to this passage are not important for the discussion and are therefore omitted, see Nestle-Aland²⁸, *ad loc*.

Latin tradition. Every Gothic reading which has a parallel in another biblical passage must be analysed in the light of these possibilities.

5.6. Transmission in two witnesses

The modifications to the Wulfilian text clearly emerge from the comparison of those passages which are transmitted by two manuscripts (*Codex Argenteus* and *Ambros.* C; *Carolinus* and *Ambros.* A⁺; *Ambros.* A⁺ and *Ambros.* B). Most differences are orthographic. The portion of text offered by the *Argenteus* and the *Ambros.* C is too small, and it is not possible to establish their relationship.[548] The ten verses in common between the *Carolinus* and the *Ambros.* A⁺, besides two orthographic divergences and two common errors, offer three further erroneous readings (one in the *Carolinus*; two in the *Ambros.* A⁺).[549]

More complex is the relationship between the *Ambros.* A⁺ and the *Ambros.* B, systematically dealt with by Friedrichsen.[550] Besides several orthographic variants,[551] the two manuscripts have in common nineteen errors, which point to a common ancestor.[552] There are also some textual divergences. Some of these involve synonyms or parallel forms; others may go back to scribal errors or misreadings, e.g.: in 2 Tim 3:13, in correspondence to Gr. ἄνθρωποι and Lat. *homines* 'men', there are two different readings: *mannans* 'men' (*Ambros.* A⁺; weak declension) and *mans* 'men' (*Ambros.* B; consonantic declension). Both are correct since they are interchangeable forms, so that it is not possible to determine Wulfila's original reading. In 1 Cor 16:2, in correspondence to τιθέτω (Lat. *ponat* 'lay'), the *Ambros.* A⁺ reads *lagjai* (pres. opt. act. from *lagjan* 'to lay') and the *Ambros.* B *taujai* (pres. opt. act. from *taujan* 'to do', 'to make'). The erroneous variant, *taujai* ᛏᛅᚢᚷᛅᛁ, might be the result of a misreading of *lagjai* (ᛚᚨᚷᛅᛁ).

Other divergences arise from the context, e.g.: in 2 Cor 2:10 the *Ambros.* A⁺ transmits *fragaf fragaf* (pret. ind.) and the *Ambros.* B *fragiba fragiba* (pres. ind.), both from *fragiban* 'to forgive', in correspondence to κεχάρισμαι [...] κεχάρισμαι (*donaui* [...] *donaui*). The reading of the *Ambros.* B was probably suggested by the preceding *fragibiþ* (pres. ind. = χαρίζεσθε/*donatis*).

---

548 See above 5.5.
549 See Falluomini 1999, 136.
550 Friedrichsen 1939, 62–127.
551 For instance the spelling *-ands* for *-and* and vice versa (see Friedrichsen 1939, 63–64).
552 See also above 2.5.

The divergent readings in 2 Tim 2:26 are difficult to assess: the *Ambros*. A⁺ reads *gafahanai habanda* against *gafahanai tiuhanda* of the *Ambros*. B, both in correspondence to ἐζωγρημένοι 'being captured' (masc. nom. plur. perf. partic. pass. of ζωγρέω 'to take, 'to capture', 'to catch').⁵⁵³ According to Friedrichsen, *habanda* is from *capti tenentur/tenentur capti* of the Latin tradition; the reading of the *Ambros*. B "seems to be a later variant"⁵⁵⁴ after 2 Tim 3:6: *frahunþana tiuhand* '(they who) took (them) prisoner', translation of αἰχμαλωτεύοντες. It is not possible to reach a definitive conclusion regarding the original Wulfilian reading and the reason for its change.

More interesting from a text-critical point of view are those readings which may reflect a different textual model. In Rom 13:1 (f. 256v, l. 26–27) there is an error in the Gothic part of the *Carolinus*: *all saiwalo waldufnjam ufarwisandam ufhausjaiþ*⁵⁵⁵ lit. 'let every of the souls be subject' (2ⁿᵈ pers. plur. pres. opt. act.) to the higher powers'. This construction is not grammatically correct, because the subject *all saiwalo* 'every of the souls' (nom. + gen. partit.) needs a third person singular. The correct reading is transmitted by the parallel manuscript *Ambros*. A⁺ (*ufhausjai*, 3ʳᵈ pers. sing.) and by the Latin part of the *Carolinus* (*subdita sit*). It should be noted that the Greek and Latin traditions are divided at this passage: πᾶσα ψυχὴ ἐξουσίαις ὑπερεχούσαις ὑποτασσέσθω is transmitted by ℵ/01, A/02, B/03, D¹/06¹, L/020, P/025, Ψ/044, 33, 1739, 𝔐, d⁽ᶜ⁾/75⁽ᶜ⁾, dem/59, e/76, z/65, vg, sy, co, Chrysostom, Rufinus, Augustine, Ambrosiaster^mss, Pelagius; against πάσαις ἐξουσίαις ὑπερεχούσαις ὑποτάσσεσθε of p⁴⁶, D*/06*, F/010, G/012, ar/61, b/89, d*/75*, f/78, g/77, m/*Speculum*, t/56, vg^mss, Ireneus, Tertullian, Ambrosiaster (*subditi estote*). It is possible that a marginal gloss *ufhausjaiþ* (or a correction to the reading of the text?), based on the variant ὑποτάσσεσθε or *subditi estote*, has replaced the original *ufhausjai*. However, a simple error in the writing cannot be excluded, i.e. the addition of þ at the end of the word.

The *Ambros*. A⁺ transmits in 1 Cor 15:54 *þanuþ þan þata diwano gawasjada undiwanein* 'and when this perishable (body) puts on imperishability' (= ὅταν δὲ τὸ φθαρτὸν τοῦτο ἐνδύσηται ἀφθαρσίαν, with p⁴⁶, ℵ*/01*, C*/04*, 088, 0121, 0243, 629*, 1175, 1739*, lat, sa^ms, bo, Ambrosiaster), against the *Ambros*. B, in which these words are omitted (with F/010, G/012, 6, 365, 614*, f/78, g/77). It is worth noting that both of them diverge from the Byzantine text and may be

---

553 The form *gafahanai* is a strong masc. nom. plur. past partic. of *gafahan* 'to take, 'to capture', 'to catch'; *habanda* is a 3ʳᵈ pers. plur. pres. ind. pass. of *haban* 'to have', 'to hold', 'to possess' and the variant *tiuhanda* is a 3ʳᵈ pers. plur. pres. ind. pass. of *tiuhan* 'to lead', 'to conduct', 'to bring'.
554 Friedrichsen 1939, 213, 250 (from here the citation).
555 Falluomini 1999, 71.

the Wulfilian reading. However, this omission in *Ambros.* B could be due to homoeoteleuton (**þanuþ þan þata diwano gawasjada undiwanein þanuh*). This fact suggests that the *Ambros.* A⁺ preserves the original reading, in agreement with old witnesses.

According to Friedrichsen,[556] in 2 Cor 4:4 the divergence between the *Ambros.* A⁺, *frisahts gudis* '(the) image of God', and the *Ambros.* B, *frisahts gudis ungasaihvani[n]s* '(the) image of (the) invisible God', reflects different textual traditions. The addition of *ungasaihvani[n]s* in the *Ambros.* B would find a parallel in τοῦ ἀοράτου (with א^c/01^c, L/020, P/025 and several Greek minuscules) and in *inuisibilis* (ar/61, m/*Speculum* and the Vulgate mss. L², O*). However, other explanations are possible: (1) this addition is due to the influence of the Gothic parallel passage Col 1:15: *frisahts gudis ungasaihvanis* (= εἰκὼν τοῦ θεοῦ τοῦ ἀοράτου); (2) *frisahts gudis ungasaihvanis* was the original (harmonised) reading; the scribe of the *Ambros.* A⁺ omitted, for reasons that are unclear, *ungasaihvanis*.

In 2 Cor 13:13 the *Ambros.* A⁺ transmits *ansts fraujins Iesuis Xristaus* '(the) grace of (the) Lord Jesus Christ' (= ἡ χάρις τοῦ κυρίου Ἰησοῦ Χριστοῦ, attested in the majority of the Greek manuscripts, and *gratia domini Iesu Christi*, passed on by d/75, e/76, g/77), which is considered the correct reading. The *Ambros.* B reads *ansts fraujins unsaris Iesuis Xristaus* '(the) grace of our Lord Jesus Christ' (= ἡ χάρις τοῦ κυρίου ἡμῶν Ἰησοῦ Χριστοῦ, attested in several minuscules, and *gratia domini nostri Iesu Christi*, witnessed by f/78, z/65, vg). It should be noted that the expression *ansts fraujins unsaris Iesuis Xristaus* is common in the Pauline Epistles,[557] so that the insertion of *unsaris* 'our' may be simply a scribal addition caused by the reminiscence of other biblical passages. It is not necessary to suppose that this reading is the result of the collation with another tradition.

The reading of Gal 6:17 is interesting. The *Ambros.* A⁺ reads *stakins Iesuis* '(the) marks of Jesus' (= τὰ στίγματα τοῦ Ἰησοῦ with p⁴⁶, A/02, B/03, C*/04*, 33, 1071, 1753, f/78, t/56, vg^st, sa^ms); the *Ambros.* B, instead, offers *stakins fraujins unsaris Iesuis Xristaus* '(the) marks of our Lord Jesus Christ' (= τὰ στίγματα κυρίου ἡμῶν Ἰησοῦ Χριστοῦ with D*/06*, F/010, G/012, 104, 1924, ar/61, b/4, g/77, sy^p (sa^mss), Chrys); both against κυρίου Ἰησοῦ of the Byzantine text. The original Wulfilian reading seems to be that of the *Ambros.* A⁺, according to the text-critical principle *lectio brevior potior est*, at least with regard to such liturgical expressions. The reading of the *Ambros.* B does not necessarily stem from another tradition. It may well be the result of an independent addition by the Gothic scribe, based on a common expression of the Pauline Epistles.

---

556 Friedrichsen 1939, 74.
557 See for instance Gal 6:18; 1 Thess 5:28; 2 Thess 3:18.

Notable also is the textual divergence in Phil 3:16: the *Ambros.* A⁺ transmitts *ei samo hugjaima [jah samo fraþjaima], samon gaggan garaideinai* lit. 'let us think (the) same [and comprehend (the) same], (in order to) walk by (the) same rule'; the *Ambros.* B offers *ei samo hugjaima [jah samo fraþjaima]* 'let us think (the) same [and comprehend (the) same]'. Friedrichsen explained this divergence as follows: "The original Gothic text has been accommodated to the Old Latin, and the actual conflations exhibited in [*Ambros.*] A and [*Ambros.*] B seem to be the result of the interpolation and substitution, respectively, of a marginal gloss."[558] He traced the history of this passage, claiming that the original reading was *samon gaggan garaideinai samo hugjan* '(to) walk by (the) same rule, (to) think (the) same' (= Byzantine text: τῷ αὐτῷ στοιχεῖν κανόνι, τὸ αὐτὸ φρονεῖν). The second part, *samo hugjan*, was subsequently adjusted both in construction and order to the Latin version: *ut idem sapiamus et in eadem permaneamus regula* (vg); *in eo ambulemus* (ar/61, Ambrosiaster, Pelagius^B).[559] The result was *ei samo hugjaima jah samon gaggan garaideinai* lit. 'let us think (the) same and walk by (the) same rule', with the conjunction *jah* 'and' and the erroneous form *gaggan* (inf., not in agreement with *hugjaima*, 1st pers. plur. pres. opt. act.). The third stage introduces a marginal gloss *samo fraþjaima* '(let us) comprehend (the) same', as the more usual alternative for *samo hugjaima*, in the margin of the ultimate ancestor of both the *Ambros.* A⁺ and the *Ambros.* B. In the fourth stage the marginal gloss has been introduced into the text of both manuscripts; the second part of the reading, i.e. *samon gaggan garaideinai*, was subsequently omitted by the *Ambros.* B. Friedrichsen proposed this schema:[560]

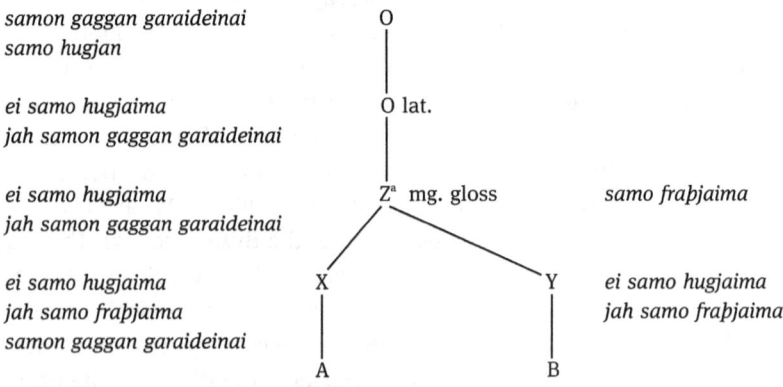

---

558 Friedrichsen 1939, 75; for the conjectural history of this passage see Friedrichsen 1939, 201–202.
559 With several variants, see VLD, *ad loc.*
560 Friedrichsen 1939, 202; see also Stutz 1972, 399–400.

Friedrichsen's explanation is, of course, possible. However, there is another explanation, which seems less complicated. The original Gothic reading was *ei samo hugjaima, samon gaggan garaideinai* 'let us think (the) same, (in order to) walk by (the) same rule', which rendered τὸ αὐτὸ φρονεῖν, τῷ αὐτῷ κανόνι στοιχεῖν, with the Greek minuscules 81, 104, 256, 263, 330, 365, 451, 459, 1175 1241^s, 1319, 1573, 2127, 2492, 1596; στοιχεῖν κανόνι D^2/06^2, 436.[561] At a later date, *samo hugjaima* was glossed with the synonymic expression *samo fraþjaima*, later incorporated into the text of the common ancestor of the *Ambros.* A$^+$ and the *Ambros.* B, with the conjunction *jah* 'and'. Subsequently, the scribe of the *Ambros.* B omitted *samon gaggan garaideinai*, perhaps because of the threefold repetition of *samo-* (*ei samo hugjaima jah samo fraþjaima samon gaggan garaideinai*).

5.7 Marginal glosses[562]

The majority of the fifteen glosses of the *Codex Argenteus* are synonyms of the readings in the text. For instance, *flodus* 'stream', 'river' (Lk 6:49, f. 146r) is a *hapax* that renders ποταμός 'stream', 'river'; it is glossed in the margin by *aƕa* 'river', 'waters', which is the usual translation of ποταμός; *mela* 'writing', 'Scriptures' (Mk 12:24, f. 45v), rendering here of γραφάς 'Scriptures', is glossed by the synonym *bokos*.

Other glosses seem to be corrections to the text: e. g. *waldaiþ*, 2nd pers. plur. pres. opt. act. of *waldan* 'to rule' (Lk 3:14, f. 129v), is in correspondence to ἀρκεῖσθε (from ἀρκέω 'to be satisfied', 'to be contented'); in the margin there is the gloss *ganohidai sijaiþ* 'be satisfied', which renders perfectly the meaning of the Greek verb. It is likely that *waldaiþ* translated ἄρχεσθε (from ἄρχω 'to rule'), which represents an error or a misreading of the *Vorlage* (rather than a later change of a Wulfilian correct reading). Indeed, the two Greek verbs are phonetically and visually very similar, and their exchange is very plausible. The gloss may be the result of the collation of the Gothic manuscript with a Latin (or Greek?) codex with the correct reading (*contenti/sufficientes estote* in the Latin versions). Another example is Lk 9:13 (f. 158r): the gloss *managein* 'multitude', 'crowd', 'people' seems to be a correction of the term of the text (*manasedai* 'mankind', 'the world of humans', 'world', for λαόν 'people').

---

[561] The rendering of the Greek infinitive with a Gothic finite construction is not unusual, see Lk 1:73 τοῦ δοῦναι ἡμῖν 'to grant us' translated *ei gebi unsis*.
[562] See also above 2.4.

In other cases, the glosses refer to a parallel passage or the close context, e.g.: in the correspondence to *mammonin* 'mammon', 'accumulation of riches' (Mt 6:24, f. 6r) is the gloss *faihuþra‹ihna›* 'accumulation of riches', attested in the parallel passage Lk 16:13; conversely, at Lk 16:13 (f. 179v), *faihuþraihna* is glossed with *mammonim* (miswriting for *mammonin*).[563]

The gloss in Lk 9:34 is notable (f. 160r): the Gothic text transmits (*faurhtidedun þan*) *in þammei jainai qemun in þamma milhmin* '(then they feared) as they entered into the cloud', translation of (ἐφοβήθησαν δὲ) ἐν τῷ ἐκείνους εἰσελθεῖν εἰς τὴν νεφέλην. In the margin, apparently written by a different hand, is the gloss *jah at im in milhmam* (for *milhman*) *atgaggandam* 'and as they entered into the clouds' (participial construction), which corresponds – with a different word order – to *et intrantibus illis in nubem*, testified by the Old Latin mss. b/4, f/10, ff²/8, l/11, q/13, r¹/14.[564] This seems to be an alternative reading, perhaps suggested by the Latin tradition.

Several of the fifty-three glosses of the *Ambros.* A⁺ are synonyms for the readings of the text, e.g.: *waira fullamma* 'a perfect man' (Eph 4:13, f. 116v/121) is glossed with *gumin fullamma* (*waira* and *gumin* are synonyms). Cross-references are the gloss *psalmo* 'psalm' in Eph 4:8, f. 116r/120 (related to Ps 67 (68):19) and *Esaïas* 'Isaiah' in 1 Cor 14:21, f. 70r/86 (related to Is 28:11).

Worth noting are the glosses in 1 Cor 13:3 (f. 67r/84) and in Eph 1:19 (f. 111v/135), which reflect different textual traditions. The text of 1 Cor 13:3, *ei gabrannjaidau* 'so that (I) may be burned', corresponds to ἵνα καυθήσωμαι, attested in K/018, Ψ/044, 𝔐, and *ut ardeam*, reported by the Latin tradition. The marginal gloss, *ei hvopau* 'so that (I) may be glorified', renders instead ἵνα καυχήσωμαι, transmitted by p⁴⁶, ℵ/01, A/02, B/03, 0150, 33, 69, 1739*, co, Origen, Jerome^mss (*glorier/glorietur*). In Eph 1:19 the gloss *in izwis* 'for you' (2ⁿᵈ pers. plur.) corresponds to ὑμᾶς (D*/06*, F/010, G/012, P/025, 33) and *uos* (f/77, r¹/14, r³/64, Ambrosiaster) / *uobis* (ar/61, d/75, e/76, f/77, Pelagius^B), against the reading of the text *in uns* 'for us', attested in the rest of the Greek and Latin witnesses. There is no doubt, in these cases, that the Gothic glossator knew other textual traditions.

In Eph 2:3 the Gothic text, transmitted by the *Ambros.* A⁺ and the *Ambros.* B, has *wiljans* lit. 'wills', as translation of θελήματα 'desires'. In the margin of the *Ambros.* A⁺ (f. 112r/88) is the gloss *lustuns* 'lusts', which – according to Bernhardt[565] – is the result of the confusion between Latin *uoluntates* (= *wiljans*)

---

[563] See above 4.2.
[564] However, Goth. *milhmam* is dat. plur. and Lat. *nubem* is acc. sing.; therefore Streitberg (1919, *ad loc.*) emended the Gothic form in *milhman* (acc. sing.).
[565] Bernhardt 1875, *ad loc.*

and *uoluptates* (= *lustuns*), attested in the Old Latin mss. d/75 (-*mpt*-), e/76, in the Vulgate mss. F, P, in Tertullian and Ambrosiaster. However, as Friedrichsen noted,[566] "the preceding *lustum* [*in lustum leikis unsaris* = ἐν ταῖς ἐπιθυμίαις τῆς σαρκὸς ἡμῶν] may be directly responsible."

The gloss in 2 Cor 1:8 (f. 82r/168) is worth noting. The text of the *Ambros*. A⁺ reads *afswaggwidai weseima*, a periphrastic form composed by the past partic. nom. plur. of *afswaggwjan* and the 1st pers. plur. pret. opt. of *wisan* 'to be'. The significance of *afswaggwjan*, a *hapax*, is not clear. According to its etymological analysis it means 'to cause to waver',[567] a meaning which does not seem to agree completely with ἐξαπορηθῆναι 'to be utterly at loss', 'to be utterly destitute of measures or resources', 'to be in despair', which is attested in the Greek text (ἐξαπορηθῆναι ἡμᾶς).[568] In the upper right margin of the manuscript, on three lines, there is the gloss

  ΝΑΙϟΕ   ⟨naide⟩
 ϟΚΑΜΑΙϟΕ ⟨skamaide⟩
  ϟΕΙΜΑ   ⟨deima⟩

First of all, it is to be noted that the reading *skamaidedeima uns* (1st pers. plur. pret. opt. act. from *skaman* 'to be ashamed for' plus 1st pers. plur. refl. pron.) is attested in the same verse of *Ambros*. B. However, this latter reading seems to be erroneous.[569] Furthermore, an autoptic examination of the gloss reveals that nothing is written before *naide*,[570] a form that does not have a proper sense. One may claim that the glossator miswrote his model (a gloss?) or perhaps he could not read the model properly and decide between -*maide*- and -*naide*-, so he likely wrote both.

---

566 Friedrichsen 1939, 68.
567 Lehmann 1986, *s.v.* (with question mark).
568 The Greek verb is attested also in 2 Cor 4:8, ἐξαπορούμενοι, where it is translated into Gothic as *afslaupidai*, from *afslaupjan* 'to perturb'.
569 According to Friedrichsen (1939, 71–72) "[t]he reading of [*Ambros*.] B is from the Latin *taederet nos*; [*Ambros*.] A has preserved the original text, with a note in the margin drawing attention to the variant." This claim is however not persuasive: the Latin meaning of *taedet* 'to be disgusted', 'to be offended', 'to be tired', 'to be sick' does not seem in agreement with the meaning of *skaman*. Both the Gothic readings seem to be inappropriate to the context.
570 Castiglioni 1834, *ad loc.*; Streitberg 1919, *ad loc.* "...*maide*"; Snædal 2013 A, I, *ad loc.* "... *naide*". They seem to suggest – erroneously – that the first part of the word is not readable.

5.8 Glosses incorporated into the text

Certain alterations in the course of the transmission of the Gothic version are represented by the insertion of glosses into the text and the conflation of variants, possibly on the basis of an ancestor with (marginal?) annotations.

Some examples are in the *Codex Argenteus*. In Mt 9:23 the manuscript transmits *jah gasaihvands swigljans jah haurnjans haurnjandans*, against the Greek and Latin traditions: καὶ ἰδὼν τοὺς αὐλητάς and *et uidisset tibicines*. In this passage, the words *jah haurnjans haurnjandans* do not correspond to the reading of any known manuscript. It is likely that they were in the margin (of *Codex Argenteus*' ancestor?) – a reminiscence of Rev 18:22, according to Streitberg[571] – and entered into the text in the course of its copying.

Another example of a gloss embodied into the text is in Lk 2:2: *wisandin kindina Swriais raginondin Saurim* lit. 'being governor of Syria governing (the) Syrians' against Gr. ἡγεμονεύοντος τῆς Συρίας and Lat. *praeside Syriae* (with some variants). *Wisandin kindina Swriais* and *raginondin Saurim* are indeed two different translations of the Greek text. On the basis of the similar expression *raginondin Puntiau Peilatau Iudaia* lit. 'governing Pontius Pilate Judaea' (Lk 3:1: ἡγεμονεύοντος Ποντίου Πιλάτου τῆς Ἰουδαίας) it is likely that *raginondin Saurim* was the original text.[572] In this case, as well as in other cases, the gloss has been inserted into the text without care for its final meaning.

The Epistles also contain possible glosses incorporated into the text, as in Rom 12:19 (*mis fraweit*) *leitaidau/letaidau* lit. '(to me vengeance) be left', attested respectively by the *Carolinus* and the *Ambros.* A⁺, without Greek or Latin correspondence. The Greek and Latin texts have only ἐμοὶ ἐκδίκησις and *mihi uindictam* (with some minor variants), that correspond to *mis fraweit*. It is also missing in the Latin text of the *Carolinus*. According to Friedrichsen,[573] it is an interpolation on the basis of Ambrosiaster's commentary:[574] *duplici igitur genere proficitur, si deo remittitur (remittatur AW) uindicta, quia et cum iracundiam uincit, perfectus fit et dei iudicio uindicabitur*. However, a free insertion of the verb by a Gothic or Greek reader/corrector cannot be excluded, in order to complete the sense of the sentence, independently from Ambrosiaster's influence.

Other examples of glosses incorporated into the text are in Gal 5:20, 1 Tim 5:4 and 2 Tim 2:2. In the first passage both *Ambros.* A⁺ and *Ambros.* B transmit *[birodeinos] hairaiseis* '[whisperings], heresies' that renders [ψιθυρισμοί], αἱρέσεις.

---

571 Streitberg 1919, *ad loc.*
572 See also Friedrichsen 1926, 221.
573 Friedrichsen 1939, 218.
574 Ambrst., *in epist. Paul., ad loc.*

It is possibly an insertion after 2 Cor 12:20. In 1 Tim 5:4 (*Ambros.* B) the gloss offers a synonym of the term transmited in the text: *þata auk ist [god jah] andanem* 'for this is [good and] pleasing', against the reading of the *Ambros.* A⁺ (*þata auk ist andanem*) that agrees with the Greek (τοῦτο γάρ ἐστιν ἀπόδεκτον). A kind of explanatory gloss is *managa weitwodja [waurda gudis]* 'many witnesses [God's words]' (*Ambros.* B, 2 Tim 2:2; *Ambros.* A⁺ is lost), in correspondence to πολλῶν μαρτύρων 'many witnesses'.

Particularly interesting are those glosses transmitted by only one manuscript where there are two, as in 2 Cor 12:20:[575] the *Ambros.* B transmits *haifsteis* 'conflics' (= ἐριθείαι), while the *Ambros.* A⁺ has *haifsteis [faiha]*[576] 'conflicts [exploitations (?)]'.[577] This insertion may be explained in several ways: (1) the common ancestor transmitted a marginal gloss, inserted into the text only by the scribe of the *Ambros.* A⁺; (2) the gloss has been written in the margin of the common ancestor after the copying of the *Ambros.* B and before the copying of the *Ambros.* A⁺; (3) it has been introduced into the *Ambros.* A⁺ without a model; (4) it has been inserted in an intermediary exemplar, from which the *Ambros.* A⁺ derives. All these explanations have the same degree of plausibility, so that it is not possible to explain how *faiha* entered into the text. Less plausible is the claim that it belonged, for some reason, to the Wulfilian text and was subsequently omitted by the scribe of the *Ambros.* B. The ancestor of the *Ambros.* A⁺ and the *Ambros.* B seems to have had marginal glosses, inserted unsystematically into the text by the copyists of these two manuscripts.[578]

5.9 Conclusions

The Gothic tradition underwent – like every other tradition – some changes during the process of copying, through the harmonisation to parallel passages, adoption of synonyms and the insertion of glosses into the text. Such changes to the Wulfilian text probably did not occur at one time, but are the result of several stages of the transmission.

Responsibility for the modifications to the original translation lies also in the readers, who occasionally added glosses into the margin, and in the scribes, who inserted the marginal glosses of the ancestor into their copy, so producing con-

---

575 The presence of different readings in 1 Tim 3:3 is to be excluded, see above, fn. 269.
576 Snædal 2013 A, I, *ad loc.* Streitberg (1919, *ad loc.*) read *bifaiha*.
577 The word *faiha* or *bifaiha* is a *hapax*; its Greek correspondence is not clear (πλεονεξίαι?). Apparently there are no parallels in the Greek or Latin tradition.
578 See above 2.5.

flated readings and, voluntarily or involuntarily, changed the text. The work of the readers is particularly significant because it testifies that the Gothic manuscripts were used not only in liturgical contexts, but also for private reading and study. They have been glossed in order to correct the text, to offer an explanation of a difficult word, to give a reference to a parallel passage or, less often, to suggest a different reading. Furthermore, some glosses show a certain text-critical effort by some cultivated readers, probably ecclesiastics, who perhaps collated their Gothic manuscript with a Greek and/or Latin (or Gothic?) exemplar and were interested to note some discrepancies. The same text-critical interest is expressed by the text of the *Praefatio*.

Another problem of Gothic criticism is the role of the Latin version(s). There are – theoretically – three possibilities: (1) Wulfila also used a Latin model for his translation (in addition to the Greek *Vorlage*); (2) the Gothic text underwent a double process of Latinisation: first at the time of translation and subsequently in the west, during the copying of the Gothic manuscripts; and finally (3) the original translation was subject to Latin influence only in the western milieu. That the Latin tradition influenced the Gothic text is undeniable: the question is how deep this influence was and at what point in the history the Latin tradition began to exercise its influence. There is nothing to contradict the claim that Wulfila used also a Latin exemplar as an aid to render some difficult expressions of the Greek text, particularly in the Epistles. Some evidence, indeed, points to the presence of Christian Latin-speaking communities and the circulation of Latin translations of the Bible in the territories where Wulfila lived.[579] On the other hand, the hypothesis of a Latin influence on the Gothic text in the post-Wulfilian period – through occasional glosses that penetrated into the text? – has to be considered as a possible explanation for some readings proper only to the Gothic and Latin versions. Beside this, another explanation may explain such agreement: that the Gothic and Latin texts reflect independently a lost Greek tradition, at least in some cases.

That all the non-Byzantine readings are post-Wulfilian modifications seems unlikely in the light of cultural reasons. Wulfila's text very probably represented an important religious symbol of identity, on which the Gothic Church based its own existence, at least in Ostrogothic Italy (no information survives with regard to the Visigoths). The production of manuscripts, among them the magnificent *Codex Argenteus*, and the building of several churches for Gothic worship reveal the determination on the part of the Ostrogothic rulers to preserve their own cultural and religious customs and to place the Gothic Arian Church on the same

---

[579] See above 1.2.

level as the Latin Catholic Church.⁵⁸⁰ A planned revision of Wulfila's translation on the basis of one or more Latin versions would seem to contradict such a picture. However, some changes to the original text did occur, consisting of additions and omissions of words, insertions of marginal annotations and harmonisation of parallel passages. These changes are typical of textual transmission and probably the result of scribal (often mechanical) activity.

---

580 See above 1.2.

6 A different approach to the problem of the *Vorlage*

As previously seen, most earlier studies of the *Vorlage* of the Gothic version are based on the assumption that Wulfila used a fourth-century recension of the New Testament and that the non-Byzantine readings of the Gothic version, in particular the so-called 'Western' readings, were later intrusions.[581]

More recent theories concerning the formation of the Byzantine text may offer a different explanation for the mixed textual character of the Gothic version. Several contemporary New Testament scholars argue that the Byzantine text type is the result of a long process of revision and standardisation, rather than the product of a recension performed at one time and place by a single editor. Already in 1937 Sir Frederic G. Kenyon suggested that the Byzantine text type – which he called α – did not originate from "a single deliberate act at a single time [...]. It was rather the result of forces and tendencies which continued to operate over a long period."[582] According to Kenyon, this process was due to both unconscious and deliberate tendencies, which led scribes to substitute familiar phrases for those less familiar, to make a passage more clear and to assimilate parallel passages, in order to render the text more intelligible. In a posthumous work of Günther Zuntz, the hypothesis of the progressive formation of the Byzantine text – included among the 'Majority text' (𝔐), because the Byzantine manuscripts always constitute the majority of the biblical manuscripts[583] – is clearly expressed.[584] Subsequently, this hypothesis has been developed particularly by Klaus Wachtel.[585] He does not identify a specific moment for the origin of the By-

---

581 See above 5.1.
582 Kenyon 1937, 199.
583 'Majority text' and 'Byzantine text' are not synonyms. 'Majority text' is a purely quantitative definition: it means the majority of the manuscripts which transmit a certain reading; 'Byzantine text' is a historical category: it represents the text of the Byzantine Church, found in Byzantine manuscripts and divergent from other forms of text, see Aland-Aland 1989, 235, 253; Wallace 2012.
584 Zuntz 1995, 14, 24–25, and at p. 40: "𝔐 ist eben eine späte, fixierte, Form dieses langlebigen und variablen 'populären' Texts, und die [...] Handschriften des 4.–6. Jahrhunderts repräsentieren frühere Formen desselben. 𝔐 gab es noch nicht, wohl aber diesen variablen 'populären' Text, und es wäre von Interesse [...] in welcher Form, oder welchen Formen, er durch die Jahrhunderte wirkte und sich wandelte, bis schließlich eine von ihnen als 'byzantinischer Mehrheitstext' 𝔐 standardisiert wurde."
585 Wachtel 1995, 180–186; regarding the formation and spread of the Byzantine text, he speaks of a "kontinuierlicher Prozeß [...]. Wahrscheinlich gab es im Zuge dieses Prozesses En-

zantine text type and prefers to assume that it is the product of a long editorial process of revision and standardisation, made in the course of the transmission of the biblical text. The Byzantine text is therefore seen as the result of the progressive establishment, in the course of the tradition, of alternative readings, often linguistically and stylistically *faciliores*.[586]

The oldest extant Greek manuscripts that exhibit an almost developed Byzantine text are the *Codex Alexandrinus* (A/02, fifth century),[587] the *Codex Washingtoniensis* (W/032, usually dated in the late fourth or early fifth century),[588] the *Codex Purpureus Petropolitanus* (N/022, sixth century),[589] the *Codex Guelferbytanus* B (Q/026, middle or end of the fifth century)[590] and the *Codex Guelferbytanus* A (P/024, of the middle or end of the sixth century).[591] The process of standardisation was still underway when they were being copied; they transmit, therefore, many readings that diverge from those of the later Byzantine witnesses. A fully-developed Byzantine text emerges only by the end of the eighth/start of the ninth century. It becomes the standard text of the Byzantine Church, transmitted by the greatest mass of the minuscules copied in its territories. Early readings, however, still persist also in the latest period.[592] Such standardisation was faster in the text of the Gospels that in the text of the Pauline Epistles, probably because the latter were copied less frequently.[593]

---

twicklungssprünge, indem Handschriften, die mehrfach kopiert werden sollten, zuvor redigiert und mit verbreiteten Lesarten angereichert wurden." (at p. 183); Wachtel 2005, 27–31 and 35; Wachtel 2009.

586 See also Racine 2004, 281; Metzger-Ehrman 2005⁴, 279: "[I]ts final form [of the Byzantine text] represents a slowly developing tradition, not one that sprang up immediately at one time and place. It was not, in other words, a textual recension created by a single person or community."; Parker 2008, 305–306. On the growing, even if not homogenous, of attestations of Byzantine readings in the manuscripts see Ralston 1992, 123; Wachtel 2009, 7–8.

587 Metzger-Ehrman 2005, 67. See also Ralston 1992, 136: "[…] the uncials, A[/02], W[/032] [in Matthew and Luke 8:13–24:53], and P[/024], should be considered strands of a 'Proto-Byzantine text' which emerged from another pre-existing textual tradition prior to the fourth century and not a hypothetical early Byzantine archetype."

588 Metzger-Ehrman 2005, 80. Schmid (2006, 244) suggests instead the middle of the sixth century.

589 Metzger-Ehrman 2005, 79.

590 Aland-Aland 1989, 122: "Kategorie V", i.e. manuscripts "mit reinem oder überwiegend byzantinischem Text" (at p. 167).

591 Aland-Aland 1989, 122: "Kategorie V", see the preceding footnote. It is a curious coincidence that both P/024 and Q/026, which evidently circulated in Italy in the period before the mid-eighth century, are bound with the Gothic leaves of the *Carolinus*, see above 2.1.4, fn. 208.

592 For the tenacity of the New Testament variants, which may appear also in late witnesses, see Aland-Aland 1989, 79.

593 See Wachtel 1995, 183.

Since the period of the earliest studies of the Gothic text, i.e. the first third of the twentieth century, the opinion concerning the origin and spread of the 'Western' readings has also changed.[594] They circulated widely not only in the west, being attested also in p^{29} (third century), p^{48} (about the end of the third century) and p^{38} (ca. 300).[595] Particularly significant – at least for the textual criticism of the Gothic version – is the consideration that the 'Western' readings which are transmitted also by non-Western witnesses[596] may represent old readings.[597]

The hypothesis of the progressive formation of the Byzantine text opens a different perspective for the evaluation of the mixed character of the Gothic text. It justifies the claim of some scholars of the past century – Jülicher, Lietzmann, Gryson[598] – according to which the non-Byzantine readings of the Gothic version were already attested in its *Vorlage*. The reason for the presence of such readings would lie in the fact that the Byzantine text was not yet established at Wulfila's time. The non-Byzantine readings, or at least many of these, would therefore represent ancient survivals, crystallised in the Gothic text, instead of later, post-Wulfilian changes.

Such a perspective would also explain the low agreement of the Gothic Epistles with the Byzantine text: Wulfila's *Vorlage* offered a text not fully standardised, in which many old, pre-Byzantine readings were still attested. The alternative view to the traditional hypothesis – sustained principally by Kauffmann, Streitberg and Friedrichsen,[599] and clearly bound to the textual criticism of their time and to the known witnesses – is exemplified by the reading of 2 Cor 1:10. The Gothic text transmits *swaleikam dauþum* (gen. plur. = τηλικούτων θανάτων). Friedrichsen explained this variant by arguing that "the secondary origin of the Gothic is almost certainly to be presumed from d[/75] e[/76] Hier. [= Hieronymus] Ambrst. [= Ambrosiaster]."[600] The picture offered by this scholar changes in the light of the modern studies and repertories of variants. The Gothic version agrees indeed not only with the witnesses cited by Friedrichsen, but also

---

594 See also Aland-Aland 1989, 61, 63–64, 78–79.
595 Metzger-Ehrman 2005, 276–277.
596 See above 5.
597 Zuntz 1946, part. 142; Gryson 1990, 27–31; Holmes 2006, 198–200.
598 See above 5.1.
599 See above 5.1. It is to be noted Friedrichsen's (1939, 41) statement, based on Kenyon's study (1937): "The Wulfilian Greek [...] presents the mid-fourth-century stage in the development of the α-text [i.e. the Byzantine text]"; but he seems not to comprehend the implications of this fact for the Gothic textual criticism. Indeed he concluded "and differs very little from the fully developed T.R. [i.e. *Textus Receptus*] of the later period", assuming that the non-Byzantine readings are not Wulfilian.
600 Friedrichsen 1939, 5.

with p⁴⁶, 630, 1611, 2200, syᵖ, syʰ, Chrysostom, Origen¹⁷³⁹ᵐᵍ, Basilᵐˢ.⁶⁰¹ Particularly significant is the agreement with p⁴⁶, which represents an old witness of the Alexandrian text type. According to Zuntz's studies, the readings which occur both in the 'Western' and in Alexandrian witnesses and foremost in p⁴⁶ may be considered ancient readings, ones that later disappeared in the Alexandrian tradition and were preserved instead in the 'Western'.⁶⁰² The possibility of a secondary origin of the Gothic reading, based on Latin influence, loses weight therefore, in favour of its old, Wulfilian, origin. In other words, the reading τηλικούτων θανάτων could already be attested in Wulfila's *Vorlage*.

This explanation applies also to other readings of the Gothic text. The following data are based on a new collation of the Gothic readings with the Greek and Latin.⁶⁰³ The analysis is concentrated on the Gospels of Matthew and John and on the Epistles to the Romans and Galatians. The reasons for these choices vary. An early Byzantine form of the texts of Matthew and John has been transmitted by the quotations of John Chrysostom's homilies.⁶⁰⁴ For the text of John, a broad apparatus of its Greek and Latin witnesses makes the comparison easier.⁶⁰⁵ The Epistle to the Romans has been chosen because the Gothic version is transmitted by two manuscripts, one of which is a bilingual Gothic-Latin, and because a collation of many Greek witnesses is offered in all its passages.⁶⁰⁶ The latter reason is also on the basis of the choice of the Epistle to the Galatians.

6.1 The Gothic Gospels

As has already been seen, about three-fifths of the Gothic Gospels are preserved, mostly in the *Codex Argenteus*. The *Ambros.* C preserves only some verses of Mat-

---

601 Against τηλικούτου θανάτου (with ℵ/01, A/02, B/03, C/04, D/06, F/010, G/012, K/018, L/020, P/025, Ψ/044, 33, 1739ᵗᵉˣᵗ, 𝔐); *tantis periculis* (lat); other variants are attested.
602 Zuntz (1946, 157), speaking about elements common to the earliest eastern and to the western traditions, claimed that they are "a survival from a pre-'Alexandrian' and pre-Western basis, the traces of which, most marked in P⁴⁶, gradually disappear from the later 'Alexandrian' tradition but often reappear in later eastern witnesses, as well as in the West."; see also Holmes 2006.
603 Aland *et al.* 1998–2005; Hodges-Farstad 1985; Houghton *et al.* forthcoming; Jülicher *et al.* 1963–1976; Nestle-Aland²⁸; Swanson 1995–2005; UBS⁴; VLD; Weber *et al.* 1994; Wordsworth-White 1889–1898; www.iohannes.com.
604 Unfortunatly, there are no critical editions of these homelies. The text used in the collation is that of the *Patrologia Graeca*.
605 See www.iohannes.com.
606 See Swanson 1995–2005.

thew, without significant text-critical divergencies.[607] Furthermore, few words of Luke are transmitted by the *Gissensis*.

6.1.1 The Byzantine readings in Matthew and John

The agreement between the Gothic and the Byzantine texts is high, as many biblical scholars have already pointed out.[608] From the analysis of the extant parts of Matthew[609] and John, for instance, the following data emerge:

Gospel	Significant readings[610]	Readings in agreement with the Byzantine text or part of its witnesses[611]
Matthew	116	72 (62%)
John	335	188 (56%)

The readings belonging to the Byzantine tradition were very likely already in Wulfila's *Vorlage*, and therefore they are not problematic from a text-critical point of view. The manuscripts which agree most closely with the Gothic text in supporting the Byzantine readings (or part of these) of Matthew are:

A/02: 94% (17/18)[612]
N/022: 84% (21/25)[613]
W/032: 75% (54/72)

---

607 See above 5.6.
608 See above 5.1.
609 Only the direct transmission of the Gospel of Matthew is here considered, not the citations transmitted by the text of the *Codex Bononiensis*.
610 A 'significant reading' is a Gothic reading that reflects clearly a single Greek reading. All readings which make no lexical or syntactical sense or are likely due to scribal errors, glosses inserted into the text or clear harmonisation inside the Gothic tradition are not considered, nor is the word order in regard to the position of personal, possessive or demonstrative pronouns (because in many cases it seems to be independent from the Greek text, following rules proper to the Gothic language, see above 4.1.2.(1)). Omission or insertion of particles and pronouns are considered when they are attested at least by two other witnesses (or by the Gothic and the *Brixianus* f/10 in the Gospels). The rendering of the proper names is not taken into account either.
611 All decimals have been rounded up or down to the nearest integer.
612 Since this manuscript is heavily mutilated, only 18 passages (out of the 72) are preserved.
613 Since several leaves of this codex are lost, only 25 passages (out of the 72) are preserved.

Θ/038: 75% (54/72)
Chrysostom: 72% (34/47)[614]

The lowest agreement is with:

ℵ/01: 17% (12/72)
B/03: 19% (14/72)
D/05: 22% (16/72)

The high agreement with A/02 and N/022 is of course less relevant (but still significant), because the number of passages available for the statistical analysis is reduced. Thus, the Gothic readings of Matthew are supported very frequently by W/032, Θ/038 and (with the limitations already mentioned) by A/02 and N/022, i.e. witnesses of an early Byzantine text (in this Gospel).[615]

The Greek manuscripts which support the Gothic version of John in its agreement with the Byzantine text (or part of its manuscripts) are:

A/02: 77% (113/146)[616]
Chrysostom: 76% (65/86)[617]
N/022: 62% (74/120)[618]
Θ/038: 60% (112/188)
Ψ/044: 57% (107/188)

The agreement with such manuscripts is not surprising, because their text is considered predominantly Byzantine in John. Also worthy of note is the agreement with the citations of Chrysostom, who transmits an early form of the Byzantine text.

The lowest level of agreement is with manuscripts that represent – to use the traditional classification – the Alexandrian and 'Western' type:

B/03: 9% (17/188)
ℵ/01: 20% (38/188)
W/032: 20% (38/188)
D/05: 30% (57/188)

---

614 It is possible to collate Chrysostom with the Gothic text only in 47 passages (out of the 72).
615 Regarding Θ/038 and its affinity with the early Byzantine witnesses, see Ralston 1992, part. 134.
616 Only 146 passages (out of the 188) are preserved.
617 The significant readings of the Gothic text of John which may be collated with Chrysostom are 86 (out of the 188).
618 Only 120 passages (out of the 188) are preserved.

The agreement of the Gothic readings with the Byzantine text is high, but very far from being complete. This is not a new observation. The turning point in respect to previous positions is how to explain or justify the presence of the non-Byzantine readings in the Gothic text.

6.1.2 The non-Byzantine readings in Matthew and John

Among the non-Byzantine readings of the Gothic text (44/116, i.e. 38% in Matthew; 147/335, i.e. 44% in John), the greatest agreement is with D/05 and/or one or more Latin manuscripts, representative of the 'Western' text.

A preliminary look at these readings permits to divide them into three groups:

1. Readings supported by D/05 and/or one or more Latin manuscripts. This group may be divided in three sub-groups:[619]

A) Readings supported also by many witnesses with which – as already seen – the Gothic text usually agrees, such as A/02, N/022, W/032, Θ/038, Ψ/044 and one or more minuscules. They are 13/116, i.e. 11% of the significant readings in Matthew and 50/335, i.e. 15% of the significant readings in John.

The agreement with A/02 and/or N/022 and/or W/032 (only in Matthew) and/or the citations of Chrysostom (witnesses of the early Byzantine text) and/or Θ/038 and/or Ψ/044 (manuscripts which support the Gothic readings in their agreement with the Byzantine ones)[620] and one or more minuscules would speak in favour of the antiquity of these Gothic readings. The fact that a great part of these readings is attested also in some late Greek manuscripts in minuscule and/or lectionaries supports the hypothesis that they represent old survivals, replaced in the course of the formation of the Byzantine text, but tenaciously retained in some Greek witnesses, besides their crystallisation in the Gothic version.

The agreement of the Gothic text with the Latin tradition might be accidental – each being dependant on a Greek *Vorlage* – and not the result of the Latin influence on Wulfila's version.

---

619 See the Appendices I.1.2.1. and I.2.2.1.
620 See above 6.1.1.

B) Readings supported also by manuscripts typologically different, among them the papyri, ℵ/01, B/03, one or more Byzantine majuscules, as well as isolated minuscules, against the usual witnesses which agree with the Gothic text. They are 4/116 of the significant readings in Matthew, i.e. 3% and 40/335, i.e. 12% of the significant readings in John.

The wide spectrum of their diffusion, which includes different textual traditions, sustains the view that they represent old Wulfilian readings which disappeared during the process of standardisation of the Byzantine text and remained as relics in the Gothic version as well as in some manuscripts of the Byzantine area.

C) Readings supported by 'Western' witnesses alone. It is worth noting that the Gothic readings are not paralleled in always the same Latin manuscript(s). They are 8/116, i.e. 7% of the significant readings in Matthew and 19/335, i.e. 6% of the significant readings in John.

In these cases it is possible both that the 'Western' Greek readings were already in Wulfila's *Vorlage* and that the Gothic version has been changed according to the Latin tradition.

2. Readings not supported by 'Western' witnesses, except the *Codex Brixianus* (f/10).[621] The possibility that they are the result of Latin influence is therefore absent or very low (otherwise one would have to assume that such readings were lost in the remaining Latin tradition). These readings, neither Byzantine nor 'Western', would represent old crystallised survival of the pre-Byzantine readings of Wulfila's *Vorlage*. They are 9/116, i.e. 8% of the significant readings in Matthew and 27/335, i.e. 8% of the significant readings in John.

3. Readings peculiar to the Gothic text, occasionally supported by the *Codex Brixianus* (f/10), against the remaining Greek and Latin tradition. They are 10/116, i.e. 9% of the significant readings in Matthew and 11/335, i.e. 3% of the significant readings in John.

Their origin is unknown. They do not seem to arise from scribal errors, glosses or harmonisation within the Gothic tradition. They may theoretically reflect lost Greek readings.

To summarise, it seems very likely that the variants of Group 2 represent pre-Byzantine readings of Wulfila's *Vorlage*. Furthermore, it is also highly plausible that

---

[621] See Appendix I.1.2.2. and I.2.2.2. On the *Brixianus*, considered the Latin part of a Gothic-Latin bilingual, see above 5.2.

the variants that belong to Group 1 A, supported by manuscripts with which the Gothic usually agree, reflect old readings of the Greek text that lay before the Gothic translator. The readings of Group 1 B, supported by some 'Western' and Alexandrian witnesses as well as isolated Byzantine majuscules and minuscules, may also represent Wulfilian readings that later disappeared in the course of the establishment of the Byzantine text and remained as relics in the Gothic text.

Making a judgement about the readings of Group 1 C is more difficult. The possibility that they have been influenced by Latin version(s) exists. However, the attestations of this group of variants are so random that the assumption of a complete revision of Wulfila's text seems unlikely. It is also possible that both the Gothic and Latin texts may independently go back to a similar Greek *Vorlage* which transmitted 'Western' readings. The origin of Group 3 is not clear. It may well reflect lost Greek readings, but it is impossible to reach a definite conclusion.

6.1.3 Significant textual features

An interesting peculiarity of the *Codex Argenteus* is the 'Western' order of the Gospels, Matthew-John-Luke-Mark. This order is found also in p^{45}, D/05, W/032, X/033, 055, 594, 256, in some Peshitta Syriac manuscripts and in the Latin witnesses.[622] It is not possible to say with confidence whether or not this order is Wulfilian. However, taking into account the claim that this manuscript is part of a Gothic-Latin Gospel book produced in the west,[623] the hypothesis of an adjustment of the text order in agreement with the Latin part and with the western usage is not to be excluded.

Important textual features in the Gospels are the omission of the story of the woman taken in adultery (*pericope adulterae*) in John 7:53–8:11 and the presence of the Long Ending of Mark (16:9–20).

The Gothic text agrees in the lacking of John 7:53–8:11[624] with p^{66}, p^{75}, א/01, B/03, L/019, N/022, T/029, W/032, X/033, Δ/037, Θ/038, Ψ/044, with the minuscules 33, 157, 565, 1241, 1424 and with the Old Latin mss. a/3, f/10, l/11 and q/13. This passage is also not contained in the Sinaitic and Curetonian manuscripts of the Old Syriac and in the best manuscripts of the Peshitta.[625] Furthermore, it is absent in the citations of John Chrysostom. The manuscripts A/02 and C/04 are

---

622 See Parker 1992, 116–118.
623 See above 2.1.1.
624 See Metzger-Ehrman 2005, 319–320; Parker 2008, 342–343.
625 Metzger-Ehrman 2005, 319.

defective at this point, but from the calculation of the available space in the missing leaves it is highly probable that these verses were lacking. The earliest extant manuscript which transmits this passage is D/05, joined by the greater part of the Old Latin witnesses and by the later Byzantine manuscripts. The Gothic version offers then further evidence that in the middle of the fourth century these verses did not yet belong to the Byzantine text tradition, but were added in a later period.

The presence of Mark 16:9–20 in Gothic is particularly noteworthy, since it is attested by Greek manuscripts only from the fifth century onwards (mss. A/02, C/04 and D/05).[626] Theoretically this passage might have been added into the Gothic version at a later date, because the *Codex Argenteus* – which transmits these verses without any mark of suspicion, such as an obelos or asterisk – is dated to the first third of the sixth century. However, there are not stylistic or linguistic grounds for doubting that this passage is part of the original Wulfilian translation. That it is a translation from the Greek emerges from the passage *þairh þos afargaggandeins taiknins* 'through the following signs', which corresponds perfectly to διὰ τῶν ἐπακολουθούντων σημείων, against Lat. *sequentibus signis*. Furthermore, the vocabulary does not diverge from that of the extant Gothic text. The only different lexical item is *farwa* 'shape', 'appearance', 'form' (Mk 16:12) rendering of Gr. μορφή, otherwise translated with -*skaunei* (Phil 2:6: *in gudaskaunein:* ἐν μορφῇ θεοῦ) and *wlits* (Phil 2:7). The Gothic version seems therefore to be the oldest witness to the Long Ending of Mark. From a text-critical point of view, it agrees particularly with 2427, f¹, A/02 and the Byzantine manuscripts.[627]

Another semantically significant variant is the inclusion of *sware* (= εἰκῇ) 'without cause' in Mt 5:22.[628] This variant is transmitted by 1449 manuscripts (vs. twenty-eight Greek manuscripts, including the oldest witnesses of this verse of Matthew, i.e. p⁶⁴, ℵ*/01*, B/03, which omit it). The oldest Greek witnesses which testify to the insertion of this word are W/032, D/05 and ℵ²/01². It was also known to Chrysostom. Furthermore, it is included in the *Vetus Latina* and in the Syriac and Coptic traditions. The presence of this reading in the Gothic text indicates its diffusion in the territory under the influence of Constantinople in the mid-fourth century. The hypothesis of its later insertion into the Gothic tradition (on the basis of the *Vetus Latina*), although theoretically possible, seems not likely, since this variant was already attested in early Byzantine wit-

---

626 Parker 2008, 341–342.
627 See Appendix II.2.
628 On this variant see Parker 2008, 336.

nesses. In many other cases, indeed, the Gothic version offers the oldest witness of a Byzantine variant.[629]

Among the readings cited by Kenyon[630] as typically Byzantine and attested also by the Gothic version, there is Mt 6:1, where the Goth. *armaion* 'compassion', 'almsgiving', 'charity' corresponds to ἐλεημοσύνην (with L/019, W/032, Z/035, Θ/038, f¹³, 33, 𝔐, f/10, k/1, sy^{p.h}, Chrys), against δικαιοσύνην (of ℵ*·²/01*·², B/03, D/05, f¹, 892, lat, sy^s). A Latin influence on the Gothic text here seems to be excluded. Again, the Gothic version is the oldest witness of this reading in the territory under the influence of Constantinople.

Furthermore, the Gothic text reports the doxology in Mt 6:13: *unte þeina ist þiudangardi jah mahts jah wulþus in aiwins. Amen* 'for yours is (the) kingdom, and (the) power, and (the) glory in (the) ages. Amen', which corresponds to ὅτι σοῦ ἐστὶν ἡ βασιλεία καὶ ἡ δύναμις καὶ ἡ δόξα εἰς τοὺς αἰῶνας. Ἀμήν. It is also attested in L/019, W/032, Θ/038, f¹³, 33, 𝔐, f/10, q/13, bo^{mss}, Chrys (in g¹/7, k/1, sy, sa with variations), against the witnesses ℵ/01, B/03, D/05, Z/035, f¹, lat, bo^{mss}, where it is omitted. The scanty attestation of this variant in the Latin tradition – and in two cases out of three it is transmitted by manuscripts connected in some ways with the Gothic text[631] – does not support the idea of a later Gothic modification.

The Gothic text adds the verse Mk 15:28 *jah usfullnoda þata gamelido þata qiþando: jah miþ unsibjaim rahniþs was* 'and the Scripture was fulfilled, which says: and with the transgressors (he) was reckoned' (= καὶ ἐπληρώθη ἡ γραφὴ ἡ λέγουσα καὶ μετὰ ἀνόμων ἐλογίσθη, with L/019, P/024, Θ/038, 083, 0250, f¹, f¹³, 33, 𝔐, lat, sy^{p.h}, bo^{mss} and some lectionaries), against its omission, testified by ℵ/01, A/02, B/03, C/04, D/05, Ψ/044, 157, 2427, d/5, k/1, sy^s, sa, bo^{mss}. The Gothic text is again one of the oldest witnesses to this reading, which is subsequently attested by the Byzantine manuscripts. The hypothesis of a later addition on the basis of the Latin tradition – even if theoretically possible – seems less plausible, given the Byzantine character of this reading.

One interesting variant that diverges from that transmitted by later Byzantine manuscripts is in Mk 1:2: *in Esaïin praufetau* 'in (the) prophet Isaiah', supported by ℵ/01, B/03, L/019, Δ/037, 22, 33, 565, 892, 1241, 2427 (ἐν τῷ Ἡσαΐᾳ τῷ προφήτῃ) or D/05, Θ/038, f¹, 205, 372, 700, 1071, 1243, 2174, 2737 (ἐν Ἡσαΐᾳ τῷ προφήτῃ), and with lat, sy^{p.hmg}, co, Ambrosiaster, against A/02, W/032, f¹³, 𝔐, vg^{ms}, sy^h, bo^{mss} (ἐν τοῖς προφήταις). This reading is more difficult to assess, because it is

---

629 See the Appendix I, *passim*.
630 Kenyon 1937, 199–200.
631 See above 5.2.

also well attested in the Latin tradition, so that the suspicion of later change cannot be eliminated completely. On the other hand, the possibility that the Gothic text retains an old reading is to be seriously considered.

It is not possible to verify the presence of the so-called 'Western non-interpolations' in the Gothic tradition, since the texts of Matthew and Luke are lacunose in those passages. It is, however, worth noting that some readings (Mt 6:15, Mt 9:34, Lk 5:39, Mk 10:2) omitted by D/05 and the most part of the Old Latin witnesses are attested in Gothic.

6.2 The Pauline Epistles

As has already been seen, long portions (about two-thirds) of the Pauline Epistles are preserved, often in two manuscripts:[632] the Epistle to the Romans is transmitted by the bilingual *Carolinus* and by the *Ambros.* A⁺, the remaining Epistles by the *Ambros.* A⁺ and the *Ambros.* B.

6.2.1 The Byzantine readings in Romans and Galatians

The analysis of Romans (6:23–16:24, with lacunae) shows that 57 (47%) out of the 120 significant readings agree with the Byzantine text type (or the majority of the manuscripts of this group).[633] In Galatians (1:1–6:18, with some lacunae) the agreement regards 42 significant readings out of the 82 (51%).[634] As previously noted, the agreement between the Gothic and the Byzantine texts is lower than in the Gospels.

6.2.2 The non-Byzantine readings in Romans and Galatians

The non-Byzantine readings of both the Epistles (63/120, i.e. 53%, in Romans; 40/82, i.e. 49%, in Galatians) may be divided into three groups:

1. Readings supported by 'Western' witnesses (D/06, F/010, G/012, Latin manuscripts, Ambrosiaster):[635]

---

[632] See above 5.6.
[633] See Appendix I.3.1.
[634] See Appendix I.4.1.
[635] See Appendix I.3.2.1 and I.4.2.1.

A) Readings supported by 'Western' and Alexandrian witnesses, with or without the support of other manuscripts, usually close to the Byzantine text.

There are 38/120 (32%) instances in Romans and 15/82 (18%) in Galatians. There is no sufficient reason to claim a Latin origin of such non-Byzantine readings. The agreement between the Gothic text and lectionaries and/or some Byzantine minuscules in the transmission of non-Byzantine readings is of the utmost relevance for sustaining the hypothesis that these readings may be old and did not become part of the Byzantine mainstream. Scholars have pointed out the conservative character of the lectionaries, which tend tenaciously to preserve pre-Byzantine readings.[636]

B) Readings attested only by 'Western' witnesses.

There are 14/120 (12%) instances in Romans and 17/82 (21%) in Galatians. This group is more difficult to assess, because of their isolation in the 'Western' tradition and in the Gothic version. Both possibilities should be taken into account: that these readings were already attested in the Greek *Vorlage*, and that they entered into the Gothic later.

2. Readings not supported by 'Western' witnesses.[637]

There are 7/120 (6%) in Romans and 7/82 (9%) in Galatians. Their Wulfilian origin is very probably, since they are not attested in the 'Western' tradition. It is worth noting that they often agree with readings attested in some Greek minuscules, but not common in Byzantine witnesses. The Gothic version testifies to the fact that these readings are old and already circulated in the mid-fourth century. Some of the agreements of the Gothic text with isolated witnesses may be accidental.

3. Isolated readings[638]

There are 4/120 (3%) in Romans. In some instances, they may reflect Greek readings, lost in the extant tradition; in others, they may be the result of variations inside the Gothic transmission.

4. Double tradition

Worth noting are the different readings of Gal 6:17 (1%) attested in the *Ambros.* A⁺ and the *Ambros.* B. Both readings diverge from the Byzantine text.[639]

---

636 Metzger-Ehrman 2005, 47.
637 See Appendices I.3.2.2 and I.4.2.2.
638 See Appendix I.3.2.3.
639 See above 5.6.

To summarise, the variants of Group 2 very probably represent pre-Byzantine readings of Wulfila's *Vorlage*. It is also possible that the readings belonging to Group 1 A, supported by typologically different manuscripts, reflect old readings of the Greek model.

Assessing the readings of Group 1 B, attested only in the 'Western' witnesses, is difficult. A later Latin influence is possible; however, the 'Western' readings may have already been present in Wulfila's *Vorlage*. The origin of Groups 3 and 4 is not clear.

6.2.3 Significant textual features

The order of the Gothic Epistles is worth noting: Romans, 1 and 2 Corinthians, Ephesians, Galatians, Philippians, Colossians, 1 and 2 Thessalonians, 1 and 2 Timothy, Titus and Philemon (Hebrews, not attested by the Gothic manuscripts, was probably never translated by Wulfila).[640] This order is only found in p^{46}, where, however, Hebrews is included (after Romans).[641]

Among the readings peculiar to the Gothic tradition is the addition of (*Iudaieis*) *wisandans* 'being (Jews)' in Gal 2:15, supported only by p^{46}: (Ἰουδαῖοι) ὄντες. According to Friedrichsen,[642] who did not know the text of the papyrus, this addition is due to the influence of the parallel expression (Gal 2:14: *Iudaius wisands* 'being Jew'). It is, however, also possible that the Gothic reading reflects a rare Greek variant (which in turn may have been influenced by the parallel expression).

The Benediction comes after Rom 16:24, in agreement with D/06, L/020, Ψ/044, 𝔐, ar/61, d/06, vg^{cl}, sy^h, Theodoret.[643] It is possible to argue that the doxology (16:25–27)[644] was placed after 14:23 by calculating the space of the missing

---

[640] The simplest explanation is that he did not translate this epistle because it was rejected by the Homoeans (on this topic, see Ellingworth 1993, 6). A different opinion was expressed by Lietzmann (1919, 218), who postulated that Wulfila used a Greek-Latin *Vorlage*, in which the Epistle to the Hebrews was missing, as in the ancestor of the bilingual 'Western' manuscripts (see Parker 2008, 256).

[641] On the order of the Pauline Epistles see Frede 1973, 122–127; Trobisch 1989, 35–37; Parker 2008, 250–256.

[642] Friedrichsen 1939, 23.

[643] From chapter 16 only the verses 21–24 are preserved, so that it is not possible to know if this Benediction was also transmitted in 16:20.

[644] On the ending of Romans see the bibliographical survey in Parker 2008, 270–274; Schmid 2013.

leaf of the *Codex Carolinus*.⁶⁴⁵ If this was really so, the Gothic version would support the reading of L/020, Ψ/044, 𝔐, vg^mss, sy^h, Chrysostom, Cyril, Theodoret and would therefore be one of the oldest witnesses to this variant.

A very interesting reading was pointed out by Antonio Piras.⁶⁴⁶ He noted that only the Gothic version translates γνήσιε σύζυγε (Phil 4:3) – which in Greek can refer to either a man or a woman – with the feminine form *waliso gajuko*, 'dear (female) companion'. This reflects an ancient textual tradition, witnessed by Clement of Alexandria and Origen, according to which Paul had a wife. Other readings transmitted by the Gothic version, joined only by a few Greek manuscripts, represent further ancient elements of this text.⁶⁴⁷

The analysis of the Gothic-Latin *Carolinus* and particularly of the portion of text which the *Carolinus* has in common with the *Ambros.* A⁺ (Rom 12:17–13:5) is significant for the history of the relationship between the Gothic version and the Latin witnesses. As previously noted, the two manuscripts go back to the same (probably monolingual) ancestor.⁶⁴⁸ It is remarkable that non-Byzantine readings are also attested in the passages transmitted by both the *Carolinus* (with the Latin gue/79) and the *Ambrosianus* A⁺. This fact is important to sustain the hypothesis that the 'Western' readings were already in their common ancestor and very probably already in the Greek *Vorlage:*

12:17 (*Ambros.* A⁺) *ni þatainei* (*Ambros.* A⁺; CC)⁶⁴⁹ *in andwairþja guþis ak jah in andwairþja*: (gue/79) *coram deo sed etiam coram*

in agreement with οὐ μόνον ἐνώπιον τοῦ θεοῦ ἀλλὰ καὶ ἐνώπιον] F/010, G/012, 629 lat, Ambrst; against ἐνώπιον] p⁴⁶, א/01, A*/02*, B/03, D/06, L/020, P/025, Ψ/044, 33, 1739, 𝔐, d/75, sy^p.h, Chrys | *var. lect.*

12:20 (*Ambros.* A⁺; CC) *jabai gredo*: (gue/79) *si esurierit*

in agreement with ἐὰν πεινᾷ] p^46vid, D*/06*, F/010, G/012, Ψ/044, 205, 209, 323, 323, 1646 (+ 26 other Greek witnesses),⁶⁵⁰ it, Ambrst; against ἀλλὰ ἐὰν πεινᾷ] א/01, A/02, B/03, P/025, 6, 81, 330, 365, 630, 1243, 1319, 1506, 1573, 1739, 1881, 2400, ar/61, t/56, vg; ἐὰν οὖν] D¹/06¹, L/020, 𝔐, sy^h

---

645 The doxology was very likely transmitted on the missing leaf between f. 255r (modern numeration), which ends with Rom 14:20, and f. 280r (modern numeration), which begins with Rom 15:3. Indeed, the number of verses usually contained in each leaf of this codex is 8/9, i.e. the missing five entire verses (14:21–15:2) and part of two verses (14:20 and 15:3) plus three verses (doxology).
646 Piras 2010.
647 See Appendices I.3.2.2. and I.4.2.2.
648 See above 2.5.
649 The *Carolinus* begins from *in andwairþja*.
650 Aland et al. 1991, 381.

13:1 (*Ambros.* A⁺; CC) *iþ þo wisandona*: (gue/79) *quae autem sunt*

in agreement with αἱ δὲ οὖσαι] ℵ/01, A/02, B/03, D*/06*, F/010, G/012, 0285ᵛⁱᵈ, 6, 81, 88, 330, 424ᶜ, 1316, 1506, 1573, 1739, 1881, 2400, latt, co, Ambrst; against αἱ δὲ οὖσαι ἐξουσίαι] D¹/06¹, L/020, P/025, Ψ/044, 33, 𝔐, sy, Chrys

13:3 (*Ambros.* A⁺; CC) *godamma waurstwa ak ubilamma*: (gue/79) *bono operi sed malo*

in agreement with τῷ ἀγαθῷ ἔργῳ ἀλλὰ τῷ κακῷ] p⁴⁶, ℵ/01, A/02, B/03, D*/06*, F²/010², G/012, P/025, 0285, 6, 256, 424ᶜ, 630, 1319, 1506, 1573, 1739, 1852, 1881, 2110, 2523, 2685, (latt), co; against τῶν ἀγαθῶν ἔργων ἀλλὰ τῶν κακῶν] D¹/06¹, L/020, Ψ/044, 33, 𝔐, (sy), Chrys, Ambrst

13:5 (*Ambros.* A⁺; CC) *ufhausjaiþ*: (gue/79) *subditi estote*

in agreement with ὑποτάσσεσθε] D/06, F/010, G/012, it, Ambrst; against ἀνάγκη ὑποτάσσεσθαι] ℵ/01, A/02, B/03, P/025, Ψ/044, 048, 33, 1739, 𝔐, ar/61, t/56, (vg), sy, co, Chrys, Ambrstᵐˢˢ | *var. lect.*

Furthermore, the Gothic text (CC) transmits a reading which diverges from its Latin counterpart (gue/79) and the remaining Latin witnesses:

15:11 (CC) *hazjaina*: (gue/79) *magnificate*

The Gothic reading is in agreement with ἐπαινεσάτωσαν] p⁴⁶, ℵ/01, A/02, B/03, C/04, D/06, Ψ/044, 81, 88, 326, 365, 1319, 1505, 1506, 1573, 1739, 1837, 1881, 2495; against ἐπαινέσατε] F/010, G/012, L/020, P/025, 33, 𝔐, latt, sy, Chrys, Ambrst

This reading is particularly significant: it offers evidence that the Gothic text transmitted non-Byzantine readings from its beginning and that the Latin tradition is not responsible for the deviation (at least in this passage).

The non-Byzantine readings of the Gothic text shared both by the *Carolinus* and the *Ambros.* A⁺ have great significance for the history of the Gothic text. They were already in the common ancestor of these two manuscripts and are therefore independent of the influence of the Latin gue/79, which in some passages diverges from the Gothic version. Friedrichsen's statement that "[t]he Gothic substitutes for the original reading that of d[/75]"[651] does not take into account the fact that these variants are occasionally also supported by non-'Western' witnesses and some minuscules. They could therefore have already been present in Wulfila's Greek *Vorlage*; decisive evidence of Latin influence is not to be found.

---

[651] Friedrichsen 1939, 54.

6.3 Conclusions

The theories that see the Byzantine text as the result of a slowly developing tradition, faster in the Gospels than in the Pauline Epistles, offer a new interpretation both of the non-Byzantine readings of the Gothic text and of the different percentage of agreement between the Gothic and the Byzantine texts (higher in the Gospels, lower in the Epistles). The non-Byzantine readings of the Gothic text (or most of them) would represent ancient survivals, later replaced in the course of the development and standardisation of the Byzantine text, rather than the result of post-Wulfilian modifications. Furthermore, the different percentage of agreement between the Gothic and the Byzantine texts reflects the different stage of standardisation and establishment of the Byzantine readings of Wulfila's *Vorlage*. In other words, the non-Byzantine readings of the Gothic Epistles (or the majority of them) are to be interpreted not as innovations but rather as conservative elements, reflecting a mid-fourth century Greek text in which the process of standardisation was still far away.

Also interesting for textual criticism is the fact that the Byzantine readings of the Gothic text represent the earliest evidence of their diffusion in the area under the influence of the Church of Constantinople. Because there is no reason to doubt that the Byzantine readings of the Gothic Bible were already in Wulfila's *Vorlage*, the Gothic version predates their attestation in the oldest surviving Greek witnesses of the early Byzantine text by at least fifty years.[652]

In summary, the following readings may safety be considered Wulfilian:

1. Readings supported by Byzantine manuscripts.[653]

2. Non-Byzantine and non-'Western' readings.[654] These readings, not suspected to be Latinised, represent old crystallised readings, i.e. readings that did not become widespread.

Furthermore, all or part of the non-Byzantine readings supported by typologically different witnesses are probably Wulfilian readings. In other words, the read-

---

[652] Otherwise one should suppose that the non-Byzantine readings of Wulfila's text were later replaced by readings agreeing with the Byzantine ones, when the Goths were in the west (or even earlier). This conjecture, however, seems too artificial. The easiest guess – i.e. that the Byzantine readings were already in Wulfila's *Vorlage* – is to be preferred.
[653] See the Appendices I.1.1., I.2.1., I.3.1. and I.4.1.
[654] See Appendices I.1.2.2., I.2.2.2., I.3.2.2. and I.4.2.2.

ings supported by 'Western' witnesses and by manuscripts of different text types, including one or more manuscripts of the early Byzantine text and other minuscules.[655] The Gothic text may preserve ancient readings that circulated in the Byzantine area.

Doubts remain when the Gothic readings agree only with the Latin witnesses, with or without the support of D/05 (Gospels) D/06 F/010 and G/012 (Epistles).[656] Either they were already present in Wulfila's Greek *Vorlage* or they entered into the Gothic text through unsystematic glosses. Difficult to assess also are the few singular readings.[657]

The genesis and transmission of the Gothic version may be outlined as follows: Wulfila, in his office of *lector*, began to translate orally the (Greek? Latin?) Bible for his people already in the trans-Danubian territory, where he first lived and where Christian communities were present. The translation was completed subsequently, after his settlement in Moesia.

It is likely that the definitive version was provided by a team under Wulfila's supervision, a fact which would explain some divergences in the translation. It is possible that the first stage of the work was an interlinear translation, in order to render the model as faithfully as possible. Wulfila probably used, beside a Greek *Vorlage* which transmitted an early Byzantine text, a Latin translation, in order to better render difficult passages of the Greek. This would justify some similar renderings in the Gothic and Latin versions.

The support of the clergy of Constantinople, with which Wulfila had several contacts, is very likely. He also needed practical aid from experts in creating a scriptorium, where parchment and ink were prepared and where scribes were trained in writing.

The Gothic Bible was in use among groups of Goths who embraced the Homoean creed and perhaps by other Germanic peoples such as the Vandals. Theoderic in particular supported the conservation and the copying of the Gothic text. In the west, it was read and occasionally annotated by readers, who added in the margin different kinds of notes, possibly on the basis of Latin variants. Subsequently, copyists inserted these notes into the text, often without deleting the original reading. The conversion of the Visigoths in Spain to the Nicene faith and the disappearance of the Ostrogothic élites in Italy, following the war with the Byzantines, brought the Gothic culture to an end.

---

655 See Appendices I.1.2.1.(A), I.2.2.1.(A), I.3.2.1.(A) and I.4.2.1.(A).
656 See Appendices I.1.2.1.(C), I.2.2.1.(C), I.3.2.1.(B) and I.4.2.1.(B).
657 See Appendices I.1.2.3., I.2.2.3., I.3.2.3. and I.4.2.3.

Apart from some limitations due to linguistic differences between Gothic and Greek, it is possible to identify the underlying Greek *Vorlage* of the Gothic text, particularly with respect to additions, omissions and, in several cases, word order. The Gothic readings may therefore gain new value for tracing the history of the oldest stage of the Byzantine text.

Appendix I 'Significant readings'

Appendix I offers a list of all significant readings[658] of the Gothic Gospels of Matthew (1.) and John (2.) and of the Pauline Epistles to the Romans (3.) and Galatians (4.).

I.1 The Gospel of Matthew

I.1.1 Byzantine readings
72/116 (62%)

5:22 sware: εἰκῇ] ℵ² D L W Θ f¹ f¹³ 33 𝔐 it sy co Chrys | *om.* p⁶⁴ ℵ* B it^aur vg
5:25 in wiga miþ imma: ἐν τῇ ὁδῷ μετ' αὐτοῦ] Θ 𝔐 lat sy^h sa^mss Chrys | 4 5 1 2 3 ℵ B D L W f¹ f¹³ 33 it sy^s.c.p sa^mss bo^mss
5:27 qiþan ist: ἐρρέθη] ℵ B D W m it sy^s.p.hmg. co | + τοῖς ἀρχαίοις L Θ 33 lat sy^c.h* Chrys
5:30 gadriusai in gaiainnan: βληθῇ εἰς γέενναν] (L) W Θ f¹³ 𝔐 it^f sy^p.h sa Chrys | εἰς γέενναν ἀπέλθῃ ℵ B f¹ 33 (lat) sy^c bo | *var. lect.*
5:31 þan: δέ] ℵ¹ B D L W Θ f¹ f¹³ 33 m latt sa Chrys | *om.* ℵ* 565 sy^s.c.p bo
5:31 þatei: ὅτι] W Θ 𝔐 sy co | *om.* ℵ B D L f¹ f¹³ 700 latt Chrys
5:36 aiþþau swart gataujan: ἢ μέλαιναν ποιῆσαι] 𝔐 sy^h | 3 1 2 ℵ B (L) W (Θ) 33 lat Chrys | *var. lect.*
5:44 þiuþjaiþ þans [...] izwis waila taujiþ þaim hatjandam izwis jah bidjaiþ bi þans usþriutandans izwis: εὐλογεῖτε τοὺς [...] ὑμᾶς καλῶς ποιεῖτε τοῖς μισοῦσιν ὑμᾶς] D^c L W Θ f¹³ 33 𝔐 it^c.d.f.h sy^(p).h bo^mss (Chrys) | *om.* ℵ B f¹ it^k sy^s.c sa bo^mss | *var. lect.*
5:47 frijonds: φίλους] L W Θ 33 𝔐 it^f.h sy^h | ἀδελφούς ℵ B D Z f¹ f¹³ lat sy^c.p co | *var. lect.*
5:47 motarjos: τελῶναι] L W Θ f¹³ 𝔐 it^h sy^p | ἐθνικοί ℵ B D Z f¹ 33 lat sy^c.h co Chrys | *var. lect.*
5:48 in himinam: ἐν τοῖς οὐρανοῖς] (D*) Θ m it sy^s.c.p | οὐράνιος ℵ B D¹ L W Z f¹ f¹³ 33 lat
6:1 *om.* δέ] B D W f¹³ 𝔐 lat sy^c bo^mss Chrys | + δέ ℵ L Z Θ f¹ 33 it^g1 sy^p.h bo
6:1 armaion: ἐλεημοσύνην] L W Z Θ f¹³ 33 𝔐 it^f.k sy^p.h Chrys | δικαιοσύνην ℵ*.² B D f¹ lat sy^s | *var. lect.*
6:4 usgibiþ: ἀποδώσει] ℵ B L Z Θ f¹³ 33 *pm* lat sy^s.c co Chrys | *praem.* αὐτός D W f¹ 565 *pm* it^h.q sy^p.h | *var. lect.*
6:4 in bairhtein: ἐν τῷ φανερῷ] L W Θ 𝔐 it sy^s.p.h Chrys | *om.* ℵ B D Z f¹ f¹³ 33 lat sy^c co | *var. lect.*
6:5 þatei: ὅτι] L W Θ 𝔐 it^f | *om.* ℵ B D Z f¹ f¹³ 33 700 lat sy co Chrys
6:6 in bairhtein: ἐν τῷ φανερῷ] L W Θ f¹³ 33 𝔐 it sy^p.h Chrys | *om.* ℵ B D Z f¹ lat sy^s.c co | *var. lect.*
6:13 unte ... amen: ὅτι ... ἀμήν] L W Θ f¹³ 33 𝔐 it^f.(g1.q) sy (sy^p) sa bo^mss Chrys | *om.* ℵ B D Z f¹ lat bo^mss | *var. lect.*
6:15 missadedins: τὰ παραπτώματα] B L W Θ f¹³ 33 𝔐 it^(b).f.q sy^c.h sa bo^mss | *om.* ℵ D f¹ 892* lat sy^p bo^mss | *var. lect.*
6:16 þatei: ὅτι] L W Θ 33 𝔐 lat | *om.* ℵ B D f¹ f¹³ 565 700 it
6:21 izwar... izwar: ὑμῶν... ὑμῶν] L W Θ f¹³ 33 𝔐 it^f sy | σου... σου ℵ B f¹ lat co

---

658 For a definition of 'significant reading' see above, fn. 610.

6:22 augo þein ainfalþ ist: ὁ ὀφθαλμός σου ἁπλοῦς ᾖ] L Θ f¹ f¹³ 33 𝔐 it Chrys | *5 1 2 3 4* ℵ B W lat
6:25 jah ƕa drigkaiþ: καὶ τί πίητε] L N Θ 𝔐 sy^{p.h} | ἢ τί πίητε B W f¹³ 33 it sa^{mss} bo | *var. lect.*
7:19 all: πᾶν] ℵ B C*^{vid} L W Θ f¹ 𝔪 lat sy^{p.h} bo^{mss} Chrys | + οὖν C¹ L Z 33 it sy^c sa bo^{mss}
7:24 galeiko ina: ὁμοιώσω αὐτόν] C L W 𝔐 it^{f.h.k.q} sy^{c.h} bo | ὁμοιωθήσεται ℵ B Z Θ (f¹) f¹³ 700 lat sy^{p.hmg.} sa Chrys
7:29 *om.* αὐτῶν] C* L 𝔐 it^b | + αὐτῶν ℵ B C² Θ f¹ f¹³ 33 lat sy co | *var. lect.*
8:7 Iesus: ὁ Ἰησοῦς] C L N W Θ f¹ f¹³ 33 𝔐 lat sy^{c.p.h} sa bo^{mss} | *om.* ℵ B it^k sy^s bo
8:10 ni in Israela swalauda galaubein: οὐδὲ ... πίστιν] ℵ C L N Θ f¹³ 33 𝔐 lat sy^{(s).p.h} Chrys | παρ' οὐδενὶ ... Ἰσραήλ B W (f¹) (892) it^{a.(g1).k.q} sy^{c.(hmg.)} co | *var. lect.*
8:13 jah²: καί] C L N Θ f¹ f¹³ 33 𝔐 lat sy^h bo^{ms} Chrys | *om.* ℵ B W it^{a.b.k} sy^{s.c.p} co
8:13 is: αὐτοῦ] C L N W Θ f¹³ 𝔐 sy sa Chrys | *om.* ℵ B f¹ 33 latt bo
8:15 imma: αὐτῷ] ℵ* B C W Θ 𝔪 it^{k.q} sy^{p.h} sa Chrys | αὐτοῖς ℵ¹ L f¹ f¹³ 33 565 lat sy^{s.c} bo | *var. lect.*
8:18 managans hiuhmans: πολλοὺς ὄχλους] ℵ² C L N Θ f¹³ 33 𝔐 lat sy^h Chrys | ὄχλον B sa^{mss} | *var. lect.*
8:21 is: αὐτοῦ] C L N W Θ f¹ f¹³ 33 𝔐 lat sy bo | *om.* ℵ B 33 (it) sa | *var. lect.*
8:25 unsis: ἡμᾶς] L W Θ 𝔐 latt sy sa bo^{mss} Chrys | *om.* ℵ B C f¹ f¹³ 33 bo^{mss}
8:28 Gairgaisaine: Γεργεσηνῶν] ℵ² C³ L W f¹ f¹³ 33 𝔐 bo | Γαδαρηνῶν (ℵ*) B C* Θ sy^{s.p.h} | *var. lect.*
8:29 Iesu: Ἰησοῦ] C³ W Θ f¹³ 𝔐 it sy^{p.h} sa bo^{mss} Chrys | *om.* ℵ B C* L f¹ 33 it^{ff1.k.l} vg sy^s bo^{mss}
8:31 uslaubei uns galeiþan: ἐπίτρεψον ἡμῖν ἀπελθεῖν] C L W f¹³ 𝔐 it^{f.h.q} sy^{p.h} | ἀπόστειλον ἡμᾶς ℵ B Θ f¹ 33 892* lat sy^s co
8:32 hairda sweine: τὴν ἀγέλην τῶν χοίρων] C³ L N W Θ f¹³ 𝔐 it^{f.h} sy^h | τοὺς χοίρους ℵ B C* f¹ 33 lat sy^{s.p} co
9:2 þus frawaurhteis þeinos: σοι αἱ ἁμαρτίαι σου] L N Θ f¹³ 𝔐 lat sy co | *4 2 3* ℵ B C W f¹ 33 Chrys | *var. lect.*
9:4 witands: εἰδώς] B f¹ 565 700 *pm* sy^p sa Chrys | ἰδών ℵ C D L W f¹³ 33 *pm* latt sy^{s.h} bo | *var. lect.*
9:4 jus: ὑμεῖς] L N W Θ f¹³ 𝔐 sy^h sa | *om.* ℵ B C D f¹ 33 bo Chrys
9:5 þus: σοι] L N f¹ f¹³ 33 *pm* it^{aur.b.d} vg | σου ℵ B C D W Θ 565 700 *pm* it^k Chrys | *var. lect.*
9:12 Iesus: Ἰησοῦς] C L N W Θ f¹ f¹³ 33 𝔐 lat sy^{p.h} bo | *om.* ℵ B D it^{a.d} sy^s sa
9:12 im: αὐτοῖς] C³ L N W Θ f¹ f¹³ 33 𝔐 it^{(a).f.h.q} sy^{p.h} bo | *om.* ℵ B C* lat sy^s sa
9:14 filu: πολλά] ℵ² C D L N W Θ f¹ f¹³ 33 𝔐 it^{d.(k)} sy^h sa^{mss} bo Chrys | *om.* ℵ* B | *var. lect.*
9:18 ains qimands: εἷς ἐλθών] (N) 33 𝔪 it^{(d).f} sy^{(s)} Chrys | εἷς προσελθών ℵ¹ B lat | *var. lect.*
9:24 qaþ du im: λέγει αὐτοῖς] C L W Θ 𝔐 it^{f.(g1)} sy | ἔλεγεν ℵ B D f¹ f¹³ 33 lat co Chrys | *var. lect.*
9:27 imma: αὐτῷ] ℵ C L N W Θ f¹ f¹³ 33 𝔐 (lat) sy | *om.* B D it^{d.k} Chrys
9:33 qiþandans: λέγοντες] ℵ B C D L N W 33 𝔪 | + ὅτι Θ sy^s
11:8 wastjom: ἱματίοις] C L N P W Θ f¹ f¹³ 33 𝔐 it^{b.f.h.l} sy co Chrys | *om.* ℵ B D Z lat
11:10 auk: γάρ] C L N P W Θ f¹ f¹³ 33 𝔐 lat sy^{p.h} sa bo^{mss} Chrys | *om.* ℵ B D Z it^{b.g1.k} sy^{s.c} bo^{mss}
11:19 barnam: τέκνων] B² C D L N Θ f¹ 33 𝔐 latt sy^{s.c.hmg.} sa^{mss} Chrys | ἔργων ℵ B* W sy^{p.h} sa^{ms} bo | *var. lect.*
11:20 dugann: ἤρξατο] ℵ B D 33 700 *pm* lat bo | + ὁ Ἰησοῦς C L N W Θ f¹ f¹³ 565 579 *pm* it^{h.(g1)} sy sa (Chrys)
11:23 ushauhida: ὑψωθεῖσα] B² (L) N (f¹³) 33 565 *pm* it^{f.(g1).h.(q)} sy^{s.p.h} Chrys | ὑψωθήσῃ ℵ B* C D W Θ (f¹) lat sy^c co | *var. lect.*
25:41 jus: οἱ] A D W Θ f¹ f¹³ 𝔐 Chrys | *om.* ℵ B L 33
26:65 is: αὐτοῦ] A C W Θ f¹ f¹³ 33 𝔐 it sy^{p.h} | *om.* ℵ B D L Z 700 lat co
26:69 uta sat: ἔξω ἐκάθητο] A C W 𝔐 sy^h | *2 1* ℵ B D L Z Θ f¹ f¹³ 33 latt sy^p | *var. lect.*
26:70 þaim: αὐτῶν] A C* W f¹ 𝔪 Chrys | *om.* ℵ B C² D L Z Θ f¹³ 33 700* | *var. lect.*
26:71 ina: αὐτόν] A C (D) W Θ f¹ f¹³ 𝔐 lat Chrys^a | *om.* ℵ B L Z 33 it^{a..n} Chrys^b

26:71 jah²: καί] A C L W Θ f¹ f¹³ 33 𝔐 latt sy^{p.h} bo Chrys | *om.* ℵ B D sy^s sa
26:75 du sis: αὐτῷ] A C W Θ f¹ f¹³ 𝔐 it^{b.f} sy sa^{ms} bo Chrys^a | *om.* ℵ B D L 0281^{vid} 33 lat sa Chrys^b
27:2 ina: αὐτόν] A (C³) W Θ f¹ f¹³ 𝔐 | *om.* ℵ B C* L 33 latt
27:2 Pauntiau: Ποντίῳ] A C W Θ f¹ f¹³ 𝔐 latt sy^h | *om.* ℵ B L 33 sy^{s.p} co
27:11 du imma: αὐτῷ] A B W Θ f¹ f¹³ 𝔐 lat sy | *om.* ℵ L 33^{vid} 700 it^{a.d} co Chrys
27:16 *om.* Ἰησοῦν] ℵ A B D L W f¹³ 33 𝔐 latt sy^{p.h} co | + Ἰησοῦν Θ f¹ 700* sy^s
27:17 *om.* Ἰησοῦν τόν] ℵ A D L W f¹³ 33 𝔐 latt sy^{p.h} co | + Ἰησοῦν τόν f¹ sy^s | *var. lect.*
27:43 ina: αὐτόν] A D W Θ f¹ f¹³ 𝔐 latt sy^{s.p.h} sa | *om.* ℵ B L 33 | *var. lect.*
27:51 in twa iupaþro und dalaþ: εἰς δύο ἀπὸ ἄνωθεν ἕως κάτω] (ℵ) A C³ W (Θ) f¹ f¹³ 𝔐 (latt) sy^{p.h} | *3 4 5 6 1 2* B C* 33 sa^{mss} bo | *var. lect.*
27:58 þata leik: τὸ σῶμα] A C D W Θ f¹³ 𝔐 latt sy^{p.h} | *om.* ℵ B L f¹ 33 bo | *var. lect.*
27:59 *om.* ἐν] ℵ A C L W f¹ f¹³ 𝔐 it^{g1} vg sa^{mss} | + ἐν B D Θ it vg^{mss} sa^{mss} bo
27:64 binimaina imma: κλέψωσιν αὐτόν] A B C* D W Θ f¹ f¹³ 33 *pm* latt sy^h co Chrys | *praem.* νυκτός C³ L 565 700 *pm* sy^s | *var. lect.*
27:65 qaþ: ἔφη] B L Θ f¹³ 33 700 *pm* lat sy^{s.p.hmg.} sa bo^{mss} | + δέ ℵ A C D W f¹ 565 579 *pm* it^d sy^{h*} bo^{mss}

I.1.2 Non-Byzantine readings
I.1.2.1 Readings supported by 'Western' witnesses
Sub-group A
13/116 (11%)

5:47 þata samo: τὸ αὐτό] ℵ B D W f¹ f¹³ 33 700 it^d sy^p Chrys | οὕτως L (Θ) 𝔪 it^h sy^{c.h} co | *var. lect.*
6:5 bidjaiþ ni sijaiþ: προσεύχησθε οὐκ ἔσεσθε] ℵ² B Z f¹ lat sy^{hmg.} co Chrys | προσεύχῃ οὐκ ἔσῃ (ℵ*) D L W Θ f¹³ 33 𝔐 it^{k.q} sy^{c.p.h}
6:14 ufar himinam: ἐν τοῖς οὐρανοῖς] Θ 700 it sy^{pmss.h} co | οὐράνιος ℵ B D L W Z f¹ f¹³ 33 𝔐 vg
8:2 durinnands: προσελθών] ℵ B Θ f¹ f¹³ 565 700 892* it^k sy^h co | ἐλθών C L W 33 𝔪 lat sy^{c.p} | *var. lect.*
8:25 siponjos is: οἱ μαθηταὶ αὐτοῦ] C* W Θ f¹ it^{b.g1.h} sy | *om.* ℵ B lat sa | *var. lect.*
8:32 so hairda: ἡ ἀγέλη] ℵ B N W Θ f¹ f¹³ 33 latt sy sa | + τῶν χοίρων C³ L 𝔐 bo | *var. lect.*
9:13 frawaurhtans: ἁμαρτωλούς] ℵ B D N W f¹ 33 565 lat sy^{p.h} bo^{mss} | + εἰς μετάνοιαν C L Θ f¹³ 𝔪 it^{c.g1} sy^{s.hmg.} sa bo^{mss} Chrys
9:27 Iesua jainþro: τῷ Ἰησοῦ ἐκεῖθεν] W 713 945 954 it^d | *3 2 1* ℵ B C D L Θ f¹ f¹³ 33 𝔐 Chrys
9:35 unhailja: μαλακίαν] ℵ¹ B C* D N W f¹ 33 565 lat sy co Chrys | + ἐν τῷ λαῷ C³ Θ f¹³ 𝔪 it^{c.g1} vg^{mss} | *var. lect.*
11:2 bi: διά] ℵ B C* D P W Z Θ f¹ 33 it^{d.q} sy^{p.h} sa | δύο C³ L f¹ 𝔐 lat sy^h bo Chrys | *var. lect.*
11:5 jah³: καί] ℵ B D L P W Θ f¹ f¹³ 565 it sy Chrys | *om.* C N 33 𝔐 lat co | *var. lect.*
11:8 þiudane sind: βασιλέων εἰσίν] ℵ² C D L P W Θ 700 f¹ f¹³ 33 latt Chrys | βασιλείων εἰσίν N 𝔪 | *var. lect.*
11:23 galeiþis: καταβήσῃ] B D W latt sy^{s.c} sa | καταβιβασθήσῃ ℵ C L N Θ f¹ f¹³ 33 𝔐 sy^{p.h} bo Chrys | *var. lect.*

Sub-group B
4/116 (3%)

8:3 imma: αὐτοῦ] ℵ B C* f¹ f¹³ 33 it^k sa^mss bo | + ὁ Ἰησοῦς C² L N W Θ 𝔐 (lat) (sy) sa^mss
9:33 swa uskunþ was: οὕτως ἐφάνη] D 33 565 1396 1424 lat sa | *2 1* ℵ B C L N W Θ f¹ f¹³ 𝔐 bo Chrys
10:42 ei: ὅτι] 440 655 it^h sy^s.c.p | *om.* ℵ B C D L P W Z Θ f¹ f¹³ 33 𝔐 lat Chrys
27:54 ist: ἐστιν] C it^f.g1 sy^(s.p) | ἦν (ℵ*²) A (B D) L W Θ f¹ f¹³ 33 𝔐 lat sy^h co

Sub-group C
8/116 (7%)

5:46 þiudo: ἐθνικοί] ethnici it^ff1 | τελῶναι *rell.*
6:25 wastjom: τῶν ἐνδυμάτων] uestimenta it^q | τοῦ ἐνδύματος *rell.*
8:5 afaruh þan þata: μετὰ δὲ ταῦτα] post haec autem it (sy^c) | *om.* ℵ B C* L N W Θ Z f¹ f¹³ 33 𝔐 lat Chrys | *var. lect.*
8:26 Iesus: ὁ Ἰησοῦς] iesus it^aur.b.c.ff1.h vg^mss sy^s.p | *om. rell.*
10:29 inuh attins izwaris wiljan: ἄνευ τοῦ πατρὸς ὑμῶν βουλῆς] sine patris uestri uoluntate it^aur | sine uoluntate patris uestri it co | ἄνευ τοῦ πατρὸς ὑμῶν *rell.*
10:42 kaldis watins þatainei: ψυχροῦ ὕδατος μόνον] *cf.* aquae frigidae tantum lat co | ὕδατος ψυχροῦ D it^d sy^s.c | ψυχροῦ μόνον *rell.*
27:65 wardjans: φυλακάς] D* it sy^p.h | κουστωδίαν *rell.*
27:65 -uh: καί] et it^f.r1 sa | *om. rell.*

I.1.2.2 Readings not supported by 'Western' witnesses
9/116 (8%)

5:31 afstassais bokos: ἀποστασίου βιβλίον] Chrys | βιβλίον ἀποστασίου Dt. 24, 1 latt | ἀποστάσιον *rell.*
5:44 usþriutandans: ἐπηρεαζόντων] 047 156 160 233 Chrys | διωκόντων ℵ B f¹ it^k sy^s.c sa bo^mss | *var. lect.*
6:24 unte: εἰ] sic ℵ L Σ 543 1675 | ἢ B W Θ f¹ f¹³ 33 𝔐 latt sy co Chrys
8:9 habands uf waldufnja meinamma: ἔχων ὑπὸ τῇ ἐξουσίᾳ μου] habens sub potestatem meam it^f sy^pal | ὑπὸ ἐξουσίαν ἔχων ὑπ' ἐμαυτόν *rell.*
9:14 om. αὐτῷ] X 478 1689 sy^s | + αὐτῷ ℵ B C D L N W Θ f¹ f¹³ 33 𝔐 latt sy^p.h co
9:15 ƕeilos: χρόνον] 66 241 252 479 480 485 517 1278 1424 | *om.* ℵ B C D L N W Θ f¹ f¹³ 33 m
10:23 ei: ὅτι] C* 245 | *om.* ℵ B D L N W Θ f¹ f¹³ 33 𝔐 Chrys
27:45 warþ riqis: ἐγένετο σκότος] U W Δ sy | *2 1* ℵ A B D L Θ f¹ f¹³ 33 𝔐 latt co Chrys
27:49 nasjan: σῶσαι] ℵ* Θ itf syp.h co | σώσων ℵ2 A B C L (W) 33 f¹ f¹³ 𝔐 it^aur.ff1.g1 vg | *var. lect.*

I.1.2.3 Isolated readings
10/116 (9%)

5:44 þiuþjaiþ þans wrikandans izwis: εὐλογεῖτε τοὺς διώκοντας ὑμᾶς] Goth | εὐλογεῖτε τοὺς καταρωμένους ὑμᾶς D^c L W Θ f^{13} 33 𝔐 it$^{c.d.f.h}$ sy$^{(p).h}$ bo^{mss} (Chrys) | *var. lect.*
5:46 (frijondans izwis) ainans: (ἀγαπῶντας ὑμᾶς) μόνον] Goth | *om. rell.*
6:24 ufhauseiþ: ὑπακούσει] obediet it^f | ἀνθέξεται *rell.*
8:18 siponjans: τοὺς μαθητάς] Goth | discipulos suos it$^{a.aur.b.c.g1.q}$ vg^{ms} | discipulis suis it$^{h.l}$ vg^{ms} sy^c | *om. rell.*
8:33 bi: κατά] Goth | τὰ κατά 118 209 | καὶ τά ℵ B C L N W Θ f^1 f^{13} 33 𝔐 latt sy co
9:8 ohtedun sildaleikjandans: ἐφοβήθησαν θαυμάσαντες] admirantes timuerunt it^f | ἐφοβήθησαν καὶ ἐθαύμασαν Diat | *var. lect.*
10:28 (leika) þatainei: (τὸ σῶμα) μόνον] Goth | *om. rell.*
11:23 izwis: ὑμῖν] Goth | σοί *rell.*
27:15 ƕarjoh] *cf* sy$^{s.p.h}$ | *om. rell.*
27:16 *om.* λεγόμενον] Goth | + λεγόμενον *rell.*

I.2 The Gospel of John

I.2.1 Byzantine readings
188/335 (56%)

5:36 ik: ἐγώ] Θ Ψ f^{13} 𝔪 lat | *om.* p^{66} ℵ A B D L N W f^1 33 it
6:2 jah laistida: καί ἠκολούθει] A Θ Ψ 𝔐 it$^{f.q}$ vg sy^h Chrys^a | ἠκολούθει δέ p$^{66.75vid}$ ℵ B (D) L N W f^1 f^{13} 33 565 579 it sa^{mss} bo^{mss} Chrys^b | *var. lect.*
6:9 ains: ἕν] A Θ 𝔪 lat sy$^{s.p.h}$ | *om.* p$^{28.66.75}$ ℵ B D L N W Ψ 565 Chrys
6:14 Iesus: ὁ Ἰησοῦς] A L N Θ Ψ f^1 f^{13} (1424) 33 𝔐 it$^{f.ff2.q}$ sy$^{p.h}$ (bo) | *om.* ℵ B D W lat sy$^{s.c}$ co | *var. lect.*
6:15 ina: αὐτόν] D Θ Ψ f^{13} 𝔐 (lat) sy Chrys | *om.* p^{75} ℵ A B L N* W 565 579 33 | *var. lect.*
6:15 aftra: πάλιν] p^{75} ℵ A B D L N Θ *pm* lat sy^c | *om.* W Ψ *pm* Chrys
6:21 skip warþ: τὸ πλοῖον ἐγένετο] ℵ (D) Θ 𝔐 it$^{a.f.ff2}$ | *3 1 2* p^{75} A B L N W Ψ f^1 f^{13} 33 565 579 lat
6:40 þis sandjandins mik: τοῦ πέμψαντός με] A 𝔪 Chrys | πατρός μου p^{75} ℵ B C D L N W Θ 565 it | *var. lect.*
6:42 sa: οὗτος] A 𝔐 | *om.* p$^{66.75}$ B C D L W Θ f^1 33 Chrys | *var. lect.*
6:43 þan: οὖν] ℵ A D N W Θ Ψ 𝔐 lat sy^h | *om.* p$^{66.75}$ B C L f^{13} 33 it^e
6:45 nu: οὖν] A Θ Ψ f^1 𝔐 it^q sy$^{c.p.h}$ | *om.* p$^{66.75}$ ℵ B C D L N W f^{13} 33 579 lat sy^s Chrys
6:47 du mis: εἰς ἐμέ] A C^2 D N Ψ f^1 f^{13} 33 𝔐 lat sy$^{p.h}$ co Chrys^a | *om.* p$^{66.75vid}$ ℵ B C* L W Θ Chrys^b | *var. lect.*
6:49 manna in auþidai: τὸ μάννα ἐν τῇ ἐρήμῳ] p^{66} ℵ A L Ψ f^1 f^{13} 33 𝔐 it^q sy^h | *3 4 5 1 2* B C W Θ it$^{(aur).c.ff2}$ vg Chrys | *var. lect.*
6:51 þatei ik giba: ἣν ἐγὼ δώσω ὑπέρ] Θ f^1 f^{13} 𝔐 it$^{f.q}$ sy$^{p.h}$ bo Chrys | *om.* p$^{66.75}$ (ℵ) B C D L W Ψ 33 579 lat sy$^{s.c}$ sa
6:55 bi sunjai... bi sunjai: ἀληθῶς... ἀληθῶς] p^{66}* (D) Θ 𝔪 lat sy | ἀληθής... ἀληθής p$^{66(c).75}$ ℵ^1 B C L W Ψ f^1 565 579 it^q co Chrys

6:58 izwarai manna: ὑμῶν τὸ μάννα] N (Θ) Ψ f¹ f¹³ 𝔐 lat sy^{p.h} Chrys | om. p^{66.75} ℵ B C L W 33 bo^{mss} | var. lect.
6:65 meinamma: μου] C³ N Ψ f¹ f¹³ 33 𝔐 lat sy^{p.h} sa^{mss} Chrys | om. p^{66} ℵ B C* D L W Θ it sy^{s.c} sa^{mss} bo
6:66 galiþun siponje is: ἀπῆλθον τῶν μαθητῶν αὐτοῦ] 𝔪 it^q | 2 3 4 1 p^{66.75} B C D L N W Θ Ψ Chrys (lat)
6:69 Xristus sunus gudis libandins: ὁ Χριστὸς ὁ υἱὸς τοῦ θεοῦ τοῦ ζῶντος] N Ψ f¹³ 𝔐 it^{f*.ff2.q.r1} sy^{p.h} bo^{mss} Chrys | ὁ ἅγιος τοῦ θεοῦ p^{75} ℵ B C* D L W it^d sa^{ms} | var. lect.
6:70 Iesus: ὁ Ἰησοῦς] p^{(66).75} B C L W Θ Ψ f¹ f¹³ 33 pm it^{f.q} vg | om. pm it sy^s | var. lect.
6:71 wisands: ὤν] p^{66} ℵ C² N W Θ Ψ f¹ f¹³ 33 𝔐 lat sy^h | om. p^{75} B C* D L it^d
7:1 jah hvarboda Iesus afar þata: καὶ περιεπάτει ὁ Ἰησοῦς μετὰ ταῦτα] 𝔪 it^q Chrys^a | 1 5 6 2 3 4 ℵ¹ C* L Θ f¹ f¹³ 33 565 lat | var. lect.
7:4 in analaugnein hva: ἐν κρυπτῷ τι] p^{66} D W Θ Ψ f¹³ 33 𝔐 lat sy^h Chrys | 3 1 2 p^{75} ℵ B L N | var. lect.
7:8 þo: ταύτην] ℵ* f¹³ 33 𝔪 lat | om. p^{66.75} ℵ^c B D L N W Θ Ψ f¹ it^b Chrys | var. lect.
7:8 ni nauh: οὔπω] p^{66.75} B L N W Θ Ψ f¹ f¹³ 33 𝔐 it^{f.q} sy^{p.h} sa bo^{mss} | οὐκ ℵ D lat sy^{s.c} bo^{mss} Chrys
7:9 du im: αὐτοῖς] p^{75} B D¹ Θ Ψ f¹³ 33 𝔪 it^{f.q.r1} sy^h Chrys^a | om. p^{66} ℵ D* L N W f¹ 565 lat co Chrys^b
7:10 þanuh jah is galaiþ in þo dulþ: τότε καὶ αὐτὸς ἀνέβη εἰς τὴν ἑορτήν] D Θ f¹ f¹³ 𝔐 lat sy^{(s).c.h} Chrys^a | 5 6 7 1 2 3 4 p^{66.75} ℵ B L N W Ψ 33 it^a sy^p | var. lect.
7:10 swe: ὡς] p^{66.75vid} B L N W Θ Ψ f¹ f¹³ 𝔐 lat sy^{p.h} bo Chrys^a | om. ℵ D it sy^{s.c} sa bo^{mss} Chrys^b
7:12 om. δέ (ἔλεγον)] p^{66} ℵ D L Ψ 𝔐 it^{b.e.q.r1} bo^{mss} | + δέ p^{75vid} B N W Θ f¹ f¹³ 33 565 lat sy^h sa bo^{mss} | var. lect.
7:15 jah sildaleikidedun: καὶ ἐθαύμαζον] N Ψ f¹³ 𝔐 it^f vg | ἐθαύμαζον οὖν p^{66.75} ℵ B D L W Θ f¹ 33 it | var. lect.
7:20 jah qeþun: καὶ εἶπεν] D N Θ Ψ f¹ f¹³ 𝔐 latt sy^{p.(h)} | om. p^{66.75} ℵ B L W 33 co
7:26 bi sunjai: ἀληθῶς] 𝔪 it^{f.q} Chrys^a | om. p^{66.75} ℵ B D L N W Θ Ψ f¹ f¹³ 33 lat Chrys^b
7:31 iþ managai þizos manageins: πολλοὶ δὲ ἐκ τοῦ ὄχλου] Ψ 𝔪 it^q (Chrys) | 3 4 5 2 1 p^{75} B L N f¹ lat | var. lect.
7:31 taiknins: σημεῖα] p^{66.75} ℵ B L N W Θ f¹ f¹³ 33 pm Chrys | + τούτων pm | var. lect.
7:32 andbahtans þai Fareisaieis jah þai auhumistans: ὑπηρέτας οἱ Φαρισαῖοι καὶ οἱ ἀρχιερεῖς] 𝔪 it^{a.q.r1} sy^h | 5 6 4 2 3 1 p^{75} B L N W Θ Ψ f¹³ 33 565 lat (co) | var. lect.
7:33 leitila hveila: μικρὸν χρόνον] (D) N Ψ f¹ 33 𝔐 (lat) Chrys | 2 1 p^{66.75} ℵ B L W Θ f¹³ it^{(e).l.q}
7:34 om. με] p^{66} ℵ D L W Θ Ψ f¹ f¹³ 33 𝔐 latt Chrys | + με p^{75} B N 565 sy
7:36 om. με] p^{66} ℵ D L N W Θ Ψ f¹³ 33 𝔐 lat | + με p^{75} B f¹ 565 vg^{ms} sy
7:40 managai þan þizos manageins: πολλοὶ οὖν ἐκ τοῦ ὄχλου] N (Θ) Ψ 0105 f¹³ 33 𝔐 it^{(f).q} sy^{(p).h} | ἐκ τοῦ ὄχλου οὖν p^{66c.75} ℵ B D L W f¹ 565 lat (co) | var. lect.
7:42 Xristus qimiþ: ὁ Χριστὸς ἔρχεται] p^{66} ℵ (D) N Θ f¹ f¹³ 𝔐 it | 3 1 2 p^{75} B L W Ψ 33 it^{aur.c} vg Chrys
7:43 in þizai managein warþ: ἐν τῷ ὄχλῳ ἐγένετο] f¹ f¹³ 𝔐 it^q | 4 1 2 3 p^{66.75} ℵ B D L N W Θ Ψ 33 lat
7:52 praufetus us Galeilaia: προφήτης ἐκ τῆς Γαλιλαίας] p^{66c} ℵ D W Θ f¹ f¹³ 33 𝔐 lat | 2 3 4 1 p^{(66*).75vid} B L N Ψ Chrys^a
8:12 du im Iesus rodida: αὐτοῖς ὁ Ἰησοῦς ἐλάλησεν] 𝔪 | 1 4 2 3 p^{66} ℵ* (B) L W Θ f¹³ it^{c.(q)} | var. lect.
8:14 aiþþau: ἤ] p^{39.66.75c} B D N Ψ f¹ pm lat sy^h sa bo | καί p^{75*} ℵ L W Θ f¹³ pm it bo^{mss} | var. lect.
8:21 Iesus: (αὐτοῖς) ὁ Ἰησοῦς] p^{66c} N Θ Ψ f¹ f¹³ 33 𝔐 lat sy sa bo | om. p^{39vid.66*.75} ℵ B D L W it^{b.d.(e)}
8:25 jah¹: καί] N Ψ f¹³ 𝔐 | om. p^{66.75} ℵ B D L W Θ f¹ 33 565 latt
8:28 im: αὐτοῖς] p^{66(c).75} ℵ D N Θ Ψ f¹³ 33 𝔐 lat sy co | om. p^{66*} B L W f¹ 565 it^a
8:28 meins: μου] B f¹ 𝔐 it^{f.q} sy^{p.h} co Chrys | om. p^{66.75} ℵ D L N T (W) Θ Ψ f¹³ 579 lat sy^s bo^{mss}
8:29 atta: ὁ πατήρ] N 𝔐 it^{f.q} sy^{(p).h} (bo^{mss}) Chrys | om. p^{66.75} ℵ B D L W Θ Ψ f¹ f¹³ 565 579 33 lat sy^s co
8:38 ik þatei: ἐγὼ ὅ] Ψ (f¹) 𝔐 lat | ἅ ἐγώ p^{66.75} ℵ B C W 565 Chrys | var. lect.
8:38 meinamma: μου] ℵ N Θ Ψ f¹ f¹³ 𝔐 it sy Chrys | om. p^{66.75} B C L it^l vg | var. lect.

8:39 weseiþ: ἦτε] C N W Θ Ψ f¹ f¹³ 𝔐 it sy^{p.h} | ἐστε p^{66.75} ℵ B D L it^{d.ff2} vg sy^s
8:41 þanuh: οὖν] p^{66.75} C D N Θ Ψ f¹³ 33 𝔐 it^{aur.(d).f} vg sy^{h**} | om. ℵ B L W f¹ it sy^{s.p} co
8:48 þan: οὖν] Ψ 𝔐 lat sy^h Chrys | om. p^{66.75} ℵ B C D L N W Θ f¹ f¹³ 33 565 579
8:52 þanuh: οὖν] p^{75} D L N Ψ f¹ f¹³ 33 𝔐 lat sy^h sa^{mss} | om. p^{66} ℵ B C W Θ 579 it sy^{s.p} sa^{mss} bo
8:54 unsar: ἡμῶν] p^{75} A B² C N W Θ f¹ f¹³ 33 𝔪 lat sy sa bo^{mss} | ὑμῶν ℵ B* D F Ψ 700 it vg^{cl} bo^{ms} Chrys
8:58 qaþ: εἶπεν] p^{66.75} A B C L W Θ Ψ 33 pm lat | + οὖν D N f¹ f¹³ pm it^d | var. lect.
8:59 usleiþands þairh midjans ins jah ƕarboda swa: διελθὼν διὰ μέσου αὐτῶν καὶ παρῆγεν οὕτως] A Θ^c f¹ f¹³ 𝔐 it^{(f).q} vg^{ms} | om. p^{66.75} ℵ* B D W Θ* lat sy^s sa bo^{ms} | var. lect.
9:4 ik: ἐμέ] ℵ¹ A C N Θ Ψ f¹ f¹³ 33 𝔐 lat sy bo^{mss} Chrys | ἡμᾶς p^{66.75} ℵ* B (D) L W it^d sa bo^{ms} | var. lect.
9:9 -h þatei: δὲ ὅτι (ὅμοιος)] A D Ψ f¹³ it^{(d).f.l.(δ)} sy^h | ἔλεγον οὐχί ἀλλά (ὅμοιος) p^{66.75} B C W it^{b.r1} sy^p | var. lect.
9:10 om. οὖν] p^{75} A B W f¹ f¹³ 33 𝔐 lat sy^{s.p} sa^{mss} bo | + οὖν p^{66} ℵ C D L N Θ Ψ it sy^{h**} sa^{mss}
9:11 jah qaþ manna: καὶ εἶπεν ἄνθρωπος] A N Ψ f¹³ 𝔐 it (bo) | om. p^{66.(75)} ℵ B (C) (D) L (W) (Θ) f¹ 33 (565) lat sa | var. lect.
9:11 om. ὅτι] p^{75} A D N W Θ Ψ f¹ f¹³ 33 𝔐 latt Chrys | + ὅτι p^{66} ℵ B L
9:12 þan: οὖν] p^{66} D N Θ Ψ f¹³ 𝔐 (it) | καί p^{75} ℵ B L f¹ 33 W 565 it^l | var. lect.
9:14 þan: ὅτε] A D N Θ Ψ f¹ f¹³ 𝔐 it^{d.f.(l).q} vg sy^{p.h} | ἐν ᾗ ἡμέρα p^{66.75} ℵ B L W 33 it | var. lect.
9:16 sa manna nist fram guda: οὗτος ὁ ἄνθρωπος οὐκ ἔστιν παρὰ θεοῦ] A 𝔪 f¹ f¹³ it^{a.(b).f.q} (Chrys) | 4 5 1 6 7 2 3 p^{66.75} ℵ B D L N W Θ Ψ 33 579 lat
9:16 om. δέ] p^{66.75} A L N Θ Ψ 𝔐 lat sy^h bo^{ms} Chrys | + δέ ℵ B D W f¹ f¹³ 565 it^c sy^{s.p} co
9:19 nu saiƕiþ: ἄρτι βλέπει] p^{66} A N Ψ f¹ f¹³ 𝔐 (lat) sy^{p.h} | 2 1 p^{75} ℵ B D L W Θ 33 (it) sy^s Chrys^b | var. lect.
9:20 þan im: δὲ αὐτοῖς] A N Ψ 𝔪 it^q sy^h | οὖν p^{66.75} ℵ B | var. lect.
9:21 silba uswahsans ist ina fraihniþ: αὐτὸς ἡλικίαν ἔχει αὐτὸν ἐρωτήσατε] A N f¹³ 𝔐 it^{l.q} (sy) | 4 5 2 3 p^{66} ℵ² B (D) L Θ Ψ f¹ 33 579 lat bo | var. lect.
9:23 fraihniþ: ἐρωτήσατε] A L N Θ Ψ f¹ f¹³ 33 𝔐 | ἐπερωτήσατε p^{66.75} ℵ B W | var. lect.
9:24 anþaramma sinþa þana mannan: ἐκ δευτέρου τὸν ἄνθρωπον] A N Ψ f¹ f¹³ 𝔐 it^{a.f.r1} vg | 3 4 1 2 p^{66.75} ℵ B L W Θ 33 (it) | var. lect.
9:26 aftra: πάλιν] p^{66} ℵ² A L N Θ Ψ f¹ f¹³ 33 𝔐 it^{f.q} sy^{p.h} | om. p^{75} ℵ* B D W 579 lat sy^s co
9:28 is siponeis: εἶ μαθητής] f¹³ 𝔐 it Chrys^a | 2 1 p^{75} ℵ A B N W Ψ f¹ 33 579 Chrys^b / var. lect.
9:31 þan: δέ] A N W Ψ f¹³ 𝔐 vg sy^{p.h} Chrys | om. p^{66.75} ℵ B D L Θ 33 it | var. lect.
9:35 du imma: αὐτῷ] p^{66} ℵ² A L Θ Ψ f¹ f¹³ 33 𝔐 lat sy co Chrys | om. p^{75} ℵ* B D W it^e bo^{ms}
9:35 gudis: θεοῦ] A L Θ Ψ f¹ f¹³ 33 𝔐 lat sy^{p.h} bo Chrys | ἀνθρώπου p^{66.75} ℵ B D W sy^s co
9:37 þan: δέ] A L f¹ f¹³ 𝔐 | om. p^{66.75} (ℵ) B (D) W Θ Ψ 33 it^{b.e} sy | var. lect.
9:40 jah¹: καί] A f¹³ 𝔐 lat sy^{p.h} | om. p^{66.75} ℵ B L W Θ Ψ 33 579 co
9:40 þai wisandans miþ imma oἱ ὄντες μετ' αὐτοῦ] A f¹³ 𝔐 | 1 3 4 2 p^{66.75} ℵ B D L W Θ Ψ 565 579 f¹ 33 (latt) Chrys
9:41 eiþan: ἢ οὖν] A f¹³ 𝔐 it^{(a).j.l.r1} sy^h | om. p^{66} ℵ * B Θ Ψ 565 (579) lat (sy^p) | var. lect.
10:4 jah¹: καί] A D f¹³ 𝔐 lat | om. p^{66.75} ℵ B L W Θ Ψ f¹ 33 565 it | var. lect.
10:7 du im: αὐτοῖς] D L Θ Ψ 𝔪 it^{a.d} sy co | om. p^{6vid.75} B | var. lect.
10:8 om. πρὸ ἐμοῦ] p^{45vid.75} ℵ* pm lat sy^{s.p} sa Chrys | + πρὸ ἐμοῦ p^{66} ℵ² A B D L W Ψ f¹³ 33 pm sy^{h**} | var. lect.
10:12 þo lamba: τὰ πρόβατα] A Ψ f¹³ 𝔐 lat sy^{p.h} | om. p^{44vid.45.66.75} ℵ B D L W Θ 33 565 it^{d.} sy^s co
10:13 iþ sa asneis afþliuhiþ: ὁ δὲ μισθωτὸς φεύγει] A^c Ψ f¹³ 𝔐 lat sy^{p.h} | om. p^{44vid.45.66.75} ℵ A*^{vid} B D L (W) Θ 33 (579) it^{d.e} co | var. lect.
10:19 þanuh οὖν] p^{66} A D Θ Ψ f¹ f¹³ 𝔐 sy^h bo Chrys | om. p^{75} ℵ B L W 579 lat sy^{s.p}

10:22 þan: δέ] p⁶⁶* ℵ A D Θ f¹³ 𝔐 lat sy^{p.h} Chrys | τότε p^{66(c).75} B L W Ψ 33 579 it^e sa^{mss} bo^{mss} | *var. lect.*
10:22 jah: καί] A f¹³ 𝔐 lat sy bo^{mss} Chrys / *om.* p^{66.75} ℵ B D L W Θ Ψ 33 565 579 it^{ff2.r1} co | *var. lect.*
10:26 unte ni: οὐ γάρ] A 𝔐 it^{a.c.e} | ὅτι οὐκ p^{66.75} ℵ B D L W Θ Ψ f¹ f¹³ 33 lat
10:26 swaswe qaþ izwis: καθὼς εἶπον ὑμῖν] A D Ψ f¹ f¹³ 𝔐 it sy bo^{mss} | *om.* p^{66(c).75} ℵ B L W Θ 33 it^{aur.c} vg sa bo^{mss} | *var. lect.*
10:28 libain aiweinon giba im: ζωὴν αἰώνιον δίδωμι αὐτοῖς] p⁶⁶* A D Θ Ψ f¹ f¹³ 𝔐 Chrys | *3 4 1 2* p^{66c} p^{75} ℵ B L W 33 | *var. lect.*
10:29 meinis: μου] A D W Θ Ψ f¹ f¹³ 33 𝔐 latt sy^{p.h} sa bo Chrys | *om.* p^{66.75vid} ℵ B L sy^s | *var. lect.*
10:32 goda waurstwa: καλὰ ἔργα (ἔδειξα ὑμῖν)] p⁶⁶ D L f¹³ 𝔪 it^d | *2 1* p^{45vid} ℵ A (Θ) Ψ f¹ 33 565 lat | *var. lect.*
10:32 meinamma: μου] p⁶⁶ ℵ² A L W Ψ f¹ f¹³ 33 𝔐 lat sy^{p.h} sa bo | *om.* p^{45vid} ℵ* B D Θ it^{d.e} sy^s
10:34 *om.* ὅτι] A f¹ f¹³ 𝔐 it^f | + ὅτι p^{66.75} ℵ B D L W Θ Ψ 33 579 (lat)
10:38 galaubjaiþ: πιστεύσητε] A Ψ f¹³ 𝔐 it^{aur.f.ff2c} vg sy^{p.h} Chrys | γινώσκητε p^{45.66.75} B L (W) Θ 33 565 it^{r1vid} co | *var. lect.*
10:38 in imma: ἐν αὐτῷ] p⁴⁵ A Θ Ψ f¹ f¹³ 𝔐 it sy^h sa^{mss} | ἐν τῷ πατρί p^{66.75} ℵ B D L W 33 lat sy^{s.(p).hmg} (sa^{mss} bo) | *var. lect.*
10:42 galaubidedun managai du imma jainar: ἐπίστευσαν πολλοὶ εἰς αὐτὸν ἐκεῖ] A Θ f¹³ sy^h 𝔪 | *2 1 3 4 5* p^{66.75} ℵ B D L (W) Ψ 33. 565 579 vg^{ms} | *var. lect.*
11:9 sind ƕeilos: εἰσιν ὧραί] Θ *pm* | *2 1* p⁶⁶ ℵ A B C L W Ψ f¹ f¹³ 33 *pm* latt | *var. lect.*
11:12 siponjos is: μαθηταὶ αὐτοῦ] C^c L Ψ f¹ 𝔪 it^{e.f} vg | μαθηταὶ αὐτῷ p^{66.75} B C* Θ f¹³ 33 it^{b.r1} | *var. lect.*
11:19 jah¹: καί] A Ψ f¹³ 𝔐 it^f | δέ p^{45vid.66.75} ℵ B C D L W Θ f¹ 33 lat
11:19 bi: τὰς περί] p^{45vid} A C² Θ Ψ f¹ f¹³ 𝔐 | πρὸς τήν p^{66.75vid} ℵ B C* L W 33
11:19 izo: αὐτῶν] A C Ψ f¹ 33 𝔐 lat | *om.* p^{45.66.75} ℵ B D L W Θ it^{d.ff2*.l}
11:44 jah¹: καί] A C³ W Θ Ψ p^{1.13} 33 𝔐 latt sy^{p.h} | *om.* p^{45vid.66.75} B C* L Ψ | *var. lect.*
11:44 *om.* αὐτόν] ℵ A C² D W Ψ f¹ f¹³ 𝔐 lat sy | + αὐτόν p^{45.59vid.66.75} B C* L Θ 33 579 it^{ff2}
12:1 sa dauþa: ὁ τεθνηκώς] p⁶⁶ A D Θ Ψ f¹ f¹³ 𝔐 it^{b.d.f.ff2} vg sy^s bo | *om.* ℵ B L W it sy^p sa Chrys
12:4 ains þize siponje is Judas Seimonis sa Iskariotes: εἷς ἐκ τῶν μαθητῶν αὐτοῦ Ἰούδας Σίμωνος ὁ Ἰσκαριώτης] A Θ (Ψ) f¹³ 𝔐 (it) sy^h (bo) | *6 8 9 1 2 3 4 5* ℵ sy^{(s).p} sa | *var. lect.*
12:6 habaida jah: εἶχε καί] p⁶⁶ A Ψ f¹³ 𝔐 it | ἔχων p⁷⁵ ℵ B D L Q W Θ 33 it^d vg | *var. lect.*
12:7 *om.* ἵνα] A f¹ 𝔐 it^f Chrys | + ἵνα p^{66.75} ℵ B D L Q W Θ Ψ 33 579 lat | *var. lect.*
12:7 fastaida: τετήρηκεν] A f¹ f¹³ 𝔐 it^f sy^{p.h} | τηρήσῃ p^{66.75vid} ℵ B D L Q W Θ Ψ 33 579 lat sy^{hmg} co
12:13 *om.* καί³] p⁶⁶ ℵ¹ A D Θ f¹ f¹³ 𝔐 sa bo^{mss} | + καί p^{75vid} ℵ*.² B L Q W Ψ 579 bo
12:16 þan: δέ] A D Ψ 0250 f¹ f¹³ 𝔐 it sy^{p.h} sa^{ms} bo | *om.* p⁶⁶ ℵ B L Q W Θ 579 lat sy^s
12:22 jah aftra: καὶ πάλιν ... *om.* καί] W Ψ f¹ f¹³ 𝔐 sy^{(p).h} | ἔρχεται ... καί p^{75vid} A B L it^a (sy^s) | *var. lect.*
12:26 jah²: καί] A 𝔐 sy^{s.h} | *om.* p^{66*.75} ℵ B D L W Θ Ψ f¹ f¹³ 33 565 lat sy^p
12:34 *om.* οὖν] A D Θ f¹ f¹³ (33) 𝔐 latt sy co Chrys | + οὖν p^{66.75} ℵ B L W Ψ 579 sy^{hmg} sa^{ms}
12:35 þande: ἕως] p⁶⁶ ℵ f¹³ 33 𝔐 lat Chrys | ὡς A B D L W Θ Ψ 565 it^{e.(d)}
12:36 þande: ἕως] p⁶⁶ f¹ f¹³ 𝔐 lat Chrys | ὡς p⁷⁵ ℵ A B D L W Θ Ψ 33 579 it^{d.e}
12:41 þan: ὅτε] D f¹³ 𝔐 sy lat Chrys | ὅτι p^{66.75} ℵ A B L Θ Ψ 33 579 it^e co | *var. lect.*
13:11 *om.* ὅτι] ℵ A Θ f¹ f¹³ 𝔐 it^{aur.(e).p} vg | + ὅτι p⁶⁶ B C L W Ψ 33^{vid} it
13:12 jah: καί] B C*.³ D W Θ f¹ f¹³ 𝔐 lat sy^h | *om.* p⁶⁶ ℵ A C² L Ψ 33 it vg^{mss} sy^{s.p}
13:12 anakumbjands: ἀναπεσών] C³ D Θ f¹ f¹³ 𝔐 it^d vg sy^h | καὶ ἀνέπεσεν ℵ* B C* W 579 it^{e.p} sy^{s.p} sa bo^{mss} | *var. lect.*
13:18 miþ mis: μετ' ἐμοῦ] p⁶⁶ ℵ A D W Θ Ψ f¹ f¹³ 33 𝔐 lat sy (bo) | μου B C L vg^{ms} sa | *var. lect.*
13:19 biþe wairþai galaubjaiþ: ὅταν γένηται πιστεύσητε] A D W Θ Ψ f¹ f¹³ 33 𝔐 it | *3 1 2* p⁶⁶ ℵ L (579) lat | *var. lect.*

13:23 þan: δέ] p⁶⁶ ℵ A C² D W Θ f¹ f¹³ 33 𝔐 latt sy^{p.h**} | om. B C* L Ψ sy^s
13:25 swa: οὕτως] p⁶⁶ B C L f¹³ 33 pm | om. ℵ A D W Θ Ψ f¹ pm latt sy co
13:28 þan: δέ] p⁶⁶ ℵ A C D L Θ f¹ f¹³ 33 𝔐 latt sy^{p.h} co | om. B W Ψ 579 sa^{ms} bo^{ms}
13:30 suns galaiþ ut: εὐθέως ἐξῆλθεν] A Θ f¹ 𝔐 it^{a.f.q} | ἐξῆλθεν εὐθύς p⁶⁶ ℵ B C D L W Ψ f¹³ 33 579 lat
13:36 ik: ἐγώ] ℵ D Ψ f¹³ 33 pm latt co (Chrys) | om. p⁶⁶ A B C L W Θ f¹ pm
14:2 om. ὅτι] p⁶⁶* C² N Θ 𝔪 it^{a.e.f.q} Chrys | + ὅτι p⁶⁶(c) ℵ A B C* D L W Ψ f¹ f¹³ 33 565 579 lat sy co
14:3 om. καί¹] A W Θ 565 pm sy^p sa^{mss} | + καί p⁶⁶ ℵ B C L N Ψ f¹ f¹³ 33 pm lat | var. lect.
14:4 jah þana wig kunnuþ: καὶ τὴν ὁδὸν οἴδατε] p⁶⁶* A C² D N Θ Ψ f¹ f¹³ 𝔐 lat sy co Chrys | τὴν ὁδόν p⁶⁶ ℵ B C* L Q W 33 579 it^{a.r1vid} sa^{ms} bo
14:5 jah: καί] ℵ A C² D N Ψ f¹ f¹³ 33 𝔐 lat sy^{p.h} Chrys | om. p⁶⁶ B C*^{vid} L W it^{a.b} sy^s
14:9 jah²: καί] A D L N Θ Ψ f¹ f¹³ 33 𝔐 it^{f.q} sy sa | om. p^{66.75} ℵ B Q W 579 lat bo
14:10 rodja: λαλῶ] p⁶⁶ ℵ A W Θ f¹ f¹³ 33 𝔐 lat sy^h Chrys | λέγω p⁷⁵ (B*) L N it^{e.q} sy^{hmg} | var. lect.
14:10 sa taujiþ þo waurstwa: αὐτὸς ποιεῖ τὰ ἔργα] A Θ Ψ f¹ f¹³ 𝔐 lat Chrys | ποιεῖ τὰ ἔργα αὐτοῦ p⁶⁶ ℵ B D it^d | var. lect.
14:14 mik: με] p⁶⁶ ℵ B W Θ f¹ f¹³ 33 pm it^{c.f} vg | om. A D L Q Ψ pm it vg^{mss} co
14:17 ina: αὐτό] p^{66c} A D^c Q Θ Ψ f¹ f¹³ 33 𝔐 lat Chrys | om. p^{66*.75} ℵ B W 579 it^a | var. lect.
14:17 iþ: δέ] A D L Θ f¹ f¹³ 33 𝔐 lat sy | om. p^{66.75} ℵ B Q W Ψ 579 it^{a.b}
14:26 om. ἐγώ] p⁷⁵ ℵ A D Θ Ψ f¹ f¹³ 𝔐 latt co | + ἐγώ B L (33)
14:28 meins: μου] ℵ*.² D² N Ψ f¹³ 𝔐 it^{a.f.q} sy^{p.h} sa^{mss} bo Chrys^a | om. ℵ¹ A B D* L Ψ 33 565 lat sa^{ms} Chrys^b
15:2 managizo akran: πλείονα καρπόν] p⁷⁵ A D Θ f¹ f¹³ 𝔐 it^{(d)} | 2 1 (ℵ) B L Ψ 33 579 lat
15:21 izwis: ὑμῖν] A D¹ N Ψ f¹³ 𝔐 lat sy^h | εἰς ὑμᾶς p⁶⁶ ℵ² B D* L Θ 33 579 it sy^{hmg} | var. lect.
15:25 gamelido in witoda ize: γεγραμμένον ἐν τῷ νόμῳ αὐτῶν] A Θ f¹³ 𝔐 | 2 3 4 5 1 p^{22vid.66cvid} ℵ^{(*)} B D L Ψ 33 565 579 latt | var. lect.
15:26 þan: δέ] A D L Θ Ψ f¹ f¹³ 33 𝔐 lat sy sa^{mss} bo^{mss} | om. p²² ℵ B 579 it^{e.l} sa^{mss} bo^{mss} Chrys | var. lect.
16:7 ik: ἐγώ] A f¹³ 33 𝔐 it vg^{mss} Chrys | om. ℵ B D L Θ Ψ lat co
16:10 meinamma: μου] A Θ f¹³ 𝔐 it^{c.f.q} sy sa^{mss} | om. ℵ B D L W (Ψ) 33 579 lat sa^{mss} bo Chrys
16:17 ik: ἐγώ] D W Θ f¹ 𝔪 it^{d.(fc)} sa bo | om. p^{5vid.66vid} ℵ A B L N Ψ f¹³ 33 565 579 700 lat
16:18 þatei qiþiþ: ὃ λέγει] ℵ² A B D² L N Θ Ψ 33 𝔐 lat sy bo | om. p^{5.66} ℵ* D* W f¹³ 565 579 it sa
16:25 akei: ἀλλ'] p^{66vid} A C³ D² N Θ Ψ f¹³ 𝔐 it^{c.f.q.r1} sy^h Chrys^a | om. p^{5vid} ℵ B C* D* L W 33 579 lat co | var. lect.
16:32 nu: νῦν] C³ D¹ N Θ Ψ f¹ f¹³ 𝔐 it^{f.q} sy^{p.h} | om. p^{22vid.66} ℵ² A B C* D* L W 33 it^b sy^s | var. lect.
17:1 uzuhhof: (καί) ἐπῆρεν] A C³ N Ψ 𝔐 (it) Chrys^a | ἐπάρας ℵ B C* D L W Θ f¹ 33 565 579 (lat)
17:1 jah: καί] A C³ N 𝔐 𝔐 it Chrys | om. ℵ B C* D L W Θ f¹ 33 565^s 579 lat
17:4 ustauh: ἐτελείωσα] D Θ Ψ f¹³ 𝔐 lat sa^{ms} Chrys | τελειώσας p⁶⁶ ℵ A B C L N (W) 33 (it^{b.ff2}) sa^{mss} bo
17:12 in þamma fairƕau: ἐν τῷ κόσμῳ] A C³ N Θ Ψ f¹³ 𝔐 it^{(a).f.q} sy bo^{ms} Chrys | om. p^{60.66} ℵ B C* D L W lat co
17:12 þanzei atgaft mis: οὓς δέδωκάς μοι] A (C³) D N Θ Ψ f¹ f¹³ 𝔐 lat sy^{p.h} (Chrys) | ᾧ δέδωκάς μοι καί (ℵ²) B (C*) L W 33 (579) co | var. lect.
17:16 us þamma fairƕau ni im: ἐκ τοῦ κόσμου οὐκ εἰμί] p⁶⁶* N Θ Ψ f¹ f¹³ 𝔐 sy^h Chrys^a | 4 5 1 2 3 ℵ A B C D L W (lat) Chrys^b
17:19 ik: ἐγώ] B C D L N Θ Ψ f¹ f¹³ 33 𝔐 it^{aur.d.f} vg Chrys | om. ℵ A W 579 700 it sa bo^{ms}
17:21 ain: ἕν] ℵ A C³ L N Ψ f¹ f¹³ 33 𝔐 lat sy^{p.h} bo | om. p^{66vid} B C* D W it^{c.d.e} sa bo^{ms}
17:22 siju: ἔσμεν] ℵ² A C³ N Θ Ψ f¹³ 𝔐 lat | om. p^{60.66} (ℵ*) B C* D L W 33 it^e
18:2 gaïddja: συνήχθη] ℵ A B C D L N W Θ f¹ f¹³ 33 pm it^{(a).q.(r1)} | + καί pm | var. lect.

18:4 usgaggands ut: ἐξελθὼν εἶπεν] p^{108vid} ℵ A C³ L N W Θ Ψ f¹³ 33 𝔐 it^f | ἐξῆλθεν καὶ λέγει B C* D 565 lat Chrys | *var. lect.*

18:5 Iesus: ὁ Ἰησοῦς] (ℵ) A C L N W Θ Ψ f¹ f¹³ 33 𝔐 lat sy^{p.h} sa bo | *om.* p^{60} B D it^{b.c.r1} sy^s

18:6 þatei: ὅτι] C f¹³ 𝔐 sy^h | *om.* ℵ A B D L N W Θ Ψ f¹ 33 565 latt

18:11 hairu: μάχαιραν] p^{66} ℵ A B C D L N W Θ Ψ f¹ 33 *pm* lat | + σου f¹³ *pm* it^e

18:13 gatauhun ina: ἀπήγαγον αὐτόν] A C³ L Θ Ψ f¹ f¹³ 𝔐 lat sy Chrys | ἤγαγον p^{66vid} ℵ* B D W 579 it^a | *var. lect.*

18:14 fraqistjan: ἀπολέσθαι] A C² N Ψ 𝔐 sy^h | ἀποθανεῖν p^{66vid} ℵ B C* D^s L W Θ f¹ f¹³ 33 565 579 latt sy^{s.p.hmg} Chrys

18:16 saei was kunþs þamma gudjin: (ἄλλος) ὃς ἦν γνωστὸς τῷ ἀρχιερεῖ] p^{66vid} ℵ A C² D^s W Θ f¹ f¹³ 33 𝔐 lat sy^{p.h} co | ὁ γνωστός B C*^{vid} L it^a | *var. lect.*

18:17 jaina þiwi so daurawardo du Paitrau: ἡ παιδίσκη ἡ θυρωρὸς τῷ Πέτρῳ] p^{66} ℵ A C³ D^s N (W) Θ Ψ f¹ f¹³ 𝔐 it^{a.(ff2).q} | 5 6 1 2 3 4 p^{59vid} B C* L 33 lat

18:18 miþ im Paitrus: μετ' αὐτῶν ὁ Πέτρος] A D^s N Θ Ψ 𝔐 lat | 4 5 2 3 p^{60.66vid} ℵ B C L (W) f¹ 33 (565) 579 it^a | *var. lect.*

18:20 sinteino: πάντοτε] C³ D^s Ψ m it^q sy^h | πάντες ℵ A B C* L N W Θ f¹ f¹³ 33 565 579 lat sy^{s.p}

18:22 andbahte atstandands: τῶν ὑπηρετῶν παρεστηκώς] A C³ D^s N (Θ) f¹ f¹³ 𝔐 it^q | 3 1 2 ℵ* B W (lat) | *var. lect.*

18:25 iþ: οὖν] C³ f¹³ m it^f | *om.* ℵ A B C* L N W Θ Ψ f¹ 33 lat

18:29 ana: κατά] p^{66} ℵ² A C D^s L N W Θ Ψ f¹ f¹³ 33 𝔐 lat Chrys | *om.* ℵ* B 579 it^e

18:30 ubiltojis: κακοποιός] A C³ D^s N Θ Ψ f¹ f¹³ 𝔐 lat Chrys | κακὸν ποιῶν ℵ² B L W it^{a.(e).r1} | *var. lect.*

18:33 in praitauria aftra: εἰς τὸ πραιτώριον πάλιν] p^{60vid} ℵ A C² (N) Θ (Ψ) f¹ 𝔐 | 4 1 2 3 p^{52vid.66vid} B C* D^s L W f¹³ 579 latt | *var. lect.*

18:36 aiþþau ... meinai usdaudidedeina: ἂν οἱ ἐμοὶ ἠγωνίζοντο] A D^s N Θ 𝔐 it^q | 2 3 4 1 p^{60vid.90vid} ℵ B² L W Ψ f¹³ 33 579 Chrys | *var. lect.*

18:37 ik: ἐγώ] A N Θ 𝔐 lat | *om.* p^{60vid} ℵ B D^s L W Ψ f¹ f¹³ 33 it Chrys

18:38 fairino...bigita in þamma: αἰτίαν εὑρίσκω ἐν αὐτῷ] ℵ A N W Θ Ψ f¹ f¹³ 33 𝔐 it^q vg^{ms} Chrys | 2 3 4 1 p^{90vid} B L 579 lat | *var. lect.*

18:40 aftra allai: πάλιν πάντες] A Θ *pm* it^f vg sy^h | πάλιν ℵ B L W 579 | *var. lect.*

19:3 *om.* καὶ ἤρχοντο πρὸς αὐτόν] A D^s Ψ f¹ m it^{f.q} sy^p | + καὶ ἤρχοντο πρὸς αὐτόν p^{66.90} ℵ B L N W Θ f¹³ 33 565 579 700 (lat) sy^h co

19:4 in imma ni ainohun fairino bigat: ἐν αὐτῷ οὐδεμίαν αἰτίαν εὑρίσκω] D^s N Θ 𝔐 sy^h | 3 4 5 1 2 (ℵ¹) B f¹ 33 565 vg^{ms} | *var. lect.*

19:6 ina: αὐτόν] p^{90vid} ℵ A D^s N Θ f¹³ 33 𝔐 (it) sy Chrys | *om.* p^{66} B L W Ψ f¹ it^{aur} vg

19:7 unsaramma: ἡμῶν] p^{60vid} A Θ f¹ f¹³ 33 𝔐 it^q sy co Chrys | *om.* p^{66vid} ℵ B D^s L N W Ψ 579 lat bo^{ms}

19:7 sik silban gudis sunu: ἑαυτὸν θεοῦ υἱόν] 700^s *pm* | 3 2 1 p^{60vid.(66)} ℵ B L (W) Ψ f¹ f¹³ 33 565 579 lat | *var. lect.*

19:10 ushramjan þuk jah waldufni aih fraletan: σταυρῶσαί σε καὶ ἐξουσίαν ἔχω ἀπολῦσαί] p^{66} D^s L W Θ (Ψ) f¹ f¹³ 33 𝔐 lat sy^h co | 6 2 3 4 5 1 p^{60} ℵ A B N it^e sy^p

19:11 *om.* αὐτῷ] p^{66c} A (f¹³) N 𝔐 lat sy^h sa^{ms} bo | + αὐτῷ p^{60vid} ℵ B D^s L N^c W Ψ f¹ 33 565 579 it^{c.j} | *var. lect.*

19:11 ainhun ana mik nih wesi þus atgiban: οὐδεμίαν κατ' ἐμοῦ] A N Θ f¹³ 𝔐 it^{ff2*} | 2 3 1 p^{66vid} ℵ B D^s L W Θ Ψ f¹ 33 lat

I.2.2 Non-Byzantine readings
I.2.2.1 Readings supported by 'Western' witnesses
Sub-group A
50/335 (15%)

5:37 ƕanhun gahausideduþ: πώποτε ἀκηκόατε] p$^{66c.75vid}$ ℵ A B D L N W f^{13} 33 579 latt | *2 1* Θ Ψ f^1 𝔐 Chrys | *var. lect.*
6:2 taiknins: τὰ σημεῖα] p$^{66.75vid}$ ℵ A B D L N W Θ Ψ 565 latt sy co Chrys^a | *praem.* αὐτοῦ 𝔐 Chrys^b
6:5 augona Iesus: τοὺς ὀφθαλμοὺς ὁ Ἰησοῦς] p$^{66.75}$ (ℵ) A B D L N W Θ Ψ 565 (latt) co sy^c | *3 4 1 2* 𝔐 | *var. lect.*
6:7 ƕarjizuh: ἕκαστος] p^{66} ℵ A B L W Θ Ψ latt Chrys | + αὐτῶν D N 𝔐
6:11 gadailida þaim anakumbjandam: διέδωκεν τοῖς ἀνακειμένοις] p$^{28vid.66.75}$ ℵ* A B L N W f^1 33 565 579 lat sy$^{c.p.h}$ sa bo^{mss} | διέδωκεν τοῖς μαθηταῖς οἱ δὲ μαθηταὶ τοῖς ἀνακειμένοις ℵ^2 D Θ Ψ f^{13} 𝔐 it$^{b.d.e}$ (sy^s) bo^{mss} | *var. lect.*
6:22 seƕun: εἶδον] p^{75} A B L W Θ 33 it sy$^{p.h}$ Chrys^a | ἰδών Ψ f^1 f^{13} 𝔐 Chrys^b | *var. lect.*
6:22 ain: ἕν] p$^{28vid.75}$ ℵ^2 A B L N W Ψ f^1 565 579 lat bo | ἕν ἐκεῖνο εἰς ὃ ἐνέβησαν οἱ μαθηταὶ αὐτοῦ Θ 𝔐 it$^{(a).(e)}$ sy$^{(c).(p).h}$ Chrys | *var. lect.*
6:33 gaf libain: διδοὺς ζωήν] A K Y 0211 27 it$^{c.f}$ vg | *2 1* p^{75} ℵ B D L N W Θ Ψ 𝔐 it Chrys
6:52 leik giban du matjan: τὴν σάρκα δοῦναι φαγεῖν] D K Θ Π 0211 f^{13} it$^{d.ff2*}$ | *3 1 2 4* L W Ψ 33 𝔐 | *var. lect.*
6:63 rodida: λελάληκα] p^{66} ℵ B C D L N W Θ Ψ 565 latt Chrys | λαλῶ 𝔐
7:16 *om.* αὐτοῖς] K N Γ Π f^{13} lat | + αὐτοῖς p$^{66.75vid}$ ℵ B D L W Θ Ψ f^1 𝔐 it | *var. lect.*
7:29 iþ: δέ] p^{66} ℵ D N Y Π f^1 33 565 1192 1194 1216 1243 it vg^{mss} sy sa^{mss} bo^{mss} | *om.* p^{75} B L W Θ Ψ f^{13} 𝔐 it vg Chrys
7:31 qeþun: ἔλεγον] p^{66} ℵ B (D) L N W Θ f^1 f^{13} 33 565 latt | + ὅτι Ψ 𝔐 Chrys
7:50 saei atiddja du imma in naht: ὁ ἐλθὼν πρὸς αὐτὸν νυκτός] K N^c Y U Δ Ψ 0211 0250 9 157 1071 lat sy^h | ὁ ἐλθὼν πρὸς αὐτὸν τὸ πρότερον p$^{(66).75}$ ℵ^2 B (L) (W) | *var. lect.*
7:53-8:11 *om.*] p$^{66.75}$ ℵ B L N W Θ Ψ 33 565 1424* it$^{a.f.l.q}$ sy sa bo^{mss} Chrys | + 7:53-8:11 D 𝔐 lat bo^{mss} | *var. lect.*
8:16 aþþan jabai stoja: ἐὰν δὲ κρίνω] N 27 1194 it$^{35.48}$ | καὶ ἐὰν κρίνω δέ p$^{39.66.75}$ ℵ B D L W Θ Ψ 33 𝔐 lat Chrys | *var. lect.*
8:20 rodida: ἐλάλησεν] p$^{39.66.75}$ ℵ B D L W Θ Ψ lat Chrys^b | + ὁ Ἰησοῦς N f^1 f^{13} 33 𝔐 it$^{r1.qc}$ Chrys^a
8:23 Iesus: ὁ Ἰησοῦς] N 28 it$^{a.f.l}$ | *om.* p$^{66.75}$ ℵ B D L W Θ Ψ f^1 f^{13} 33 𝔐 lat Chrys
8:26 rodja: λαλῶ] p$^{66.75}$ ℵ B D L N W Θ Ψ f^1 f^{13} 33 latt | λέγω 𝔐 Chrys
8:42 qaþ: εἶπεν] p$^{66.75}$ B C L N W Θ Ψ f^1 33 565 579 it | + οὖν ℵ D f^{13} 𝔐 it$^{aur.d.f}$ vg sa^{mss}
8:46 *om.* δέ] p$^{66.75}$ ℵ B C D L N W Θ Ψ f^1 f^{13} 565 579 latt | + δέ 𝔐
9:8 bidagwa: προσαίτης] p$^{66.75}$ ℵ A B C* D L N W Θ Ψ f^1 33 565 579 it$^{d.f.ff2.q}$ vg Chrys | τυφλός C^3 f^{13} 𝔐 | *var. lect.*
9:9 iþ: δέ] p^{66} ℵ*.^{2} A C^2 K N U Γ Π 0211 f^{13} 33 579 1216 1243 1519 (it) | *om.* p^{75} ℵ^1 B C* D L W Θ Ψ f^1 𝔐 it^d vg
9:15 jah^2: καί] A 0211 f^{13} 124 788 1346 it^q | *om.* p$^{66.75}$ ℵ B D L N W Θ Ψ f^1 𝔐 | *var. lect.*
9:31 guþ frawaurhtaim: ὁ θεὸς ἁμαρτωλῶν] B D Θ Ψ it$^{a.e}$ Chrys^b | *3 1 2* p$^{66.75}$ ℵ A L W f^1 f^{13} 33 𝔐 lat Chrys^a | *var. lect.*
10:5 laistjand: ἀκολουθήσουσιν] A B D E F G Y Δ 2 461 475 700 1192 1210 1212 1505 lat | ἀκολουθήσωσιν p$^{6vid.66.75}$ ℵ L W Θ Ψ f^1 f^{13} 33 𝔐 Chrys
10:21 iþ: δέ] p^{66} ℵ (W) Θ f^{13} it^d vg^{ms} sy$^{s.p}$ sa^{mss} bo | *om.* p$^{45.75}$ A B D L Ψ f^1 𝔐

10:33 Iudaieis: Ἰουδαῖοι] p⁴⁵·⁶⁶·⁷⁵ ℵ A B L W Θ Ψ f¹ f¹³ 33 565 579 lat | + λέγοντες D 𝔐 it^d.(e) vg^ms bo^mss | var. lect.
10:41 gatawida taikne: ἐποίησεν σημεῖον] K M W Π Ψ 69 124 157 475 565 579 788 1346 f¹ f¹³ 33 Chrys it^g2 | 2 1 p⁴⁵·⁶⁶·⁷⁵ ℵ A B D Θ 𝔐 lat
11:30 nauhþanuh: ἔτι] p⁶⁶·⁷⁵ ℵ B C F W Ψ f¹ f¹³ 33 579 lat | om. p⁶⁵ A D L Θ 𝔐 it^d.l sy
11:35 jah: καί] ℵ* D Θ f¹³ l²⁵³ latt | om. p⁶⁶ ℵ² A B C L W Ψ f¹ 33 𝔐 Chrys | var. lect.
11:45 gatawida: ἐποίησεν] p⁶·⁴⁵·⁶⁶ A B C* L W Θ Ψ f¹ lat | + ὁ Ἰησοῦς (ℵ) C² D f¹³ 33 𝔐 it^a.d.f.ff2
12:35 in izwis: ἐν ὑμῖν] p⁶⁶·⁷⁵ ℵ B D K L M W Θ Π Ψ 0211 f¹ f¹³ 33 565 latt | μεθ' ὑμῶν A 𝔐 sy^s.p sa Chrys
13:33 mel: χρόνον] ℵ L Θ Ψ 0211 461 f¹³ it^c.f.l sy^h sa^mss bo^mss Chrys^a | om. p⁶⁶ A B C D W f¹ 33 𝔐 lat Chrys^b
14:12 attin: πατέρα] p⁶⁶·⁷⁵ ℵ A B D L Q W Θ Π Ψ f¹ 33 0211 1192 1210 lat | + μου f¹³ 𝔐 it^e.27 Chrys
14:16 sijai miþ izwis du τὸν αἰῶνα: ᾗ μεθ' ὑμῶν εἰς τὸν αἰῶνα] L Q Ψ 33^vid it^e sy^hmg Chrys^b | 2 3 4 5 6 7 1 p⁷⁵ B it^b | var. lect.
14:22 om. καί¹] p⁶⁶*·⁷⁵ A B D E L M Θ 0211 33 35 700 1212 1241 1243 1505 lat sy^s.c.p co | + καί p⁶⁶c ℵ W Ψ f¹ f¹³ 𝔐 it^q sy^h
15:11 sijai: ᾗ] A B D Θ Π Ψ 0211 (33) 565 579 lat sy | μείνῃ ℵ L f¹³ 𝔐 it^f.r1
16:4 ize: αὐτῶν] p⁶⁶vid ℵ¹ A B L Θ Π f¹³ 0211 33 (lat) sy^p.h bo^ms | om. ℵ* D Ψ 𝔐 it^a.ff2 sy^s co | var. lect.
16:16 nauh ... ni: οὐκέτι] p⁶⁶vid ℵ B D L N W Θ Ψ 0211 33 1216 1243 lat sy^h Chrys^b | οὐ A f¹³ 𝔐 it^a.d.e sy^s.p
16:22 þan ... auk nu saurga: οὖν νῦν μὲν λύπην] p⁵·²²vid·⁶⁶ ℵ² B C* D L M W Ψ f¹ 33 565 lat | 1 4 3 2 A C³ N Θ 𝔐 | var. lect.
16:23 þatei þisƕah þei: ὅτι ὅ ἐάν] (ℵ) Θ X Y Π 0211* 33 1241 it^a.c.r1 | ἄν τι p⁵ B C (D*) L (Ψ) lat | var. lect.
16:29 qeþun: λέγουσιν] p⁵* ℵ² B C* N Θ Π Ψ 0211 565 it^e.q vg^mss sy^h | + αὐτῷ p⁵cvid (ℵ*) A C³ D L W f¹³ 33 𝔐 lat sy^s.p.hmg co
17:1 ei sunus þeins: ἵνα ὁ υἱός σου] A D X Θ 579 lat sy | ἵνα ὁ υἱός ℵ B C* W it^d.e.ff2 bo^mss | var. lect.
17:8 om. καὶ ἔγνωσαν] ℵ* A D W 0211 it^a.d.e.q | + καὶ ἔγνωσαν ℵ¹ B C L N Θ Ψ f¹ f¹³ 33 𝔐 lat
17:17 sunjai: ἀληθείᾳ] p⁶⁶ (ℵ*) A B C* D L W Θ 579 lat co | + σου ℵ² C³ N Ψ f¹³ 33 𝔐 it^q sy bo^mss Chrys
17:19 sijaina jah eis: ὦσιν καὶ αὐτοί] p⁶⁰vid·⁶⁶cvid ℵ A B C* D L N W Θ Ψ f¹ f¹³ 33 565 lat | 2 3 1 C³ 𝔐 sy^h | var. lect.
18:28 ak: ἀλλά] p⁶⁰vid ℵ A B C* D^s N W Θ 565 579 lat | + ἵνα C² L Ψ f¹ f¹³ 33 𝔐 it^e.f.ff2.r1 sy^h Chrys
18:34 Iesus: Ἰησοῦς] A B C* D^s L N W Θ 33 565 579 700 lat sy^h | praem. αὐτῷ (ὁ) ℵ C³ f¹³ 𝔐 it^c sy^p sa^ms bo^ms
18:34 abu þus silbin: ἀπὸ σεαυτοῦ] p⁶⁶ ℵ B C* L N Ψ 579 latt Chrys | ἀφ' ἑαυτοῦ A C² D^s W Θ f¹ f¹³ 33 𝔐

Sub-group B
40/335 (12%)

6:7 om. τι] p⁷⁵ B D it | + τι p⁶⁶ ℵ A L N W Θ Ψ f¹ f¹³ 33 𝔐 it^c.f vg sy^h Chrys
6:17 ni...nauhþan: οὔπω (ἐληλύθει πρὸς αὐτοὺς ὁ Ἰησοῦς)] (L) W 33 it bo | οὐκ A Θ f¹ 𝔐 lat sy sa Chrys | var. lect.
6:24 om. αὐτοί] ℵ* S it^(c).(e) (vg) | + αὐτοί p⁷⁵ ℵ² B L N W Ψ (33) 579 | var. lect.
6:36 om. καί¹] K Λ it^e.f | + καί p⁷⁵vid ℵ A B D L N W Θ Ψ 𝔐 lat Chrys

6:46 attin: τοῦ πατρός] ℵ it^μ Did | τοῦ θεοῦ p^66.75 A (B) C D L N W Θ Ψ 33 𝔐 lat Chrys
6:58 iþ: δέ] it^b.f Chrys^a | om. p^66.75 ℵ B C L N W Θ Ψ 𝔐 Chrys^b
7:12 in managein: ἐν τῷ ὄχλῳ] p^66 ℵ D 33 latt sa^mss bo^mss | ἐν τοῖς ὄχλοις p^75 B L N W Θ Ψ f^1 f^13 𝔐 Chrys
7:51 faurþis hauseiþ: πρῶτον ἀκούσῃ] X it^f.μ | 2 1 p^66.75 ℵ B D L N W Θ Ψ 33 lat | var. lect.
8:15 iþ: δέ] p^75 it^d.f sa^mss bo | om. p^39.66 ℵ B D L N W Θ Ψ f^1 f^13 33 𝔐 lat Chrys
9:7 om. οὖν] 1210 it | + οὖν p^66.75 ℵ A C D L N W Θ Ψ f^1 f^13 33 𝔐 it^d.e.f vg | var. lect.
10:10 iþ: δέ] p^45 D it^a.d Chrys | om. p^45.66.75 ℵ A B D L W Θ Ψ f^1 f^13 33 𝔐 lat
10:14 kunnun mik þo meina: γινώσκουσί με τὰ ἐμά] p^45.66.75 ℵ B (D) L W latt (sy^s) | γινώσκομαι ὑπὸ τῶν ἐμῶν A Θ Ψ f^1 f^13 33 𝔐 sy^p.h Chrys
10:25 om. αὐτοῖς] p^66 ℵ* D l^640 it^d.r1 sa^ms bo^ms | + αὐτοῖς p^75 ℵ^2 A B*.2 L W Ψ f^1 f^13 33 𝔐 lat | var. lect.
10:29 þatei ... maizo: ὃ ... μεῖζόν] (B* lat bo) | ὃς ...μείζων p^66 f^1 f^13 33 𝔐 | var. lect.
10:29 þo: αὐτά] 0211 475* 1424 l^640 it Chrys | om. p^66.75 ℵ A B D L W Θ Ψ f^1 f^13 33 𝔐 it^d.ff2.l.r1
10:30 meins: μου] W* Δ 27 1243 700 it^e sy^s.p co | om. p^66.75 ℵ A B D L Θ Ψ f^1 f^13 33 𝔐 lat Chrys
11:3 is: αὐτοῦ] D S Ω f^1 f^13 28 157 565 579 1346 it | om. p^6.45.66 ℵ A B L W Θ Ψ 33 𝔐 it^b.ff2c vg
11:16 seinaim: αὐτοῦ] D Π^c 579 28 1071 l^253 it^d.f | om. p^66.75 ℵ A B C L W Θ Ψ f^1 f^13 33 𝔐 lat Chrys
11:17 juþan fidwor dagans: ἤδη τέσσαρας ἡμέρας] p^66 it^(a).ff2*c.l vg^ms | 2 1 3 p^75 B C* Θ f^13 vg^ms | var. lect.
11:21-22 ni þau gadauþnodedi broþar meins; akei: οὐκ ἂν ἀπέθανεν ὁ ἀδελφός μου ἀλλά] ℵ^2 L W it^l | 1 2 3 4 5 6 p^75 ℵ* B C* | var. lect.
12:18 om. τοῦτο] 0211 lat | + τοῦτο p^(66).75(ℵ) A B D L W Θ Ψ f^1 f^13 33 𝔐
12:18 om. καί] p^66*.75(*vid).c E H Δ Λ 2 27 461 1194 1203 1243 1505 1519 it | + καί p^66c A (B^2) L Θ Ψ f^1 f^13 𝔐 it^aur.f.ff2 vg sy^h | var. lect.
12:21 om. οὖν] L 1216 it^a.e | + οὖν p^66.75 ℵ A B D L W Θ Ψ f^1 f^13 33 𝔐 lat
12:29 om. καί] ℵ D f^1 69 565 1216 it^d.ff2*.l.r1* | + καί p^66.75 A B L W Θ Ψ f^13 33 𝔐
12:29 -h: δέ] W it^e.(l) | om. p^66.75 ℵ A B D L Θ Ψ f^1 f^13 33 𝔐
12:32 alla: πάντα] p^66 ℵ* latt | πάντας ℵ^2 A B L W Θ Ψ f^1 f^13 33 𝔐 Chrys | var. lect.
12:37 om. δέ] G it^a.e | + δέ p^66.75 ℵ A B D L W Θ Ψ f^1 f^13 33 𝔐 Chrys
13:34 ik: ἐγώ] p^66 it Chrys^a | om. ℵ A B L W Θ Ψ f^1 33 𝔐 lat | var. lect.
13:38 þu mik afaikis kunnan: σύ με ἀπαρνήσῃ] W (it^a.b.ff2.r1) | οὐ ἀρνήσῃ με p^66 B D 565 579 lat | var. lect.
14:23 jah^2: καί] 0233 it^r1 | om. p^66.75 ℵ A B D L W Θ Ψ f^1 f^13 33 𝔐
14:28 ik: ἐγώ (πορεύομαι)] f^13 it^a.e.q sa^mss | om. ℵ A B D L Θ Ψ 33 565 579 lat | var. lect.
15:5 iþ: καί] et it^aur.c.f.ff2; CyrJ | om. p^66.75 ℵ A B D L Θ Ψ f^1 f^13 33 𝔐 lat Chrys
15:5 swa: οὕτως] M 788 it^e | οὗτος p^66.75 ℵ A B D L Θ Ψ f^1 f^13 33 𝔐 lat
16:20 jus: ὑμεῖς] p^5 ℵ* B D 1 it sy^s co | + δέ ℵ^2 A L N W Θ Ψ f^13 33 𝔐 it^aur.ff2c vg sy^h sa^ms bo^ms
17:5 at þus faurþizei sa fairƕus wesi: παρὰ σοί πρὸ τοῦ τὸν κόσμον εἶναι] p^66 it^a.f GrNy | 3 4 5 6 7 1 2 ℵ A B C L N W Θ Ψ f^1 f^13 33 𝔐 (lat) Chrys | var. lect.
17:11 þanzei atgaft mis: ἵυς δέδωκάς μοι] D^1 N^c 69 76 205 209 892^s 1009 1192 1195 1210 1230 1505 1646 lat | ᾧ δέδωκάς μοι p^60 A B C Θ Ψ f^13 𝔐 | var. lect.
17:23 jah^2: καί] p^66 ℵ W 579 lat | ἵνα B C D L 33 it^a.e.r1 sy^s Chrys | var. lect.
18:33 om. οὖν] 788 it^q | + οὖν ℵ A B C D^s L N W Θ Ψ f^1 f^13 33 𝔐
19:4 om. καί^1] p^90 ℵ D^s Γ 0211 565 1519 f^1 latt sy^h | + καί A B L 33 vg^ms sy^p | var. lect.
19:12 framuh þamma sokida Peilatus fraletan ina: (ἐκ τούτου) οὖν ἐζήτει ὁ Πιλᾶτος (ἀπολῦσαι αὐτόν)] 565 1210 (it^aur.f.g2) | (1 2) 5 6 4 (7 8) p^66vid ℵ B L W Ψ it | var. lect.

Sub-group C
19/335 (6%)

6:8 om. αὐτῷ] it^{ff2*.9A} | + αὐτῷ p^{66.75} ℵ A B C D L N W Θ Ψ f¹ f¹³ 33 𝔐 lat
6:26 jah fauratanja: καὶ τέρατα] D it^{a.b.d.9A*.f*.gat.μ} | om. p⁷⁵ ℵ A B L N W Ψ Θ 𝔐 lat Chrys | var. lect.
6:35 jah¹: καί] et it^{f.ff2} | om. p^{75vid} B L W 579 it^{a.b.e.rl.j} sy^{s.c.p} co | δέ A f¹ 𝔐 it^{c.d} vg sy^{h(mg)} | var. lect.
6:50 om. καί] D* lat | + καί p⁶⁶ ℵ A B C L W Θ Ψ 𝔐 it^d
7:39 sa weiha ana im: ἅγιον ἐπ' αὐτοῖς] D* it^{d.(f)} | om. p^{66(c).75} ℵ N* Θ Ψ sy^{s.c.p} lat | var. lect.
9:19 om. οὖν] it^{a.e.q} | + οὖν p^{66.75} ℵ A B C D L N W Θ Ψ f¹ f¹³ 33 𝔐 lat Chrys
9:28 siponjos sijum: μαθηταί ἐσμέν] discipuli sumus lat | 2 1 p^{66.75} ℵ A B C D L N W Θ Ψ f¹ f¹³ 33 𝔐 it^{(e).d.q.δ.47} Chrys
11:33 Iudaiuns þaiei qemun miþ izai: Ἰουδαίους τοὺς συνελθόντας αὐτῇ] Iudaeos qui uenerant cum ea lat | συνελθόντας αὐτῇ Ἰουδαίους pm | var. lect.
12:36 galaiþ jah: ἀπῆλθεν καί] D latt | ἀπελθών p^{66.75} ℵ A B L W Θ Ψ f¹ f¹³ 33 𝔐 Chrys
13:13 om. καί²] it^{r1.p.μ} | + καί p⁶⁶ ℵ A B C D L W Θ Ψ f¹ f¹³ 33 𝔐 lat Chrys
13:14 om. ἐγώ] it^{b.r1.p.gat.μ} | + ἐγώ p⁶⁶ ℵ A B C D L W Θ Ψ f¹ f¹³ 33 𝔐 lat Chrys
13:18 usfulliþ waurþi þata gamelido: πληρωθῇ ἡ γραφή] D lat | 2 3 1 p⁶⁶ ℵ A B C L W Θ Ψ f¹ f¹³
13:36 (andhafjands Iesus) qaþ: (ἀποκριθεὶς Ἰησοῦς) εἶπεν/ἔφη] (respondit Iesus et) dixit it^{ff2} | om. rell.
13:38 þei: ὅτι] D* it^{c.d.r1} | om. p⁶⁶ ℵ A B C L W Ψ f¹ f¹³ 33 𝔐 lat
15:7 aþþan: δέ] D it^{d.f} | om. ℵ A B L Θ Ψ f¹ f¹³ 33 𝔐
15:24 mik: ἐμέ] me it^{e.l.μ} | om. ἐμέ p⁶⁶ ℵ A B C D L W Θ Ψ f¹ f¹³ 33 𝔐 lat
17:20 om. καί] it^{a.b.9A.q.gat.48} | + καί ℵ A B C D L N W Θ Ψ f¹ f¹³ 33 𝔐 lat Chrys
18:23 om. αὐτῷ] it^{9A.gat.} | + αὐτῷ (ℵ) A B C D L N W Θ Ψ f¹ (f¹³) 33 𝔐 lat
19:2 jah²: καί] et it^{(e).f.q} | om. καί p⁶⁶ ℵ A B C D L N W Θ Ψ f¹ f¹³ 33 𝔐 lat

I.2.2.2 Readings not supported by 'Western' witnesses
27/335 (8%)

6:1 jah: καί] V 9 183 190 247 280 350 it^f | om. p^{66(c).75vid} ℵ A B L W Ψ f¹ f¹³ 33 𝔐 it sy^{s.c.p.h} co | var. lect.
6:8 Paitraus Seimonaus: Πέτρου Σίμωνος] Θ Bas / 2 1 p^{28.66.75} ℵ A B D L N W Ψ 𝔐 latt sy co
7:12 mikila was: πολὺς ἦν] 416 1053 1424 1644 2549* | περὶ αὐτοῦ ἦν πολύς p⁷⁵ B L W | var. lect.
7:15 manageins: ὄχλοι] 047 it^f | Ἰουδαῖοι p^{66.75} ℵ B D L N W Θ Ψ f¹ f¹³ 33 𝔐 lat sy
7:46 (rodida) manna swaswe sa manna: (ἐλάλησεν) ἄνθρωπος ὡς οὗτος ὁ ἄνθρωπος] 28 700 | (ἐλάλησεν) οὕτως ἄνθρωπος p^{66(c).75} ℵ² B L W vg^{ms} bo | var. lect.
8:38 hausideduþ fram attin izwaramma: ἠκούσατε παρὰ τοῦ πατρὸς ὑμῶν] (ℵ²) C Θ f¹ f¹³ 33 565 it^f Chrys | ἠκούσατε παρὰ τοῦ πατρός p⁷⁵ B C (L) W | var. lect.
8:50 om. δέ] 69 124 788 1210 1505 Chrys | + δέ p^{66.75} ℵ B C D L N W Θ Ψ f¹ f¹³ 33 𝔐 latt
9:11 afþwahan in þata swumfsl Siloamis: νίψαι εἰς τὴν κολυμβήθραν τοῦ Σιλωάμ] K Π f¹³ 9 28 (33) 1071 1424 it^f Chrys | εἰς τὸν Σιλωάμ καὶ νίψαι p^{66.75} ℵ B D L W Θ f¹ 565 it | var. lect.
10:4 om. πάντα] ℵ* | + πάντα p^{66c.75} ℵ² B D L W Θ Ψ f¹ f¹³ 33 565 it^{a.d.e} | var. lect.
10:31 aftra: πάλιν] ℵ B L W 33 l^{1073} sy^p sa^{mss} | + οὖν p⁶⁶ A Ψ f¹ f¹³ 𝔐 it^f sy^h sa^{ms} | var. lect.
10:39 ina aftra gafahan: αὐτὸν πάλιν πιάσαι] Ω 9 | οὖν αὐτὸν πάλιν πιάσαι ℵ² A L W Ψ f¹ 33 565 it^f | var. lect.
11:41 þarei was: οὗ ἦν] A K Π 0211 0250 1 579 1582* (it^f) sy^h | om. p⁶⁶ ℵ B C* D L W Θ Ψ 33 | var. lect.

12:3 fotuns is skufta seinamma: τοὺς πόδας αὐτοῦ ταῖς θριξὶν ἑαυτῆς] M | ταῖς θριξὶν αὐτῆς τοὺς πόδας αὐτοῦ p⁶⁶·⁷⁵ ℵ A B D L Q W Ψ 33 𝔐 | var. lect.
12:43 mais hauhein manniska: μᾶλλον τὴν δόξαν τῶν ἀνθρώπων] 579 1424 | 2 3 4 5 1 p⁶⁶·⁷⁵ ℵ A B D L W Θ Ψ f¹ f¹³ 33 𝔐 latt
12:47 galaubjai: πιστεύσῃ] S 0211 1424* itf | μὴ φυλάξῃ p⁶⁶*·⁷⁵ ℵ A B L Ψ f¹ f¹³ 33 565 itff2c.lc vg sy
13:18 ƕarjans: τίνας] ℵ B C L M 33 | οὕς p⁶⁶ A D W Θ Ψ f¹ f¹³ 𝔐
13:31 þan galaiþ ut. Qaþ þan Iesus: ὅτε ἐξῆλθεν. Λέγει οὖν ὁ Ἰησοῦς] U Ψ 047 | 1 4 2 3 (5) 6 p⁶⁶ ℵ B C D L W Θ f¹ f¹³ 33 | var. lect.
14:11 ni galaubeiþ mis: μὴ πιστεύετέ μοι] G | πιστεύετε p⁶⁶·⁷⁵ ℵ D L W 33 (579) lat syc·p sa | var. lect.
14:30 om. γάρ] 0211 69 | + γάρ p⁶⁶ ℵ A B D L Θ Ψ f¹ f¹³ 𝔐 latt
14:30 bigitiþ: εὑρήσει] K Y Π itf syhmg | ἔχει p⁶⁶ ℵ A B D L Θ Ψ f¹ f¹³ 33 𝔐
14:31 meinana: μου] l⁶⁴⁰ itf | om. rell.
15:16 om. καὶ ἔθηκα ὑμᾶς] Δ 565 1424 f¹³ | + καὶ ἔθηκα ὑμᾶς ℵ A B D L N Θ Ψ f¹ 33 𝔐 (latt) | var. lect.
16:16 unte ik gagga du attin ὅτι ἐγὼ ὑπάγω πρὸς τὸν πατέρα] 9c 33 1192 1210 1212 1505 l⁶⁶³·⁷³⁵·¹⁰⁷³·¹⁰⁷⁵·¹⁰⁷⁶s·¹⁰⁸²⁽¹⁾·¹⁰⁹¹·¹⁶⁹² | om. ὅτι ἐγὼ ὑπάγω πρὸς τὸν πατέρα p⁵·⁶⁶ ℵ B D L W it sa bomss | var. lect.
17:14 us þamma fairƕau ni im: ἐκ τοῦ κόσμου οὐκ εἰμί] M 0211 9 1243 l¹⁰⁷⁵·¹⁰⁹¹⁽³⁾ | 4 5 1 2 3 ℵ A B C L N W Θ Ψ f¹ 33 𝔐 (latt)
18:38 so: ἤ] f¹ | om. p⁶⁶ ℵ A B Ds L N W Θ Ψ f¹³ 33 𝔐
18:38 om. πάλιν] 0290 | + πάλιν p⁶⁶ ℵ A B Ds L N W Θ Ψ f¹ f¹³ 33 𝔐
18:39 ei: ἵνα (ἀπολύσω ὑμῖν)] ℵ K U W Π 27s 475s 700 | om. p⁶⁰vid A B C Ds L N Θ Ψ f¹ f¹³ 33 latt | var. lect.

I.2.2.3 Isolated readings
11/335 (3%)

7:7 ins: αὐτῶν¹] illis itf | αὐτοῦ rell.
7:7 ize: αὐτῶν²] eorum itf | αὐτοῦ rell.
7:12 sunjeins: ἀληθής] uerax itf | ἀγαθός rell.
7:23 iþ: δέ] autem itf | om. rell.
9:6 imma ana augona þata fani þamma blindin: αὐτοῦ ἐπὶ τοὺς ὀφθαλμοὺς τὸν πηλὸν τοῦ τυφλοῦ] Goth | αὐτοῦ τὸν πηλὸν ἐπὶ τοὺς ὀφθαλμούς pm | var. lect.
10:37 wajamerjau: βλασφημῶ] Goth | βλασφημεῖς rell.
12:9 Iesus: Ἰησοῦς] Iesus itf | om. rell.
15:2 goþ: καλόν] Goth | om. rell.
18:5 andhafjandans imma qeþun: ἀποκριθέντες αὐτῷ εἶπαν] respondentes ei dixerunt itf | ἀπεκρίθησαν αὐτῷ rell.
18:10 sah þan haitans was namin Malkus: ἦν δὲ ὄνομα ἐκείνῳ Μάλχος] Goth | ἦν δὲ ὄνομα τῷ δούλῳ ἐκείνῳ Μάλχος 27s l²⁵³ l¹⁰⁹⁶ | ἦν δὲ ὄνομα τῷ δούλῳ Μάλχος rell.
18:32 fraujins: (ὁ λόγος) κυρίου (πληρωθῇ)] Goth | (πληρωθῇ ὁ λόγος) τοῦ κυρίου Chrys | Ἰησοῦ rell.

I.3 The Epistle to the Romans

I.3.1 Byzantine readings
57/120 (47%)

7:6 gadauþnandans: ἀποθανόντες] ℵ A B C K L P Ψ 33 1739 𝔐 vg^ww Chrys | του θανάτου D F G it vg^cl Ambrst
7:13 frawaurhta frawaurhts: ἁμαρτωλὸς ἡ ἁμαρτία] ℵ A B C K L P Ψ 33 1739 𝔐 (lat) Chrys | 2 3 1 D F G it^ar.d.f.(g) vg^mss Ambrst
7:20 ik: ἐγώ] ℵ A K L P Ψ 33 1739 𝔐 bo Ambrst^mss | om. B C D F G latt sa Ambrst | var. lect.
7:23 in witoda: ἐν τῷ νόμῳ] ℵ B D F G K P Ψ 33 pm latt Ambrst | τῷ νόμῳ (A) L 1739 pm sy^p Chrys
7:25 awiliudo guda: εὐχαριστῶ τῷ θεῷ] ℵ* A K L P 1739 𝔐 sy | χάρις δὲ τῷ θεῷ ℵ¹ Ψ 33 | var. lect.
8:2 mik: με] A D K L P 1739^c 𝔐 lat sy^h sa Ambrst^mss | σε ℵ B F G 1739* it sy^p Ambrst | var. lect.
8:38 aggeljus: ἄγγελοι] ℵ A B C K L P Ψ 33 1739 𝔐 vg Chrys Ambrst^mss | ἄγγελός D F G it vg^ms Ambrst
8:38 ni mahteis nih andwairþo nih anawairþo: οὔτε δυνάμεις οὔτε ἐνεστῶτα οὔτε μέλλοντα] K L 33 𝔐 it^b.mon sy^p Ambrst^ms Chrys | 1 4 3 6 5 2 p^27vid.(46) ℵ A B C D F G 1739 (lat) co | var. lect.
9:4 triggwos: αἱ διαθῆκαι] ℵ C K Ψ 33 1739 𝔐 it vg^ww vg^st sy bo Ambrst Chrys | ἡ διαθήκη p^46 B D F G it^ar.b.dem vg^cl sa bo^mss Ambrst^mss | var. lect.
9:4 gahaita: αἱ ἐπαγγελίαι] ℵ A B C K L P Ψ 33 1739 𝔐 lat Chrys (Ambrst) | (ἡ) ἐπαγγελία p^46vid D F G it^ar bo^mss
9:6 Israel: Ἰσραήλ] p^46 ℵ A B K L Ψ 1739 𝔐 it^b vg^mss Chrys | Ἰσραηλῖταί D F G lat Ambrst
9:20 þannu nu jai manna: μενοῦνγε ὦ ἄνθρωπε] ℵ² D² K L P Ψ 33 𝔐 sy^h Chrys 2 3 1 ℵ* A (B) 1739 | var. lect.
9:26 qiþada im: ἐρρέθη αὐτοῖς] ℵ A D K L P Ψ 33 (1739) 𝔐 vg sy^h co | (ε)ἂν κληθήσονται p^46 F G it vg^mss sy^p Ambrst | var. lect.
9:28 gamaurgjands in garaihtein unte waurd gamaurgiþ: συντέμνων ἐν δικαιοσύνῃ ὅτι λόγον συντετμημένον] ℵ² D F G K L P Ψ 33 𝔐 lat sy^h Chrys Ambrst | συντέμνων p^46 ℵ* A B 1739 sy^p co | var. lect.
9:31 bi witoþ garaihteins: εἰς νόμον δικαιοσύνης] ℵ² F K L P Ψ 𝔐 lat sy Ambrst^mss | εἰς νόμον p^46vid ℵ* A B D G 1739 it^b.d*.g co Ambrst | var. lect.
9:32 us waurstwam witodis: ἐξ ἔργων νόμου] ℵ² D K L P Ψ 33 𝔐 it^d vg^ms sy Ambrst^ms | ἔργων ℵ* A B F G 1739 lat co Ambrst
10:3 seina garaihtein: ἰδίαν δικαιοσύνην] p^46 ℵ F G K L Ψ 33 𝔐 it^(b).d*.f.g Chrys Ambrst^mss | ἰδίαν A B D P 1739 it^ar vg co Ambrst
10:5 þo garaihtein us witoda þatei: τὴν δικαιοσύνην τὴν ἐκ τοῦ νόμου ὅτι] p^46 (ℵ²) (B) D² F G K L P (Ψ) 𝔐 it (sy^p) Chrys Ambrst | 7 1 2 3 4 5 6 (D*) (33*) 1739 vg co Ambrst^mss | var. lect.
10:8 qiþiþ: λέγει] p^46 ℵ A B K L P Ψ 1739 𝔐 lat | λέγει ἡ γραφή D (F) (G) 33 it^ar.d.(f.g) vg^cl bo Ambrst
10:9 in munþa þeinamma fraujin Iesu: ἐν τῷ στόματί σου κύριον Ἰησοῦν] ℵ D F G K L P Ψ 33 1739 𝔐 lat sy bo Chrys Ambrst | ἐν τῷ στόματί σου κύριον Ἰησοῦν Χριστόν p^46 A it^t | var. lect.
10:15 þize spillondane gawairþi þize spillondane: τῶν εὐαγγελιζομένων εἰρήνην τῶν εὐαγγελιζομένων] ℵ² D F G K L P Ψ 33 pm lat sy Ambrst | τῶν εὐαγγελιζομένων p^46 ℵ* A B C 1739 pm it^ar co Ambrst^mss
10:20 anananþeiþ jah: ἀποτολμᾷ καί] p^46 ℵ A B C D¹ L P Ψ 33 1739 𝔐 lat Chrys Ambrst | om. D* F G it^d.f.g
11:16 jabai: εἰ] ℵ A B C D L P¹ Ψ 33 1739 𝔐 lat sy co Chrys Ambrst | om. p^46 F G P* it^f.g

11:17 þizai waurhtai jah smairþra: τῆς ῥίζης καὶ τῆς πιότητος] ℵ² A D¹ L P 33 1739 𝔐 it^ar vg sy Chrys Ambrst^ms | τῆς ῥίζης τῆς πιότητος ℵ* B C Ψ it^b | *var. lect.*
11:21 ibai aufto ni: μή πως οὐδέ] p⁴⁶ D F G L Ψ 33 𝔐 latt sy Chrys Ambrst | οὐδέ ℵ A B C P 1739 co | *var. lect.*
11:22 ƕassein: ἀποτομίαν] ℵ^2a D F G L Ψ 33 𝔐 latt Chrys | ἀποτομία p⁴⁶ ℵ*^.cvid A B C 1739
11:22 selein: χρηστότητα] D² F G L Ψ 33 𝔐 latt Ambrst | χρηστότης θεοῦ p⁴⁶ (ℵ) A B C D* 1739 | *var. lect.*
11:25 daubei: πώρωσις] p⁴⁶ ℵ A B C D F G L Ψ 33 1739 𝔐 Ambrst | caecitas latt sy Ambrst^mss
11:31 eis gaarmaindau: αὐτοὶ ἐλεηθῶσιν] p^46vid A D¹ F G L Ψ 1739 𝔐 latt Ambrst | αὐτοὶ νῦν ἐλεηθῶσιν ℵ B D*^.c bo | *var. lect.*
11:32 allans: τοὺς πάντας] ℵ A B D¹ L Ψ 33 1739 𝔐 Chrys Ambrst^mss | τὰ πάντα p^46vid D* (F) (G) latt Ambrst
12:1 waila galeikaidana guda: εὐάρεστον τῷ θεῷ] (p⁴⁶) ℵ² B D F G L Ψ 33 1739 𝔐 it^d.f.g.gue vg^ms Chrys Ambrst | *2 3 1* ℵ* A P lat
12:2 fraþjis izwaris: νοός ὑμῶν] ℵ D¹ L P Ψ 33 𝔐 latt sy Chrys Ambrst | νοός p⁴⁶ A B D* F G 1739
12:4 liþjus allai: μέλη πολλά] A L P Ψ 33 1739 𝔐 Chrys | *2 1* p^31.46 ℵ B D F G latt Ambrst
12:11 fraujin: κυρίῳ] p⁴⁶ ℵ A B D¹ L P Ψ 33 1739 𝔐 lat sy^p sy^h co Chrys Ambrst | καιρῷ D*^.c F G it^d*.fc.g Ambrst | *var. lect.*
12:14 wrikandans izwis: διώκοντας ὑμᾶς] ℵ A D L P Ψ 33^vid 𝔐 it^(b).d.t vg^cl sy Chrys (Ambrst^mss) | διώκοντας p⁴⁶ B 1739 vg^ww.st | *var. lect.*
13:1 (*Ambros.* A⁺) all saiwalo waldufnjam ufarwisandam ufhausjai: πᾶσα ψυχὴ ἐξουσίαις ὑπερεχούσαις ὑποτασσέσθω] ℵ A B D¹ L P Ψ 33 1739 𝔐 lat sy co Chrys Ambrst^mss / πάσαις ἐξουσίαις ὑπερεχούσαις ὑποτάσσεσθε p⁴⁶ D* F G it vg^mss Ambrst
13:4 fraweitands in þwairhein: ἔκδικος εἰς ὀργήν] p⁴⁶ ℵ² A B L P Ψ* 1739 *pm* it^ar.b.gue.t vg^mss Ambrst | *2 3 1* ℵ* D¹ Ψ^c 33 *pm* | *var. lect.*
13:7 nu: οὖν] ℵ² A D¹ F G L P 33 1739 𝔐 it vg^mss Chrys Ambrst | *om.* p⁴⁶ ℵ* A B D* 1739 vg Ambrst^ms
13:9 ni hlifais nih faihugeigais: οὐ κλέψεις οὐκ ἐπιθυμήσεις] p⁴⁶ A B D F G L Ψ 33 1739 *pm* it^d.f.g vg^ww.st sy^p sa Ambrst | οὐ κλέψεις οὐκ ψευδομαρτυρήσεις οὐκ ἐπιθυμήσεις ℵ (P) *pm* it^ar.b vg^cl (sy^h) bo Chrys Ambrst^mss | *var. lect.*
13:9 þamma: ἐν τῷ] ℵ A D L P Ψ 33 1739 𝔐 sy^h co Chrys | *om.* p^46vid B F G latt Ambrst
13:11 þatei mel ist uns ju: ὅτι ὥρα ἡμᾶς ἤδη] F G L Ψ 33 𝔐 it^ar.f.g.t Chrys Ambrst | ὅτι ὥρα ἤδη ὑμᾶς ℵ* B C lat Ambrst^mss | *var. lect.*
14:5 sums raihtis: ὃς μέν] p⁴⁶ ℵ² B C² D F G L Ψ 33 1739 𝔐 sy Chrys | + γάρ ℵ* A P latt Ambrst
14:10 þeinamma: σου] ℵ A B C D¹ L P Ψ 33 1739 𝔐 it^gue vg Chrys Ambrst^mss | + ἐν τῷ μὴ ἐσθίειν D* (G) (F) it Ambrst
14:10 Xristaus: Χριστοῦ] ℵ² C² L P Ψ 33 𝔐 it^gue.r3 vg^cl sy Chrys Ambrst | θεοῦ ℵ* A B C* D F G 1739 lat co Ambrst^mss
14:11 þatei: ὅτι] ℵ A B C D¹ L P Ψ 33 1739 𝔐 (lat) Chrys Ambrst | εἰ μή D*^vid F G
14:12 nu: οὖν] ℵ A C D¹ P^c Ψ 33 𝔐 sy^h Chrys | *om.* B D* F G L P* 1739 lat
14:12 guda: τῷ θεῷ] ℵ A C D¹ L P Ψ 33 𝔐 lat sy co Chrys Ambrst | *om.* B F G 1739 it^f.g.r3 Ambrst
14:14 fraujin: κυρίῳ] ℵ A B C D F G Ψ 1739 *pm* lat Chrys | Χριστῳ L P 33 *pm* | *var. lect.*
14:18 in þaim: τούτοις] ℵ² D¹ L Ψ 33 𝔐 it^b.gue vg^mss sy Chrys Ambrst | τούτῳ ℵ* A B C D* F G P 1739 lat
14:19 laistjaima: διώκωμεν] C D Ψ 33 1739 𝔐 latt co Chrys Ambrst | διώκομεν ℵ A B F G L P
14:19 in uns misso: εἰς ἀλλήλους] ℵ A B C D¹ L P Ψ 33 1739 𝔐 it^r Chrys | + φυλάξωμεν D* F G (lat) Ambrst

15:4 fauragameliþ warþ: προεγράφη] ℵ A C D F G L 1739 𝔐 it^{gue.(r3)} Chrys Ambrst^{mss} | προεγράφη πάντα P Ψ 33 | *var. lect.*
15:5 Xristu Iesu: Χριστὸν Ἰησοῦν] B D G L Ψ 33 1739 𝔐 it^{d.g.gue} vg^{mss} Chrys Ambrst | *2 1* ℵ A C F P lat sy Ambrst^{mss}
15:7 izwis: ὑμᾶς] ℵ A C D¹ F G L Ψ 33 1739 *pm* lat sy bo Chrys Ambrst | ἡμᾶς B D* P *pm* it^{ar.b.d*.r3} sa
15:8 Xristu Iesu: Χριστὸν Ἰησοῦν] L P 33 𝔪 it^{ar.gue.t} vg Chrys | Χριστόν p^{46} ℵ A B C Ψ 1739 it^{b.r3} Ambrst | *var. lect.*
15:9 frauja: κύριε] ℵ² 33 *pm* it^{ar.gue.t} vg^{cl} sy^h bo^{mss} Chrys | *om.* ℵ* A B C D F G L P Ψ 1739 *pm* lat Ambrst
16:25-16:27 Τῷ... ἀμήν] (only after Romans 14:23) Goth^{vid} L Ψ 𝔐 it^{guevid.mvid} sy^h Chrys | (here) p^{61} ℵ B C D 81 630 1739 2200 it^{ar.b.d*.f} vg sy^p co Ambrst | *var. lect.*

I.3.2 Non-Byzantine readings
I.3.2.1 Readings supported by 'Western' witnesses
Sub-group A
38/120 (32%)

7:4 swaei nu jah jus broþrjus meinai: ὥστε καὶ ὑμεῖς ἀδελφοί μου] ℵ 1735 Ambrst^{mss} | *1 4 5 2 3* A B C D K L P Ψ 33 1739 𝔐 latt Chrys Ambrst | *var. lect.*
7:7 unte lustu: τὴν γὰρ ἐπιθυμίαν] F G 1506 latt Ambrst^{mss} | τήν τε γὰρ ἐπιθυμίαν ℵ A B C D K L P Ψ 33 1739 𝔐 Ambrst | *var. lect.*
7:13 warþ: ἐγένετο] ℵ A B C D P 330 365 1270 1319 1573 1739 1881 vg | γέγονεν K L Ψ 33 𝔐 it Ambrst | *var. lect.*
7:15 þatei waurkja: ὃ κατεργάζομαι] 999 it^{d*} | ὃ γὰρ κατεργάζομαι ℵ A B C D F G K L P Ψ 33 1739 𝔐 lat Chrys Ambrst
8:34 saei ist: ὃς ἐστιν] ℵ* A C 131 323 424 440 460 547 618 796 945 1242 1315 1734 1738 1506 1836 2125 Chrys it vg^{ww} bo | ὃς καί ἐστιν p^{27.46} ℵ² B D F G K L Ψ 33 𝔐 it^{b.f.g} vg^{st} sy^h sa | *var. lect.*
8:39 nih gaskafts: οὔτε κτίσις] p^{46} D F G 1505 2495 lat sy Ambrst | οὔτε τις κτίσις ℵ A B C K L Ψ 33 1739 𝔐 (it^t) | *var. lect.*
9:3 anaþaima wisan silba ik: ἀνάθεμα εἶναι αὐτὸς ἐγώ] p^{46} A B D F G Ψ 1505 1735 2495 it^{b.d*.f.g} Chrys Ambrst^{mss} | *3 4 1 2* ℵ C K L 33 1739 𝔪 vg | *var. lect.*
9:19 aþþan ƕa: τί οὖν] p^{46} B D F G it vg^{mss} | τί ℵ A K L P Ψ 33 1739 𝔐 vg sy Chrys Ambrst
9:22 þata mahteigo: τὸ δυνατόν] 205 it^{ar} vg^{ms} | τὸ δυνατὸν αὐτοῦ p^{46} ℵ A B D F G K L P Ψ 33 1739 𝔐 lat Chrys Ambrst
9:23 ei: ἵνα] B 6^c 69 326 424 436 1837 1912 1739^{mg} it^{ar.b} vg Ambrst^{mss} | καὶ ἵνα p^{46vid} ℵ A D F G K L P Ψ 33 1739* it^{d.g} vg^{ms} Ambrst Chrys
9:32 bistuggqun: προσέκοψαν] p^{46} ℵ A B D* F G 1739 it^{d.g} vg Ambrst^{mss} | προσέκοψαν γάρ D² K L P Ψ 33 𝔐 it^{ar.b.f} vg^{ms} Chrys Ambrst
9:33 jah sa: καὶ ὁ] ℵ A B D F G it sy^p co Ambrst | καὶ πᾶς ὁ K L P Ψ 33 1739 𝔐 it^{ar} vg sy^h Chrys Ambrst^{mss}
10:1 ins: αὐτῶν] p^{46} ℵ* A B D F G it sy^p co Ambrst | τοῦ Ἰσραήλ ἐστιν K L 𝔐 | *var. lect.*
10:5 in izai: ἐν αὐτῇ] ℵ* A B 33 1739 vg co | ἐν αὐτοῖς p^{46} ℵ² D F G K L P Ψ 𝔐 it sy Ambrst
10:17 Xristaus: Χριστοῦ] p^{46vid} ℵ* B C^{vid} D* 1739 lat co Ambrst^{mss} | θεοῦ ℵ¹ A D¹ K L P Ψ 33 𝔐 sy Chrys | *var. lect.*

10:19 ibai Israel ni fanþ: Ἰσραὴλ οὐκ ἔγνω] p⁴⁶ ℵ A B C D F G P 1739 latt Chrys Ambrst | *2 3 1* L Ψ 33 𝔐
11:1 arbja: τὴν κληρονομίαν] p⁴⁶ F G it^(b.f.g) Ambrst | τὸν λαόν ℵ A B C D L P Ψ 33 1739 𝔐 it^(ar.d) vg sy^(p.h) co Chrys Ambrst^(mss)
11:26 sa lausjands: ῥυόμενος] p⁴⁶ ℵ A B C D* F G 1739 | + καί D¹ L Ψ 33 𝔐 latt Chrys Ambrst
11:30 raihtis: γάρ] p⁴⁶ ℵ¹ A B C D* F G 1739 it^(d.f.g.t) co Ambrst^(mss) | + καί ℵ² D¹ L Ψ 33 𝔐 lat sy Chrys Ambrst | *var. lect.*
12:2 ni: μή] 424^c 1739 it^(d*.gue) Chrys | καὶ μή p⁴⁶ ℵ A B D F G L P Ψ 33 𝔐 lat Ambrst | *var. lect.*
12:3 anst gudis: χάριτος τοῦ θεοῦ] L 049 69 81 205 209 323 330 424 547 796 945 999 1241 1315 1448 1506 1735 1827 1854 1891 2400 it^(gue.t) vg^(ms) sy^h | χάριτος p⁴⁶ ℵ A B D F G P Ψ 33 1739 𝔪 lat Chrys Ambrst
12:4 taui haband: πρᾶξιν ἔχει] p⁴⁶ F lat sy^(p.h) (Ambrst^(mss)) | *2 1* ℵ A B D G L P Ψ 33 1739 𝔐 it^(d.f.g) vg^(mss) Chrys (Ambrst)
12:15 faginondam: χαιρόντων] p⁴⁶ ℵ B D* F G 1739 latt sy^h Ambrst | + καί A D² L P 𝔐 sy^p Chrys
12:20 jabai gredo: ἐὰν πεινᾷ] p^(46vid) D* F G Ψ (+ 31 other Greek witnesses)⁶⁵⁹ it Ambrst | ἀλλὰ ἐὰν πεινᾷ ℵ A B P 1739 it^(ar.t) vg | *var. lect.*
12:20 iþ jabai: ἐὰν δέ] D¹ Ψ 517 1505 1735 2495 sy^h | ἐάν ℵ A B D F G P Ψ 1739 𝔐 lat Chrys Ambrst | *var. lect.*
13:1 iþ þo wisandona fram: αἱ δὲ οὖσαι ὑπό] ℵ A B D* F G 1739 latt co Ambrst | αἱ δὲ οὖσαι ἐξουσίαι ὑπό D¹ L P Ψ 33 𝔐 sy Chrys
13:3 godamma waurstwa ak ubilamma: τῷ ἀγαθῷ ἔργῳ ἀλλὰ τῷ κακῷ] p⁴⁶ ℵ A B D* F² G P 1739 (latt) co | τῶν ἀγαθῶν ἔργων ἀλλὰ τῶν κακῶν D¹ L Ψ 33 𝔐 (sy) Chrys Ambrst
13:8 izwis misso frijoþ: τὸ ἀλλήλους ἀγαπᾶν] p⁴⁶ ℵ A B D F G P 1739 latt Ambrst | *3 1 2* L Ψ 33 𝔐
13:12 uswairpam: ἀποβαλώμεθα] p⁴⁶ D*.² F G latt Ambrst | ἀποθώμεθα ℵ A B C D¹ L P Ψ 33 1739 𝔐
13:14 fraujin unsaramma Xristau Iesua: τὸν κύριον ἡμῶν Ἰησοῦν Χριστόν] 1827 it^(ar.t) Chrys | τὸν κύριον Ἰησοῦν Χριστόν ℵ A C D F G L P Ψ 33 𝔐 lat sy Ambrst | *var. lect.*
14:9 jah qiwaim jah daubaim: καὶ ζώντων καὶ νεκρῶν] 056 0142 1739 it^(ar.d.gue) vg^(mss) Ambrst | *1 4 3 2* ℵ A B C D F G L P Ψ 33 1739 𝔐 lat Chrys Ambrst^(mss)
14:11 andhaitiþ all razdo: ἐξομολογήσεται πᾶσα γλῶσσα] p^(46vid) B D*.² F G it vg^(mss) Ambrst | *2 3 1* ℵ A C D¹ L P Ψ 33 1739 𝔐 vg Chrys
14:12 usgibiþ: ἀποδώσει] B D* F G P^c 326 1837 latt Chrys Ambrst | δώσει ℵ A C D² L (P) Ψ 33 1739 𝔐
15:4 gameliþ warþ: ἐγράφη] ℵ B C D F G 1739 latt sy^p Ambrst | προεγράφη A L P Ψ 33 𝔐 sy^h Chrys
15:11 aftra qiþiþ: πάλιν λέγει] B D F G 1 1505 1735 2495 it sy Ambrst | πάλιν ℵ A C L P Ψ 33 1739 𝔐 it^(ar.t) vg Ambrst^(mss)
15:11 allos þiudos fraujan: πάντα τὰ ἔθνη τὸν κύριον] p^(46vid) ℵ A B D P Ψ 1739 it^(b.gue) vg sy^h Chrys Ambrst | *4 5 1 2 3* C F G L 33 𝔐 it vg^(mss) | *var. lect.*
15:11 hazjaina: ἐπαινεσάτωσαν] p⁴⁶ ℵ A B C D Ψ 81 88 326 365 1319 1505 1506 1573 1739 1837 1881 2495 | ἐπαινέσατε F G L P 33 𝔐 latt sy Chrys Ambrst
16:23 allaizos aikklesjons: ὅλης τῆς ἐκκλησίας] ℵ A B C D P 1739 latt (Ambrst) | *2 3 1* L Ψ 33 𝔪 Chrys | *var. lect.*

---

659 Aland *et al.* 1991, 381.

Sub-group B
14/120 (12%)

7:3 haitada horinondei: χρηματίσει μοιχαλίς] D F G (latt) (Ambrst) | *2 1* א A B C K L P Ψ 33 1739 𝔐 Chrys

7:15 wiljau tauja: θέλω πράσσω] D F G it$^{d.f.g}$ Ambrst^{ms} | θέλω τοῦτο πράσσω א A B C K L P Ψ 33 1739 𝔐 lat Ambrst | *var. lect.*

9:1 qiþa: λέγω] vg^{ms} | + ἐν Χριστῷ p^{46} א A B C D^2 K L Ψ 33 1739 𝔐 lat Chrys | *var. lect.*

9:3 þans samakunjans: τῶν συγγενῶν] D* F G it$^{b.d*.(g)}$ Ambrst | + μου p^{46} א A B C D^2 K L P Ψ 33 1739 𝔐 lat Ambrst^{mss}

9:4 witodis garaideins jah triggwos: ἡ νομοθεσία καὶ αἱ διαθῆκαι] Ambrst | *4 5 3 1 2* p^{46} א B C D F G K P Ψ 33 1739 𝔐 Chrys Ambrst^{mss}

9:11 aiþþau: ἤ] F G latt Ambrst | μηδέ p^{46} א A B D K L P Ψ 1739 𝔐 Chrys

9:21 kasja waldufni: ὁ κεραμεὺς ἐξουσίαν] Ambrst^{ms} | *3 1 2* p^{46} א A B C D F G K L P Ψ 33 1739 𝔐 latt Chrys Ambrst | *var. lect.*

9:22 bi kasam: εἰς σκεύη] F G (it) Ambrst | σκεύη א A B D K L P Ψ 33 1739 𝔐 vg Chrys

10:14 aiþþau: ἤ] F G (latt) | *om.* p^{46} א A B D K L P Ψ 33 1739 𝔐

11:13 swa lagga swe ik im: ἐφ' ὅσον ἐγὼ εἰμι] F G it$^{d*.f.g}$ vg^{ms} | ἐφ' ὅσον μὲν οὖν εἰμι ἐγώ p^{46} א A B C P Chrys | *var. lect.*

11:23 jah jainai: κἀκεῖνοι] it$^{b.d*.f.g}$ Ambrst^{mss} | κἀκεῖνοι δέ א A B C D F G L Ψ 33 1739 𝔐 vg Chrys Ambrst

12:17 ni þatainei in andwairþja gudis ak jah in andwairþja: οὐ μόνον ἐνώπιον τοῦ θεοῦ ἀλλὰ καὶ ἐνώπιον] F G 629 lat Ambrst | ἐνώπιον p^{46} א A* B D L P Ψ 33 1739 𝔐 it^d sy$^{p.h}$ Chrys | *var. lect.*

13:5 ufhausjaiþ: ὑποτάσσεσθε] D F G it Ambrst | ἀνάγκη ὑποτάσσεσθαι א A B L P Ψ 048 33 1739 𝔐 it$^{ar.t}$ (vg) sy co Chrys Ambrst^{mss} | *var. lect.*

14:16 ni wajamerjaidau unsar: μὴ βλασφημείσθω ἡμῶν] F G it^g sy^p Ambrst | μὴ βλασφημείσθω οὖν ὑμῶν א A B C L P 33 1739 𝔐 lat sy^h co Chrys | *var. lect.*

I.3.2.2 Readings not supported by 'Western' witnesses
7/120 (6%)

7:18 ni: οὔ] א A B C 6 81 424^c 436 1739 1852 1881 2200 co | οὐχ εὑρίσκω D F G K L P Ψ 33 1506 𝔐 latt sy Ambrst Chrys | *var. lect.*

7:25 skalkino gahugdai: δουλεύω τῷ (μὲν) νοΐ] 1505 2495 | *2 3 4 1* א^2 A B D K L P Ψ 33 1739 𝔐 latt Chrys Ambrst |*var. lect.*

9:26 þai haitanda: αὐτοὶ κληθήσονται] Ψ 1504 2495 | ἐκεῖ κληθήσονται p^{46} א A B D F G K L P Ψ 33 1739 𝔐 lat Ambrst | *var. lect.*

9:32 ak: ἀλλ'] 1874 2344 2400 | ἀλλ' ὡς א A B D F G K L P Ψ 33 1739 𝔐 latt Ambrst

12:17 manne allaize: ἀνθρώπων πάντων] Chrys | *2 1* א A* B D^1 L P Ψ 33 1739 𝔐 it$^{b.f}$ vg | *var. lect.*

14:4 frauja: ὁ κύριος] p^{46} א A B C P Ψ sy^p co | ὁ θεός D F G L 33 1739 𝔐 latt sy^h Chrys Ambrst | *var. lect.*

14:11 all kniwe biugiþ: πᾶν γόνυ κάμψει] 330 2400 | *3 1 2* א A B C D F G L P Ψ 33 1739 𝔐 (latt) Chrys (Ambrst)

I.3.2.3 Isolated readings
4/120 (3%)

9:3 usbida: εὔχομαι] Goth | ηὐχόμην rell.
11:33 unusspilloda sind: ἀνεκδιηγήτα] Goth | ἀνεξεραύνητα rell.
12:19 mis fraweit leitaidau: ἐμοὶ ἐκδίκησις ἀφεθῇ?] Goth | ἐμοὶ ἐκδίκησις rell.
16:24 ansts fraujins unsaris Iesuis Xristaus miþ ahmin izwaramma. amen: ἡ χάρις τοῦ κυρίου ἡμῶν Ἰησοῦ Χριστοῦ μετὰ τοῦ πνεύματος ὑμῶν. ἀμήν] Goth | om. p⁴⁶.⁶¹ ℵ A B C 1739 it^b vg^ww.st co Ambrst | var. lect.

I.4 The Epistle to the Galatians

I.4.1 Byzantine readings
42/82 (51%)

1:3 jah fraujin unsaramma: καὶ κυρίου ἡμῶν] p⁴⁶.⁵¹ᵛⁱᵈ B D F G K L 1739 𝔐 lat sy sa bo^mss | 3 1 2 ℵ A P Ψ 33 it^ar.b vg^mss Chrys Ambrst | var. lect.
1:4 andwairþin aiwa: ἐνεστῶτος αἰῶνος] ℵ² D F G K L P Ψ 𝔐 latt Chrys Ambrst | αἰῶνος τοῦ ἐνεστῶτος p⁴⁶.⁵¹ᵛⁱᵈ ℵ* A B 33 1739
1:6 Xristaus: Χριστοῦ] p⁵¹ ℵ A B F^c K L P Ψ 33 1739 𝔐 it^f vg sy^p bo Chrys | om. p⁴⁶ᵛⁱᵈ F* G it^ar.b.g Ambrst | var. lect.
2:5 þaimei ni(h): οἷς οὐδέ] p⁴⁶ ℵ A B C D² F G K L P Ψ 33 1739 𝔐 (lat) sy^h co Chrys | om. D* it^b.d vg^ms Ambrst | var. lect.
2:9 weis: ἡμεῖς] ℵ* B F G K L Ψ 33 pm lat Chrys Ambrst | + μέν ℵ² A C (D) 1739 pm it^r3
2:10 þizei unledane ei gamuneima: τῶν πτωχῶν ἵνα μνημονεύωμεν] ℵ A B C K L P Ψ 33 1739 𝔐 Chrys | 3 1 2 4 D F G (latt) Ambrst
2:11 Paitrus: Πέτρος] D F G K L 𝔐 it vg^mss sy^h Chrys Ambrst | Κηφᾶς ℵ A B C P Ψ 33 1739 vg sy^hmg
2:12 qemun: ἦλθον] A C D¹ K L P Ψ 1739 𝔐 it^ar.f.r3 vg sy co Chrys Ambrst | ἦλθεν p⁴⁶ ℵ B D* F G 33 it^b.d.g
2:14 Paitrau: Πέτρῳ] D F G K L P 𝔐 it vg^mss sy^h Chrys Ambrst | Κηφᾷ p⁴⁶ ℵ A B C 33 vg co
2:16 aþþan: δέ] ℵ B C D* F G L pm lat Ambrst | om. p⁴⁶ A D² K P Ψ 33 1739 pm sy^h vg^ms Chrys | var. lect.
2:16 Iesuis Xristaus: Ἰησοῦ Χριστοῦ] p⁴⁶ ℵ C D F G K L P Ψ 1739 𝔐 lat Chrys Ambrst | 2 1 A B 33 vg^mss
2:16 Xristau Iesua: Χριστὸν Ἰησοῦν] ℵ A C D F G Ψ 𝔐 (lat) Ambrst | 2 1 p⁴⁶ B K L P 33 1739 it^ar.d sy
2:16 unte ni wairþiþ garaihts us waurstwam witodis: διότι οὐ δικαιωθήσεται ἐξ ἔργων νόμου] 𝔐 it^f vg | ὅτι ἐξ ἔργων νόμου οὐ δικαιωθήσεται p⁴⁶ ℵ A B D* F G 33 1739 it Ambrst | var. lect.
2:20 sunus gudis: υἱοῦ τοῦ θεοῦ] ℵ A C D¹ K L P Ψ 33 1739 𝔐 lat sy bo Chrys Ambrst | θεοῦ καὶ Χριστοῦ p⁴⁶ B D* F G it^d.g | var. lect.
3:1 sunjai ni ufhausjan: τῇ ἀληθείᾳ μὴ πείθεσθαι] C D² K L P Ψ 33^c 𝔐 it^f vg^cl sy^h | om. ℵ A B D* F G 33* 1739 lat sy^p co
3:1 in izwis: ἐν ὑμῖν] D F G K L 33^c 𝔐 it vg^cl sy^h Chrys Ambrst | om. ℵ A B C P Ψ 33* 1739 it^f.r3 vg^st co
3:2 wiljau witan fram izwis: θέλω μαθεῖν ἀφ' ὑμῶν] ℵ A B C K L Ψ 33 1739 𝔐 Chrys it^ar.b.r3 Ambrst | 2 1 3 4 D F G it^d.g | var. lect.

3:29 Xristaus þannu: Χριστοῦ ἄρα] ℵ A B C K L Ψ 33 1739 𝔐 lat Chrys | ἐν Χριστῷ Ἰησοῦ ἄρα οὖν D F G it^{d.g} vg^{mss} Ambrst

3:29 jab bi: καὶ κατ'] F G K L Ψ 𝔐 it^g Chrys | κατ' ℵ A B C D 33 1739 lat Ambrst

4:6 izwara: ὑμῶν] D² K L Ψ 33 𝔐 vg^{cl} sy bo^{mss} Chrys | ἡμῶν p^{46} ℵ A B C D* F G P 1739 lat sa bo^{mss} Ambrst

4:7 gudis þairh Xristu: θεοῦ διὰ Χριστοῦ] ℵ² C³ D K L 𝔐 it^{ar.d} Chrys | διὰ θεοῦ p^{46} ℵ* A B C* 33 1739*^{vid} lat bo Ambrst | *var. lect.*

4:10 melam jah aƕnam: καιροὺς καὶ ἐνιαυτούς] p^{46} ℵ A B C K L Ψ 33 1739 𝔐 lat Chrys Ambrst | *3 2 1* D F G it

4:15 ƕileika was nu: τίς οὖν ἦν] D K 𝔪 it^{b.d.r3} Chrys Ambrst | ποῦ οὖν p^{46} ℵ A B C Ψ 33 1739 lat | *var. lect.*

4:17 aljanoþ: ζηλοῦτε] ℵ A B C D² K L Ψ 33 1739 𝔐 vg Chrys | + ζηλοῦτε δὲ τὰ κρείττω χαρίσματα D* F G it Ambrst

4:19 barnilona: τεκνία] ℵ² A C D¹ K L Ψ 33 𝔐 lat Chrys | τέκνα ℵ* B D* F G 1739 it^{d.g} Ambrst

4:21 hauseiþ: ἀκούετε] p^{46} ℵ A B C K L Ψ 33 1739 𝔐 Chrys | ἀναγινώσκετε D F G latt Ambrst

4:28 weis...sium: ἡμεῖς...ἐσμέν] ℵ A C D² K L P Ψ 𝔐 lat sy bo Chrys | ὑμεῖς...ἐστέ p^{46} B D* F G 33 1739 it^{b.d.g.t} sa Ambrst

4:30 miþ sunau frijaizos: μετὰ τοῦ υἱοῦ τῆς ἐλευθέρας] p^{46} ℵ A B C D² K L P Ψ 33 1739 𝔐 it^{f.r3} Chrys | μοῦ Ἰσαάκ D* F G it vg^{ms} Ambrst

5:7 ni ufhausjan: μὴ πείθεσθαι] p^{46} ℵ A B C D K L Ψ 33 1739 𝔐 it^d vg Ambrst | + μηδενὶ πείθεσθε F G it^{ar.b.f.g} vg^{mss}

5:8 so gakunds ni: ἡ πεισμονὴ οὐκ] p^{46} ℵ A B C D² F G K L Ψ 33 1739 𝔐 lat Chrys | ἡ πεισμονή D* it^{b.d} | *var. lect.*

5:14 usfulljada: πληροῦται] D F G K L Ψ 𝔐 latt Chrys Ambrst | πεπλήρωται p^{46} ℵ A B C 33 1739

5:14 in þamma: ἐν τῷ] p^{46} ℵ A B C D² Ψ 33 1739 𝔐 Chrys | *om.* D* F G latt Ambrst

5:15 izwis misso beitiþ jah fairinoþ: ἀλλήλους δάκνετε καὶ κατεσθίετε] p^{46} ℵ A B C K L Ψ 33 1739 𝔐 (lat) Chrys | *2 3 4 1* D F G it^{(b.d).f.g} | *var. lect.*

5:19 horinassus kalkinassus: μοιχεία πορνεία] ℵ² D (F G) K L Ψ 1739^{mg} 𝔐 it^{b.d.g} sy^h | πορνεία ℵ* A B C P 33 1739* it^{ar} vg sy^p co | *var. lect.*

5:21 neiþa maurþra: φθόνοι φόνοι] A C D F G K L Ψ 1739 𝔐 lat (sy^p) bo Chrys | φθόνοι p^{46} ℵ B P 33 vg^{mss} sa Ambrst | *var. lect.*

5:24 Xristaus: Χριστοῦ] p^{46} D F G K L P 𝔐 latt sy Chrys Ambrst | + Ἰησοῦ ℵ A B C P Ψ 33 1739 co | *var. lect.*

5:25 libam ahmin: ζῶμεν πνεύματι] p^{46} ℵ A B C F K L P Ψ 33 1739 𝔐 lat Ambrst | *2 1* D G it^{d.g} vg^{mss} Ambrst^{mss}

6:1 þu: σύ] p^{46} ℵ A B C D² K L P Ψ 33 1739 𝔐 lat Chrys Ambrst | αὐτός D* F G it^{d.g}

6:3 sis silbin fraþjamarzeins ist: ἑαυτὸν φρεναπατᾷ] D F G K L Ψ 𝔐 (latt) Ambrst | *2 1* p^{46} ℵ A B C 33 1739 Chrys

6:8 us þamma leika: ἐκ τῆς σαρκός] ℵ A B C D² K L P Ψ 33 1739 𝔐 lat Ambrst | + αὐτοῦ D* F G it^{d.g} Chrys

6:13 bimaitanai sind: περιτεμνόμενοι] ℵ A C D K P 33 1739 *pm* it^{ar.f} vg sy Chrys | περιτετμημένοι p^{46} B (F G) L Ψ *pm* it^{b.d.g.r3} co Ambrst

6:16 gudis: θεοῦ] p^{46} ℵ A B C D² K L P Ψ 33 1739 𝔐 lat Chrys Ambrst | κυρίου D* F G it^d vg^{ms}

I.4.2 Non-Byzantine readings
I.4.2.1 Readings supported by 'Western' witnesses
Sub-group A
15/82 (18%)

2:9 Paitrus jah Iakobus: Πέτρος καὶ Ἰάκωβος] D F G 629 1175 it vg^{mss} Ambrst | Ἰάκωβος καὶ Κηφᾶς ℵ B C K L P Ψ 33 1739 𝔐 vg sy co Chrys | *var. lect.*

2:13 imma: αὐτῷ] p^{46} B 6 630 1739 1881 it$^{ar.f}$ vg bo | + καί ℵ A C D F G P Ψ 33 𝔐 it$^{b.d.g.r3}$ vg^{ms} sy sa Ambrst

2:13 þizai litai ize: τῇ ὑποκρίσει αὐτῶν] D F G P Ψ 33 it$^{ar.(g)}$ Ambrst | *3 1 2* p^{46} ℵ A B C K L 1739 𝔐 it^{r3} Chrys | *var. lect.*

2:14 libais jah ni iudaiwisko ƕaiwa: ζῇς καὶ οὐκ Ἰουδαϊκῶς πῶς] D^1 330 1270 1837 2400 2464 vg^{mss} | καὶ οὐχὶ Ἰουδαϊκῶς ζῇς πῶς ℵ A B C P Ψ 33 it$^{f.g}$ | *var. lect.*

3:28 nih qinakund: οὐδὲ θῆλυ] lat Ambrst | καὶ θῆλυ ℵ A B C D F G K L Ψ 33 1739 𝔐 it$^{d.g.r3}$ | *var. lect.*

3:28 ain sijuþ in Xristau: ἕν ἐστε ἐν Χριστῷ] F G 33 latt Ambrst | εἷς ἐστε ἐν Χριστῷ ℵ^2 B C D K L P Ψ 1739 𝔐 Chrys | *var. lect.*

4:25 gamarkoþ: συστοιχοῦσα] D* F G (latt) Ambrst | συστοιχεῖ δέ p^{46} ℵ A B C K L P Ψ 33 1739 𝔐

4:26 unsara: ἡμῶν] p^{46} ℵ* B C* D F G Ψ 33 1739 lat sy$^{p.h(mg)}$ co Ambrst | πάντων ἡμῶν ℵ^2 A C^3 K L P 𝔐 it$^{ar.b.t}$ vg^{mss} sy^h

5:1 þammei freihals uns Xristus frijans brahta standaiþ nu: ᾗ ἐλευθερίᾳ ἡμᾶς Χριστὸς ἠλευθέρωσεν στήκετε οὖν] F G it$^{g.r3}$ (sy$^{p.h}$) Ambrst | τῇ ἐλευθερίᾳ ἡμᾶς Χριστὸς ἠλευθέρωσεν στήκετε οὖν ℵ* A B P 33 sa (bo) | *var. lect.*

5:3 aþþan weitwodja: μαρτύρομαι δέ] D* F G 1739 1881 it Chrys Ambrst | + πάλιν p^{46} ℵ A B C D^2 K L Ψ 33 𝔐 vg

5:11 jabai bimait: εἰ περιτομήν] D* F G 0278 6 1739 1881 it vg^{mss} Ambrst | + ἔτι p^{46} ℵ A B (C) D^2 K L Ψ 33 𝔐 lat Chrys

5:13 ahmins: τοῦ πνεύματος] D F G 104 (it) vg^{cl} sa bo^{ms} Ambrst | *om.* p^{46} ℵ A B C K L Ψ 33 1739 𝔐 vgst

5:17 sis misso andstandand: ἀλλήλοις ἀντίκειται] A B C D F G P 075 33 1739 (lat) Ambrst | *2 1* ℵ K L Ψ 𝔐 Chrys | *var. lect.*

6:15 unte ni(h): οὔτε γάρ] p^{46} B Ψ 33 1739* it^{r3} (sy^p) sa^{mss} Chrys Ambrst | ἐν γὰρ Χριστῷ Ἰησοῦ οὔτε ℵ A C D F G K L P 1739^c 𝔐 lat sy^{h*} sa^{mss} bo

6:15 ist: ἔστιν] p^{46} ℵ* A B C D* F G 33 1739 it$^{d.g.r3}$ sy$^{p.hmg}$ co Ambrst | ἰσχύει ℵ^2 D^2 K L P Ψ 𝔐 lat sy^h Chrys

Sub-group B
17/82 (21%)

1:24 in mis mikilidedun: ἐν ἐμοὶ ἐδόξαζον] D F G (latt) Ambrst | *3 1 2* p^{46} ℵ A B C K L P Ψ 33 1739 𝔐 Chrys

2:1 usiddja aftra: ἀνέβην πάλιν] D F G it$^{ar.b.d.g}$ Ambrst^{ms} | *2 1* p^{46} ℵ A B K L P Ψ (33*) 1739 𝔐 lat sy$^{(p).h}$ sa Ambrst^{ms} | *var. lect.*

2:6 guþ mans andwairþi: θεὸς ἀνθρώπου πρόσωπον] D*c F G it^(d.g) Au (Pel^B) | πρόσωπον (ὁ) θεὸς ἀνθρώπου p^46 ℵ A B C D^2 K L P 33 1739 𝔐 | var. lect.
2:7 gatrauaida was mis: πεπίστευταί μοι] F G (lat) Ambrst | πεπίστευμαι p^46 ℵ A B C D^2 K L Ψ 33 1739 𝔐 Chrys | var. lect.
2:16 us galaubeinai Xristaus Iesuis: ἐκ πίστεως Χριστοῦ Ἰησοῦ] Goth per fidem Christi Iesu Au^var Pel^B | ἐκ πίστεως Χριστοῦ p^46 ℵ A B C D F G K L Ψ 33 1739 𝔐 lat Ambrst^mss | var. lect.
4:6 sunjus gudis: υἱοὶ θεοῦ] D F G it vg^mss Ambrst | υἱοί p^46 ℵ A B C K L P Ψ 33 1739 𝔐 vg Chrys
4:8 þaim þoei wistai ni sind guda skalkinodeduþ: τοῖς φύσει μὴ οὖσιν θεοῖς ἐδουλεύσατε] D F G it^(f.(r3)) vg | ἐδουλεύσατε τοῖς φύσει μὴ οὖσιν θεοῖς p^46 ℵ A B C 33 1739 | var. lect.
4:13 wituþ: οἴδατε] D* F G it Ambrst | + δέ p^46 ℵ A B C D^2 K L P 33 1739 𝔐 lat Chrys
4:31 þannu nu: διὸ οὖν] F G | διό ℵ B D K L 33 1739 𝔐 lat Ambrst | var. lect.
5:1 þammei freihalsa uns Xristus frijans brahta standaiþ nu: ᾗ ἐλευθερίᾳ ἡμᾶς Χριστὸς ἠλευθέρωσεν στήκετε οὖν] F G it^g | τῇ ἐλευθερίᾳ ἡμᾶς Χριστὸς ἠλευθέρωσεν· στήκετε οὖν ℵ* A B 33 sa (bo) | var. lect.
5:1 skalkinassaus jukuzja: δουλείας ζυγῷ] D F G it Ambrst | 2 1 ℵ A B C K L P^vid Ψ 33 1739 𝔐 lat Chrys | var. lect.
5:9 distairiþ: δολοῖ] D* lat Ambrst | ζυμοῖ p^46 ℵ A B C D^2 F G K L P Ψ 33 1739 𝔐 vg^ms Chrys
5:13 leikis taujaiþ: τῆς σαρκὸς δῶτε] carnis detis it^(ar.b.f) Ambrst Au Pel^B | τῇ σαρκί p^46 ℵ A B C D^2 K L Ψ 33 1739 𝔐 Chrys | var. lect.
5:14 witoþ in izwis: νόμος ἐν ὑμῖν] D* F G it^(ar.b.d.g) Ambrst | νόμος p^46 ℵ A B C D^2 Ψ 33 1739 m lat Chrys | var. lect.
5:23 gahobains swiknei: ἐγκράτεια ἁγνεία] D* F G it^(b.f.g) vg^cl Ambrst | ἐγκράτεια p^46 ℵ A B C D^2 K L P Ψ 33 1739 𝔐 vg^st sy co Chrys | var. lect.
5:24 sein: αὐτῶν] F G lat Ambrst | om. p^46 ℵ A B C D K L P Ψ 33 1739 𝔐 it^(b.d) vg^mss Chrys
6:4 in sis silbin: εἰς ἑαυτόν] 2464 it^gig | + μόνον p^46 ℵ A B C D F G K L P Ψ 33 1739 𝔐 (latt) Chrys Ambrst

I.4.2.2 Readings not supported by 'Western' witnesses
7/82 (9%)

1:5 du aiwam: εἰς τοὺς αἰῶνας] 1 209 460 796 1243 1245 1735 1837 Chrys | + τῶν αἰώνων p^46 ℵ A B D F G K L P Ψ 33 1739 𝔐 latt Ambrst
2:15 weis raihtis: ἡμεῖς δέ] 1505 1611 2495 | ἡμεῖς p^46 ℵ A B C D F G K L P Ψ 33 1739 𝔐 latt Chrys Ambrst
2:15 Iudaieis wisandans: Ἰουδαῖοι ὄντες] p^46 | Ἰουδαῖοι ℵ A B C D F G K L P Ψ 33 1739 𝔐 latt Chrys Ambrst
4:14 fraistubnjai: τὸν πειρασμόν] ℵ^2 0278 5 38 69 81 88 104 326 436 459 1241^s 1837 1984 1985 2464 (+ 62 other witnesses[660]) sy^p | + ὑμῶν ℵ* A B C^2 D* F G P 33 lat bo Ambrst | var. lect.
4:25 Seina: Σινᾶ] 61* 90 465* 1243 1352 1874* 2344 | δὲ Ἁγὰρ Σινᾶ A B D sy^hmg bo^mss | var. lect.
5:20 haifsteis aljan: ἔρεις ζῆλος] P | ἔρις ζῆλος B D* 1739 | var. lect.
6:1 jabai: ἐάν] K 440 | + καί p^46 ℵ A B C D F G L P Ψ 33 1739 𝔐 latt Chrys Ambrst

---

660 Aland et al. 1991, 155.

I.4.2.3 Double tradition
1/82 (1%)

6:17 Iesuis (*Ambros.* A⁺): Ἰησοῦ] p⁴⁶ A B C* 33 629 1071 1241ˢ 1753 it^{f.t} vg^{st} sa^{ms} | κυρίου Ἰησοῦ C³ D² K L 1739 𝔐 vg^{cl} sy^p
fraujins unsaris Iesuis Xristaus (*Ambros.* B): κυρίου ἡμῶν Ἰησοῦ Χριστοῦ] D* F G 104 1924 it^{ar.b.g} (sa^{mss}) Chrys Ambrost^{var} Pel^B | *var. lect.*

Appendix II

II.1 Table of the main codicological features of the Gothic manuscripts of the Gospels and Pauline Epistles

Legenda: '+': *membra disiecta*; '?' not verifiable; '??' in doubt; '–': not in agreement with other features of the manuscript.

	Codex Argenteus	Codex Carolinus	Codex Gissensis	Codex Ambros. A⁺	Codex Ambros. B	Codex Ambros. C
Number of folios	187+1	4	fragm. of a bifolio	102+4	78	2
Language	Goth.	Goth. and Lat.	Goth. and Lat.	Goth.	Goth.	Goth.
Columns per page	1	2 Goth. and Lat.	1	1	1	1
Marginal bounding lines	single	double	double	double (first part)/ single (second part)	single	single
Latin shape of ‹s›	yes	yes	yes	yes	no	yes
Suspension for ‹m›	yes	yes	?	yes	no	yes (apparently with the same mark of ‹n›)
Quire numbering in the last folio of each quire	yes	yes	?	yes	yes	yes
Current titles	yes	?	??	yes	no	yes
Superscriptions and subscriptions	yes	?	?	yes	yes	?
Enlarged letters in the middle of the line	occasionally (first hand)	–	–	occasionally (second hand)	occasionally	no
Punctuation	yes	–	–	yes (second part)	yes	yes
Graphic division of *cola et commata*	no	yes	yes	yes (first part)	no	no

II.2 The Long Ending of Mark

The *Codex Argenteus* transmits the Long Ending of Mark (16:9–20) after the verses 16:8, with A/02, C/04, D/05, L/19, W/032, Θ/038, Ψ/044, f¹ (marked by an obelos), f¹³, 33, 2427, 𝔐, aur/15, c/6, ff²/8, l/11, n/16 (down to v. 13), o/16 (from v. 14), q/13, vg, sy$^{c.p.h}$, bo. It is transmitted in part by the last Uppsala leaf (f. 187v, 16:9–12) and in part by the Speyer leaf (16:12–20). In the margin of v. 9 is the Ammonian Section 'sld' (= 234).

Legenda
Text

1st line: Greek text, according to Nestle-Aland^{28}

2nd line: Commentary line. It offers the Greek equivalent of the Gothic text, in case of divergence from Nestle-Aland^{28}.

| | indicates one or more Greek readings, which are equivalent with the Nestle-Aland^{28} reading in respect to the Gothic text. It is used when, for linguistic reasons, it is not possible to determine the underlying Greek reading of the Gothic text. Such readings are therefore worthless from a text-critical point of view and no information is given about the witnesses that support them.

–   indicates the absence in the Gothic version of a reading of the Nestle-Aland^{28} text.

{ }   indicates an unattested Greek reading, reconstructed on the basis of the Gothic text.

3rd line: Gothic text, according to Streitberg-Scardigli 2000, 504–507.

Apparatus

The apparatus is based on that of Nestle-Aland^{28}, with some additions according to Hodges-Farstad 1985, Jülicher *et al.* 1963–1976 (1970), Legg 1935, Swanson 1995–2005 (1995 B), VLD. The first reading always supports the Gothic text. Only the variants which are significant for the Gothic text are indicated. The witnesses always cited are: A/02, C/04, D/05, L/19, W/032, Θ/038, Ψ/044, f¹, f¹³, 33, 2427, 𝔐, aur/15, c/6, ff²/8, l/11, n/16 (until v. 13), o/16 (from v. 14), q/13, vg. In the cases in which the Gothic text diverges from 𝔐, all the manuscripts in agreement with the Gothic are indicated.⁶⁶¹

[16:9] Ἀναστὰς   δὲ   πρωῒ   πρώτῃ σαββάτου ἐφάνη   πρῶτον Μαρίᾳ
[16:9] Usstandands þan in maurgin frumin sabbato   ataugida ‹sik› frumist Marjin

---

661 Other symbols are listed above, see b. Symbols.

16:9 αναστας δε] A D L W Θ Ψ f¹ 33 2427 𝔐 it^{n.q} vg sy bo | αναστας C* it¹ | αναστας δε ο Ιησους F *pm* it^{aur.c.ff2} vg^s | αναστας ο Ιησους f¹³ *pc* — 16:9 εφανη πρωτον] A C L Θ Ψ f¹ f¹³ 33 2427 𝔐 latt sy bo | εφανη W | εφανερωσεν πρωτοις D

τῇ   Μαγδαληνῇ, παρ'   ἧς ἐκβεβλήκει ἑπτὰ δαιμόνια.   [16:10]   Ἐκείνη πορευθεῖσα
                        | ἀφ' |
þizai Magdalene, af þizaiei uswarp   sibun unhulþons. [16:10] Soh gaggandei

ἀπήγγειλεν τοῖς   μετ' αὐτοῦ γενομένοις πενθοῦσι καὶ κλαίουσιν· [16:11] κἀκεῖνοι
            | αὐτοῖς τοῖς |
gataih   þaim⁶⁶²   miþ imma wisandam qainondam jah gretandam. [16:11] jah eis

16:10 τοις μετ' αυτου] A C (αυτοις μετ' αυτου D) L W Ψ f¹ f¹³ 33 2427 𝔐 (latt) | τοις μαθηταις αυτου Θ — 16:10 και κλαιουσιν] A C D L Θ Ψ f¹ f¹³ 33 2427 𝔐 latt sy bo | *om*. W — 16:11 κακεινοι] A D W Θ Ψ f¹ f¹³ 33 2427 𝔐 it^{aur.l.n} vg sy bo | εκεινοι δε C* it^{c.ff2.q} bo | εκεινοι L U *pc* vg^{mss}

ἀκούσαντες ὅτι   ζῇ   καὶ   ἐθεάθη   ὑπ' αὐτῆς ἠπίστησαν. [16:12] Μετὰ δὲ
                                                                    | Καὶ μετὰ δὲ |
hausjandans þatei libaiþ jah gasaiƕans warþ fram izai ni galaubidedun. [16:12] Afaruh⁶⁶³ þan

16:11 αὐτῆς] A C D L W Θ Ψ f¹ f¹³ 33 2427 𝔐 latt sy bo | αὐτοῖς Θ — 16:11 ηπιστησαν] A C L W Θ Ψ f¹ f¹³ 33 2427 𝔐 lat sy^{c.h} bo | και ουκ επιστευσαν αυτη D^{(*)} | + eis vg^{ms} sy^p

ταῦτα δυσὶν ἐξ αὐτῶν περιπατοῦσιν ἐφανερώθη   ἐν ἑτέρᾳ   μορφῇ πορευομένοις εἰς
                                              —
þata twaim ize   ataugiþs warþ in anþaramma farwa gaggandam du

16:12 *om*. περιπατουσιν] f¹ arm^{ms} | περιπατουσιν A C D L W Θ Ψ f¹³ 33 2427 𝔐 latt sy bo

ἀγρόν· [16:13] κἀκεῖνοι ἀπελθόντες   ἀπήγγειλαν τοῖς λοιποῖς·   οὐδὲ ἐκείνοις
wehsa: [16:13] jah jainai galeiþandans gataihun þaim anþaraim; niþ þaim

16:13 εκεινοις] A C D W Θ Ψ f¹ f¹³ 33 2427 𝔐 lat sy bo | εκεινοι L it^{ff2}

ἐπίστευσαν. [16:14] Ὕστερον   [δὲ] ἀνακειμένοις   αὐτοῖς τοῖς ἕνδεκα ἐφανερώθη καὶ
                              δὲ | — |
galaubidedun. [16:14] Bi spedistin þan anakumbjandam þaim⁶⁶⁴ ainlibim ataugida, jah

16:14 δε] A D Θ f¹ 244 472 565 579 892 1424 2427 it^{aur.c.ff2.o.q} vg^s sy^{p.h**} co | *om*. δε C L W Ψ f¹³ 33 2427 𝔐 it¹ vg sa^{ms}

ὠνείδισεν τὴν ἀπιστίαν   αὐτῶν καὶ σκληροκαρδίαν ὅτι   τοῖς θεασαμένοις αὐτὸν
idweitida   ungalaubein ize   jah harduhairtein unte þaim gasaiƕandam ina

16:14 σκληροκαρδιαν] A C D L W Θ Ψ f¹ f¹³ 33 2427 𝔐 it^{aur.l} vg sy^{c.p.h} bo | + illorum it^{ff2.o.q} vg^{mss} | + eorum it^c vg^{ms}

---

662 See above 4.1.3.(4).
663 See above 4.1.2.(6).
664 See above 4.1.3.(4).

ἐγηγερμένον οὐκ ἐπίστευσαν.   [16:15] Καὶ εἶπεν αὐτοῖς·   Πορευθέντες εἰς τὸν κόσμον
                                              | πρὸς αὐτούς |
urrisanana   ni galaubidedun. [16:15] Jah qaþ du im: Gaggandans in þo manaseþ

16:14 εγηγερμενον] C³ D L W Θ Ψ 𝔐 lat sy^p sa bo^mss | εγηγερμενον εκ νεκρων A C* Δ f¹ f¹³ 28 33 565 579 892 1241 1424 (2427) *l*^844 *l*^211 vg^ms sy^h bo^mss | + et (- it° vg^mss) nuntiantibus it^o.q (+ illis vg^mss) — 16:14–15 επιστευσαν. και ειπεν αὐτοις] A C L Θ Ψ f¹ f¹³ 33 2427 𝔐 it^aur.ff2.l.q vg sy^c.p.h bo | crediderant. dicit eis it^c.o | επιστευσαν. και ειπεν προς αυτους D | επιστευσαν. κακεινοι απελογουντο λεγοντες οτι ο αιων ουτος της ανομιας και της απιστιας υπο τον σαταναν εστιν, ο μη εων τα (τον μη εωντα?) υπο των πνευματων ακαθαρτα (-των?) την αληθειαν του θεου καταλαβεσθαι (+ και? vel αληθινην pro αληθειαν) δυναμιν· δια τουτο αποκαλυψον σου την δικαιοσυνην ηδη, εκεινοι ελεγον τω χριστω. και ο χριστος εκεινοις προσελεγεν οτι πεπληρωται ο ὅρος των ετων της εξουσιας του σατανα, αλλα εγγιζει αλλα δεινα· και υπερ ων εγω αμαρτησαντων παρεδοθην εις θανατον ινα υποστρεψωσιν εις την αληθειαν και μηκετι αμαρτησωσιν ινα την εν τω ουρανω πνευματικην και αφθαρτον της δικαιοσυνης δοξαν κληρονομησωσιν. αλλα W

ἅπαντα κηρύξατε τὸ   εὐαγγέλιον   πάσῃ τῇ   κτίσει.   [16:16]   Ὁ πιστεύσας καὶ
                                                   { Καὶ }   { — }
alakjo merjaiþ   þo aiwaggeljon   allai þizai gaskaftai. [16:16] Jah sa galaubjands

16:15 απαντα] A C L W Θ Ψ f¹ f¹³ 33 2427 𝔐 lat sy | om. D 579* vg^ms bo — 16:15 κηρυξατε] A C L W Θ Ψ f¹ f¹³ 33 2427 𝔐 latt sy bo | και κηρυξατε D — 16:16 και¹] et qui it^ff2.q | qui autem it^c | οτι D^s 565 pc | om. A C L W Θ Ψ f¹ f¹³ 33 2427 𝔐 it^aur.l.<o> vg sy bo — 16:16 jah sa galaubjands ufdaupiþs] *pro* sa galaubjands jah ufdaupiþs?[665]

βαπτισθεὶς σωθήσεται, ὁ δὲ ἀπιστήσας   κατακριθήσεται. [16:17] Σημεῖα δὲ τοῖς
ufdaupiþs   ganisiþ,   iþ saei ni galaubeiþ   afdomjada. [16:17] Aþþan taikns þaim

16:16 κατακριθησεται] A C D^s L Θ Ψ f¹ f¹³ 33 2427 𝔐 latt sy bo | κατακριθεις ου σωθησεται W

πιστεύσασιν ταῦτα παρακολουθήσει·   ἐν   τῷ ὀνόματί μου   δαιμόνια   ἐκβαλοῦσιν,
           | παρακολουθήσει ταῦτα | | ἐπὶ | | ἐκβαλλοῦσιν |
           | ἀκολουθήσει ταῦτα |
galaubjandam þata[666] afargaggiþ: in   namin   meinamma unhulþons uswairpand[667],

γλώσσαις λαλήσουσιν καιναῖς, [16:18] [καὶ ἐν ταῖς χερσὶν] ὄφεις   ἀροῦσιν   κἂν
                                              —
razdom   rodjand   niujaim,   [16:18]   waurmans nimand, jah jabai

16:17 λαλησουσιν] A C L W Ψ f¹ f¹³ 33 2427 𝔐 latt sy bo | λαλησωσιν D^s Θ —
16:17 καιναις] A C² D^s W Θ f¹ f¹³ 33 2427 𝔐 (latt) sy | om. C* L Δ Ψ pc co —

---

[665] Scardigli 1973, 367.
[666] See above 4.1.1.(10), 4.1.2.(1) and 4.1.3.(8).
[667] See above 4.1.3.(2).

16:18 om. και εν ταις χερσιν] A D^s W Θ f^{13} 2427 𝔐 latt sy^p | και εν ταις χερσιν C L Δ Ψ 1 33 565 579 892 1424* *l*^{844} (*l*^{2211}) sy$^{c.h**}$ co

θανάσιμόν τι πίωσιν οὐ μὴ αὐτοὺς βλάψῃ, ἐπὶ ἀρρώστους χεῖρας ἐπιθήσουσιν καὶ
| αὐτοῖς | | βλάψει |
| βλάψῃ αὐτοὺς |
ingibe hva drigkaina, ni þauh im⁶⁶⁸ agljai, ana unhailans handuns uslagjand, jah

καλῶς ἕξουσιν. [16:19] Ὁ μὲν οὖν κύριος Ἰησοῦς μετὰ τὸ λαλῆσαι αὐτοῖς
waila wairþiþ im. [16:19] Þanuh þan frauja Iesus afar þatei rodida du im,

16:19 ουν] A D^s Θ Ψ f^1 f^{13} 33 2427 𝔐 sy bo | et latt | om. C* L W *l*^{844} *pc* — 16:19 Ιησους] C* K L Δ f^1 33 124 565 579 1071 1241 1424 2427 *l*^{844} *l*^{2211} it$^{aur.c.ff2.q}$ vg^{cl} sy co | Ιησους Χριστος W it^o bo^{mss} | om. A C^3 D^s Θ Ψ 𝔐 f^{13} it^l vg$^{st.ww}$

ἀνελήμφθη εἰς τὸν οὐρανὸν καὶ ἐκάθισεν ἐκ δεξιῶν τοῦ θεοῦ. [16:20] Ἐκεῖνοι δὲ
usnumans warþ in himin jah gasat af taihswon gudis. [16:20] Iþ jainai

16:19 εις τον ουρανον] A C D^s L W Θ Ψ f^1 33 2427 𝔐 it$^{aur.ff2.l}$ vg sy bo | εις τους ουρανους f^{13} it$^{c.o.q}$ — 16:19 εκ δεξιων] A (D^s) L W Θ Ψ f^1 f^{13} 33 2427 𝔐 it$^{aur.l}$ vg sy$^{c.p.h}$ bo | εν δεξια C Δ *pc* it$^{c.ff2.o.q}$

ἐξελθόντες ἐκήρυξαν πανταχοῦ, τοῦ κυρίου συνεργοῦντος καὶ τὸν λόγον βεβαιοῦντος
usgaggandans meridedun and allata, miþ fraujin gawaurstwin jah þata waurd tulgjandin

διὰ τῶν ἐπακολουθούντων σημείων.
                                                          Ἀμήν.
þairh þos afargaggandeins taiknins. Amen.

16:20 εκηρυξαν] A C D^s L W Θ Ψ f^1 f^{13} 33 2427 𝔐 lat sy co | praedicauerunt et docuerunt it^o — 16:20 διά] A C D^s W Θ Ψ f^1 f^{13} 33 2427 𝔐 sy bo | om. L sa — 16:20 αμην] C* D^s L W Θ Ψ f^{13} 2427 𝔐 it$^{c.o}$ vg^{ww} bo | om. A C^2 f^1 33 *l*^{844} *l*^{2211} *pc* it$^{aur.l.q}$ vg$^{cl.st}$ sy sa

II.3 The *Praefatio* to the *Codex Brixianus*

The text is preserved by a bifolio bound with the Latin Gospels text f/10 in the ms. Brescia, Biblioteca Queriniana, s.n. It is here reported in the edition of Henss (1972), with some modifications;⁶⁶⁹ the English translation that follows is by Michael Metlen (1938).

(1) S(an)c(tu)s Petrus Apostolus, discipulus saluatoris D(omi)ni nostri Ihu Xpi (Iesu Cristi), edocens fideles propter diuersitatem adsertionis linguarum admonet cunctos, ut in octauo libro Clementis continet scribtum, dicens sic: (2) 'Audite me conserui dilectissimi. Bonum est ut unusquisque uestrum secundum quod potest prosit acce[n]dentibus ad fidem religio-

---

668 See above 4.1.2.(1) and 4.1.3.(8).
669 Editorial signs are used according to b. Symbols.

nis nostrae. (3) Et ideo non uos pigeat secundum sapientiam quae uobis per D(e)i prouidentiam conlata est disserentes instruere, ignaros edocere, ita tamen ut his quae a me audistis et tradita sunt uobis uestri tantum sermonis eloquentiam societis, nec aliquid proprium et quod uobis non est traditum proloquamini, etiamsi uobis uerisimile uideatur. (4) Sed ut dixi quae ipse a uero propheta suscepta uobis tradidi prosequimini, etiamsi minus plenae adsertionis esse uidebuntur'. (5) Et ideo ne in interpraetationibus linguarum secundum quae [in] interiora libri ostenduntur legenti uideatur aliud in Graeca lingua aliud in Latina uel Gotica designata esse conscribta, illud aduertat quis. (6) Quodsi pro disciplina linguae discrepationem ostendit ad unam tamen intentionem concurrit. (7) Quare nullus exinde titubare debet de quod ipsa auctoritas manifestat secundum intentione⟨m⟩ linguae. (8) Propter declinationes sonus uocis diligenti perceptione statuta sunt, ut in subsequentibus conscribta leguntur. (9) Haec res fecit probanter publicare propter aliquos qui falsa adsertione secundum uolumtate⟨m⟩ sua⟨m⟩ mendacia in lege uel in euangeliis per interpraetationem propria⟨m⟩ posuerunt. (10) Quare illa declinantes haec posita sunt quae antiquitas legis in dictis Graecorum contineri inueniuntur, et ipsas etymologias linguarum conuenientes sibi conscribtas ad unum sensum concurrere demonstra⟨n⟩tur. (11) Nam et ea conuenit indicare pro quod in uulthres factu⟨m⟩ est latina uero lingua adnotatio significatur. (12) Quare id positum est agnosci possit ubi littera .gr. super uulthre inuenitur. (13) Sciat qui legit quod in ipso uulthre secundum quod Graecus continet scribtum est. (14) Ubi uero littera .la. super uulthre inuenitur secundum latina⟨m⟩ lingua⟨m⟩ in uulthre ostensum est. (15) Et ideo ista instructio demonstrata[ta] est ne legentes ipsos uulthres non perciperent pro qua ratione positi sint. (16) Sed quod...

(1) Saint Peter, the apostle and disciple of the Saviour our Lord Jesus Christ, teaching the faithful, on account of the diversity of expression in the various languages admonishes all – as is written in the eighth book of Clement – saying: (2) 'Listen to me, beloved fellow servants [of the Lord]. It is a good thing that every one of you according to his ability should help those who are joining the faith of our religion. (3) And thus you should not become weary, according to the wisdom which is given to you through God's providence, instructing by discussion, teaching the ignorant, in such a way, however, that you add only the eloquence of your own speech to that which you have heard from me and which has been handed down to you, without adding anything of your own and which has not been handed down to you, although it may appear plausible to yourselves. (4) But as I have said, pass on what I myself have received from the true prophet and handed down to you, although it may seem to be stated less fully' [than you would do]. (5) And thus, in order that (6) what is contained in this book should not, on the basis of the different versions (in interpraetationibus linguarum: Greek, Gothic, Latin), appear to the reader to mean something different in the Greek, Latin, and Gothic language, let him note that what is different from the standpoint of idiomatic usage (si pro disciplina [sua] lingua dis crepationem ostendit), yet expresses the same sense. (7) On which account nobody should be in doubt concerning the original meaning (de quod ipsa auctoritas manifestat), expressed idiomatically (secundum intentione linguae). (8) [For] in virtue of this idiomatic translation (propter declinationes sonus uocis) it (viz., the original sense) is stated with clearness the way it is hereinafter rendered. (9) The nature of the case (res) made it advisable to call attention (publicare) to this (haec) because some who, by wrongly interpreting (falsa adsertione) according to their whims (i.e. for lack of understanding) have introduced errors into the Laws (Old Testament) or their own ideas, through their translations, into the Gospels. (10) Hence,

declining those [errors], we have furnished the sense of what is found to be contained in the old Greek texts, and it is likewise being shown that the correct idiomatic forms (etymologias linguarum conuenienter sibi conscribtas) [of the languages here concerned] exhibit one and the same sense. (11) In this connection (nam) it will also be useful (conuenit) to explain these [idiomatic expressions, etymologias linguarum] in a measure (i.e., where it is particularly necessary for the understanding) by adding wulthres – which means in Latin adnotatio –, so that it may be understood why a particular [Gothic] rendering (etymologia = it) was used. (12) [Hence] where the symbol .gr. is found on top of a wulthre, (13) the reader may know that the corresponding wulthre is a [literal] rendering of the Greek text. (14) Where, on the other hand, the symbol .la. is found above a wulthre, the latter exhibits the Latin form. (15) The foregoing explanation has been given lest those who read these wulthres fail to understand the reason for the same. . . .

Bibliography

I. Ancient sources

Agn., *lib. pont.* = *Codex Pontificalis ecclesiae Ravennatis. I. Agnelli Liber Pontificalis*, a cura di A. Testi Rasponi. Bologna: Zanichelli 1924 (*Rerum Italicarum Scriptores*, N. S. 2, 3).
Ambrst., *in epist. Paul.* = Ambrosiaster, *Commentarius in Epistulas Paulinas*, hrsg. von H. J. Vogels. Wien: Österreichische Akademie der Wissenschaften 1966 (Corpus Scriptorum Ecclesiasticorum Latinorum, 81, 1).
Athan., *de incarn.* = Athanasius, *Contra gentes and* De incarnatione, ed. by R. W. Thomson, Oxford: Clarendon Press 1971.
Aug., *contra adv. leg. et proph.* = *Sancti Aurelii Augustini Contra aduersarium legis et prophetarum*, ed. K.-D. Daur. Turnhout: Brepols 1985, 35–131 (Corpus Christianorum, Serie Latina, 49).
Bas., *epist.* = *Basilii Magni Epistolae*, ed. J.-P. Migne. Paris: Garnier 1886, 219–1112 (Patrologia Graeca, 32).
Cassiod., *var.* = *Magni Aurelii Cassiodori Variarum libri XII*, cura et studio Å. J. Fridh. Turnholt: Brepols 1973, 3–499 (Corpus Christianorum, Serie Latina, 96).
Hier., *epist.* = *Sancti Eusebii Hieronymi Epistulae*, II. *Epistulae LXXI-CXX*, rec. I. Hilberg. Wien: Österreichische Akademie der Wissenschaften 1912, 247–289 (Corpus Scriptorum Ecclesiasticorum Latinorum, 55).
Hier., *in Is.* = Eusebius Hieronymus, *Commentarii in Isaiam*, ed. by M. Adriaen, Turnhout: Brepols 1963 (Corpus Christianorum, Serie Latina, 73–73 A).
Joh. Chrys., *epist.*= Johannes Chrysostomos, *Epistulae*, ed. J.-P. Migne. Paris: Garnier 1862 (Patrologia Graeca, 52).
Joh. Chrys., *hom.* = Johannes Chrysostomos, *Homiliae*, ed. J.-P. Migne. Paris: Garnier 1862, 499–511 (Patrologia Graeca, 63).
Jord., *Get.* = *Jordanis de origine actibusque Getarum*, ed. Th. Mommsen. Berlin: Weidmann 1882, 53–138 (Monumenta Germaniae Historica, Auctores Antiquissimi, V, 1).
Max., *diss.* = "Maximini episcopi dissertatio contra Ambrosium", in *Scripta Arriana Latina I*, éd. par R. Gryson. Turnhout: Brepols 1982, 149–171 (Corpus Christianorum, Serie Latina, 87).
Orig., *in Matth.* = Origenes, *Commentarii in Mattheum*, hrsg. von E. Klostermann – E. Benz. Berlin: Akademie Verlag 1935 (Griechische Christliche Schriftsteller, 40).
Oros., *hist.* = Paulus Orosius, *Historiarum adversus paganos libri VII*, hrsg. von C. Zangemeister. Wien: Österreichische Akademie der Wissenschaften 1982, 1–600 (Corpus Scriptorum Ecclesiasticorum Latinorum, 5).
Passio S. Sabae = *Passio S. Sabae Gothi*, éd. par H. Delehaye, *Analecta Bollandiana* 31 (1912), 216–221.
Patrum Nicaen. Nom. = *Patrum Nicaenorum Nomina latine, graece, coptice, syriace, arabice, armeniace*, hrsg. von H. Gelzer *et al.* Leipzig: Teubner 1898 (Scriptores sacri et profani II).
Pel., *exp. epist.* = Pelagius, *Expositiones XIII Epistularum sancti Pauli*, ed. by A. Souter, *Pelagius's Expositions of Thirteen Epistels of St. Paul. II: Text and Apparatus Criticus*. Cambridge: Cambridge University Press 1922–1931 (Texts and Studies, 9).

Pelagius[B] = Readings of the *Codex Collegii Balliolensis Oxon*. 157 (*Arch*. E. 5. 2) in Pelagius, *Expositiones XIII Epistularum sancti Pauli*, ed. by A. Souter, *Pelagius's Expositions of Thirteen Epistels of St. Paul. II: Text and Apparatus Criticus*. Cambridge: Cambridge University Press 1922–1931 (Texts and Studies, 9).
Philost., *HE* = Philostorgius, *Kirchengeschichte*, hrsg. von J. Bidez – F. Winkelmann. 3., durchges. Aufl. Berlin-New York: de Gruyter 1981 (Griechische Christliche Schriftsteller, 21).
Proc., *BG* = Procopius Caesarensis, "Bellum Gothicum", in *Opera omnia* (II), rec. J. Haury, add. et corr. G. Wirth. Leipzig: Teubner 1963.
Proc., *BV* = Procopius Caesarensis, "Bellum Vandalicum", in *Opera omnia* (I), rec. J. Haury, add. et corr. G. Wirth. Leipzig: Teubner 1962.
Pseudo-Augustinus, *Liber de divinis scripturis sive speculum quod fertur sancti Augustini*, hrsg. von F. Weihrich. Wien: Akademie der Wissenschaften 1887: 287–700 (Corpus Scriptorum Ecclesiasticorum Latinorum, 12).
Pseudo-Fredegar., *chron.* = *Chronicarum quae dicuntur Fredegarii Scholastici Libri IV*, ed. B. Krusch. Hannover: Hahn 1888 (Monumenta Germaniae Historica, Scriptores Rerum Merovingicarum II).
Salv., *gub.* = *Saluiani Massiliensis Presbyteri De gubernatione Dei libri VIII*, éd. par G. Lagarrigue. Paris: Editions du Cerf 1975 (Sources Chrétiennes, 220).
Socr., *HE* = Sokrates, *Kirchengeschichte*, hrsg. von G. Ch. Hansen – M. Širinjan. Berlin: Akademie-Verlag 1995 (Griechische Christliche Schriftsteller, N. F., 1).
Sozom., *HE* = Sozomenus, *Kirchengeschichte*, hrsg. von J. Bidez – G. Ch. Hansen. 2., durchges. Aufl., Berlin: Akademie-Verlag 1995 (Griechische Christliche Schriftsteller, N. F., 4).
Tert., *adv. Jud.* = Tertullianus, *Adversus Iudaeos*, hrsg. von E. Kroymann. Turnhout: Brepols 1954, 1337–1396 (Corpus Christianorum, Serie Latina, 2).
Theod., *HE* = Theodoret, *Kirchengeschichte*, hrsg. von G. Ch. Hansen. 3., durchges. Aufl., Berlin: Akademie-Verlag 1998 (Griechische Christliche Schriftsteller, N. F., 5).
Wal. Strabo, *exord.* = *Libellus de exordiis et incrementis rerum ecclesiasticarum*, hrsg. von A. Boretius – V. Krause, Berlin: Hahn 1897 (Monumenta Germaniae Historica, Capitularia II).
Zeno, *tract.* = Zeno Veronensis, *Tractatus Sancti Zenonis Veronensis episcopi*, hrsg. von B. Löfstedt. Turnhout: Brepols 1971 (Corpus Christianorum, Serie Latina, 22).

II. Secondary bibliography

Abraham, W. (1989), "Zu den distributionellen Eigenschaften von *wairðan* 'werden' und *wisan* 'sein' im gotischen Passiv", in W. Tauber, *Aspekte der Germanistik. Festschrift fur Hans-Friedrich Rosenfeld zum 90. Geburtstag*. Göppingen: Kümmerle, 601–620 (Göppinger Arbeiten zur Germanistik, 521).
Achelis, H. (1900), "Der älteste deutsche Kalender". *Zeitschrift für die neutestamentliche Wissenschaft und Kunde der älteren Kirche* 1: 308–335.
Agati, M.L. (2003), *Il libro manoscritto. Introduzione alla codicologia*. Roma: "L'Erma" di Bretschneider (Studia Archaeologica, 124).

Aimi, C. – Modesti, M. – Zuffrano, A. (2013), "Il frammento bolognese del *De civitate Dei* di S. Agostino: un nuovo palinsesto goto-latino. Considerazioni paleografiche e cronologiche, edizione e analisi filologica del testo". *Scriptorium* 67: 319–358.

Aland, K. (1974), "Der Schluß des Markusevangeliums", in M. Sabbe, *L'Évangile selon Marc. Tradition et rédaction*. Louvain: Louvain University Press, 435–470.

Aland, K. – Aland, B. (1989), *Der Text des Neuen Testaments. Einführung in die wissenschaftlichen Ausgaben sowie in Theorie und Praxis der modernen Textkritik*, 2. verb. u. erw. Aufl. Stuttgart: Deutsche Bibelgesellschaft.

Aland et al. (1991) = *Text und Textwert der griechischen Handschriften des Neuen Testaments.* II. *Die Paulinischen Briefe*. 1. *Allgemeines, Römerbrief und Ergänzungsliste*; 2. *Der 1. und der 2. Korintherbrief*; 3. *Galaterbrief bis Philipperbrief*; 4. *Kolosserbrief bis Hebräerbrief*, hrsg. von K. Aland in Verbindung mit A. Benduhn-Mertz, G. Mink, H. Bachmann. Berlin-New York: de Gruyter (Arbeiten zur neutestamentlichen Textforschung, 16–19).

Aland et al. (1998–2005) = *Text und Textwert der griechischen Handschriften des Neuen Testaments*. IV. *Die synoptischen Evangelien*. Berlin-New York: de Gruyter. 1. *Das Markusevangelium*, hrsg. von K. Alandt und B. Aland in Verbindung mit K. Wachtel und K. Witte. 1,1. *Handschriftenliste und vergleichende Beschreibung*; 1,2. *Resultate der Kollation und Hauptliste*. 2. *Das Matthäusevangelium*, hrsg. von K. Alandt, B. Aland, K. Wachtel in Verbindung mit K. Witte. 2,1. *Handschriftenliste und vergleichende Beschreibung*; 2,2. *Resultate der Kollation und Hauptliste sowie Ergänzungen*, 1999; 3. *Das Lukasevangelium*, hrsg. von K. Alandt, B. Aland, K. Wachtel in Verbindung mit K. Witte. 3,1. *Handschriftenliste und vergleichende Beschreibung*; 3,2. *Resultate der Kollation und Hauptliste sowie Ergänzungen*, 1999; V. *Das Johannesevangelium*. 1. *Teststellenkollation der Kapitel 1–10*, hrsg. von K. Alandt, B. Aland, K. Wachtel in Verbindung mit K. Witte. 1,1. *Handschriftenliste und vergleichende Beschreibung*; 1,2. *Resultate der Kollation und Hauptliste*, 2005 (Arbeiten zur neutestamentlichen Textforschung, 26–31; 35–36).

Alcamesi, F. (2009), "Il commento dell'Ambrosiaster e la traduzione gotica delle Epistole Paoline". *Filologia Germanica/Germanic Philology* 1: 1–27.

Alexianu, M. (2004), "La situation linguistique de la province romaine Scythie Mineure. Repères d'une recherche", in S. Santelia, *Italia e Romania: storia, cultura e civiltà a confronto. Atti del IV convegno di studi italo-romeno (Bari, 21–23 ottobre 2002)*. Bari: Edipuglia, 145–156 (Quaderni di "Invigilata lucernis", 21).

Amory, P. (1997), *People and Identity in Ostrogothic Italy, 489–554*. Cambridge: Cambridge University Press (Cambridge Studies in Medieval Life and Thought, 33).

Andersson-Schmitt, M. (1975–1976), "Anmerkungen zur Bedeutung des Haffner-Blattes für die Geschichte des *Codex Argenteus*". *Nordisk tidskrift för bok- och biblioteksväsen* 62–63: 16–21.

Antonelli, A. (2009), "Un inedito frammento del VI secolo del *De civitate Dei* di Sant'Agostino (con un lacerto dei secc. VIII-IX anch'esso sconosciuto)". *Giornale italiano di filologia* 61: 205–220.

Balg, G.H. (1891), *The First Germanic Bible translated from the Greek by the Gothic Bishop Wulfila in the Fourth Century and the other Remains of the Gothic Language. Edited with an Introduction, a Syntax and a Glossary*. New York: B. Westermann & Co.

Bardy, G. (1948), *La question des langues dans l'Église ancienne*. Paris: Beauchesne.

Barnea, I. (1977), *Les monuments paléochrétiens de Roumanie*. Città del Vaticano: Pontificio Istituto di Archeologia Cristiana (Sussidi allo studio delle antichità cristiane, 6).

Barnea, I. (1987), "Le christianisme des premiers six siècles au nord du Bas-Danube à la lumière des sources littéraires et des découverts archéologiques", in V. Gjuzelev – R. Pillinger, *Das Christentum in Bulgarien und auf der übrigen Balkanhalbinsel in der Spätantike und im frühen Mittelalter. II. Internationales Symposium Haskovo (Bulgarien), 10.-13. Juni 1986*. Wien: Verein 'Freunde des Hauses Wittgenstein', 39–50 (Miscellanea Bulgarica, 5).

Barnes, T.D. (1990), "The Consecration of Ulfila". *Journal of Theological Studies* 41: 541–545.

Beeson, F.H. (1946), "The Palimpsests of Bobbio", in *Miscellanea Giovanni Mercati VI*. Città del Vaticano: Biblioteca Apostolica Vaticana, 162–184 (Studi e testi, 126).

Bellocchio, S. – Dolcetti Corazza, V. (2009), "Il *Codex Taurinensis* F. IV 1 fr. 10", in V. Dolcetti Corazza – R. Gendre, *Le Rune. Epigrafia e letteratura, IX Seminario avanzato in Filologia Germanica*. Alessandria: Edizioni dell'Orso, 65–115 (Bibliotheca Germanica. Studi e testi, 26).

Bennett W.H. (1960), *The Gothic Commentary on the Gospel of John*. Skeireins aiwaggeljons þairh Iohannen: *A Decipherment, Edition and Translation*. New York: Modern Language Association of America (Monograph series, 21).

Bernhardt, E. (1864), *Kritische Untersuchungen über die gothische Bibelübersetzung. Ein Beitrag zur deutschen Literaturgeschichte und zur Kritik des Neuen Testaments*. Meiningen: Brückner & Renner.

Bernhardt, E. (1868), *Kritische Untersuchungen über die gothische Bibelübersetzung. Ein Beitrag zur deutschen Literaturgeschichte und zur Kritik des neuen Testaments. II. Heft*. Elberfeld: Lucas.

Bernhardt, E. (1875), *Vulfila oder die gotische Bibel. Mit dem entsprechenden griechischen Text und mit kritischem und erklärendem Commentar nebst dem Kalender, der Skeireins und den gotischen Urkunden*. Halle: Verlag der Buchhandlung des Waisenhauses (Germanistische Handbibliothek, 3).

Bertelli, C. (1998), "The Production and Distribution of Books in Late Antiquity", in R. Hodges – W. Bowden, *The Sixth Century: Production, Distribution and Demand*. Leiden-Boston: Brill, 41–60 (Transformation of the Roman World, 3).

Beševliev, V. (1964), *Spätgriechische und spätlateinische Inschriften aus Bulgarien*. Berlin: Akademie Verlag (Berliner byzantinistische Arbeiten, 30).

Petersen, Ch.T. (2005), ed. *Gotica Minora. V. Bibliographia gotica amplificata*. Hanau: Syllabus.

Bischoff, B. (1980), *Die süddeutschen Schreibschulen und Bibliotheken in der Karolingerzeit, II. Die vorwiegend österreichischen Diözesen*. Wiesbaden: Harrassowitz.

Bischoff, B. (1984), "Ein karolingisches Denkmal des Gotischen (zweite Hälfte des neunten Jahrhunderts)", in Anecdota novissima – *Texte des vierten bis sechzehnten Jahrhunderts*. Stuttgart: Hiersemann, 256–258 (Quellen und Untersuchungen zur lateinischen Philologie des Mittelalter, 7).

Bolognesi, G. (1999), "La scoperta e l'edizione dei testi gotici ambrosiani a 150 anni dalla morte di Carlo Ottavio Castiglioni". *Rendiconti dell'Istituto Lombardo – Accademia di Scienze e Lettere* 133: 493–518.

Boüüaert, J. (1950), "Oorsprong en vorming van het gotisch alphabet". *Revue Belge de Philolologie et Histoire* 28: 423–437.

Braun, W. (1898), "Die Lese- und Einteilungszeichen in den gotischen Handschriften der Ambrosiana in Mailand". *Zeitschrift für deutsche Philologie* 30: 433–448.

Braune-Heidermanns (2004) = Braune, W., *Gotische Grammatik. Mit Lesestücken und Wörterverzeichnis*, 20. Aufl., neu bearb. von F. Heidermanns, Tübingen: Niemeyer Verlag (Sammlung kurzer Grammatiken germanischer Dialekte A, 1).

Brennecke, H.Ch. (2007), "Christianisierung und Identität. Das Beispiel der germanischen Völker", in H.Ch. Brennecke *et al.*, Ecclesia est in re publica: *Studien zur Kirchen- und Theologiegeschichte im Kontext des Imperium Romanum*. Berlin-New York: de Gruyter, 145–156 (Arbeiten zur Kirchengeschichte, 100).

Brown T.S. (2007), "The Role of Arianism in Ostrogothic Italy: The Evidence from Ravenna", in S. Barnish – F. Marazzi, *The Ostrogoths from the Migration Period to the Sixth Century: An Ethnographic Perspective*. Woodbridge: Boydell Press, 417–441 (Studies in Historical Archaeoethnology, 7).

Burkitt, F.C. (1899), "The Vulgate Gospels and the *Codex Brixianus*". *Journal of Theological Studies* 1: 129–134.

Burkitt, F.C. (1927), "Review of G. W. S. Friedrichsen, *The Gothic Version of the Gospels*". *Journal of Theological Studies* 28: 90–97.

Burns, Th.S. (1980), *The Ostrogoths: Kingship and Society*. Wiesbaden: F. Steiner (Historia, 36).

Burns, Th.S. (1984), *A History of the Ostrogoths*. Bloomington-Indianapolis: Indiana University Press.

Burton, Ph. (1996 A), "*Fragmentum Vindobonense* 563: Another Latin-Gothic Bilingual?". *Journal of Theological Studies* 47: 141–156.

Burton, Ph. (1996 B), "Using the Gothic Bible. Notes on Jared S. Klein 'On the Independence of Gothic Syntax'". *Journal of Indo-European Studies* 24: 81–98.

Burton, Ph. (2000), *The Old Latin Gospels: A Study of their Texts and Language*. Oxford: Oxford University Press.

Burton, Ph. (2002), "Assessing Latin-Gothic Interaction", in J. N. Adams, M. Janse *et al.*, *Bilingualism in Ancient Society: Language Contact and the Written Text*. Oxford: Oxford University Press, 393–418.

Butzmann, H. (1964), *Die Weissenburger Handschriften*. Frankfurt am Main: Klostermann (Kataloge der Herzog-August-Bibliothek Wolfenbüttel, 10).

Buzzoni, M. (2009), "*Ibai mag blindana tiuhan?* (Luke, 6.39): Pragmatic Functions and Syntactic Strategies in the Gothic Left Sentence Periphery". *Filologia Germanica/Germanic Philology* 1: 29–62.

Casaretto, A. (2004), *Nominale Wortbildung der gotischen Sprache: Die Derivation der Substantive*. Heidelberg: Winter (Indogermanische Bibliothek, 3. Untersuchungen).

Casaretto, A. (2010), "Evidence for Language Contact in Gothic", in H.F. Nielsen – F.T. Stubkjær, *The Gothic Language. A Symposium* (= NOWELE 58/59). Odense: University Press of Southern Denmark, 217–237.

Castiglioni, C.O. (1829), ed. *Ulphilae Gothica versio Epistolae Divi Pauli ad Corinthios Secundae quam ex Ambrosianae Bibliothecae Palimpsestis depromptam cum interpretatione adnotationibus glossario*. Mediolani: Regii Typis.

Castiglioni, C.O. (1834), ed. *Gothicae versionis epistolarum Divi Pauli ad Romanus, ad Corinthios primae, ad Ephesios quae supersunt ex Ambrosianae Bibliothecae palimpsestis depromta cum adnotationibus*. Mediolani: Regiis Typis.

Castiglioni, C.O. (1835), ed. *Gothicae versionis epistolarum Divi Pauli ad Galatas, ad Philippenses, ad Colossenses, ad Thessalonicenses primae, quae supersunt ex*

Ambrosianae Bibliothecae palimpsestis deprompta cum adnotationibus. Mediolani: Regiis Typis.
Castiglioni, C.O. (1839), ed. *Gothicae versionis epistolorum Divi Pauli ad Thessalonicenses secundae, ad Timotheum, ad Titum, ad Philemon quae supersunt, ex Ambrosianae Bibliothecae palimpsestis deprompta cum adnotationibus*. Mediolani: Regiis typis.
Căţoi, M.O. (2009), "Le christianisme au Bas-Danube à la veille de la Grande Persécution", in *The Christian Mission on the Romanian Territory during the First Centuries of the Church (1600 Years since the Falling Asleep in the Lord of Saint Theotim I of Tomis). The Acts of the International Symposium at the Center for Studies and Historic-Religious Researches of the European South-East Area "Holy Apostle Andrew", Ovidius University, 27 November 2007*. Constanţa: Editura Arhiepiscopiei Tomisului, 186–215.
Cavallo, G. (1967), *Ricerche sulla maiuscola biblica*. Firenze: Le Monnier.
Cavallo, G. (1983), "La cultura a Ravenna tra Corte e Chiesa", in *Le sedi della cultura nell'Emilia Romagna. I. L'alto Medioevo*. Milano: Silvana editoriale, 29–51.
Cavallo, G. (1984), "Libri e continuità della cultura antica in età barbarica", in G. Pugliese Caratelli, Magistra Barbaritas. *I barbari in Italia*. Milano: Scheiwiller, 613–662.
Cavallo, G. (1992), "La cultura scritta a Ravenna tra antichità tarda e alto medioevo", in A. Carile, *Storia di Ravenna. II.2 Dall'età bizantina all'età ottoniana. Ecclesiologia, cultura e arte*. Ravenna: Marsilio, 79–125.
Cecchelli, C. (1960), "L'arianesimo e le chiese ariane d'Italia", in *Le chiese nei regni dell'Europa occidentale e i loro rapporti con Roma sino all'800 (7–13 Aprile 1959, Spoleto)*. Spoleto: Centro Italiano di Studi sull'Alto Medioevo, 742–774 (Settimane di studio del Centro Italiano di Studi sull'Alto Medioevo, 3).
Cercignani, F. (1988), "The Elaboration of the Gothic Alphabet and Orthography". *Indogermanische Forschungen* 93: 168–185.
Chrysos, E. (1992), "Von der Räumung der Dacia Traiana zur Entstehung der Gothia". *Bonner Jahrbücher* 192: 175–193.
Cipolla, M.A. (1990), "Matteo XXVI,70-XXVII, 1: interpretazione ed edizione di un frammento della Bibbia gotica". *Annali dell'Istituto Orientale di Napoli (Filologia Germanica)* 30–31: 215–236.
CLA = Lowe, E.A. (1934–1971), Codices Latini Antiquiores: *A Palaeographical Guide to Latin Manuscripts prior to the Ninth Century*. Vols. I-XI and Supplement. Oxford: Clarendon Press.
Comfort, Ph.W. (2005), *Encountering the Manuscripts: An Introduction to New Testament Paleography and Criticism*. Nashville (TN): Broadman & Holman.
Corazza, V. (1969), "Le parole latine in gotico". *Atti dell'Accademia Nazionale dei Lincei. Memorie* 14: 3–109.
Curcă, R.-G. (2009), *Elenism şi romanitate. Interferenţe etnice şi lingvistice în spaţiul Moesiei Inferior oglindite în sursele literare şi epigrafice*. Diss. Univ. Iaşi.
Curme, G.O. (1911), "Is the Gothic Bible Gothic?". *Journal of English and Germanic Philology* 10: 151–190; 335–377.
D'Alquen, R.J.E. (1974), *Gothic "ai" and "au": A Possible Solution*. The Hague: Mouton & Co (Janua linguarum. Series practica).
Dahl, N.A. (1979), "0230 (= PSI 1306) and the Fourth-Century Greek-Latin Edition of the Letters of Paul", in E. Best – R. McLachlan Wilson, *Text and Interpretation: Studies in the New Testament presented to Matthew Black*. Cambridge: Cambridge University Press, 79–98.

Daris, S. (2000), "I papiri e gli ostraca latini d'Egitto". *Aevum* 74: 105–175.
Dawson, H. (2002), "Deviations from the Greek in the Gothic New Testament", in M.R.V. Southern, *Indo-European Perspectives*. Washington DC: Institute for the Study of Man, 9–18 (Journal of Indo-European Studies Monographs, 43).
Deichmann, F.W. (1980), "La corte dei re goti a Ravenna", in *XXVII corso di cultura sull'arte ravennate e bizantina (Ravenna, 9–18 marzo 1980)*. Ravenna: Edizioni del girasole, 41–53.
Del Pezzo, R. (1973), "Le citazioni bibliche nella *Skeireins*". *Annali dell'Istituto Orientale di Napoli (Filologia Germanica)* 16: 7–15.
Del Pezzo, R. (1974), "L'arianesimo nella *Skeireins*". *Annali dell'Istituto Orientale di Napoli (Filologia Germanica)* 17: 243–255.
Delehaye H. (1912), "Saints de Thrace et de Mésie". *Analecta Bollandiana* 31: 194–209.
Diaconu, G. (1975), "On the Socio-Economic Relations between Natives and Goths in Dacia", in M. Constantinescu, Ş. Pascu *et al.*, *Relations between the Autochthonous Population and the Migratory Populations on the Territory of Romania: A Collection of Studies*. Bucureşti: Editura Academiei, 67–75.
Dolcetti Corazza, V. (1997), *La Bibbia gotica e i* bahuvrīhi. Alessandria: Edizioni dell'Orso (Bibliotheca Germanica. Studi e testi, 5).
Dolcetti Corazza, V. (2004), "La Bibbia Gotica e i Goti. Interferenze linguistiche e vicende storiche", in V. Dolcetti Corazza – R. Gendre, *I Germani e gli altri. II Parte. IV Seminario avanzato in Filologia Germanica*. Alessandria: Edizioni dell'Orso, 59–93 (Bibliotheca Germanica. Studi e testi, 17).
Dolcetti Corazza, V. (2011), "I Goti e la 'germanizzazione' del Vangelo", in P. Lendinara, F.D. Raschellà *et al.*, *Saggi in onore di Piergiuseppe Scardigli*. Bern: Lang, 63–74 (Jahrbuch für Internationale Germanistik, Reihe A: Kongressberichte, 105).
Ebbinghaus, E.A. (1974), "The Usage of *atta* to translate πατήρ and *fadar* as a *mot de caractère religieux*". *General Linguistics* 14: 97–101.
Ebbinghaus, E.A. (1976), "The First Entry of the Gothic Calendar". *Journal of Theological Studies* 27: 140–145.
Ebbinghaus, E.A. (1979 A), "Gothic Names in the Menologies". *General Linguistics* 19: 69–73.
Ebbinghaus, E.A. (1979 B), "The Origin of Wulfila's Alphabet". *General Linguistics* 19: 15–29.
Ebbinghaus, E.A. (1989), "Some Observations on *Codex Gissensis*". *General Linguistics* 29: 276–278.
Ebbinghaus, E.A. (1991), "Ulfila(s) or Wulfila?". *Historische Sprachforschung* 104: 236–38.
Ebbinghaus, E.A. (1992), "Some Remarks on the Life of Bishop Wulfila". *General Linguistics* 32: 95–104.
Ebbinghaus, E.A. (1997 [1995]), "Wulfila's Script: Facts and Inferences". *General Linguistics* 35: 81–96.
Ellingworth, P. (1993), *The Epistle to the Hebrews: A Commentary on the Greek Text*. Grand Rapids: Eerdmans (New International Greek Testament Commentary).
Ellis, L. (1996), "Dacians, Sarmatians, and Goths on the Roman-Carpathian Frontier: Second-Fourth Centuries", in R.W. Mathisen – H.S. Sivan, *Shifting Frontiers in Late Antiquity: Papers from the First Interdisciplinary Conference on Late Antiquity. The University of Kansas, March 1995*. Aldershot: Variorum, 105–119.

Ene, I. (2009), "Episcopia Gothiei și Dunărea de Jos", in *Istorie bisericească, misiune creștină și viață cultural. I. De la începuturi până în secolul al XIX-lea*. Galaţi: Editura Arhiepiscopiei Dunării de Jos, 116–141.

Fairbanks, S. – Magoun, F.P. (1940), "On Writing and Printing Gothic. I". *Speculum* 15: 313–330.

Falluomini, C. (1999), *Der sogenannte* Codex Carolinus *von Wolfenbüttel* (Codex Guelferbytanus 64 Weissenburgensis). *Mit besonderer Berücksichtigung der gotisch-lateinischen Blätter (255, 256, 277, 280)*. Wiesbaden: Harrasowitz (Wolfenbütteler Mittelalter-Studien, 13).

Falluomini, C. (2006), "Kodikologische Bemerkungen über die Handschriften der Goten". *Scriptorium* 60: 3–37.

Falluomini, C. (2008), "Il testo gotico nella tradizione biblica", in V. Dolcetti Corazza – R. Gendre, *Intorno alla* Bibbia gotica. *VII Seminario avanzato in Filologia Germanica*. Alessandria: Edizioni dell'Orso, 249–288 (Bibliotheca Germanica. Studi e testi, 21).

Falluomini, C. (2010 A), "Il codice gotico-latino di Gießen e la Chiesa vandalica", in A. Piras, Lingua et ingenium. *Studi su Fulgenzio di Ruspe e il suo contesto*. Ortacesus: Sandhi, 309–340 (Studi e Ricerche di Cultura Religiosa. N.S., VII).

Falluomini, C. (2010 B), "Zur Schrift der *Gotica Vindobonensia*". *Zeitschrift für deutsches Altertum und deutsche Literatur* 139: 26–35.

Falluomini, C. (2012), "The Gothic Version of the New Testament", in B.D. Ehrman – M.W. Holmes, *The Text of the New Testament in Contemporary Research: Essays on the Status Quaestionis*, 2nd rev. edition. Leiden-Boston: Brill, 329–350 (New Testament Tools. Studies and Documents, 42).

Falluomini, C. (2014), "Zum gotischen Fragment aus Bologna". *Zeitschrift für deutsches Altertum und deutsche Literatur*.

Felle, A.E. (2009), "Le citazioni bibliche nella documentazione epigrafica dei cristiani: i casi in territorio romeno e sulla sponda europea del Mar Nero". *Classica et Christiana* 4: 233–264.

Ferraresi G. (2005), *Word Order and Phrase Structure in Gothic*. Leuven: Peeters (Orbis/Supplementa, 25).

Ferrari, M. (1976), "Libri e maestri tra Verona e Bobbio", in *Storia della cultura veneta. I. Dalle origini al Trecento*. Vicenza: Neri Pozza, 271–278.

Finazzi, R.B. – Tornaghi, P. (2013), "*Gothica Bononiensia*. Analisi linguistica e filologica di un nuovo documento". *Aevum* 87: 113–153.

Fischer, B. (1972), "Das Neue Testament in lateinischer Sprache", in K. Aland, *Die alten Übersetzungen des Neuen Testaments, die Kirchenväterzitate und Lektionare*. Berlin-New York: de Gruyter, 1–92 (Arbeiten zur neutestamentlichen Textforschung, 5).

Forlin Patrucco, M. – Roda, S. (1979), "Religione e cultura dei Goti transdanubiani nel IV-V secolo". *Augustinianum* 19: 167–187.

Francini, M. (2009 A), *Edizione sinottica del Vangelo di Giovanni in gotico del* Codex Argenteus. Bergamo: Sestante edizioni.

Francini, M. (2009 B), "Key Words of the Gospel of John: The Gothic Version". *Filologia Germanica/Germanic Philology* 1: 89–112.

Junius, F. (1665), ed. *Quatuor Domini Nostri Iesu Christi Evangeliorum Versiones perantiquae duae, Gothica scilicet et Anglo-Saxonica* [...]. Dordrecht: Junius.

Francovich Onesti, N. (2002), *I Vandali. Lingua e storia*. Roma: Carocci.

Francovich Onesti, N. (2007), "Interferenze latine nella scrittura del gotico", in E. Fazzini – E. Cianci, *I Germani e la scrittura. Atti del XXXIII Convegno dell'Associazione Italiana di Filologia Germanica (Pescara 7–9 giugno 2006)*. Alessandria: Edizioni dell'Orso, 1–12.

Francovich Onesti, N. (2011), "La romanizzazione dei Goti: i risvolti linguistici", in C. Ebanista – M. Rotili, *Archeologia e storia delle migrazioni. Europa, Italia, Mediterraneo fra tarda età romana e alto medioevo. Atti del Convegno internazionale di studi (Cimitile-Santa Maria Capua Vetere, 17–18 giugno 2010)*. Cimitile: Tavolario Edizioni, 199–218 (Giornate sulla tarda-antichità e il medioevo, 3).

Frede, H.J. (1964), *Altlateinische Paulus-Handschriften*. Freiburg: Herder (*Vetus Latina*. Aus der Geschichte der lateinischen Bibel, 4).

Frede, H.J. (1973), "Die Ordnung der Paulusbriefe", in E. A. Livingstone, *Studia Evangelica*, VI. Berlin: Akademie-Verlag, 122–127.

Frede, H.J. (1974), *Ein neuer Paulustext und Kommentar. II. Die Texte*. Freiburg: Herder (*Vetus Latina*. Aus der Geschichte der lateinischen Bibel, 8).

Friedrichsen, G.W.S. (1926), *The Gothic Version of the Gospels: A Study of its Style and Textual History*. London: Oxford University Press.

Friedrichsen, G.W.S. (1939), *The Gothic Version of the Epistles: A Study of its Style and Textual History*. London: Oxford University Press.

Friedrichsen, G.W.S. (1959), "The Greek Text underlying the Gothic Version of the New Testament. The Gospel of St. Luke", in *Mélanges de linguistique et de philologie. Fernand Mossé in Memoriam*. Paris: Didier, 161–184.

Friedrichsen, G.W.S. (1961), *Gothic Studies*. Oxford: Blackwell (Medium Aevum Monographs, 6).

Friedrichsen, G.W.S. (1964–1965), "The Gothic Text of Luke in its Relation to the *Codex Brixianus* (f) and the *Codex Palatinus* (e)". *New Testament Studies* 11: 281–290.

Friedrichsen, G.W.S. (1977), "Limitations of Gothic in representing Greek", in B.M. Metzger, *The Early Versions of the New Testament: Their Origin, Transmission and Limitations*. Oxford: Clarendon Press, 388–393.

von Friesen, O. – Grape, A. (1927), *Codex Argenteus Upsaliensis jussu Senatus Universitatis phototypice editus*. Uppsala: Almqvist & Wiksell.

von Friesen, O. – Grape, A. (1928), *Om Codex Argenteus, dess tid, hem och öden. Med ett appendix av Hugo Andersson*. Uppsala: Svenska Litteratursällskapet (Skrifter utgivna av Svenska Litteratursällskapet, 27).

von der Gabelentz, H.G – Löbe, J. (1836), eds. *Ulfilas. Veteris et Novi Testamenti versionis gothicae fragmenta quae supersunt ad fidem codd. castigata, latinitate donata, adnotatione critica instructa, cum glossario et grammatica linguae gothicae*. Altenburg-Leipzig: Brockhaus.

Gaebeler, K. (1911), "Die griechischen Bestandteile der gotischen Bibel". *Zeitschrift für deutsche Philologie* 43: 1–118.

Gamber, K. (1988), *Die Liturgie der Goten und der Armenier. Versuch einer Darstellung und Einführung*. Regensburg: Pustet (Beiheft zu den Studia patristica et liturgica, 21).

Gamble, H.Y. (1995), *Books and Readers in the Early Church: A History of Early Christian Texts*. New Haven-London: Yale University Press.

Gendre, R. (1976), "Il fuþark e l'alfabeto gotico", in *Scritti in onore di Giuliano Bonfante*. Brescia: Paideia, I. 309–323.

Gerhard, A. (1984), *Goten in Konstantinopel. Untersuchung zur oströmischen Geschichte um das Jahr 400 n. Chr.* Paderborn: Schöningh (Studien zur Geschichte und Kultur des Altertums, 1. N.F.; Theologie, 2).

Gerov, B. (1980), "Die lateinisch-griechische Sprachgrenze auf der Balkanhalbinsel", in G. Neumann, *Die Sprachen im römischen Reich der Kaiserzeit. Kolloquium vom 8. bis 10. April 1974.* Köln: Rheinland, 147–165 (Beihefte der Bonner Jahrbücher, 40).

Girardi, M. (2004), "Basilio di Cesarea, la *passio* di s. Saba 'il goto' e la propagazione del Cristianesimo nella regione del basso Danubio fra III e IV sec.", in S. Santelia, *Italia e Romania: storia, cultura e civiltà a confronto. Atti del IV convegno di studi italo-romeno (Bari, 21–23 ottobre 2002).* Bari: Edipuglia, 157–172 (Quaderni di "Invigilata lucernis", 21).

Girardi, M. (2009), "La *passio* del 'goto' Saba. Ideologia universalistica sui confini dell'impero fra memoria storica e trafigurazione biblica". *Classica et Christiana* 4: 279–294.

Girardi, M. (2012), "Dinamiche multietniche ed interreligiose sul *limes* danubiano nel IV secolo: il martirio di Saba il goto". *Classica et Christiana* 7: 117–141.

Glaue, K.L. – Helm, K. (1910), "Das gotisch-lateinische Bibelfragment der Großherzoglichen Universitätsbibliothek Gießen". *Zeitschrift für die neutestamentliche Wissenschaft und Kunde der älteren Kirche* 11: 1–38.

Goswell, G.R. (2009), "Early Readers of the Gospels: The *Kephalaia* and *Titloi* of Codex Alexandrinus". *Journal of Greco-Roman Christianity and Judaism* 6: 134–74.

Granberg, A. (2010), "Wulfila's Alphabet in the Light of Neighbouring Scripts", in H.F. Nielsen – F.T. Stubkjær, *The Gothic Language. A Symposium* (= NOWELE 58/59). Odense: University Press of Southern Denmark, 169–193.

Green, D.H. (1998), *Language and History in the Early Germanic World.* Cambridge: Cambridge University Press.

Gregory, C.R. (1894), ed. *Novum Testamentum Graece. Ad antiquissimos testes denuo recensuit, apparatum criticum apposuit. Editio octava critica maior. III: Prolegomena.* Leipzig: Hinrichs.

Gregory, C.R. (1902), *Textkritik des Neuen Testamentes. II. Die Übersetzungen, die Schriftsteller, Geschichte der Kritik.* Leipzig: Hinrichs.

Griepentrog, W. (1988), *Synopse der gotischen Evangelientexte.* München: Kitzinger (Münchener Studien zur Sprachwissenschaft N. F., 14).

Griepentrog, W. (1990), *Zur Text- und Überlieferungsgeschichte der gotischen Evangelientexte.* Innsbruck: Institut für Sprachwissenschaft der Universität (Innsbrucker Beiträge zur Sprachwissenschaft, 49).

Grimm, W. (1828), "Zur Literatur der Runen. Nebst Mittheilung runischer Alphabete und gothischer Fragmente aus Handschriften". *Wiener Jahrbücher der Literatur* 43: 1–42.

Gryson, R. (1980), *Scolies ariennes sur le concile d'Aquilée.* Paris : Edition du Cerf (Sources chrétiennes, 267).

Gryson, R. (1982 A), *Le recueil arien de Vérone (MS. LI de la Bibliothèque capitulaire et feuillets inédits de la collection Giustiniani Recanati). Étude codicologique et paléographique.* Steenbrugis: Abbatia Sancti Petri (Instrumenta patristica, 13).

Gryson, R. (1982 B) ed., *Scripta Arriana Latina I.* Turnhout: Brepols (Corpus Christianorum Serie Latina, 87).

Gryson, R. (1990), "La version gotique des évangiles. Essai de réévaluation". *Revue théologique de Louvain* 21: 3–31.

Gudea, N. – Chiu, D. (2005), "Descoperiri creștine timpurii (până la 313 p. Chr.) în provinciile romane din jurul Daciilor. Contribuții la istoria creștinismului impuri (preconstantinian)". *Studia Universitatis Babes-Bolyai. Theologia Catholica* 50: 9–84.
Gusmani, R. (1971), "Integrazione morfologica dei prestiti latini e greci in gotico". *Rendiconti dell'Istituto Lombardo di Scienze e Lettere* 105: 123–148.
Gwynn, D.M. (2010), "Archaeology and the 'Arian Controversy' in the Fourth Century", in D.M. Gwynn – S. Bangert, *Religious Diversity in Late Antiquity*. Leiden-Boston: Brill, 229–263 (Late Antique Archaeology, 6).
Harmatta, J. (1996), "Fragments of Wulfila's Gothic Translation of the New Testament from Hács Béndekpuszta". *Acta Antiqua Hungarica* 37: 1–24.
Heather, J.P. (1991), *Goths and Romans. 332–489*. Oxford: Clarendon Press.
Heather, J.P. – Matthews, J. (1991), *The Goths in the Fourth Century*. Liverpool: Liverpool University Press (Translated Texts for Historians, 11).
Heil, U. (2011), *Avitus von Vienne und die homöische Kirche der Burgunder*. Berlin-Boston: de Gruyter (Patristische Texte und Studien, 66).
Hen, Y. (2007), *Roman Barbarians: The Royal Court and Culture in the Early Medieval West*. New York: Palgrave Macmillan.
Henning, H. (1913), *Der Wulfila der Bibliotheca Augusta zu Wolfenbüttel. Codex Carolinus*. Hamburg: Behrens.
Henss, W. (1957), "Gotisches *jah* und *-uh* zwischen Partizipium und Verbum finitum. Zur Herleitung der gotischen und altlateinischen Version des Neuen Testaments". *Zeitschrift für die neutestamentliche Wissenschaft und Kunde der älteren Kirche* 48: 133–141.
Henss, W. (1973), *Leitbilder der Bibelübersetzung im 5. Jahrhundert. Die Praefatio im Evangelienkodex Brixianus (f) und das Problem der gotisch-lateinischen Bibelbilinguen*. Heidelberg: Winter (Abhandlungen der Heidelberger Akademie der Wissenschaften. Philosophisch-historische Klasse).
Hodges, Z.C. – Farstad, A.L. (1985), eds. *The Greek New Testament according to the Majority Text*. 2nd ed., Nashville (TN): Thomas Nelson.
Holmes, M.W. (2006), "The Text of P[46]: Evidence of the Earliest 'Commentary' of Romans?", in Th.J. Kraus – T. Nicklas, *New Testament Manuscripts: Their Texts and their World*. Leiden-Boston: Brill, 189–206
Houghton et al. (forthcoming) = Houghton, H.A.G. – Kreinecker, C.M. – MacLachlan, R.F. – Smith, C.J., *The Principal Pauline Epistles: A Collation of the Old Latin Evidence*. Piscataway NJ: Gorgias (Texts and Studies 3rd series).
Hunter, M.J. (1969), "The Gothic Bible", in G.W.H. Lampe, *The Cambridge History of the Bible*. II. *The West from the Fathers to the Reformation*. Cambridge: Cambridge University Press, 338–362.
Hurtado, L.W. (2006), *The Earliest Christian Artifacts: Manuscripts and Christian Origins*. Grand Rapids (MI): Eerdmans.
IGNTP 1984–1987 = *The Gospel According to St. Luke*, ed. by the American and British Committees of the International Greek New Testament Project. 2 vols. Oxford: Clarendon Press.
Ioniţa, I. (1997), "Archéologie des Goths en Roumanie: paganisme et christianisme", in M. Rouche, *Clovis, histoire et mémoire. Actes du Colloque International d'Histoire de Reims, du 19 au 25 septembre 1996*. Paris: Presses de l'Université de Paris-Sorbonne, I. 159–170.

Ivanov, R. (1998) "Nicopolis ad Istrum. Eine römische und frühbyzantinische Stadt in Thrakien und Niedermösien". *Antike Welt. Zeitschrift für Archäologie und Kulturgeschichte* 29: 143–153.

Jellinek, M.H. (1923), "Zur christlichen terminologie im Gotischen". *Beiträge zur Geschichte der deutschen Sprache und Literatur* 47: 434–447.

Jellinek, M.H. (1926), *Geschichte der gotischen Sprache*. Berlin-Leipzig: de Gruyter (Grundriss der germanischen philologie, 1).

Johnson, M. (1988), "Towards a History of Theodoric's Building Program". *Dumbarton Oaks Papers* 42: 73–96.

Jülicher, A. (1910), "Die griechische Vorlage der gotischen Bibel". *Zeitschrift für deutsches Altertum und deutsche Literatur* 52: 365–387.

Jülicher, A. (1912), "Ein letztes Wort zur Geschichte der gotischen Bibel". *Zeitschrift für deutsches Altertum und deutsche Literatur* 53: 369–381.

Jülicher et al. (1963–1976) = *Itala. Das Neue Testament in altlateinischer Überlieferung*, hrsg. von A. Jülicher, durchgeseh. W. Matzkowt und K. Aland, Berlin: de Gruyter. IV. Johannes-Evangelium, 1963; I. Matthäus-Evangelium. 2. verb. Aufl., 1972; II. Marcus-Evangelium. 2. verb. Aufl., 1970; III. Lucas-Evangelium. 2. verb. Aufl., 1976.

Kapteijn, J.M.N. (1911–1912), "Die Übersetzungstechnik der gotischen Bibel in den Paulinischen Briefen". *Indogermanische Forschungen* 29: 260–367.

Kauffmann, F. (1898), "Beiträge zur Quellenkritik der gotischen Bibelübersetzung. II. Das Neue Testament". *Zeitschrift für deutsche Philologie* 30: 145–183.

Kauffmann, F. (1899 A), *Aus der Schule des Wulfila*. Auxenti Dorostorensis epistula de fide vita et obitu Wulfilae *im Zusammenhang der* Dissertatio Maximini contra Ambrosium. Strassburg: Trübner (Texte und Untersuchungen zur altgermanischen Religionsgeschichte. Texte, 1).

Kauffmann, F. (1899 B), "Beiträge zur Quellenkritik der gotischen Bibelübersetzung". *Zeitschrift für deutsche Philologie* 31: 178–194.

Kauffmann, F. (1900), "Beiträge zur Quellenkritik der gotischen Bibelübersetzung. 5. Der Codex Brixianus". *Zeitschrift für deutsche Philologie* 32: 305–335.

Kauffmann, F. (1903), "Beiträge zur Quellenkritik der gotischen Bibelübersetzung. 6. Die Corintherbriefe". *Zeitschrift für deutsche Philologie* 35: 433–463.

Kauffmann, F. (1911 A), "Beiträge zur Quellenkritik der gotischen Bibelübersetzung. 7. Der Codex Carolinus". *Zeitschrift für deutsche Philologie* 43: 401–428.

Kauffmann, F. (1911 B), "Zur Textgeschichte der gotischen Bibel". *Zeitschrift für deutsche Philologie* 43: 118–132.

Kauffmann, F. (1919), "Der Stil der gotischen Bibel". *Zeitschrift für deutsche Philologie* 48: 7–80; 165–235; 349–388.

Kauffmann, F. (1923), "Der Stil der gotischen Bibel". *Zeitschrift für deutsche Philologie* 49: 11–57.

Kenyon, F.G. (1937), *The Text of the Greek Bible*. London: Duckworth.

Kiss, A. (1995), "Das germanische Gräberfeld von Hács-Béndekpuszta (Westungarn) aus dem 5.–6. Jahrhundert". *Acta Antiqua Academiae Scientiarum Hungaricae* 36: 275–342.

Klein, J.S. (1992), "On the Independence of Gothic Syntax, I: Interrogativity, Complex Sentence Types, Tense, Mood, and Diathesis". *Journal of Indo-European Studies* 20: 339–379.

Knittel, F.A. (1758), ed. *Ulphilae versionem gothicam nonnullorum capitum Epistolae Pauli ad Romanos* […]. Brunsvigae: Orphanotropheus.

Kokowski, A. (2007), "The Agriculture of the Goths between the First and Fifth Centuries AD (Central and Eastern Europe – the Roman Period and the Early Migration Period)", in S. Barnish – F. Marazzi, *The Ostrogoths from the Migration Period to the Sixth Century: An Ethnographic Perspective*. Woodbridge: Boydell Press, 221–236 (Studies in Historical Archaeoethnology, 7).

Krahe-Seebold 1967 = Krahe, H., *Historische Laut- und Formenlehre des Gotischen. Zugleich eine Einführung in die germanische Sprachwissenschaft*. 2. Aufl. bearb. v. E. Seebold. Heidelberg: Winter.

Krašovec, J. (2010), *The Transformation of Biblical Proper Names*. New York: T&T Clark (Library of Hebrew Bible/Old Testament Studies, 418).

Krause, W. (1968), *Handbuch des Gotischen*. 3. rev. Aufl. München: Beck.

Lambdin, Th.O. (2006), *An Introduction to the Gothic Language*. Eugene, OR: Wipf & Stock.

La Rocca, M.C. (1993), "Una prudente maschera 'antiqua'. La politica edilizia di Teoderico", in *Teoderico il Grande e i Goti d'Italia. Atti del XIII Congresso internazionale di studi sull'Alto Medioevo, Milano, 2–6 nov. 1992*. Spoleto: Centro Italiano di Studi sull'Alto Medioevo, 451–515 (Atti dei congressi del Centro Italiano di Studi sull'Alto Medioevo, 13).

Legg, S.C.E. (1935) ed. *Novum Testamentum Graece [...]. Evangelium secundum Marcum cum apparatu critico*. Oxford: Clarendon Press.

Legg, S.C.E. (1940) ed. *Novum Testamentum Graece [...]. Evangelium secundum Matthaeum cum apparatu critico*. Oxford: Clarendon Press.

Lehmann, W.P. (1986), *A Gothic Etymological Dictionary: Based on the Third Edition of Vergleichendes Wörterbuch der gotischen Sprache by Sigmund Feist*. Leiden: Brill.

Lendinara, P. (1992), "Wulfila as the Inventor of the Gothic Alphabet: The Tradition in Late Antiquity and the Middle Ages". *General Linguistics* 32: 217–225.

Lenski, N.E. (1995), "The Gothic Civil War and the Date of the Gothic Conversion". *Greek, Roman and Byzantine Studies* 36: 51–87.

Lenski, N.E. (2002), *Failure of Empire: Valens and the Roman State in the Fourth Century A.D.* Berkeley: University of California Press (The Transformation of the Classical Heritage, 34).

Liebeschuetz, J.H.W.G. (1990), *Barbarians and Bishops: Army, Church, and State in the Age of Arcadius and Chrysostom*. Oxford: Clarendon Press.

Lietzmann, H. (1919), "Die Vorlage der gotischen Bibel". *Zeitschrift für deutsches Altertum und deutsche Literatur* 56: 249–278.

Llamas Pombo, E. (2002), "Visual Construction of Writing in the Medieval Book". *Diogenes* 49: 31–40.

Lo Monaco, F. (1996), "*In codicibus ... qui Bobienses inscribuntur*: scoperte e studio di palinsesti bobbiesi in Ambrosiana dalla fine del Settecento ad Angelo Mai (1819)". *Aevum* 70: 657–719.

Lo Monaco F. (2006), "De fatis palimpsestorum bibliothecae Sancti Columbani Bobiensis", in Á. Escobar, *El palimpsesto grecolatino como fenómeno librario y textual*. Zaragoza: Intistución "Fernando el Católico", 53–62.

Lowe, E.A. (1925), "Some Facts about our Oldest Latin Manuscripts". *The Classical Quarterly* 19: 197–208 (reprint in L. Bieler, *Palaeographical Papers 1907–1965*. Oxford: Clarendon Press, 1972: 251–274).

Lowe, E.A. (1961), "Greek Symptoms in a Sixth-Century Manuscript of St. Augustine and in a Group of Latin Legal Manuscripts", in S. Prete, Didascaliae. *Studies in Honor of Anselm*

M. Albareda. New York: Rosenthal, 279–289 (reprint in L. Bieler, *Palaeographical Papers 1907–1965*. Oxford: Clarendon Press, 1972: 466–474).

Lühr, R. (1985), "Zur Deklination griechischer und lateinischer Wörter in Wulfilas gotischer Bibelübersetzung". *Münchener Studien zur Sprachwissenschaft* 46: 139–155.

Luiselli, B. (1982), "La società dell'Italia romano-gotica", in *Atti del VII Congresso internazionale di studi sull'Alto Medioevo, Norcia-Subiaco-Cassino-Montecassino, 29 sett.–5 ott. 1980*. Spoleto: Centro Italiano di Studi sull'Alto Medioevo, 49–116 (Atti dei congressi del Centro Italiano di Studi sull'Alto Medioevo, 7).

Luiselli, B. (1992), *Storia culturale dei rapporti tra mondo romano e mondo germanico*. Roma: Herder.

Lungu, V. (2000), *Creştinismul în Scythia Minor în contextul vest-pontic*. Sibiu-Constanţa: Sen.

Lusuardi Siena, S. (1984), "Sulle tracce della presenza gota in Italia: il contributo delle fonti archeologiche", in G. Pugliese Caratelli, Magistra Barbaritas. *I barbari in Italia*. Milano: Scheiwiller, 509–558.

Madgearu, A. (2001), *Rolul creştinismului în formarea poporului român*. Bucureşti: Editura All.

Madgearu, A. (2004), "The Spreading of the Christianity in the Rural Areas of Post-Roman Dacia (4th-7th Centuries)". *Archaevs. Études d'histoire des religions* 8: 41–59.

Mai, A. – Castiglioni, C.O. (1819), eds. *Ulphilae partium ineditarum in Ambrosianis palimpsestis ab Angelo Maio repertarum specimen*. Mediolani: Regiis Typis.

Marchand, J.W. (1956), 'The Gothic Evidence for 'Euthalian Matter'". *Harvard Theological Review* 49: 159–167.

Marchand, J.W. (1957), 'Review of *Manuel de la langue gotique: grammaire, textes, notes, glossaire*, 2nd ed. by F. Mossé'. *Language* 33: 231–240.

Marchand, J.W. (1959), "Les Gots ont-ils vraiment connu l'écriture runique?", in *Mélanges de linguistique et de philologie. Fernand Mossé in memoriam*. Paris: Didier, 277–291.

Marchand, J.W. (1973 A), "On the *Gotica Veronensia*". *New Testament Studies* 19:465–468.

Marchand, J.W. (1973 B), *The Sounds and Phonemes of Wulfila's Gothic*. The Hague-Paris: Mouton (Janua Linguarum, Series Practica, 25).

Maßmann, H.F. (1857), ed. *Ulfilas. Die heiligen Schriften alten und neuen Bundes in gothischer Sprache – mit gegenüberstehenden griechischem und lateinischem Texte, Anmerkungen, Wörterbuch, Sprachlehre und geschichtlicher Einleitung*. Stuttgart: Liesching.

Mastrelli, C.A. (1963), "La tecnica delle traduzioni della Bibbia nell'Alto Medioevo", in *La Bibbia nell'Alto Medioevo. X Settimana di studio del Centro Italiano di Studi sull'Alto Medioevo (26 aprile-2 maggio 1962)*. Spoleto: Centro Italiano di Studi sull'Alto Medioevo, 657–681 (Settimane di studio del Centro Italiano di Studi sull'Alto Medioevo, 10).

Mastrelli, C.A. (1980), *Grammatica gotica*, 2. ed. riv. e ampl. Milano: Mursia.

Mauskopf Deliyannis D. (2010), *Ravenna in Late Antiquity*. Cambridge-New York: Cambridge University Press.

McGurk, P. (1961), "Citation Marks in Early Latin Manuscripts". *Scriptorium* 15: 3–13.

McGurk, P. (1994), "The Oldest Manuscripts of the Latin Bible", in R. Gameson, *The Early Medieval Bible: Its Production, Decoration and Use*. Cambridge: Cambridge University Press, 1–23.

McLynn, N. (2007), "Little Wolf in the Big City: Ulfila and his Interpreters", in J. Drinkwater – B. Salway, *Wolf Liebeschuetz reflected. Essays presented by Colleagues, Friends, & Pupils*. London: Institute of Classical Studies, 125–135.

Mees, B. (2002–2003), "Runo-Gothica: The Runes and the Origin of Wulfila's Script". *Die Sprache* 43: 55–79.
Merrills, A.H. (2005), *History and Geography in Late Antiquity*. Cambridge, Cambridge University Press.
Meslin, M. (1967), *Les Ariens d'Occident 335–430*. Paris: Édition du Seuil (Patristica Sorbonensia, 8).
Metlen, M. (1933), "What a Greek Interlinear of the Gothic Bible can teach us". *Journal of English and Germanic Philology* 32: 530–548.
Metlen, M. (1938), "A Natural Translation of the *Praefatio* attached to the *Codex Brixianus*". *Journal of English and Germanic Philology* 37: 355–366.
Metzger, B.M. (1964), *The Text of the New Testament: Its Transmission, Corruption, and Restoration*. Oxford: Clarendon Press
Metzger, B.M. (1977), *The Early Versions of the New Testament: Their Origin, Transmission, and Limitations*. Oxford: Clarendon Press.
Metzger, B.M. – Ehrman, B.D. (2005), *The Text of the New Testament: Its Transmission, Corruption, and Restoration*. 4th ed. Oxford-New York: Oxford University Press.
Mierow, Ch.C. (1915), *The Gothic History of Jordanes*. Princeton: Princeton University Press.
Mihăescu, H. (1978), *La langue latine dans le sud-est de l'Europe*. București: Editura Academiei; Paris: Les Belles Lettres.
Milde, W. (1972), *Mittelalterliche Handschriften der Herzog August Bibliothek*. Frankfurt am Main: Klostermann.
Minis, C. (1977), "Über die *wulthres* in der *Praefatio* des Kodex *Brixianus*", in F. Maurer – C. Minis, *Altgermanistische Beiträge. Jan van Dam zum 80. Geburtstag gewidmet*. Amsterdam: Rodopi, 11–28.
Mirarchi, G. (1976 A), "Sul testo originale greco delle lettere paoline in gotico". *Annali dell'Istituto Orientale di Napoli (Filologia Germanica)* 19: 111–126.
Mirarchi, G. (1976 B), "L'arianesimo nei frammenti della Bibbia gotica". *Annali dell'Istituto Orientale di Napoli (Filologia Germanica)* 19: 165–184.
Mitrea, I. (2009), "The First Christian Communities from the Central Area of Moldavia", in *The Christian Mission on the Romanian Territory during the First Centuries of the Church (1600 Years since the Falling Asleep in the Lord of Saint Theotim I of Tomis), The Acts of the International Symposium at the Center for Studies and Historic-Religious Researches of the European South-East Area "Holy Apostle Andrew", Ovidius University, 27 November 2007*. Constanța: Editura Arhiepiscopiei Tomisului, 133–144.
Mohrmann, Ch. (1968), "Sakralsprache und Umgangssprache". *Archiv für Liturgiewissenschaft* 10: 344–354.
Moorhead, J. (1978), "Boethius and Romans in Ostrogothic Service". *Historia* 27: 604–612.
Moorhead, J. (1986), "Culture and Power among the Ostrogoths". *Klio* 68: 112–122.
Moorhead, J. (1992), *Theoderic in Italy*. Oxford: Clarendon Press.
Morin, G. (1937), "L'évêque Laurent de 'Novae' et ses opuscoles théologiques (attribué à tort à un Laurent de Novare)". *Revue des sciences philosophiques et théologiques* 2: 307–317.
Mossé F. (1956), *Manuel de la langue gotique. Grammaire, textes, glossaire*. Nouv. éd. Paris: Aubier (Bibliothe`que de philologie germanique, 2).
Müller, R.W. (1964), *Rhetorische und syntaktische Interpunktion. Untersuchungen zur Pausenbezeichnung im antiken Latein*. Diss. Tübingen.

Munkhammar, L. (2011 A), "Theoderic, Ravenna and the *Codex Argenteus*", in R. Milev, *Gotite III*. Sofia: Balkan Media, 241–245.

Munkhammar, L. (2011 B), *The Silver Bible: Origins and History of the* Codex Argenteus. Västerås: Edita Västra Aros.

Nestle-Aland[28] = *Novum Testamentum Graece*. Based on the work of Eberhard and Erwin Nestle, ed. by B. and K. Aland, J. Karavidopoulos, C.M. Martini, B.M. Metzger. 28th rev. edition, ed. by the Institute for New Testament Textual Research Münster/Westphalia under the direction of H. Strutwolf. Stuttgart: Deutsche Bibelgesellschaft, 2012.

Nigro, G. (2012), "Dinamiche multietniche e interreligiose oltre il *limes* danubiano: Niceta, Inna e altri martiri goti". *Classica et Christiana* 7: 201–220.

Nordenfalk, C. (1938), *Die spätantiken Kanontafeln. Kunstgeschichtliche Studien über die eusebianische Evangelien-Konkordanz in den vier ersten Jahrhunderten ihrer Geschichte*. Göteborg: Isacson (Die Bücherornamentik der Spätantike, 1).

Odefey, P.G. (1908), *Das gotische Lukasevangelium. Ein Beitrag zur Quellenkritik und Textgeschichte*. Diss. Kiel. Flensburg: Meyer.

Pagliarulo, G. (2008), "Innovazione e conservazione nel passivo gotico", in V. Dolcetti Corazza – R. Gendre, *Intorno alla* Bibbia *gotica*. Alessandria: Edizioni dell'Orso, 329–339 (Bibliotheca Germanica. Studi e testi, 21).

Pagliarulo, G. (2011), "Su alcuni casi di cattivo accordo in perifrasi passive gotiche". *Alessandria* 4: 95–101.

Pakis, V.A. (2010), "Praesens Historicum and the Question of Old Latin Influence on the Gothic Bible", in H.F. Nielsen – F.T. Stubkjær, *The Gothic Language. A Symposium* (= NOWELE 58/59). Odense: University Press of Southern Denmark, 239–254.

Parker, D.C. (1992), Codex Bezae: *An Early Christian Manuscript and its Text*. Cambridge: Cambridge University Press.

Parker, D.C. (2008), *An Introduction to the New Testament Manuscripts and their Texts*. Cambridge: Cambridge University Press.

Parkes, M.B. (1992), *Pause and Effect: An Introduction of the History of Punctuation in the West*. Aldershot: Scolar Press.

Pecere, O. (1993), "La cultura greco-romana in età gota tra adattamento e trasformazione", in *Teoderico il Grande e i Goti d'Italia. Atti del XIII Congresso internazionale di studi sull'Alto Medioevo, Milano, 2–6 nov. 1992*, Spoleto: Centro Italiano di Studi sull'Alto Medioevo, 355–394 (Atti dei congressi del Centro Italiano di Studi sull'Alto Medioevo, 13).

Petitmengin, P. (1985), "Les plus anciens manuscrits de la Bible latine", in J. Fontaine – Ch. Pietri, *Le monde latin antique et la Bible*. Paris: Beauchesne, 89–123 (Bible de tous les temps, 2).

Petrucci, A. (1973), "La concezione cristiana del libro fra VI e VII secolo". *Studi medievali* 14: 961–984.

Piras, A. (2007), *Manuale di gotico. Avviamento alla lettura della versione gotica del Nuovo Testamento*. Roma: Herder.

Piras, A. (2009), "La resa di alcuni semitismi sintattici indiretti nella versione gotica della Bibbia". *Filologia Germanica/Germanic Philology* 1: 159–180.

Piras, A. (2010), "γνήσιε σύζυγε in Phil 4,3 und seine gotische Übersetzung. Ein Beitrag zur Text- und Interpretationsgeschichte". *Zeitschrift für die neutestamentliche Wissenschaft und Kunde der älteren Kirche* 101: 78–92.

Pollak, H. (1973), "Weiterer Kommentar zum *Fragmentum Spirense*". *Zeitschrift für deutsche Philologie* 92: 61–65.
Popescu, E. (1973), "Das Problem der Kontinuität in Rumänien im Lichte der epigraphischen Entdeckungen". *Dacoromania* 1: 69–77.
Popescu, E. (1976), *Inscripţiile greceşti şi latine din secolele IV-XIII descoperite în România*. Bucureşti: Editura Academiei.
Popescu, E. (1987), "Le christianisme en Roumanie jusqu'au VIIe siècle à la lumière des nouvelles recherches". *Mitropolia Banatului* 4 (1987), 34–49.
Popescu, E. (1990), "Byzanz und die Christianisierung Südost- und Osteuropas", in A.M. Ritter, *Die Anfänge des Christentums unter den Völkern Ost- und Südosteuropas. Referate und Materialien des IX. Theologischen Südosteuropaseminars (Heidelberg, 21.–27. August 1989)*. Heidelberg: Lehrstuhl für Histor. Theologie, 6–20 (Theologisches Südosteuropaseminar, 9).
Popescu, E. (2006), "Das Frühchristentum in Rumänien zwischen Byzanz und Rom", in R. Harreither, P. Pergola *et al.*, Acta Congressus Internationalis XIV Archaeologiae Christianae: Vindobonae 19.-26.9.1999 / *Frühes Christentum zwischen Rom und Konstantinopel. Akten des XIV. Internationalen Kongresses für Christliche Archäologie in Wien vom 19. bis 26. September 1999*. Città del Vaticano: Pontificio Istituto di Archeologia Cristiana, 621–637 (Studi di antichità cristiana, 62).
Popescu, E. (2013), "Creştinismul în vremea împăratului Constantin cel Mare pe teritoriul românesc la populaţia autohtonă şi barbară", in E. Popescu – V. Ioniţă, *Cruce şi Misiune. Sfinţii Împăraţi Constantin şi Elena – promotori ai libertăţii religioase şi apărători ai Bisericii*. Bucureşti: Basilica a Patriarhiei Române, II, 595–614.
Porter, S.E. (2009), "Pericope Markers and the Paragraph: Textual and Linguistic Implications", in R. de Hoop, M.C.A. Korpel, S.E. Porter, *The Impact of Unit Delimitation on Exegesis*. Leiden-Boston: Brill, 175–195 (Pericope. Scripture as Written and Read in Antiquity, 7).
Possnert, G. – Munkhammar, L. (1999–2000), "Silverbibelns ålder och bindningshistoria i ljuset av C14-analys". *Annales Academiae Regiae Scientiarum. Kungliga Vetenskapssamhällets i Uppsala Årsbok* 33: 53–65.
Poulter A. (2000), "The Roman to Byzantine Transition in the Balkans: Preliminary Results on Nicopolis and its Hinterland". *Journal of Roman Archeology* 13: 347–358.
Poulter, A. (2007), "Invisible Goths within and beyond the Roman Empire", in J. Drinkwater – B. Salway, *Wolf Liebeschuetz reflected. Essays presented by Colleagues, Friends, & Pupils*. London: Institute of Classical Studies, 169–182.
Prostko-Prostyński J. (1997), "Theodoric the Great in Novae: Some Remarks on the Chronology of Events", in A.B. Biernacki – P. Powlak, *Late Roman and Early Byzantine Cities on the Lower Danube from the 4th to the 6th Century A. D. International Conference, Poznań, Poland 15–17 November 1995. Studies and Materials*. Poznań: Instytut Historii Uniwersytetu im. Adama Mickiewicz, 21–30.
Raffaelli, R. (1984), "La pagina e il testo. Sulle funzioni della doppia rigatura verticale nei codici latini antiquiores", in C. Questa – R. Raffaelli, *Atti del convegno internazionale sul tema: Il libro e il testo (Urbino, 20–23 sett. 1982)*. Urbino: Universita degli Studi di Urbino, 3–26.
Ralston, T.R. (1992), "The 'Majority text' and Byzantine Origins". *New Testament Studies* 38: 122–137.

Rapp, C. (2005), *Holy Bishops in Late Antiquity: The Nature of Christian Leadership in an Age of Transition*. Berkeley-Los Angeles (CA): University of California Press (The Transformation of the Classical Heritage, 37).

Raschellà, F.D. (2008), "Vulfila e il fuþark: la componente runica dell'alfabeto gotico", in V. Dolcetti Corazza – R. Gendre, *Intorno alla* Bibbia *gotica*. Alessandria: Edizioni dell'Orso, 3–39 (Bibliotheca Germanica. Studi e testi, 21).

Raschellà, F.D. (2011), "Models and Principles of Wulfila's Gothic Alphabet: Some Methodological Remarks", in E. Glaser, A. Seiler *et al.*, *LautSchriftSprache. Beiträge zur vergleichenden historischen Graphematik*. Zürich: Chronos, 109–124 (Medienwandel – Medienwechsel – Medienwissen, 15).

Rauch, I. (2003), *The Gothic Language: Grammar, Genetic Provenance and Typology, Readings*. New York: Lang.

Reichert, H. (1989), "Die Bewertung namenkundlicher Zeugnisse für die Verwendung der gotischen Sprache. Methodendiskussion an Hand der Namen der Märtyrer aus der Gothia des 4. Jahrhunderts", in H. Beck, *Germanische Rest- und Trümmersprachen*. Berlin-New York: de Gruyter, 119–142 (Ergänzungsbände zum Reallexikon der germanischen Altertumskunde, 3).

Robinson, M.A. – Pierpont, W.G. (2005), eds. *The New Testament in the Original Greek: Byzantine Textform*. Southborough (MA): Chilton Book Publishing.

Rubin, Z. (1981), "The Conversion of the Visigoths to Christianity". *Museum Helveticum* 38: 34–54.

Rusu, M. (1991), "Paleocreştinismul din Dacia romană". *Ephemeris Napocensis* I: 81–112.

Saitta, B. (1993), *La* civilitas *di Teoderico. Rigore amministrativo, 'tolleranza' religiosa e recupero dell'antico nell'Italia ostrogota*. Roma: "L'Erma" di Bretschneider (Studia Historica, 128).

Salamon, Á. (1977 [1978]), "Grave 5 from the Cemetery at Hács-Béndekpuszta". *Mitteilungen des Archäologischen Instituts der Ungarischen Akademie der Wissenschaften* 7: 37–40.

Scardigli, B. (1979), "*Conveniunt itaque Gothi Romanique* ... (Ein Forschungsbericht über die römisch-gotischen Beziehungen im 4. Jahrhundert n. Chr.: 1950–1975)". *Romanobarbarica* 4: 255–340.

Scardigli, B. (1982–83), "*Conveniunt itaque Gothi Romanique* ... (Einzelne Aspekte der römisch-gotischen Beziehungen im 3. und 4. Jhh. – Abschluss des Forschungsberichtes)". *Romanobarbarica* 7: 355–433.

Scardigli, B. – Scardigli, P. (1976), "I rapporti fra Goti e Romani nel III e IV secolo". *Romanobarbarica* 1: 261–295.

Scardigli, P. (1967), "La conversione dei Goti al cristianesimo", in *La conversione al cristianesimo nell'Europa dell'Alto Medioevo. XIV Settimana di studio del Centro Italiano di Studi sull'Alto Medioevo (14–19 aprile 1966)*. Spoleto: Centro Italiano di Studi sull'Alto Medioevo, 47–86 (Settimane di studio del Centro Italiano di Studi sull'Alto Medioevo, 14).

Scardigli, P. (1971), "Unum Redivivum Folium". *Studi germanici* n. s. 9: 1–15.

Scardigli, P. (1973), *Die Goten. Sprache und Kultur*. München: Beck.

Scardigli, P. (1994), "Zur Typologie der gotischen Handschriftüberlieferung", in H. Uecker, *Studien zum Altgermanischen. Festschrift für Heinrich Beck*. Berlin-New York: de Gruyter, 527–538 (Ergäzungsbände zum Reallexikon der germanischen Altertumskunde, 11).

Scardigli, P. (1998), "Gotische Schrift", in *Reallexikon der germanischen Altertumskunde*. 2. rev. Aufl., Bd. 12. Berlin-New York: de Gruyter, 455–458.

Scardigli, P. (2003), "Zum Thema gotische Bibel: Streitberg und Sievers an Lietzmann", in W. Heizmann – A. van Nahl, Runica – Germanica – Mediaevalia, *Festschrift Klaus Düwel*. Berlin-New York: de Gruyter, 707–718 (Ergäzungsbände zum Reallexikon der germanischen Altertumskunde, 37).

Schäferdiek, K. (1979), "Wulfila. Vom Bischof von Gotien zum Gotenbischof". *Zeitschrift für Kirchengeschichte* 90: 253–292.

Schäferdiek, K. (1981), "Die Fragmente der *Skeireins* und der Johanneskommentar des Theodor von Herakleia". *Zeitschrift für deutsches Altertum und deutsche Literatur* 110: 175–193.

Schäferdiek, K. (1988), "Das gotische liturgische Kalenderfragment. Bruchstück eines Konstantinopeler Martyrologs". *Zeitschrift für die neutestamentliche Wissenschaft und Kunde der älteren Kirche* 79: 116–137.

Schäferdiek, K. (1990 [1991]), "Gotien. Eine Kirche im Vorfeld des frühbyzantinischen Reichs". *Jahrbuch für Antike und Christentum* 33: 36–52.

Schäferdiek, K. (1992), "Das gotische Christentum im vierten Jahrhundert", in K-F. Kraft, E.-M. Lill *et al.*, Triuwe. *Studien zur Sprachgeschichte und Literaturwissenschaft (Gedächtnisbuch für Elfriede Stutz)*. Heidelberg: Heidelberger Verlagsanstalt, 19–50 (Heidelberger Bibliotheksschriften, 47).

Schäferdiek, K. (1993), "Märtyrerüberlieferungen aus der gotischen Kirche des vierten Jahrhunderts", in H.Ch. Brennecke, E.L. Grasmück *et al.*, *Logos. Festschrift für Luise Abramowski*. Berlin-New York: de Gruyter, 328–360 (Beihefte zur *Zeitschrift für die neutestamentliche Wissenschaft und Kunde der älteren Kirche*, 67).

Schäferdiek, K. (2001), "Die Anfänge des Christentums bei den Goten und der sogenannte gotische Arianismus". *Zeitschrift für Kirchengeschichte* 112: 295–310.

Scherbenske, E.W. (2013), *Canonizing Paul: Ancient Editorial Practice and the Corpus Paulinum*. Oxford-New York: Oxford University Press.

Scherer, Ph. (1964), "The Theory of the Function of the Gothic Preverb *ga-*". *Word* 20: 221–245.

Schmid, U.B. (2006), "Reassessing the Palaeography and Codicology of the Freer Gospel Manuscript", in L.W. Hurtado, *The Freer Biblical Manuscripts: Fresh Studies of an American Treasure Trove*. Atlanta: Society of Biblical Literature, 227–250 (Text Critical Studies, 6).

Schmid, U.B. (2013), "Marcion and the Textual History of *Romans*: Editorial Activity and Early Edition of the New Testament", in M. Vinzent, *Papers presented at the Sixteenth International Conference on Patristic Studies held in Oxford 2011. 17: Latin Writers – Nachleben*. Leuven: Peeters, 99–113 (Studia Patristica, 54).

Schröder, W. (1957), "Die Gliederung des gotischen Passivs". *Beiträge zur Geschichte der deutschen Sprache und Literatur* (H) 79: 1–105.

Schuhmann, R. (forthcoming), *Gotisch*. Wiesbaden: Reichert Verlag.

Schwarcz, A. (1987), "Die Anfänge des Christentums bei den Goten", in V. Gjuzelev – R. Pillinger, *Das Christentum in Bulgarien und auf der übrigen Balkanhalbinsel in der Spätantike und im frühen Mittelalter. II. Internationales Symposium Haskovo (Bulgarien), 10.–13. Juni 1986*. Wien: Verein 'Freunde des Hauses Wittgenstein", 107–118 (Miscellanea Bulgarica, 5).

Schwarcz, A. (1999), "Cult and Religion among the Tervigi and the Visigoths and their Conversion to Christianity", in P. Heather, *The Visigoths from the Migration Period to the*

Seventh Century: An Ethnographic Perspective. Woodbridge: The Boydell Press, 447–459 (Studies in Historical Archaeoethnology, 4).
Seppänen, A. (1985), "On the Use of the Dual in Gothic". *Zeitschrift für deutsches Altertum und deutsche Literatur* 114: 1–41.
Simonetti, M. (1976), "L'arianesimo di Ulfila". *Romano Barbarica* 1: 297–323.
Sivan, H. (1996), "Ulfila's own Conversion". *Harvard Theological Review* 89: 373–386.
Snædal, M. (2002), "Naples, Arezzo, Verona", in Ch.T. Petersen, *Gotica minora. I. Miscellanea de lingua Wulfilae collecta.* Hanau: Syllabus, 1–6.
Snædal, M. (2003), "The Gothic Text of *Codex Gissensis*", in Ch. T. Petersen, *Gotica Minora. II. Scripta nova & vetera.* Hanau: Syllabus, 1–20.
Snædal, M. (2007), "The Consequence of Syncretism", in N.S. Babeiko – A.L. Zeleneckij, Lingua gotica. *Novye Issledovanija. Kaluga: Rossijskaja Akademija Nauk*, 92–96.
Snædal, M. (2013 A), *A Concordance to Biblical Gothic, I: Introduction-Texts; II: Concordance*, 3rd rev. ed. Reykjavík: University of Iceland Press.
Snædal, M. (2013 B), "Text-critical remarks initiated by the Folium Spirense", in Ch.T. Petersen, *Gotica Minora. VIII. Spirensia & Synoptica.* Aschaffenburg: Syllabus. s.n [10 pp.]
von Soden, H. (1902–1913), ed. *Die Schriften des Neuen Testaments in ihrer ältesten erreichbaren Textgestalt hergestellt auf Grund ihrer Textgeschichte.* I, 1–3. *Untersuchungen.* Berlin: Glaue, 1902–1910; II. *Text mit Apparat.* Göttingen: Vandenhoeck & Ruprecht, 1913.
Sörries, R. (1983), *Die Bilder der Orthodoxen im Kampf gegen den Arianismus. Eine Apologie der orthodoxen Christologie und Trinitätslehre gegenüber der arianischen Häresie, dargestellt an den ravennatischen Mosaiken und Bildern des 6. Jahrhunderts. Zugleich ein Beitrag zum Verständnis des germanischen Homöertums.* Frankfurt/M.-Bern: Lang (Europäische Hochschulschriften. R. 23, Th. 186).
Solari R. (1974), "Le trascrizioni gotiche di parole greche". *Rendiconti dell'Accademia Nazionale dei Lincei. Scienze morali, storiche e filologiche* 29: 335–361.
Staab, F. (1976), "Ostrogothic Geographers at the Court of Theodoric the Great: A Study of Some Sources of the Anonymous Cosmografer of Ravenna". *Viator* 7: 27–64.
Stamm, F.L. (1858), ed. *Ulfilas oder die uns erhaltenen Denkmäler der gothischen Sprache. Text, Grammatik und Wörterbuch.* Paderborn: Schöningh (Bibliothek der ältesten deutschen Literaturdenkmäler, 1).
Stolzenburg, H. (1905), *Zur Übersetzungstechnik des Wulfila.* Halle a S.: Buchdruckerei des Waisenhauses.
Streeter, B.H. (1924), *The Four Gospels: A Study of Origins, Treating of the Manuscript Tradition, Sources, Auhorship & Dates.* London: McMillan.
Streitberg, W. (1891). "Perfektive und imperfektive Aktionsart im Germanischen. Einleitung und 1. Teil: Gotisch". *Beiträge zur Geschichte der deutschen Sprache und Literatur* 15: 70–177.
Streitberg, W. (1908), ed. *Die gotische Bibel, I. Der gotische Text und seine griechische Vorlage. Mit Einleitung, Lesarten und Quellennachweisen sowie den kleineren Denkmälern als Anhang.* Heidelberg: Winter (Germanische Bibliothek, II. 3, 1).
Streitberg, W. (1919), ed. *Die gotische Bibel, I. Der gotische Text und seine griechische Vorlage. Mit Einleitung, Lesarten und Quellennachweisen sowie den kleineren Denkmälern als Anhang*, 2. verb. Aufl. Heidelberg: Winter (Germanische Bibliothek, II. 3, 1).

Streitberg, W. (1920), *Gotisches Elementarbuch*. 5./6. neubearb. Aufl. Heidelberg: Winter (Germanische Bibliothek, I. 1, 2).
Streitberg-Scardigli 2000 = W. Streitberg (ed.), *Die gotische Bibel*. I. *Der gotische Text und seine griechische Vorlage. Mit Einleitung, Lesarten und Quellennachweisen sowie den kleineren Denkmälern als Anhang*. 7. Aufl. Mit einem Nachtrag von P. Scardigli. Heidelberg: Winter (Germanistische Bibliothek, 3).
Streitberg-Stopp 1981 = Streitberg, W., *Gotische Syntax*, hrgs. von H. Stopp. Heidelberg: Winter (Germanische Bibliothek, N. F. 1.).
Stutz, E. (1966), *Gotische Literaturdenkmäler*. Stuttgart: J. B. Metzlersche Verlagsbuchhandlung (Sammlung Metzler, 1684).
Stutz, E. (1971), "Ein gotisches Evangelienfragment in Speyer". *Zeitschrift für vergleichende Sprachforschung* 85: 85–95.
Stutz, E. (1972), "Das Neue Testament in gotischer Sprache", in K. Aland, *Die alten Übersetzungen des Neuen Testaments, die Kirchenväterzitate und Lektionare*. Berlin-New York: de Gruyter, 375–402 (Arbeiten zur neutestamentlichen Textforschung, 5).
Stutz, E. (1973), "Fragmentum Spirense – verso". *Zeitschrift für vergleichende Sprachforschung* 87: 1–15.
Sumruld, W.A. (1994), *Augustine and the Arians: The Bishop of Hippo's Encounters with Ulfilan Arianism*. London: Selinsgrove/Toronto: Susquehanna University Press.
Swanson 1995–2005 = Swanson, R.J. (ed.), *New Testament Greek Manuscripts: Variant Readings Arranged in Horizontal Lines against Codex Vaticanus*. Sheffield, Sheffield Acad. Press.: *Matthew*, 1995 A; *Mark*, 1995 B; *John*, 1995 C; *Luke*, 1995 D; *Galatians*, 1999; *Romans*, 2001; *1 Corinthians*, 2003; *2 Corinthians*, 2005.
Székely, D. (1977 [1978]), "A Lead Tablet with Inscriptions from Hács-Béndekpuszta". *Mitteilungen. Archäologisches Institut der ungarischen Akademie der Wissenschaften* 7: 41–43.
Thompson, E.A. (1955), "The *Passio S. Sabae* and the Early Visigothic Society". *Historia. Zeitschrift für alte Geschichte* 4: 331–338.
Thompson, E.A. (1966), *The Visigoths in the Time of Ulfila*. Oxford: Clarendon Press.
Thompson, E.M. (1912), *An Introduction to Greek and Latin Palaeography*. Oxford: Clarendon Press.
Tischendorf, C. (1869–1872), ed. *Novum Testamentum Graece. Ad antiquos testes recensuit apparatum criticum multis modis auctum et correctum apposuit commentationem isagogicam praemisit Constantinus Tischendorf. Editio octava critica major*. Leipzig: J.C. Hinrichs.
Tjäder, J-O. (1954), ed. *Die nichtliterarischen Papyri Italiens aus der Zeit 445–700. III. Tafeln*, Lund: Gleerup (Acta Instituti Romani Regni Sueciae, 19. 3).
Tjäder, J-O. (1972), "Der *Codex Argenteus* in Uppsala und der Buchmeister Viliaric in Ravenna", in U.E. Hagberg, Studia Gotica. *Die eisenzeitlichen Verbindungen zwischen Schweden und Südosteuropa. Vorträge beim Gotensymposion im Statens historiska Museum (Stockholm 1970)*. Stockholm: Almqvist & Wiksell, 144–164 (Kungl. Vitterhets-, historie- och antikvitetsakademiens handlingar. Antikvariska serien, 25).
Tjäder, J-O. (1974), "Studier till *Codex Argenteus*' historia". *Nordisk tidskrift för bok och biblioteksväsen* 61: 51–99.
Tov, E. (1998), "Sense Divisions in the Qumran Texts, the Masoretic Text and Ancient Translations of the Bible", in J. Krasovec, *Interpretation of the Bible: International Symposium on the Interpretation of the Bible on the Occasion of the Publication of the*

New Slovanian Translation of the Bible. Ljubljana: Slovenska akademija znanosti in umetnosti, 121–146.

Tovar, A. (1946), *Lengua gótica: paradigmas gramaticales, textos, léxico*, Madrid: Ediciones Nueva Época.

Traube, L. (1907), Nomina sacra. *Versuch einer Geschichte der christlichen Kürzung*. München: Beck (Quellen und Untersuchungen zur lateinischen Philologie des Mittelalters, 2).

Trobisch, D. (1989), *Die Entstehung der Paulusbriefsammlung. Studien zu den Anfängen christlicher Publizistik*. Freiburg/Schweiz: Universitätsverlag.

Trovato, A. (2009), "Sulla funzione del prefisso *ga-* nella morfologia verbale del gotico". *Filologia Germanica/Germanic Philology* 1: 215–242.

Tudor, D. (1973), "Preuves archéologiques attestantes la continuité de la domination romaine au Nord du Danube après l'abandon de la Dacie sous Aurélian (IIIe-Ve siècles)". *Dacoromania* 1: 149–161.

Turner, C.H. (1924), "The *Nomina Sacra* in Early Christian Latin Mss", in *Miscellanea Francesco Ehrle. Scritti di storia e paleografia*, IV. Roma: Biblioteca Apostolica Vaticana, 62–74 (Studi e testi, 40).

UBS^4 = *The Greek New Testament*. Ed. by B. Aland, K. Aland, J. Karavidopoulos, C.M. Martini, and B.M. Metzger in collaboration with the Institute for New Testament Textual Research, Münster/Westphalia, 4th rev. ed., 11th impr., Stuttgart: Deutsche Bibelgesellschaft, 2006.

Unterkircher, F. (1969), ed. *Alkuin-Briefe und andere Traktate*. Epistolae *im Auftrage des Salzburger Erzbischofs Arn um 799 zu einem Sammelband vereinigt*. Codex Vindobonensis 795 der Österreichischen Nationalbibliothek. Graz: Akad. Druck- u. Verl.-Anst (Codices selecti phototypice impressi, XX).

Uppström, A. (1854), ed. *Codex Argenteus sive sacrorum evangeliorum versionis gothicae fragmenta quae iterum recognita adnotationibusque instructa per lineas singulas ad fidem codicis additis fragmentis evangelius codicum ambrosanorum et tabula lapide expressa*. Uppsala: Leffler.

Uppström, A. (1857), ed. *Decem codicis argentei rediviva folia cum foliis contiguis et intermediis*. Uppsala: Leffler.

Uppström, A. (1864–1868), ed. *Codices Gotici Ambrosiani sive Epistolorum Pauli Esrae Nehemiae versionis Gothicae fragmenta quae iterum recognovit per lineas singulas descripsit adnotionibus instruxit Andreas Uppström*. Stockholm – Leipzig: Samson et Wallin.

van den Hout, M. (1952), "Gothic Palimpsests of Bobbio". *Scriptorium* 6: 91–93.

Velkov, V. (1989), "Wulfila und die *Gothi minores* in Moesien". *Klio* 71: 525–527.

Velkov, V. (1995), "Altchristliche Inschriften vom unterdonauländischen Limes (Provincia Moesia Secunda)", in E. Dassmann – J. Engemann, *Akten des XII. internationalen Kongresses für Christliche Archäologie, Bonn 22.–28. September 1991*. Münster: Aschendorffsche Verlagsbuchhandlung, 1251–1254 (Jahrbuch für Antike und Christentum. Ergänzungsband, 20.2).

Velten, H.V. (1930), "Studies in the Gothic Vocabulary with Especial Reference to Greek and Latin Models and Analogues". *Journal of English and Germanic Philology* 29: 332–351, 489–509.

Vezin, J. (1987), "Les divisions du texte dans les Évangiles jusqu'à l'apparition de l'imprimerie", in A. Maierù, *Grafia e interpunzione del latino nel medioevo (Seminario*

Internazionale, Roma, 27–29 settembre 1984). Roma: Edizioni dell'Ateneo, 53–68 (Lessico intellettuale europeo, 41).

Viehmeyer, L.A. (1971), *The Gothic Alphabet: A Study and Derivation*. Diss. University of Illinois at Urbana-Champaign (IL).

Vladkova, P. (2007), "The Late Roman Agora and the State of Civic Organization". *Proceedings of the British Academy* 141: 203–217.

VLD = *Vetus Latina Database*, ed. by *Vetus Latina* Institut (Beuron). Turnhout: Brepols, 2002.

Vööbus, A. (1954), *Early Versions of the New Testament. Manuscript Studies*. Stockholm: Estonian Theological Society in Exile (Papers of the Estonian Theological Society in Exile, 6).

Vogels, H.J. (1913), ed. Codex Rehdigeranus. *Die vier Evangelien nach der lateinischen Handschrift R 169 der Stadtbibliothek Breslau*. Roma: Pustet (Collectanea Biblica Latina, 2).

de Vries, J. (1936), ed. *Wulfilae Codices Ambrosiani rescripti epistularum evangelicarum textum Goticum exhibentes*. Torino: Molfese.

Wachtel, K. (1995), *Der Byzantinische Text der Katholischen Briefe. Eine Untersuchung zur Entstehung der Koine des Neuen Testaments*. Berlin-New York: de Gruyter (Arbeiten zur neutestamentlichen Textforschung, 24).

Wachtel, K. (2005), "Varianten in der handschriftlichen Überlieferung des Neuen Testamens", in Ch. Jansohn – B. Plachta, *Varianten-Variants-Variantes*. Tübingen: Niemeyer, 25–38 (Beihefte zu *Editio*, 22).

Wachtel, K. (2009), "The Byzantine Text of the Gospels: Recension or Process?". Paper prepared for the NTTC session 23–327 at SBL 2009 (http://www.uni-muenster.de/INTF/ByzTextDownload/).

Wagner, N. (1994), "Zu den *Gotica* der Salzburg-Wiener Alcuin-Handschrift". *Historische Sprachforschung* 107: 262–283.

Wallace, D.B. (1995), "The Majority Text Theory: History, Methods, and Critique", in B.D. Ehrman – M.W. Holmes, *The Text of the New Testament in Contemporary Research. Essays on the Status Quaestionis*. Grand Rapids (MI): Eerdmans, 297–320 (Studies and documents, 46).

Weber *et al.* (1994) = *Biblia Sacra iuxta Vulgatam versionem*, ed. R. Weber, rev. R. Gryson, B. Fischer, H. I. Frede *et alii*, 4. Aufl., Stuttgart: Deutsche Bibelgesellschaft.

Werth, R. (1967), "Criteria for Sentence Delimitation in Wulfilian Gothic'. *Orbis* 16: 519–527.

Westcott, B.F. – Hort, F.J.A. (1882), eds. *The New Testament in the Original Greek*. II. *Introduction, Appendix*. London: Macmillan.

Wiles, M.F. (1996), *Archetypal Heresy: Arianism through the Centuries*. Oxford: Clarendon Press.

Willard, L.Ch. (2009), *A Critical Study of the Euthalian Apparatus*. Berlin-New York: de Gruyter (Arbeiten zur neutestamentlichen Textforschung, 41).

Wolfram, H. (1990), *Die Goten. Von den Anfängen bis zur Mitte des sechsten Jahrhunderts. Entwurf einer historischen Ethnographie*. 3. neubearb. Aufl. München: Beck.

Wolfram, H. (2013), "Vulfila *pontifex ipseque primas Gothorum minorum*", in A. Kaliff – L. Munkhammar, *Wulfila 311–2011. International Symposium, Uppsala University, June 15–18, 2011*. Uppsala: Uppsala Universitet, 25–32 (Acta Universitatis Upsaliensis, 48).

Wood, I. (2007), "Theoderic's Monuments in Ravenna", in S. Barnish – F. Marazzi, *The Ostrogoths from the Migration Period to the Sixth Century: An Ethnographic Perspective*. Woodbridge: Boydell Press, 249–63 (Studies in Historical Archaeoethnology, 7).

Wordsworth, J. – White, H.J. (1889–1898), eds. *Novum Testamentum* [...] *secundum editionem Sancti Hieronymi* [...], 1. *Quattuor evangelia.* Oxford: Clarendon Press.
Wright-Sayce = J. Wright, *Grammar of the Gothic Language.* 2nd ed. by O. L. Sayce. Oxford: Clarendon Press, 1954.
Zeev, R. (1981), "The Conversion of the Visigoths to Christianity". *Museum Helveticum* 38: 34–54.
Zeiller, J. (1905), "Étude sur l'arianisme en Italie". *Mélanges d'Archéologie et d'Histoire* 25: 127–146.
Zgusta, L. (1980), "Die Rolle des Griechischen im römischen Kaiserreich", in G. Neumann *et al.*, *Die Sprachen im römischen Reich der Kaiserzeit. Kolloquium vom 8. bis 10. April 1974.* Köln: Rheinland-Verlag, 121–145 (Beihefte der Bonner Jahrbücher, 40).
Zironi, A. (1997), "Verona und die arianische Kultur in dem ostgotischen Reich". *Speculum Medii Aevi* 3: 139–158.
Zironi, A. (2004), *Il monastero longobardo di Bobbio. Crocevia di uomini, manoscritti e culture.* Spoleto: Centro Italiano di Studi sull'Alto Medioevo (Istituzioni e società, 3).
Zironi, A. (2005), "I *Gotica Parisina* nel codice Bibliothèque Nationale de France, lat. 528", in L. Sinisi, *Il plurilinguismo in area germanica nel medioevo. Atti del XXX Convegno Associazione Italiana di Filologia Germanica (Bari, 4–6 giugno 2003).* Bari: Palomar, 301–339.
Zironi, A. (2007), "La ricezione della scrittura gotica in età carolingia: il caso dei *Gotica Vindobonensia*", in E. Fazzini – E. Cianci, *I Germani e la scrittura. Atti del XXXIII Convegno dell'Associazione Italiana di Filologia Germanica (Pescara 7–9 giugno 2006).* Alessandria: Edizioni dell'Orso, 13–38.
Zironi, A. (2008), "Testimonianze gotiche e l'età carolingia", in V. Dolcetti Corazza – R. Gendre, *Intorno alla* Bibbia *gotica. VII Seminario avanzato in Filologia Germanica.* Alessandria: Edizioni dell'Orso, 127–164 (Bibliotheca Germanica. Studi e testi, 21).
Zironi, A. (2009), *L'eredità dei Goti. Testi barbarici in età carolingia.* Spoleto: Fondazione Centro Italiano di Studi sull'Alto Medioevo (Istituzioni e società, 11).
Zugravu, N. (1997), *Geneza creştinismului popular al românilor.* Bucureşti: Ministerul Educaţiei, Institutul Român de Tracologie (Bibliotheca Thracologica, 18).
Zuntz, G. (1946), *The Text of the Epistles: A Disquisition upon the* Corpus Paulinum. London: Oxford University Press.
Zuntz, G. (1995), *Lukian von Antiochien und der Text der Evangelien*, hrsg. von B. Aland – K. Wachtel. Heidelberg: Winter.

Websites (last consultation: January 2014)

http://app.ub.uu.se/arv/codex/faksimiledition/contents.html
http://bibd.uni-giessen.de/papyri/images/pbug-inv018–1.jpg
http://bibd.uni-giessen.de/papyri/images/pbug-inv018–2.jpg
http://homepage.uibk.ac.at/~c30310/gotwbhin.html
http://www.iohannes.com. = *An Electronic Version of the New Testament in Greek IV. The Gospel according to St. John. II. The Majuscules*, ed. for the International Greek New Testament Project by U.B. Schmid with W.J. Elliott and D.C. Parker, 2007; Vetus Latina Iohannes. *The Verbum Project: The Old Latin Manuscripts of John's Gospel*, ed. by P.H.

Burton, J. Balserak, H.A.G. Houghton, D.C. Parker, 2010; *An Electronic Edition of the Gospel according to John in the Byzantine Tradition*, ed. for the United Bible Societies by R.L. Mullen with S. Crisp and D.C. Parker and in association with W.J. Elliott, U.B. Schmid, R. Kevern, M.B. Morrill, C.J. Smith, 2007.
http://www.ub.uu.se/samlingar/verk-och-samlingar-i-urval/silverbibeln
http://www.uni-muenster.de/INTF/ECM.html
http://www.wulfila.be/

Index of biblical citations

Old Testament

Deuteronomy		Psalms	
24:1	116	67 (68):19	124

Nehemiah		Isaiah	
5:13–18	25	1:4	113
6:14–7:3	25	14:20	113
7:13–45	25	28:11	124
		45:24	116

New Testament

Matthew			
3:11	115	8:16	84
5:16	88	8:28	84, 90
5:22	139	8:33	84
5:23	45	9:2	114
5:23–24	82	9:8	58, 101, 117
5:31	116	9:9	86
5:37	58	9:11	78
5:39	76, 78	9:12	86
5:44	118	9:13	74
6:1	140	9:20	87
6:2	85	9:23	126
6:5	45	9:27	71
6:9	62	9:32	84
6:10	81	9:34	141
6:13	140	9:37	78
6:15	141	10:23	72
6:19	88	10:32	79
6:24	46, 85, 92, 101, 124	11:17	58
6:26	106	11:22	72
6:28	79	12:4	115
6:31	61	17:19–21	109
7:15	69, 88	19:7	116
7:24	72	25:38–46	34
7:26	78	26:1–3	34
7:28	54	26:65–75	34
7:29	58	26:70	117
8:12	58	26:70–27:1	34
8:14	73, 87	26:71	71, 76
		26:72	117–118

26:75	117–118	5:42	87
27:1	34, 76	6:3	89
27:3	117	6:5	73
27:42	116	8:1	73
27:46	89	8:31	61
27:49	76	9:28–29	109
		9:39	45, 118
Mark		9:50	112
1:2	140	10:2	141
1:6	46	10:4	116
1:7	74	10:18	45
1:8	115	12:10	53
1:11	46	12:24	46, 123
1:17	71	14:10	88
1:30	79, 87	14:70	117–118
1:32	84	14:72	118
1:42	45	15:28	140
1:45	77	15:32	116
2:4	73	15:34	89
2:5	114	16:9–20	2, 138–139, 175–178
2:6	75	16:12	139
2:8	77		
2:9	114	Luke	
2:12	117	1:3	107
2:13	46	1:9	104
2:14	80, 86	1:10	92
2:17	86	1:29	107
2:20	76	1:46–47	71
2:25	53	1:63	108
2:26	115	1:73	123
3:8	76	2:1	61
3:11	79	2:2	126
3:18	88	2:8	110
3:19	88, 117	2:14	17
3:20	76	2:48	71
4:1	75	2:49	71
4:9	77	3:1	126
4:13	70	3:6	116
4:24	101	3:14	46
4:37	88	3:16	115
4:40	76	3:23–38	59
5:4	46, 86	3:26	80
5:9	76	3:33	89
5:15	77, 84–85	3:36	89
5:16	84–85	4:2	69
5:18	85	4:9	70
5:25	69	4:15–16	85

4:16	53	23:4	103
4:17	71	23:5	103
4:23	74	23:11–14	35
4:28	72	24:5–9	35
4:35	77	24:6	103
5:4	87	24:7	103
5:13	76	24:9	103
5:20	114	24:13–17	35
5:26	117	24:49	16–17
5:27	86		
5:28	46	John	
5:31	86	1:1–14	41
5:39	141	1:26	115
6:3	53	5:45	78
6:9	77	5:46	74
6:14	88	6:19	69
6:14–16	58	6:20	70
6:15	80	6:27	78
6:16	88–89	6:60	78
6:25	70	6:66	101
6:27	46	6:71	88
6:40	46	7:6	79
6:49	46	7:12	101
7:25	70	7:32	83
7:32	46	7:45	83
7:48	114	7:53–8:11	138
7:50	74	9:15	104
8:13–24:53	131	10:1	111
8:27	46	10:16	112
8:29	86	10:18	44
8:36	84	10:21	85
8:42	87	10:30	15
9:10	88	11:24	76
9:13	46, 123	11:47	83
9:28	43	12:3	71
9:34	46, 72	12:4	88
9:43	109	12:10	83
9:50	118	12:14	73
10:13	88	12:21	88
10:26	53	13:26	88
15:32	43	13:29	45
16:13	46, 85, 124	13:38	118
17:26–27	89	14:9	75
17:27	17	14:22	88
19:33	63	15:16	44
20:23	74	15:17	72
23:3–6	35	16:11	76

16:22	70	14:20	144
17:11–12	41	14:23	143
18:1	45, 78	15:3	144
18:2	117	15:8	102
18:3	83	15:9	102
18:10	83	15:11	145
18:13	83	16:22	61
18:15	83	16:24	61, 143
18:16	83	16:25–27	143
18:19	83		
18:20	82, 104	1 Corinthians	
18:22	72, 83	1:22	81
18:24	83	5:4	38, 49, 58–59
18:25	72, 74	9:6	71
18:26	83	9:7	47
18:35	83	9:9	47
19:2	73	9:19	47
19:3	44	9:21	47
19:5	44	9:22	47
19:6	83	10:25	87
		10:30	47
Acts		11:23	69
1:8	17	13:3	47, 124
15:28	107	13:5	47
		13:12	112
Romans		14:21	47, 72, 124
7:2	75	15:33	47
7:25	92	15:49	82
8:35	61	15:54	120
9:13	47	16:1	72
9:27	88	16:2	119
11:33	79, 111	16:13	17
12:2	60		
12:3	71	2 Corinthians	
12:9	74	1:8	47
12:14	118	1:10	132
12:17	37–38, 48, 59	1:19	45
12:18	17	2:10	119
12:19	126	2:11	47
12:20	59, 144	2:15	47
13:1	61, 70	3:7	88
13:3	69	3:14	47
13:5	37–38, 48, 59	3:15	53
14:11	116	4:4	63, 121
14:14	79	4:8	125
14:17	63	4:17	111
14:18	102	5:12	47

6:8	75	Philippians	
6:16	47	2:6	15, 139
7:8	77	2:7	139
10:2	45	2:10	116
11:10	71	3:16	122
11:25	71, 113	4:3	144
12:7	47		
12:15	47	Colossians	
12:18	45	1:15	121
12:20	127	1:22	84
13:13	121	2:16	88
		3:5	47
Galatians		4:16	53
2:5	47		
2:6	47	1 Thessalonians	
2:8	47	5:27	53
2:13	71	5:28	121
2:14	143		
2:15	143	2 Thessalonians	
4:3	47	3:18	121
4:6	84		
4:13	47	1 Timothy	
4:19	47	1:5	47
4:21	47	1:9	47
5:6	68	1:18	47
5:20	126	1:19	113
6:3	47	3:3	48
6:11	72	3:11	47
6:17	121, 142	5:4	126–127
6:18	121	5:18	47
		5:23	47
Ephesians		6:6	47
1:9	47		
1:14	47	2 Timothy	
1:19	47	2:2	126–127
1:20	70	2:21	63
2:3	47	2:26	120
2:10	47	3:2	47, 87
3:4	53	3:8	90
3:10	47	3:9	47
4:8	47	3:10	47
4:13	47	3:13	47
4:32	17	4:6	47
5:25	74		
6:11	47	Titus	
		1:16	47

Philemon
12   47
14   47

Revelation
18:22   128

Index of manuscripts

Ann Arbor/MI, University Library, Inv. Nr. 1571	(p^{38}) 132
Ann Arbor/MI, University Library, Inv. Nr. 6238⁺	(p^{46}) 133, 143
Athōs, Monē Megistēs Lavras, B' 52	(Ψ/044) 135–136
Basel, Universitätsbibliothek, A.N. III. 12	(E/07) 95
Berlin, Staatsbibliothek, Preußischer Kulturbesitz, Depot Breslau, 5	(l/11; *Codex Rehdigeranus*) 54
Bologna, Archivio della Fabbriceria della Basilica di San Petronio, Cart. 716/1, n 1	(*Codex Bononiensis*) 20, 25, 26, 40, 42, 52, 63–64, 67, 89, 91, 134
Brescia, Biblioteca Queriniana, s. n.	(f/10; *Codex Brixianus*) 17, 27, 33, 94, 101, 104–105, 107–109, 116–117, 134, 137, 178
Cambridge, Trinity College, B. XVII. 1	(F/010) 93–94, 141, 147
Cambridge, Trinity College, B. XVII. 20⁺	(G/011) 95
Cambridge, Trinity College, Nn. II. 41	(D/05; *Codex Bezae*) 55–56, 59, 62, 93, 103, 135–136, 139, 141, 147
Dresden, Sächsische Landesbibliothek, A 145ᵇ	(G/012) 93–94, 141, 147
Dublin, P. Chester Beatty II⁺	(p^{46}) 133, 143
Florence, Biblioteca Medicea Laurenziana, Pluteo LXV. 1	31
Florence, Biblioteca Medicea Laurenziana, PSI X 1165	(p^{48}) 132
Giessen, Universitätsbibliothek, 651/20	(*Codex Gissensis*) 20, 25–27, 29, 35–36, 48, 50–51, 53, 55, 59–60, 62, 102–103, 134, 174, 211
Hamburg, Staats- und Universitätsbibliothek, Cod. 91 in scrin.	(H/013) 95
London, British Library, Add. 43725	(א/01; *Codex Sinaiticus*) 21, 55, 59, 135, 137
London, British Library, Harley 5684⁺	(G/011) 95
London, British Library, Royal 1 D VIII	(A/02; *Codex Alexandrinus*) 59, 94–95, 131, 134–136, 138–139
Milan, Biblioteca Ambrosiana, C 73 inf.	30
Milan, Biblioteca Ambrosiana, E 147 sup.⁺	(*Codex Ambros.* E⁺) 26, 64
Milan, Biblioteca Ambrosiana, G 82 sup.	(*Codex Ambros.* D) 20
Milan, Biblioteca Ambrosiana, I 61 sup.	(*Codex Ambros.* C) 20, 26, 31, 54–55, 57, 76, 117, 119, 133, 174
Milan, Biblioteca Ambrosiana, S 36 sup.⁺	(*Codex Ambros.* A⁺) 10, 20, 26, 31, 37, 39, 45–49, 52, 54–63, 72–73, 75, 77, 82, 87, 90, 92, 106, 113, 119–127, 141–142, 144–145, 174

Milan, Biblioteca Ambrosiana, S 45 sup.	(*Codex Ambros.* B) 20, 26, 31, 38, 45, 48–49, 54–57, 62–65, 72, 75, 77, 82, 87, 90, 106, 119–127, 141–142, 173–174, 213
Moscow, Gosudarstvennyj Istoričeskij Musej, V. 9	(V/031) 95
Moscow, Gosudarstvennyj Istoričeskij Musej, V. 93	(K/018) 56, 96, 99
Munich, Bayerische Staatsbibliothek, Clm 6224	(q/13; *Codex Monacensis*) 17, 104
Naples, Biblioteca Nazionale 'Vittorio Emanuele', s.n.	(pap. 34) 20, 30
Oxford, Bodleian Library, Auct. T. infr. 1.1	(Λ/039) 95
Oxford, Bodleian Library, Auct. T. infr. 2.2	(Γ/036) 95
Oxford, Bodleian Library, Gr. bibl. g. 4 (P)	(p^{29}) 132
Oxford, Bodleian Library, Laudianus Gr. 35 [S.C. 1119]	(E/08; *Codex Laudianus*) 29
Paris, Bibliothèque Nationale de France, Gr. 9	(C/04; *Codex Ephraemi Rescriptus*) 138–139
Paris, Bibliothèque Nationale de France, Gr. 48	(M/0121+0243) 96, 99
Paris, Bibliothèque Nationale de France, Gr. 63	(K/017) 95
Paris, Bibliothèque Nationale de France, Gr. 107 + 107 AB	(D/06; *Codex Claromontanus*) 56, 93–94, 99, 141, 147; (d/75) 132
Paris, Bibliothèque Nationale de France, Lat. 528	43
Paris, Bibliothèque Nationale de France, Nouv. acq. Lat. 2171	(t/56; *Liber Comicus Toletanus*) 103
Rome, Biblioteca Angelica, 39	(L/020) 96, 99
Saint Petersburg, Rossijskaja Nacional'naja Biblioteka, Gr. 20	(e/76) 132
Saint Petersburg, Rossijskaja Nacional'naja Biblioteka, Gr. 33	(Γ/036) 95
Saint Petersburg, Rossijskaja Nacional'naja Biblioteka, Gr. 34	(Π/041) 95
Saint Petersburg, Rossijskaja Nacional'naja Biblioteka, Gr. 225	(P/025) 96, 99
Saint Petersburg, Rossijskaja Nacional'naja Biblioteka, Gr. 537	(N/022; *Codex Purpureus Petropolitanus*) 131, 134–136
Sankt Gallen, Stiftsbibliothek, 48	(δ/27) 104
Speyer, Historisches Museum der Pfalz, s.n.[+]	(*Codex Argenteus*) 32, 50–51, 56, 175
Tbilisi, Inst. rukop., Gr. 28	(Θ/038) 135–136
Trent, Museo Nazionale, s.n.	(e/2; *Codex Palatinus*) 87, 104, 108, 110

Turin, Biblioteca Nazionale Universitaria, (*Codex Ambros.* A⁺) 38–39
F. IV. 1 Fasc. 10⁺

Uppsala, Universitetsbiblioteket, D G 1⁺ (*Codex Argenteus*) 1, 20–21, 25–27, 29, 31–35, 41, 44–48, 51–55, 57–59, 61–63, 76, 87, 98, 100–102, 104, 109, 117, 119, 123, 126, 128, 133, 138–139, 174–175, 210

Utrecht, Universiteitsbibliotheek, 1 (F/09) 95

Vatican City, Biblioteca Apostolica Vaticana, (S/028) 95
Vat. Gr. 354

Vatican City, Biblioteca Apostolica Vaticana, (B/03; *Codex Vaticanus*) 21, 55, 135, 137
Vat. Gr. 1209

Vatican City, Biblioteca Apostolica Vaticana, (*Codex Ambros.* E⁺) 26, 64
Vat. Lat. 5750⁺

Venice, Biblioteca Giustiniani Recanati, 25
s. n. ⁺

Venice, Biblioteca San Marco, 1397 [I.8] (U/030) 95

Verona, Biblioteca Capitolare, LI (49)⁺ 20, 25, 30, 111

Vienna, Österreichische Nationalbibliothek, 103
563

Vienna, Österreichische Nationalbibliothek, 43
795

Washington/DC, Smithsonian Institution, (W/032; *Codex Washingtonianus*) 21, 62, 131, 134–136
Freer Gallery of Art, 06.274

Wolfenbüttel, Herzog August Bibliothek, (*Codex Carolinus*) 20, 25–27, 31, 36–38, 48–49, 51–52, 54–55, 57, 59–63, 102–103, 111, 116, 119–120, 126, 131, 134, 141, 144–145, 174, 212; (gue/79) 37, 111, 144–145; (P/024; *Codex Guelferbytanus* A) 38, 131; (Q/026; *Codex Guelferbytanus* B) 38, 131
Guelf. 64 Weiss.

Index of names and subjects

Aachen 33
Absolute dative 72
Acts of the Apostles 25
Africa 9, 35
Agnellus, archbishop of Ravenna 29
Alans 10
Alcuin of York 33
Alexandrian
– text type 93, 133, 135
– witnesses 138, 142
Alliteration 87–88
Alpha privativum 87
Alphabet (Gothic) 4, 15, 18–21, 24, 43
Alsace 38
Amalafrida 35
Amalasuintha 30
Ambrosiaster 38, 90, 112–114, 120, 122, 124–126, 132, 140–141
Ammonian Sections 21, 32, 34, 36, 46, 53–54, 57–58, 61–62, 64, 175
Antinoopolis 35–36
Antiochian text, see Byzantine text
Anton Ulrich, Duke of Braunschweig-Lüneburg 38
Aorist (Greek) 75–76, 115
Aquileia 54
Arezzo, deed of 20, 25, 67
Arian
– buildings 29
– Church 28, 35, 128
– texts 25, 30, 104
Arians 29–30, see also Homean Goths
Armenian 96, 99
Article (definite)
– Gothic 66, 76–77, 83
– Greek 74, 76
Asia Minor 6, 12
Athanaric 14
Athanasius 12
Audius 12
Augustinus 42
Auxentius of Durostorum 4–7, 13, 16

Basil of Caesarea 13

Batwins (Βαθοῦσης) 10
Belisarius 30
Biertan 11
Bilingual manuscripts 1, 27, 29–31, 33, 36–37, 51, 56, 59–61, 63, 93, 102–104, 111, 116, 133, 137, 141–143
Black Sea 8, 10–11
Bobbio 31, 34, 38–40
Boethius 28
Bologna 42
Bounding lines 27, 36–38, 59, 174
Brescia 27, 32, 94, 178
Bulgaria 1, 7, 9
Burgunds 9
Byzantine
– readings 1, 103, 131, 134, 141, 146, 149, 153, 164, 169
– text 1, 17, 81, 92, 95–97, 99–101, 103, 111, 120–122, 130–139, 141–142, 146–148
Byzantium 100, see also Constantinople

Calendar, Gothic 10, 15, 25
Cappadocia 6, 13, 94
Carolingian
– period 25
– readers 52
Carolingians 33
Cases of the Gothic noun 68
Cassiodorus 28, 30
Celts 10
Charlemagne 33
Cherneakov culture 15
Christianity 6, 11–14, 22
Christina, Queen 34
Chrysostom, John 13, 16, 94–96, 99, 101, 113, 116, 120, 133, 135–136, 138–139, 144
Ciprianus, *patricius* 30, 37
Citation, mark of 21, 63
Clement of Alexandria 144
Cola et commata 36–38, 48–49, 59–61, 174
Cologne 33

Columban 31
Conflation 46, 56, 101, 108, 122, 126
Conjunctions 45, 60, 73, 75, 108, 122–123
Constanţa 8
Constantine 6, 13
Constantinople 6–8, 13, 21, 93, 99, 139–140, 146–147
Constantius II 6–7
Coptic 96, 139
Crimea 13
Curetonian 93, 138
Cyril 144

Dacia 4–5, 10, 16
Dacians 10
Daco-Romans 11
Danube 1, 4–5, 8, 11, 13–15, 24, 93
David, King 5
Diaeresis 65
Diatessaron 117
Diple 57, 63
Dittography 44
Dniester 5
Domninus of Marcianopolis 16
Don 5
Doxology 140, 143–144
Dual 15, 68, 71

Egypt 35, 95
Ekthesis 53, 65
Eusebian Canons 53–54, 62, 64
Eusebius of Caesarea 54, 95
Eusebius of Nicomedia 5–6
Euthalian Apparatus 21, 36, 38, 40, 54–55, 58, 64
Euthalius 54, 60
Eutyches 13
Evagrius 54, 60

Figura etimologica 88
Foederati ware 15
France 43, 100
Fritigern 14
Friþila (Fretela) 106
Future
 – Gothic 70
 – Greek 70

Gaatha 14
Galen 37
Gaul 1, 9, 25, 43
Gepidae 8
Gepids 10
Germanic
 – languages 1, 16, 70, 113
 – peoples 1, 8–10
Giessen 35
Glosses 18, 20–21, 25, 39, 46–48, 86, 91, 105, 111, 123–128, 134, 137, 147
Goddas 14
Golden Section 32
Gothi minores 1, 7–9
Gothia 5, 12–13
Gothica Bononiensia 42, see also Bologna, Archivio della Fabbriceria della Basilica di San Petronio,
 – Cart. 716/1, n°1
Gotica Parisina 40, 43, 50, see also Paris, Bibliothèque Nationale de France, Lat. 528, f. 71v.
Gotica Veronensia 25, 40, see also Verona, Biblioteca Capitolare, LI (49)⁺
Gregory the Great 39
Greuthungi 5
Guþþika 14

Hács-Béndekpuszta 8, 18, 25, 40–41, 50
Hapax 45, 81–84, 106, 112–113, 123, 125, 127
Haplography 44–45
Harmonisation 45–46, 86, 107, 114–118, 127, 129, 134, 137
Hebrews, epistle to the 25, 38–39, 143
Hesychius 96
Hieronymus, see Jerome
Hispano-Mozarabic lectionary 103
Historical present 75
Holland 34
Homoean
 – faith 5, 7–8, 13–15, 147
 – Goths 11, 14–15, 143
Homoeoteleuton 44, 104, 121

Imperfect (Greek) 75
Indo-European 17, 68, 70, 84

Innas 13
Intermarriage 30
Isidore of Sevilla 37
Itala, see *Vetus Latina*
Italy 1, 9, 20–21, 24–25, 27, 30–31, 33–37, 39–40, 42–43, 54, 93–94, 100, 104–105, 128, 131, 147

Jerome 40, 60, 106, 124
Jesus' genealogy 43, 59
Jordanes 7–8, 28

Karl I, Duke of Braunschweig-Lüneburg 38
Koine, see Byzantine text

Langobards 9
Laurentius, bishop of Novae 16
Letters (Gothic)
– addition 44–45, 60, 120
– confusion 44–45
– omission 44–45
Liber Comicus Toletanus 103
Liturgical indications 54, 65
Liturgy 9, 29, 31, 37, 39–40, 42, 52, 65, 67, 91, 121, 128
Liutger 33
Loan meanings 22–23
Loan translations 22–23, 112
Loan words 10–12, 16, 22–23, 85, 91
Long Ending of Mark 32, 138–139, 175–177
Lord's Prayer, see *Pater noster*
Lucian of Antioch 95

Majority text, see Byzantine text
Maximinus 16
Mediopassive (Greek) 70
Milan 25–26, 30, 32, 34, 38–39
Moesia Inferior 1, 7–9, 15, 17, 24, 93, 147
Moldavia 5
Moods of the Gothic verb 68
Moses 7
Mount Haemus 7

Naples, deed of 15, 20, 25, 67
Nehemiah 1, 4, 25, 95
Nicaea, council of 5

Nicene
– bishops 12, 14
– faith 13, 147
– Goths 11, 13–15
– historians 5
Nicetas 13
Nicopolis ad Istrum 7, 15–16
Nikyup 7
Nomina sacra 21, 27, 45, 63–64
Novae 9, 16
Numerals 18, 31, 43, 64, 69

Old Church Slavonic 99
Old Latin 17, 33, 54, 66, 73–74, 80–81, 83, 85, 93, 96, 98–100, 102–103, 107–109, 111, 114, 116–118, 122, 125, 138–139, 141, see also *Vetus Latina*
Old Testament 1, 4, 20, 25, 53, 60, 63, 95, 179
Optative (Gothic) 68, 70, 74
Origen 124, 133, 144
Orosius 31
Ostrogothic Geographers 28
Ostrogoths 1, 8, 9, 28

Palatinian Bilingual 104, 108, 110
Pamphilus 95
Pannonia 8–9, 104
Paragraphs 37, 57, 61
Parallel passages 45–46, 54, 58, 85–86, 91, 97, 109, 114–118, 121, 124, 127–130
Participle
– Gothic 70, 73–74, 76, 117
– Greek 73–74, 76–78
Passive
– Gothic 68, 70
– Greek 70–71
Pater noster 62, 81
Pavia 32
Pelagius 102, 113, 120, 122, 124
Perfect (Greek) 75, 79
Pericope adulterae 138
Peshitta 117, 138
Petrus, bishop of Ravenna 30
Philostorgios 4–7
Piacenza 31
Pinnas 13

Pluperfect (Greek) 75
Praefatio to the *Codex Brixianus* 105–106, 128, 178–179
Praesens historicum (Greek) 77, 79
Prague 33
Procopius 30, 35
Pronouns (Gothic) 45, 60, 67, 69–72, 74–78, 83, 90–91, 109, 115, 117–118, 134
Psalms 17, 25, 106
Pseudo-Clement 105
Punctuation 21, 38–39, 58–59, 65, 174

Ravenna 27–31, 33, 39, 42, 52
Reccared 9
Relative clause
– Gothic 77–78
– Greek 77
Rimas 13
Roman Empire 1, 4, 6, 13–14
Romania 1, 4, 11
Romans 10–11, 28–30
Rudolf II 33
Rufinus 102, 105, 120
Runes 18–19, 24, 41
Running titles 31, 55

Sabas 10, 13–14
Sadagolthina 6
Salvian of Marseille 9
Sant'Anastasia, church 30
Sant'Apollinare Nuovo, Church 29
Sântana de Mureş 4, 10, 12, 15
Sarmatians 10
Schema Atticum 79
Script (Gothic)
– sloping type 20–21, 39, 41–42, 47
– upright type 20–21, 33–36, 38, 41, 43, 46–47
Script (Greek)
– biblical majuscule 21
– sloping majuscule 21
Script (Latin)
– cursive 19
– uncial 19–20, 35–37, 109
Scriptio continua 49, 53, 65
Scythia 12
Selenas (Σελῖνας) 8, 10

Semitisms 22
Shêkh 'Abâde 35
Skeireins 25, 67, 115
Socrates 4–5, 13–14
Sondersprache 91
Sozomen 4–5, 14
Spain 1, 9, 103, 147
Speyer 32, 50–51, 56, 175
Spirito Santo, church 29
Subscriptions 25, 31, 55–56, 174
Suebes 9
Sunnja (Sunnia) 106
Superscriptions 31, 55–56, 174
Suspensions 33–36, 38
Svishtov 9
Symmachus 28
Syriac 74, 93, 96, 99, 138–139
Syrian text, see Byzantine text

Tabella Hungarica 19, 41
Tenses of the Gothic verb 68, 71
Tervingi 5
Textus Receptus 99, 132
Theodahad 30
Theoderic the Great 1, 9, 27–30, 32–33, 35, 147
Theodore of Heraclea 26
Theodoret 5, 7, 143–144
Theophilos 5, 13
Thracian language 16
Thracians 10
Thrasamund 35
Toledo 103
Tomi 8
Turin 38–39

Uiliaric 31
Unila 13
Uppsala 27, 32, 34, 175
Uulthres 105–106, 179

Valens, bishop of Oescus 16
Valens, Emperor 6, 14
Vandalic language 9
Vandals 1, 9, 29, 147
Variatio 83, 87, 91
Verona 20, 25, 30, 32, 40, 42, 111

Vetus Latina 17, 36–37, 60, 67, 93, 96–98, 139
Visigoths 1, 8–9, 128, 147
Vulgate 17, 33, 36, 51, 54, 66–67, 102–103, 107, 121, 125

Walafrid Strabo 9
Wallachia 5
Waw-conversive 71
Werden 33
Wereka (Οὐήρικας) 10, 14
'Western'
– non-interpolations 141
– readings 1, 93, 97, 100, 110–111, 130, 132, 137–138, 143–144
– text type 93, 103, 135–136
witnesses 93–94, 111, 133, 137, 141–143, 147, 151–152, 159, 162, 166, 168, 171–172
Wissembourg 38
Wolfenbüttel 36
Word order (Gothic) 66–68, 72–73, 77, 90–91, 115–116, 118, 124, 134, 148

Zeno Veronensis 111

Index of words

Gothic forms

abba 22, 84
aggilus 22, 81
ahma 23
aibr 45, 82
aipiskaupus 14, 22
aipistaule 23, 56
aipistula 23
airus 81
aiwaggeli 23
aiwaggelista 22
aiwaggeljo 22–23, 56
aiwlaugia 22
aiwxaristia 22
Aizoris 89
ak 60
alabrunsts 23
alhs 82
allwaldands 23
anakaurjan 80
anakumbjan 11
anastodeiþ 56–57
anaþaima 22
anno 11
apaustaulus 22, 24
arka 17
armahairts 17
armaion 140
atta 84
aþþan 60, 69, 82
aurali 11
awistr 112

Baiþsaidan (with variants) 88
birodeinos 126
boka/bokos 21, 53, 71
bruta 16
bwssaun 22

daimonareis 84
daupjan 23
diabaulus/diabulus 22

diakaunus 14
duginnan 70
dustodeiþ 57
duþþe 60

fadar 84
faiha (or bifaiha) 127
faihuþraihna 85, 124
farwa 139
fotubandjom 86
frasts 16
frauja 23, 63–64

ga- 70, 85
gaguþs 23
Gairgaisaine 90
galeiks 15
galiug 24
galiugaapaustaulus 24
gaqumþs 85
garda 112
garuns 85
gawairþeigai sijaiþ 112
gawairþi habandans 17
gazaufwlakio 22
gibai 45
giban 45, 70
gibau 45
godis wiljins 17
gudhūs 82
gudja 83
guþ 23, 56, 63–64

haban 70, 84, 120
habanda 120
habandans 84–86, 112
hairaiseis 22
hleiþra 23
hleiþrastakeins 23

ibna 15
Iesus 40, 45, 64, 109
Iskariotes (with variants) 88
iþ 60, 69, 82

jah 73, 82, 109, 122–123

Kafarnaum 89
Kajafa 90
kalkjo 16
kapillon 11
karkara 11
kaurban 22
kaurei 80
kauriþa 80
kaurjan 80
kaurus 80
Kreks 81
kubitus 11

laiktsjo/laiktjo 40, 54, 65
laustim/laistim 45
leik 84
lima 89
liugan 81
liugna 80
liugnawaurds 80
lukarn 11

maimbrana 21
Mambres 90
mammo 84
mammonin 85, 124
managein 123
manasedai 123
manna 22
Maria/Mariam/Marja 89
meljan 21
merjan 23
mes 11
militon 11
mota 86
motastaþs 86
munan 70

Nauel 89

paintekuste 22
papa 15
parakletus 22
paraskaiwe 22
pasxa/paska 22
praufetes 23
praufetja 22
psalmo 22, 124

qens 81
qino 81

rabbei 22
raþjo 81

sagiþa 81
sein- 78
siggwan 53
silbasiuneis 80
siponeis 16
skulan 70
staks 23
sulja 11
sunus 59, 80
swartizl 21
swnagoge 85

Teimauþaiu 45, 56
tibr 45, 82
tiuhanda 120

þairh 55
þan 82
þanuh 82
þaruh 69, 82
þiuda 81
þiudangardi 81
þiudans 81
þiudinassus 81

ufargudja 83
-uh 73, 75, 82, 90
un- 80, 87
unhulþons 84, 112
unkaureins 80
unte 60, 69
usbruknan 81

ushrainjan 81
usletan 81
ussiggwan 53
ustauh 56–57

wailamerjan 23
wairaleiko 17
wairþan 70–71

waurd 80–81, 108, 127
waurstweiga 68
weiha 83
wisan 70–71, 79, 125
woþs 85

Xristus 40, 64

Greek forms

ἀβαρής 80
ἀββα 22, 84
ἄγγελος 22, 81
αἱρέσεις 22, 126
ἀναγινώσκω 53
ἀνάθεμα 22
ἀνδρίζεσθε 17
ἀπόστολος 22
ἀρχιερεύς 83
αὐλή 112
αὐτός 76

βαπτίζω 23, 115
βαρέω 80
Βαρθολομαῖον 88
βάρος 80
βαρύς 80
βασιλεία 81
Βηθσαϊδά(ν) 88
βύσσος 22

γαζοφυλάκιον 22
γαμέω 81
γάρ 69, 75
Γεργεσηνῶν 90
γυνή 81

δαιμόνια 84–85
δαιμονιάρι(ο)ς 84
δαιμονιζόμενος 84
δέ 66, 69, 75, 82
διάβολος 22
διάκονος 14
δῷ 45

δῷ 45

εἰρηνεύοντες 17
ἐκεῖνος 76
ἐκκαθαίρω 81
ἐκκλάω 81
ἐκκλείω 81
Ἕλληνες 81
ἐπιβαρέω 80
ἐπίσκοπος 14, 22
ἐπιστολή 23
ἐπισυναγωγή 85
Ἑσρώμ (with variants) 89
εὐαγγελίζω 23
εὐαγγέλιον 22
εὐαγγελιστής 22
εὐδοκίας 17
εὐλογία 22
εὔσπλαγχνος 17
εὐσχήμων 23
εὐχαριστία 22

θεός 23

Ἰαμβρῆς 90
ἱερόν 82

καί 73, 75
Καϊάφας 90
Καπερναούμ 89
Καφαρναούμ 89
κιβωτόν 17
κορβᾶν 22
κύριος 23

λαόν 123
λεμά/λειμά/λιμά 89
λόγος 81

Μαμβρῆς 90
μαμ(μ)ωνᾶς 85
μάννα 22
Μαρία(μ) 89
μεμβράνα 21
μορφή 139

Νῶε 89

ὁλοκαύτωμα 23
ὅμοιος 15
οὖν 69, 75, 77
οὗτος 76, 78

παντοκράτωρ 23
παπᾶς 15
παράκλητος 22
παρασκεύη 22

πάσχα 22
πατήρ 84
πέδη 86
πεντηκοστή 22
πλεονεξίαι 127
πνεῦμα 23
προφητεία 22
προφήτης 23
πτῶμα 84

ῥαββεί 22

σάρξ 84
σκηνοπηγία 23
συναγωγή 85
συνέδριον 85
σῶμα 84

ψαλμός 22
ψευδαπόστολος 24
ψευδολόγος 80
ψιθυρισμοί 126

Latin forms

accumbo 11
angelus 22
annōna 11
apostolus 22
arca 17

bonae uoluntatis 17

Capharnaum 89
capillus 11
cohortem 112
cubitus 11

daemonarius 84
daemonia 84–85, 112
daemoniaci 84
diabolus 22
diaconus 14

ecce 17
episcopus 14, 22
epistula
ēuangelista 22

Gerasenorum 90

Hierusalem 17

lectio 40, 65
lucerna 11

Maria 89
membrāna 21
mīlito 11
misericors 17

Noah 89
nuntius 81
nurus 16

pacem habentes 17
pontifex 83
princeps 83
prophētia 22

sacerdos 83
scēnopēgia 23

solea 11

templum 82

uiriliter agite 17

Vulgar Latin

*carcara 11
*ēuangeli(o) 22
*lucarna 11

*mēsa 11
*ōrārium 11

Plates

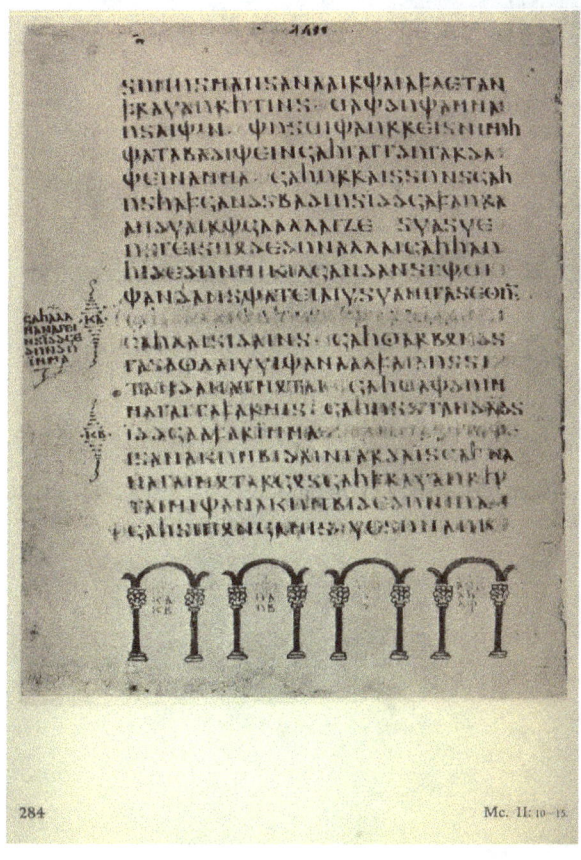

1. *Codex Argenteus*: Uppsala, Universitetsbiblioteket, D G 1, f. 61v; Mk 2:10-15 (picture from <http://app.ub.uu.se/arv/codex/faksimiledition/jpg_files/284mc2f.html>).

2. *Codex Gissensis*: Giessen, Universitätsbibliothek, 651/20 (now lost), flesh side; Lk 23:11-14 (Gothic), Lk 24:5-9 (Latin) (picture from <http://bibd.uni-giessen.de/papyri/images/pbug-inv018-1.jpg>).

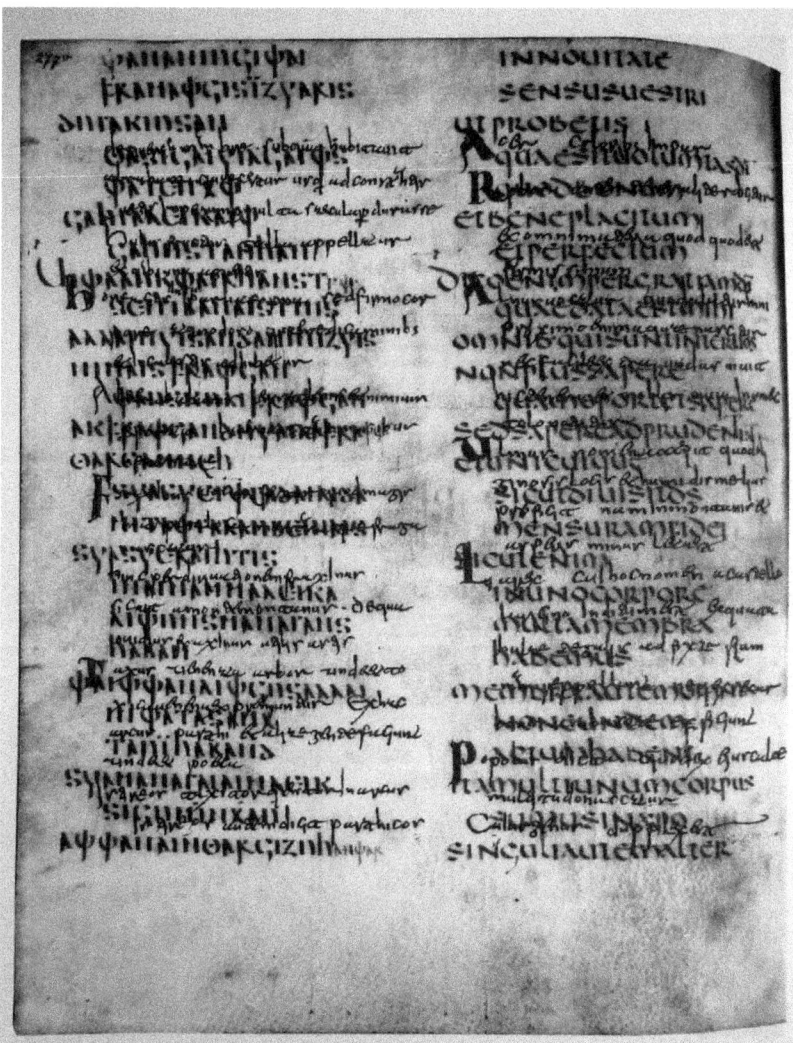

3. *Codex Carolinus*: Wolfenbüttel, Herzog August Bibliothek, Guelf. 64 Weiss., f. 277v; Rom 12:2-5 (picture from <http://diglib.hab.de/mss/64-weiss/start.htm>).

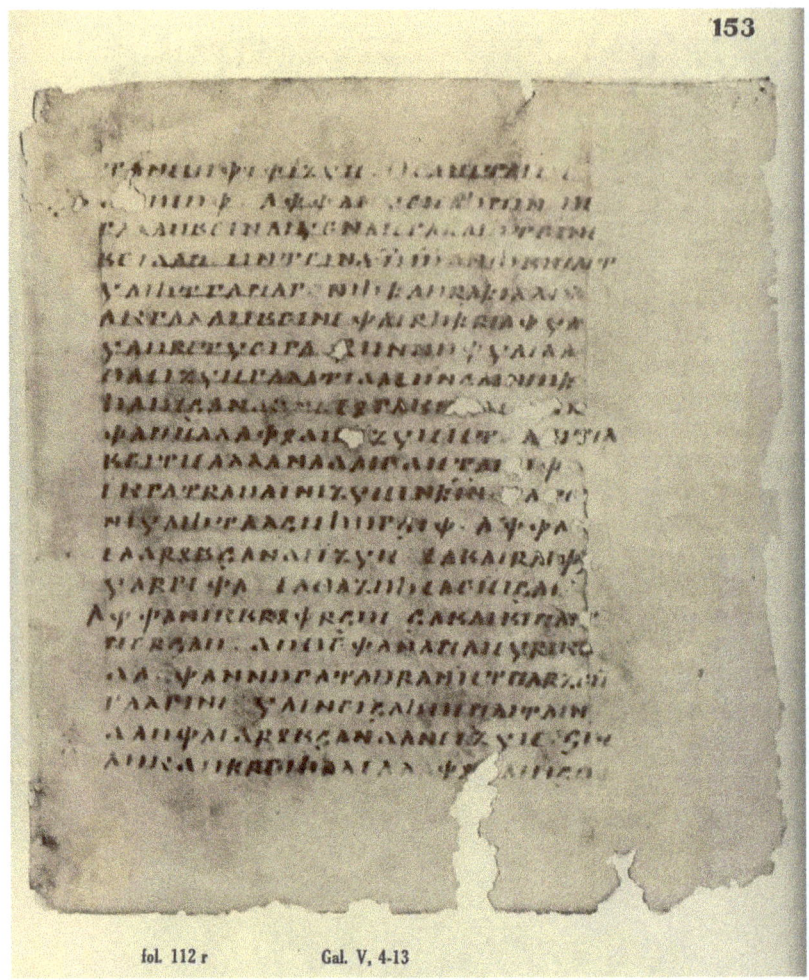

4. *Codex Ambrosianus* B: Milan, Biblioteca Ambrosiana, S 45 sup., f. 112r; Gal 5:4-13 (picture from de Vries 1936, 153).

www.ingramcontent.com/pod-product-compliance
Lightning Source LLC
Chambersburg PA
CBHW070610170426
43200CB00012B/2643